Dr Rudolph Brasch, born in Berlin of British parents, is not only an acclaimed author with twenty books to his credit, he is also a popular and respected telecaster, broadcaster and scriptwriter and a firm believer in the promotion of understanding among people of all faiths.

Dr Brasch worked in London, Dublin and South Africa after receiving his Ph.D. in 1938. He came to Australia in 1949 and was Chief Minister of the Temple Emanuel in Sydney for the next thirty years.

Among his many honours are the Coronation Medal (1952), the Order of the British Empire (1967), the Silver Jubilee Medal (1977) and the Order of Australia (1979).

His books, which are read for pleasure and are used as textbooks in the USA, Japan and many other countries, include HOW DID IT BEGIN?, HOW DID SEX BEGIN?, HOW DID SPORTS BEGIN?, THERE'S A REASON FOR EVERYTHING!, MISTAKES, MISNOMERS AND MISCONCEPTIONS and PERMANENT ADDRESSES.

Dr Brasch presently lives in Sydney. He travels extensively to research his books and when not writing, continues his busy schedule of public speaking and lecturing.

STOC DYNNWYD YMAITH
LLYFRGELL COLEG MENAI
WITHDRAWN LIBRARY STOCK

LLYFRGELL COLEG MENAI LIBRARY

055501

By the Same Author

The Star of David

The Eternal Flame

How Did It Begin?

Mexico — A Country of Contrasts

The Unknown Sanctuary

The Judaic Heritage

How Did Sex Begin?

The Supernatural and You!

Australian Jews of Today

There's a Reason for Everything

Mistakes, Misnomers and Misconceptions

Strange Customs

How Did Sports Begin?

Thank God I'm an Atheist

Permanent Addresses

How Did Sports Begin?

R. BRASCH

ST NO	
ACC NO	
CLASS	
DATE	
STAFF	

Tynron Press
Scotland

© R. Brasch 1986

First published in 1970 by David McKay Co. Inc., New York
This edition first published in 1990 by
Tynron Press
Stenhouse
Thornhill
Dumfriesshire DG3 4LD
by arrangement with
Collins/Angus & Robertson Publishers Australia

ISBN 1-871948-92-4
All rights reserved

ST NO	1871948924 £7.99
ACC NO	055501
CLASS	796.09
DATE	21/5/03
STAFF	EW

Printed in Singapore by Chong Moh Offset Printing Pte Ltd

055501

LLYFRGELL COLEG MENAI LIBRARY
SAFLE FFRIDDOEDD SITE
BANGOR GWYNEDD LL57 2TP

To James D. Wolfensohn,
a very dear friend, whose mother
introduced my wife
to me and thereby gave two people
supreme happiness.

We are grateful to the following for permission to reproduce illustrations in this book:

The All Japan Karate Association, Tokyo, and Masanao Takazawa; the American Bowling Congress, Wisconsin, U.S.A.; the Archiv für Kunst und Geschichte, Berlin; Frank Arthur and the Empire Speedway Pty Ltd; the Ashmolean Museum; Bruce Austin; the Basketball Hall of Fame, Springfield, Mass., U.S.A.; the British Museum; G. M. Cowie; the Kodokan Institute, Tokyo; Longman Group Ltd; the Mitchell Library, Sydney; the National Baseball Library, Cooperstown, N.Y., U.S.A.; the National Maritime Museum, Greenwich, England; the Pergamonmuseum, Berlin; the Prins Hendrik Maritime Museum, Rotterdam; the Public Library of N.S.W.; the Radio Times Hulton Picture Library, London; the Staatliche Museen, Berlin; the Trotting Control Board, Melbourne; and Mr and Mrs Dennis Zines.

CONTENTS

Foreword

1   How Did Sports Begin?   1

2   Archery   8

3   Badminton   20

4   Baseball   27

5   Basketball   40

6   Billiards and Snooker   45

7   Boxing   54

8   Bullfighting   61

9   Cock-Fighting   72

10   Cricket   83

11   Croquet   89

12   Curling   95

13   Cycling   108

14   Dog-Racing   120

15   Fencing   130

16   Football   137
    Soccer   143
    Rugby Union   145
    Rugby League   148
    American Football   151
    Australian Rules   153

17   Golf   159

18   Hockey   172

19   Horse-Racing   179

20   Hunting   206

21 Ice Hockey 216
22 Ice Skating 221
23 Jai Alai (*Pelota*) 231
24 Judo 234
25 Karate 244
26 Lacrosse 248
27 Lawn Bowling (*Bowls*) 254
28 Motorcycle Speedway Racing 259
29 Mountaineering 262
30 Polo 273
31 Racquets 278
32 Roller Skating 282
33 Rowing 286
34 Sailing 300
35 Skiing 316
36 Squash 323
37 Surfing 329
38 Swimming 339
39 Table Tennis (*Ping-Pong*) 349
40 Tennis 354
41 Ten-Pin Bowling 364
42 Trotting 371
43 Water Polo 377
44 Water Skiing 383
45 Wrestling 389
46 Olympics 399
47 Australian Beginnings 411
   Index 423

FOREWORD

Sport is adventure, personal and vicarious. It is challenge, endeavour, and relaxation. It is, too, universal, and very few people have not succumbed to its lure, either as participant or spectator. Fewer, probably, have given thought to how the various popular sports originated, a many-sided, fascinating subject and the very topic of this book.

Sports are as old as time and the story of their rise and evolution into present-day form, a form often in sharp contrast to the original, is a richly coloured narrative that encompasses numerous and diverse lands and peoples.

Everything in life has a reason for its being, even the smallest detail, though often we are prone to forget this fact. This is especially true of sports. What, for instance, determined the specific dimension of the cup in golf, and the 'odd' number of eighteen holes? How did 'love' find its way into scoring in tennis, and the sheep-pen into cricket? And why do we speak of a 'bull's-eye' in archery and shooting?

Football, horse-racing, and cycling are self-explanatory in their nomenclature. But how did squash, jai alai, and badminton get their names? The answers to these and scores of other questions are in this book whose range extends to the impact of sports on culture, and our very way of speaking.

Many everyday idioms were born of sport, although today they are completely divorced from their source. Thus, 'to come up to scratch' originated in the boxing ring, 'to peg out' on the croquet lawn, and 'to show the white feather' in the cockfighting pit.

For the sake of giving as complete a picture as possible, I have also included the fascinating stories of the 'birdie', 'duck' and 'heat', although I have explained these, as well as some other sporting terms and practices, in a previous book.

I have always been curious about the origins of things. Over many years I researched the history of superstitions and customs. I found it equally intriguing and rewarding to delve into the roots of the many trees in the vast domain of sport. As a theologian who is much concerned with the history of faith, I was amazed, in the process, to discover how greatly religion, and even humble clergymen, have influenced sports. It is a fact that many modern sports descend from ancient religious rites.

Finally, and not least, as an Australian living in a country in which sport of almost every kind is a part of life, indeed almost a religion, I could not but be drawn to explore the many unusual facts of our sporting heritage through the whole alphabet, from archery to wrestling.

Frequently, sports 'just happened'—whoever invented them did so unintentionally, and certainly left no record. And so it is that in the case of many sports first played thousands of years ago, the roots are ill-defined and subject to much conjecture. Even comparatively modern sports (as baseball testifies) have been the cause of much controversy as to how they really started. All the more absorbing then was my task of inquiring 'how sports began', and it is my wish that readers will share with me the joy and excitement of discovery.

R.B.

Chapter 1

HOW DID SPORTS BEGIN?

In the beginning, sport was a religious cult and a preparation for life. Its roots were in man's desire to gain victory over foes seen and unseen, to influence the forces of nature, and to promote fertility among his crops and cattle.

Sport, as a word, is an abbreviation: the shortened form of disport, a diversion and an amusement. Rooted in Latin, it literally means 'carry away' (from *des-porto*). In our time millions of people, whether spectators or participants, amateurs or professionals, are carried away by the sport they love from the cares of their daily toil, their anxieties and frustrations, to a world of relaxation and emulation, excitement and thrill.

However, going back to the very beginning of sport as such, we find that far from being restricted, it started as part of man's history and is bound up closely with his very being. Sport was not merely a diversion or pastime, but an essential feature of man's existence.

An inborn impulse and a basic need caused primitive man to play games, even though it might be only hitting a stone with a branch. It eased his tension, helped him to get aggressiveness out of his system, and, altogether, served as an innocuous outlet for otherwise harmful urges. After all, to hit an object was so much better than to hit a friend.

Thus sport fulfilled a primary want of man, and, spontaneously taken up, games catered to it, giving satisfaction and a sense of achievement and overcoming.

Sport was a natural result of a universal love of play and man's innate desire to compete with and to excel, if not dominate, others.

Another mainspring of sport was man's need effectively to defend himself, his tribe, and later on, his country. In panic and fear when escaping from danger, he learned to run, jump, and swim. To avoid defeat, or to subdue opponents, he invented archery, judo, and karate. And in order to be ready for combat, at all times he practised them, and new sports evolved out of his martial training. Even football and baseball carry vestiges of battles between tribes.

Muscular strength and alertness served well in the repulse or conquest of foes. Sports taught man endurance and courage, essential qualities in a fighter, and man was a fighter from the very beginning.

However, in some parts of the world where the severity of the elements and a low protein diet endangered his life, man's healthy instinct led him to create sports for yet another reason. In cold climates, games provided vital exercise, making the blood course through the veins and keeping man warm and resistant to the hazards of nature and the harshness of the weather.

Man's wish to survive, in this world and the next, explains the origin of a majority of sports. They were not deliberately invented but arose, almost inevitably, out of man's quest to exist and to overcome the countless enemies that threatened him: natural and supernatural, man and beast. He had to ward them off everywhere.

Most of all, sports began as fertility magic, to ensure birth, growth, and the return of spring. Therefore, sport to begin with was mainly a magical rite. It tried to attain human survival by supernatural means. Numerous examples of this are at hand in ancient records and the practices of primitive races.

For instance, for the Zuñis, a Mexican tribe that lived in arid zones, rain was the prime necessity for life. Droughts were frequent and it was because of them that the Zuñis first played games. They were convinced that these would magically bring rain for the crops.

Other primitive tribes established a fraternity of rain-making priests. The sole task of this first team of professional players was to join in games of chance which, they believed, would force nature to precipitate rain.

With the approach of the whaling season, Makah Indians played a primitive type of hockey, using whalebone for ball and bat, the latter symbolizing the war-god's club. A hill tribe in Assam, India, arranged a regular tug-of-war to expel demons. The ceremony — it was not then a sport — took place at a fixed time each year. Two bands of men (the original teams) stood on opposite banks of a river, each tugging at the end of a rope stretched across the water. One team represented the forces of evil, the other those of increase in nature. On the result of the struggle depended whether trouble would haunt the tribe or the sun would shine, literally.

Wrestling bouts were practised in southern Nigeria. They took the form also of a religious act to strengthen the growth of the crop by sympathetic magic. In suspense, huge crowds watched the contestants. They were not reluctant to interfere should either of the fighters show weakness, anger, or fatigue, lest these deficiencies cause any ill-effect on the reproductive forces of nature.

Games were highly important in winter and at the coming of spring. They were considered essential to hasten the return of the sun, and ensure a fruitful season. Some of the games took place between groups of single men and women, representing the unprolific, and married people, symbolizing fecundity.

The Wichita tribe, on the Red River of Oklahoma, conducted a sporting event very similar to modern field hockey. This, too, enacted symbolically a contest between winter and spring, to assist in the renewal of life and the conquest of the evil forces of winter.

For a similar reason, some Eskimos had seasonal games. In spring, the players used a kind of cup and ball — to catch the sun. In the autumn, when the sun was going south, a sort of cat's cradle of sealgut was used to enmesh the sun and delay its departure.

Sport thus assumed even cosmic significance. Definite rules in primitive ball games were religiously observed to direct the winds, the bringers of life. The two teams represented earth and sky, and as no one would dare to cheat the gods, an umpire was unnecessary.

No wonder that primitive man believed that sport if not divine itself, was a gift of the gods. He was firmly convinced that 'to play the game' meant to accelerate the revival of nature and the victory of vegetation. The association of games with religious worship continued from prehistoric times well into the classical period. The Olympic Games were centred on the magnificent temple of Zeus at Olympia, and were played in his honour. The Pythian Games were closely linked with the oracle of Apollo and his shrine at Delphi.

It was from those magical roots of primitive faith that our sports mainly grew. With the passing of time, and frequent repetition of games, their original purpose was forgotten and people enjoyed the contests for their own sake, discovering in them a source of excitement, amusement, and strength.

All these pursuits can be called 'natural' sports, as they 'naturally' evolved from early rites, training for warfare, and defence against threats of nature, whether of the animate or inanimate kind. Equally prominent in this class are sports now taken up for mere pleasure, which developed out of man's search for sustenance: hunting for food, catching fish, rowing and sailing across rivers and the sea.

In the practice of these skills, he acquired as well a liking for them, independent of their primary aim, and pursued them even after their original purpose no longer applied. A means to an end here became an end in itself. And that is how hunting, angling, yachting, and shooting became sports. There is no doubt that the present-day probing of outer space sooner or later will create a modern twentieth — (or twenty-first) — century sport, perhaps called cosmonautics.

Finally, of course, there are those sports which do not constitute relics of man's previous preoccupation with his fate or which are not the by-products of vital tasks. They were artificially created and from the very beginning designed as sports, and nothing else. New technological advance may account for the origin of such sports as car-racing and flying. Mostly, the motive was to present a new type of exercise, demanding different skills, and a novel kind of recreation when older games could not be played or, for one reason or another, had lost their appeal. In one case, however, ten-pin bowling, a new sport was devised simply as a legal subterfuge. And yet, unconsciously, even the latest of sports continues to answer some of the identical needs that had urged our ancestors in the dim past to play games.

Some of the earliest statues emphasized the power and agility of man. Sporting pictures adorned the walls of Egyptian temples. The Pharaohs and their nobles enjoyed sport, not merely as spectators, but as participants. A hieroglyphic inscription lauds Pharaoh Amenophis II as a perfect athlete — 'strong of arm', 'long of stride', 'a skilled charioteer', an efficient oarsman, and a powerful archer.

Gradually, sport became part and parcel of man's social life. Even the Bible, though interested mainly in the spiritual aspect of existence, could not ignore sporting activities altogether.

Hebrew Scripture mentions the use of the sling and the bow. Some authorities have even suggested that it contains certain allusions to weightlifting, either as a test of strength or a means to toughen one's muscles (Zechariah XII:3). Contests and tournaments were known, and with them, the selection of champions.

The New Testament abounds in references to games and St Paul, especially, aware of how much they belonged to everyday life, makes frequent metaphorical use of them. In the Epistle to the Corinthians, for instance, he recalls the spirit of contest to illustrate the strenuous and glorious issue of the Christian fight. Footraces, boxing, and wrestling alike supplied him with memorable phrases to express essential lessons. Paul thus speaks of man's wrestling against the powers of darkness, his fighting the good fight, and finishing the race. Describing his mission and the task of the faithful Christian, he could say: 'I do not run aimlessly, I do not box as one beating the air, but I pommel my body to subdue it'. A notable passage in the Epistle to the Hebrews compares the vast multitude of men and women who have borne testimony to their faith in God, to the enormous crowd of spectators at a foot-race in which the contestant discards all unnecessary encumbrance. He needs patience to go forward perseveringly and to gain the prize conferred by the Umpire, who judges all.

The terminology of sports has its own story. The word 'game' recalls an Old English and Teutonic term that referred to 'participation' and a 'gathering' — for fun. The scoring of points is linked with primitive methods of counting and recording. 'Score' is derived from an Old Norse word for 'notch'. Notches made on a stick served to register the correct number of hits, wins, or killings. Score also came to indicate units of twenty. In earliest days, dents were cut into pieces of wood to mark every twenty, possibly, first of all, when sheep were being counted. Originally, 'umpire' — from the Latin *non-par* — described an 'odd' man who was called upon to settle differences. Amateurs (from the Latin *amare*, 'to love') played for the love of the game.

Civilization has been defined as what man does with his leisure time. Its wise use for the practice of sports has had its beneficial effect not only on his physical health and the promotion of numerous skills, but on his moral character.

All sports, irrespective of their origin, developed in man faculties that have enriched his life manifold. They trained him in endurance, hard work, and vigorous self-control, gave him stamina and the will to do his best, no matter what.

Some of the greatest lessons of life have come out of the world of sport. They have taught man to be undaunted by any challenge. Athletics, from the Greek, embodies the 'prize' (*athlon*) awarded to the winning contestant. Yet, failing to gain it, the true sportsman also knows how to take defeat. He will always be ready to try again and strive to attain what has never before been achieved.

Sports, not least, have had their impact on the social ethics of man. Not accidentally do we speak of 'playing the game', it 'not being cricket', to 'abide by the rules of the game', or 'hitting below the belt' and being a 'spoilsport'. As such a great number of sports owe their existence to the realm of religion, it is well to end this introductory chapter with the 'Ten Commandments of Sport', originally published for Table Tennis players, but applying to every true sportsperson:

TEN COMMANDMENTS OF SPORT

1 Thou shalt not quit.
2 Thou shalt not alibi.
3 Thou shalt not gloat over winning.
4 Thou shalt not sulk over losing.
5 Thou shalt not take unfair advantage.
6 Thou shalt not ask odds thou art unwilling to give.
7 Thou shalt always be willing to give thine opponent the benefit of the doubt.
8 Thou shalt not underestimate an opponent or over-estimate thyself.
9 Remember that the game is the thing and he who thinks otherwise is no true sportsperson.
10 Honour the game thou playest, for he who plays the game straight and hard wins even when he loses.

Chapter 2

ARCHERY

Archery is a sport that goes back to the earliest times. It helped man to survive and to create his civilization, and enabled Britain to become a world power.

The importance of archery has been compared to that of the wheel and fire. Only when man had learned to use the bow and arrow was he able to confront the mighty beasts of the jungle. Without archery, man might well have died of starvation or as the victim of the animals that exceeded him so much in strength.

That is why some of the most ancient races believed that the art of archery was a divine gift to man for his survival.

No one knows exactly when, where, and by whom bows were first used. However, archery was practised in almost every part of the world by the most primitive tribes—among American Indians, African pygmies, and races of the Asian steppes. Hence it is assumed that archery did not spread from one source, but was taken up independently in various places.

Archaeological excavations proved its existence over at least 10,000 years. Stone arrowheads were found in the skeletons of prehistoric beasts killed by the first hunters. They have been discovered embedded in the bones of extinct, giant bisons, elks, and huge rhinoceroses of the pre-glacial era. Such fossils had been buried under the ice for many millennia.

The earliest cave-paintings extant, found in Spain and south-western France, show dramatic pictures of men hunting animals with bow and arrow.

Different legends have tried to explain how man first got the idea and acquired the art of archery. He had seen the porcupine shoot off its quills, which led him to construct a device that could do the same sort of thing. This is one explanation. (Surely a myth, as a porcupine never shoots its quills but merely raises them.)

Indian lore links the beginning of archery with an early hunting expedition. Chasing bears with a spear in dense jungle, a tribesman suddenly found himself alone in thick undergrowth, face to face with an enraged bear.

While making his escape he slipped and fell. Convinced it was the best thing to do, he lay still.

When nothing happened, he looked around, to discover the bear's dead body close by. He realized what had saved him. When he slipped, the butt of his spear had struck an overhanging vine which, acting like a bowstring, had 'fired' the spear and killed the bear.

Returning to his tribe, the hunter brought back with him not only his trophy but also archery—the result of an accident.

Primitive man called on magic to re-inforce the results of his prowess in archery. To his fearful mind, merely to hit a foe with a poisoned arrow was insufficient. The effect had to be prolonged and secured by what is now called contagious or sympathetic magic.

A man who had inflicted a wound thus, would drink hot juice, chew highly spiced plants or heat the bow which had shot the arrow. All these acts, the bowman was convinced, would irritate the wound and make it burn. If he could retrieve the arrowhead, he would throw it into the fire to achieve the same purpose. Similarly, the bowman kept his bow strung tight, hoping thereby to cause his foe to become tense.

The victim, for his part, tried to use magic to ease the pain and undo the effects of the arrow. His friends, after carefully removing its head, would bury it among wet leaves or in a damp spot to cool the wound.

Magic and archery were also linked in a completely

different way—to secure the perpetuation of the life-giving force, whether on earth or in the heavens. Sir James Frazer cited examples of this connection in his *Golden Bough.*

At an eclipse of the sun, men were greatly worried lest this source of all life, as they regarded it, would vanish forever. So they shot arrows toward the disappearing disc, believing that, magically, they would bring it back.

Some tribes held that evil forces and fearsome beasts were trying to destroy and devour the celestial body and that, by shooting arrows at them, they could drive them away and save the sun. Others, again, thinking that for some unknown reason the heavenly light was dying, to revive it, shot fire-tipped missiles at it.

Archery was also used at times of drought to precipitate rain, and to restore sexual power. Among the ancient Hittites, for instance, it was part of a magic rite to cure impotence or homosexuality. A treatise gave a detailed account of the treatment.

The patient had to don a giant black cloak. After chants intoned by a priest, the man was asked to disrobe and stark naked then, to walk with a spindle in his hand (symbolizing womanhood), through a sacred gateway. The moment he had passed through it, he discarded the spindle, taking in its stead a war-bow (expressive of manhood). A magical formula then confirmed, as it were, the man's return to his proper sex and the expurgation of all female demeanour.

The Japanese believed that the sound produced by lightly drawing the bowstring and letting it flick back several times would magically drive away evil spirits.

Bows and arrows were among the earliest weapons of warfare and hunting. They were used by the ancient Egyptians, Assyrians, Persians, Scythians, and Parthians. Archers on horseback or in chariots were man's first mobile artillery. A famous frieze excavated in the former Mesopotamia pictures Assurbanipal, the Assyrians' mighty king, hunting lions with a bow from his chariot.

Greek legend refers to archery many times, and Homer's Odysseus used it most skilfully. Well known is the story of his return home after twenty years' absence to find his wife Penelope besieged by a hundred suitors, eating and drinking at his expense. In the guise of a beggar, he cleverly planned the things to come.

Penelope had just decided that she could no longer wait for her husband's return, and was ready to wed one of the men. All that remained was to select the right spouse. She would make her choice by means of a trial.

Odysseus's bow had lain idle for twenty years. She would choose for her husband the man able to string it and shoot an arrow at a target through the eyes of twelve axe-heads, set up in a row, just as her husband used to do.

One by one, the suitors tried the feat, but could not even string the bow. When all had failed, Odysseus, still in rags, was handed the bow, over the violent protest of the other men. Without effort, he strung the great bow, took a sharp arrow which lay on a table before him, and shot it through the tops of all the axes to the target. Then, stripping off his rags, he revealed himself, took aim at his wife's suitors, and struck them down one by one.

However, neither the Greeks nor the Romans were notable archers. They made frequent use of skilled bowmen from Crete and Asia, whom they enlisted as mercenaries in their armies. In fact, the Parthians so excelled in archery that they defeated the Roman legions.

It was only toward the decline of their empire that the Romans themselves became adept in the art, and even kings took it up with zeal and, at times, sadistic enjoyment. It is told of Emperor Commodus that he shot ostriches with a special type of arrow and how, at gladiatorial combats, he sat in his royal box equipped with a bow and arrows. From there he watched the cruel spectacle of men being chased by lions and leopards, and at the very moment when a beast was about to spring on its prey, he took aim and killed it.

Archery occupies a prominent place in the Bible and in the history of the early Hebrews. It is said of Ishmael, Abraham's son and the ancestor of the Arabs, that 'God was with the lad and he grew ... and became an archer'.

Prince Jonathan, King Saul's son, engaged in the sport and, on one occasion, used it to convey a message to his friend David, the future king. To tell him that his life was threatened and that he should make his escape, Jonathan shot arrows far beyond the usual target, calling out to the boy who stood ready at the customary distance to retrieve them, that they were much farther afield. This was a pre-arranged signal for David that he, too, had to go far beyond, out of King Saul's reach.

Much later, after the fatal battle of Gilboa, David lamented the deaths of Saul and Jonathan in a dirge that became known as 'The Song of the Bow'.

Archery was so common in biblical times that frequently the bow, arrow, and quiver were used as figures of speech by the poets and prophets of Israel. The Psalmist thus spoke of the armed might of the wicked, 'who have bent their bow, to cast down the poor and needy, to slay such as are upright', but whose 'bows shall be broken'.

In powerful realism, suffering Job pictured himself as the target of archers who compassed him round about. God shoots at him, first letting His arrows whistle all about him, keeping him in fearful suspense, dreading that every shaft would strike the mark. Eventually, his apprehension comes true and each arrow hits his very vitals.

In Japan, archery became closely linked with the metaphysical system of Zen Buddhism. It became part of the education of the noble Samurai and was practised not for such purposes as the hunt or war or purely aesthetic enjoyment, but to discipline the mind. Archery was considered a lesson in effortless self-control, perfect equanimity, and the attainment of utter detachment.

It is not known definitely when archery started in Britain. The Roman occupation forces, as well as the Danes, have been credited with its introduction there, and certainly the 'wild Welsh' became expert shots.

Until the Norman invasion the Saxons had regarded fighting with the bow and arrow as unworthy of Saxon warriors. Only close combat between individual men with hand-held weapons such as the sword and battle-axe was considered appropriate. Any impersonal shooting of missiles from a distance lowered the noble art of war. It was disreputable because it lacked valour and personal courage, the Saxons reasoned.

All this suddenly changed. The Normans, resolved to keep the Saxons a subject race and to prevent rebellion, made the carrying of arms illegal. However, they had not reckoned with the Saxons' gift of improvisation and their determination to regain freedom.

The people realized that the only military pursuit left open to them was archery, so long despised and practised only by hunters, and as a sport. Equipment could be easily made from material near at hand.

Thus, in the eleventh century, the English took up archery with zeal and were well tutored by the proficient Welsh. Through a national emergency, it gained a new status in Britain. It was practised for 350 years, and as time passed it made England a first-class military power. Folktales celebrated tremendous feats with the bow and arrow by such legendary figures as Robin Hood.

Archery became part of British compulsory military training. Every man was obliged to keep a bow. Officers, appointed by the Crown, inspected homes to ensure that the law was obeyed and that the weapon was in good order and ready for instant use.

The people had to keep up regular practice. When other sports became overly popular and threatened to take up too much of the people's spare time and so interfere with archery, those sports were banned. Anyone daring to take part in them was liable to severe punishment. To make certain of a continuous supply of raw material for bows, the growing of yew trees in cemeteries was made obligatory. That is how those trees found their permanent place in English churchyards!

The English people became so well trained that they

began to excel all other nations in archery. It was their superb use of the long bow that led them to victory over France, especially during the Hundred Years War (which started in 1340 and actually lasted 116 years). The celebrated victories of Crécy, Poitiers, and Agincourt, in 1415, were largely due to the Englishman's mastery of the long bow.

A chronicler of the time spoke of the devastation it wrought, saying how 'our archery was such that the arrows, flying in the air, as thick as snow with a terrible noise, much like a tempestuous wind preceding a tempest, they did leave no disarmed place of horse or man unstricken'. At Agincourt, it is said, a mere 6000 archers, under the command of King Henry V, faced and beat triumphantly the massed forces of 85,000 Frenchmen, thereby changing the course of history.

Shakespeare was an archery expert and, according to some, his plays can be fully understood only by those versed in its art, as many of his expressions and terms stem from it.

Kings and noblemen as well as the people came to delight in shooting the arrow, and it was said of King Henry VIII that 'His Grace shotte as stronge and as greate a lengthe as anie of his garde'.

It was during his reign that (in 1545) the classic work on archery was published (indeed, it was the first book on the subject ever written in English). Its very title, *Toxophilus*, gave the sport its technical name. Ever since, archery has been known among experts as *toxophily* (from the Greek, meaning 'the love of the bow'), and those who indulge in it as a pastime as *toxophilites*. The book's author was Roger Ascham who, in fact, occupies in the world of archery a similar place to that of Izaak Walton's in fishing. They both share the merit of having written the authoritative treatise in their field of sport and Ascham's *Toxophilus* can be compared to Walton's *Compleat Angler*.

Ascham was an enthusiastic archer and erudite Cambridge scholar, whom Henry VIII chose as tutor of the future Queen Elizabeth. He dedicated his work to the king and prefaced it with these words:

> ...although to have written this book either in Latin or Greek had been more easy and fit for my trade in study; yet nevertheless, I, supposing it no point of honesty, that my commodity should stop and hinder any part of the pleasure or profit of many, have written this English matter, in the English tongue, for Englishmen.

Ascham composed his work specifically in the vernacular so that the greatest possible number of people could read and learn about archery, and become, as the book's title indicated, true 'lovers of the bow'.

Two centuries later (in 1761), in a preface to a new edition of Ascham's classic, Dr Johnson related a delightful story on what prompted the Cambridge don to write this work. Ascham's continuous research and study rather exhausted him and, to relieve his mental fatigue, he took up archery as a pastime. Some of his colleagues resented this and, somewhat unkindly, suggested that the hobby was undignified for a man of his station. Moreover, it took up too much of his valuable time which he could use to much better purpose. Their final dart was that he set a bad example to others engaged in educational matters.

To justify himself, Ascham had written this book to show both the merits and precepts of archery. Whether his critical friends approved of it is doubtful. However, the king was most favourably impressed. As Ascham recorded, Henry 'did so well like and allow it' that he gave him 'a living for it'—an annual allowance of £10.

Such was the popularity of the sport at the time that at a two-day meeting at Shoreditch, London, in 1583, some 3000 people actively participated. They were so keen that they began shooting at daybreak and did not cease until it had become too dark to distinguish the target.

Inevitably, after the invention of gunpowder and the subsequent revolution in methods of warfare, archery became redundant in combat. It changed into a pure sport and as such almost died out. It revived in the 1780s when it was given a great impetus by the formation of the Royal Toxophilite Society (in 1781).

Its foundation was due, so it is said, to Sir Ashton Lever, an extraordinary man of many pursuits and an all-round sportsman. He collected wild birds and prided himself on an aviary containing about 4000 of them. Then he became an enthusiastic animal trainer. His next hobby was the gathering of fossils and shells.

Eventually, he opened a museum which attained such popularity that it was always so crowded that Sir Ashton felt compelled to restrict admission. He made a rule that anyone arriving on foot was excluded! The story goes that a man who had been refused entry as a pedestrian, procured a cow, rode back to the museum, and was duly admitted.

Associated with the museum was a man named Waring who suffered from a chest complaint. No doctor could cure it. He himself felt that all he needed was exercise. He took up archery and soon was well again!

Sir Ashton, feeling somewhat off colour himself, thought that archery might also do him much good. With some of his friends, he formed the Royal Toxophilite Society for that purpose. The society met at Leicester Square, London, and became the parent body of future archery organizations. In fact, it was through its activities that the sport became a vogue.

Most famous among the other clubs was 'The Woodmen of Arden'. Scotland, however, had led the way many years before when, in 1676, the Royal Company of Archers was established as a semi-military group acting as the Queen's bodyguard in Scotland. In 1861, the Grand National Archery Association became the sport's governing body.

The first archery championship was held in 1864. Of all those who took up the pastime, no one equalled Horace A. Ford. He eclipsed all previous records and was twelve times champion of England.

The secret of his achievements was his scientific approach. He paid meticulous attention to every aspect of shooting the arrow. He advised students to 'use your brains as well as your muscles'. His enthusiasm was so great that frequently he rose at 4 a.m. to have a round of archery.

On Sundays, however, when religious scruples did not permit him to shoot, he still went out to the targets, 'just to look at them'. We can well imagine his frustration that this was all he could do. To convey his methods and art to people of his own time and future generations, he produced the second great classic on archery, *Its Theory and Practice*.

Archery has thus played an active part in everyday life from the early Stone Age onward. Indeed, some of its addicts felt impelled to call it 'the sport of man since time began'. In our modern atomic age it is well to remember that earliest man had mastered the art (by means of his strung bow) to accumulate and store energy and then to release it, all of a sudden, not haphazardly but fully under control.

Archery's vocabulary of terms is misleading at times, as some of the expressions used do not actually mean what they at first suggest. On the other hand, the sport has created some metaphors which, now completely divorced from their original source, belong to everyday speech.

A *self-bow* is not one produced by the archer himself for his personal use. It is a bow made from a single piece of wood or metal.

Free-flight shooting does not refer to aiming at flying birds. It has become the technical description of a position in which the archer, lying on his back, straps the bow to his feet and, with both his hands, draws back the string.

Poundage has nothing to do with the weight of the bow but indicates its strength by the number of pounds required to pull the string twenty-eight inches (71.12 cm) from the bow.

A *fletcher* manufactures bows and arrows or merely fixes feathers to the latter.

To hit the *bull's eye* is every archer's desire. He little realizes that his target's description is derived from a completely different and most brutal sport, once very popular among the British, and outlawed as late as 1835.

It goes back to the days of bull-baiting, the cruel practice of making dogs attack and pin down a bull by his nose, and the wagers associated with the game. Spectators chose their favourites (either bull or dog) and placed their bet accordingly. If they backed the bull, they expressed this by saying that they had put their money on 'the bull's eye', just as today racegoers bet on a horse's 'nose'.

As the usual unit of money wagered was a crown, with the passing of time the actual coin was identified in people's minds with the bull's eye. The fact that the crown piece and the bull's eye were approximately of the same size, probably contributed to this development. Eventually, the coin itself was called a bull's eye, and when target-shooting came into fashion, the small black spot (which became golden in archery) indicating the target's centre, came to be known as the bull's eye. It is a strange and complex story, linking bovine and canine, betting and baiting, vision and target.

Arrow-root is a plant so called because its root-starch was applied by American Indians to absorb the poison from wounds caused by arrows.

Tall stories, not unlike those told by fishermen, of superb marksmanship created the idiom of *drawing the long bow* for giving an exaggerated account of anything.

The modern word *toxic* owes its origin to archery's technical name, toxophily. Toxic really means 'pertaining to the bow' (from the Greek *toxon*), but was associated specifically with the poison used for smearing arrows to ensure their deadly effect.

Sometimes people who are unnerved and full of apprehension are called 'unstrung'. This expression, too, comes straight from archery. Bowmen realized that it was inadvisable to keep the bow constantly strung, as the perpetual tension weakened its resilience. The obvious thing to do, after using the bow, was to loosen the bowstring by unhooking it at one end.

This, however, had a great disadvantage. In an unexpected attack, the archer was unprepared, and the time it took to restring the bow could make all the difference between victory and defeat, life and death. Those caught with an *unstrung* bow had every reason to be tense and nervy, and 'unstrung' became the colloquial term for that state of mind.

Chapter 3

BADMINTON

Uniquely among all sports, badminton is named after a country seat of nobility. Badminton was the residence and estate of the Duke of Beaufort, situated in the southern part of the county of Gloucestershire, England. Because the Duke and his friends (all sports lovers) played the game in its precincts during a weekend house party around 1870, it has ever since been called after the Duke's domicile. This also gave the name to a famous collection of sporting books, the *Badminton Library.*

Its association with the game and sport generally made the village and the manor world-renowned and beloved in the hearts of many.

The Duke of Beaufort did not invent the game; he merely put it on the map, as it were, by introducing it into society. The game itself was an adaptation of an earlier pastime which, in turn, has its roots in an ancient divination ritual: to hit an object into the air as often as possible with the hand or some sort of bat, the number of throws achieved without a miss indicated the length of one's life. A maximum score of 'catches' was viewed as a happy omen of longevity. No wonder that people tried to attain record performances. Magical formulae were sung to accompany the rite, and eventually the 'ball game' (to which it amounted) and the chant were believed not simply to reveal the future but, by sympathetic magic, to influence it.

The secularization of this magical rite created the game of battledore and shuttlecock. Its principle, if played individually, was to hit a shuttle with some sort of racket into the air as many times as possible, without letting it drop to the ground. Played by two persons the shuttle was hit backwards and forwards between them, a point being scored for each miss on the part of the opponent.

In one version or another, the pastime became popular in many parts of the world, in Europe and Asia, from England to China. It was played by the noble as much as by the common man, by adults as enthusiastically as by boys and girls. No doubt people at first used the outstretched palm as a racket. (Of course, to close the hand around the missile when catching it was counted a miss.) The palm was replaced by a small bat, initially made of wood, then of skin, and finally of catgut strings, stretched over a frame. The name battledore is derived from the bat used in washing laundry.

The shuttlecock was originally a rounded piece of cork, with feathers stuck around its flattened top. Probably the early use of cocks' feathers, responsible for its name, was a survival of the bird's employment for purposes of divination. To begin with, shuttles were not uniform but varied greatly in size, weight, and characteristics of flight.

The game was first mentioned in England in the fourteenth century. It had become a most fashionable pastime during the reign of James I, so much so that in 1609 a writer could say, 'to play Shuttlecok methinkes is the game now'. A story tells of an unfortunate mishap when the king's son, Prince Henry, playing the game 'with one farr taller than himself', accidentally hit him with the shuttlecock upon the forehead. A pastime suitable for confined spaces, it must have brought some solace to the Earl of Northumberland while held prisoner in the Tower of London for his alleged complicity in the gunpowder plot. Among moneys paid on his behalf was one amount for the purchase of shuttlecocks.

Children especially enjoyed the 'toy', particularly so on Shrove Tuesday. Playing became so popular that in Leicester the day came to be known as 'shuttlecock day'. The streets were crowded with people of all ages batting their feathered corks into the air and toward each other.

Typical of the rhymes chanted as an accompaniment to the game was the verse:

> Shuttlecock, shuttlecock, tell me true
> How many years have I to go through?
> One, two, three . . .

Counting ended, of course, when the player missed a catch — an obvious indication of the toy's roots in the ancient practice of divination.

Divinatory rhymes (identical with those that were sung during similar games with cherry stones, balls made of daisy petals or cowslip) dealt with the year of one's marriage, the social position of one's future spouse, or the size of one's family-to-be:

> Grandmother, grandmother
> Tell me no lie,
> How many children
> Before I die?
> One, two, three . . .

An adaptation of this simple amusement gave birth to a new game that — with progressive elaboration — came to differ in essential features from its predecessor. In the older pastime, two persons playing together were stationary and protected a target area within reach of the outstretched arm in which they held the battledore. In the new and improved version, however, the playing field was extended to the size of a court, divided by a cord or some sort of net to enforce a fair return of the shuttle.

English army officers, serving in India in the 1860s, were very much taken by a game which was similar, and yet far superior, to battledore and shuttlecock, known as Poona. (It has been suggested that possibly the sport reached the subcontinent by earlier English expeditionary forces.) They enjoyed it so much that they took it home, together with some of the Indian equipment, chiefly shuttlecocks.

Some of the officers on leave were friends of the Duke of Beaufort, who invited them to play the game at Badminton. (One tradition says that the guests played in the manor's picture gallery, very much to the hurt of the paintings.) Thus badminton got its name.

Yet another version of the origin of the sport exists, linking it to an even greater degree with the Duke of Beaufort and his weekend party. According to this tradition, wet weather forced the guests indoors where, at a loss as to how to pass the time, someone fetched battledores and shuttlecocks from the nursery. Stretching a cord across the width of the drawing room, they improvised the new game, proposing there and then to call it by the estate's name, which was the obvious thing to do.

The army officers then took the sport to India (thus reversing direction), where they played it first in Karachi. One of the earliest games they organized was played in a hall the size of which was little more than that of a court. A peculiar feature of the hall was that its doors were centrally situated on the longer walls, and opened inward. People entering inevitably had to trespass on the playing area and thereby disturbed any game in progress. To remedy this situation, some unknown person put up a semi-circular barricade around the doors on either side. This resulted in creating the most unusual hourglass shape of the court. It was from Karachi and the badminton played there on a court of the oddest shape because of fortuitous architectural circumstances, that Major Wingfield derived the initial, wasp-waisted shape of his tennis court. Another version, however, asserts that all this happened not in far-off India but in the Duke's own drawing room, in which the doors were built in that fashion.

Whichever the true facts, no longer ascertainable, the sport assumed wide popularity in India, where its first rules were printed in Karachi in 1877. Also, there is no doubt that English army personnel were largely

LLYFRGELL COLEG MENAI LIBRARY

responsible (whether first in India or England really does not matter) for the adoption of the sport and the formation of the earliest English clubs in seaside resorts, such as Southsea and Bath, where they spent their leave and retirement.

To achieve uniformity in the game, particularly in the shape and size of the court, the Badminton Association of England was formed in 1893. Its fourteen foundation members, meeting at Southsea, laid down the first rules which they based on those drawn up at Karachi. As late as 1901, the Association decided that courts must be rectangular. From England, touring players and teams pioneered and fostered badminton throughout the British Commonwealth and carried enthusiasm for it to Denmark and the United States. The International Badminton Federation dates back to 1934.

The missile used in badminton was not at first exclusively the shuttlecock, but frequently a woollen ball. It was soon realized that the shuttle (which then completely superseded the ball) and, at first was a piece of cork into which an unspecified number of feathers were stuck, was most unpredictable in its flight. With good reason, it was referred to by some as a wobbler. Around 1900 it was replaced by a barrel-shaped shuttle, still made of cork but with chicken feathers in their natural curve inserted around the flattened top — which gave it its distinctive appearance.

The straight-feather shuttle was introduced in 1909. The number of suitable feathers which could be obtained from the wings of the goose ranged from fourteen to sixteen. As a whole army of geese would be needed to supply the required raw material, this was not only impracticable but uneconomic, even if the remainder of the bird could be sold for mattresses and the dining table.

Inevitably, the need arose for a substitute, non-feather shuttle, and this led to numerous experiments and inventions: from fabric and papier mâché, to the modern plastic 'bird' first made of polythene and then of nylon.

Of course, each material, because of its different properties of texture, smoothness, and weight, to mention merely a few, and the essential consideration of trajectory, length of flight, and wind resistance, demanded painstaking research to attain an ideal shape and construction of the shuttle. The many patents taken out in the course of the years in many countries reflect the metamorphosis of the shuttle in the short history of the sport.

The unique flight of the shuttle (often called a bird in the United States) has given the game perhaps its greatest appeal. Its range of possible speeds excels that of almost any other missile. Gently tapped, the shuttle merely floats. Hit hard, it can travel at a terrific pace, with an initial velocity exceeding 100 mph (160 km) though, because of its peculiar make-up, this speed is quickly spent.

Badminton also became the name of a famous series of sports books, the first of its kind in the world. Oddly enough, this does not include the very game that bears the identical name.

The story of the origin of the Badminton Library testifies to the Duke's fame as a sportsman of most diverse tastes. Early in the spring of 1882, Longmans, Green & Co., the old established publishing firm in London, was considering a new edition of Blaine's *Encyclopedia of Sports*, then out of print. However, while discussing the project, it became apparent that the text as it then existed was largely out of date and required revision. New sports had arisen and others had changed considerably.

On further examination, Mr C. J. Longman suggested it was evident that to do justice to the subject it would be preferable to publish a number of separate volumes, each devoted to an individual sport and written by an expert.

This was decided on. The next question was who would be best qualified to edit the new works. A thorough knowledge of many sports was essential. It did not take long for it to be realized that 'of all English sportsmen none fulfilled every essential condition so fully as the Duke of Beaufort'. He was 'the hereditary master of one of the most famous packs of hounds in England, a member of the Jockey Club, a keen lover of the turf, a coachman of unequalled skill, an admirable shot and a most expert fisherman'.

All agreed that, 'if only his Grace could be induced to lend his invaluable aid, success was assured'. Moreover, 'a peculiarly attractive and appropriate title for the library, The Badminton, naturally followed'.

Wisely, a member of the firm who was also a friend of the Duke undertook to place the project before him. He agreed at once and, enthusiastic from the beginning, called at Longman's offices at Paternoster Row, London, to discuss the details. He himself promised to write the hunting volume, which was to appear first — in May 1885.

The Library of Sports and Pastimes was dedicated to His Royal Highness the Prince of Wales, and in a foreword the editor-in-chief explained its objective in these words:

> There is no modern encyclopedia to which the inexperienced man, who seeks guidance in the practice of the various . . . sports and pastimes, can turn for information. The Badminton Library is offered to supply the want . . . written by men who are in every case adepts at the sport or pastime of which they write.

For some time Badminton was also the name of a pleasant, iced drink, a concoction of claret, soda, spices, and sugar. This used to be served at the Ducal parties on the Beaufort estate, no doubt at first to refresh players. Benjamin Disraeli wrote of those fragrant cups of Badminton which 'soothed and stimulated'. They are now of the past. But not so their namesake, the sport, the ultimate result of an ancient, magical rite of divination.

Chapter 4

BASEBALL

Baseball, America's national game (at first spelled base ball), is second to none in the fame it enjoys, the millions of its loyal fans, and the confusion that surrounded claims about its origin.

A commission appointed to trace its beginnings gave a report that was proved to be completely erroneous. Nevertheless, as the result of its 'findings' Americans erected — at the wrong place — a shrine to commemorate in perpetuity the birth of the game, and honoured the wrong man as its inventor, at a date which was equally unauthentic.

It all started when American baseball lovers conjected how, where and when it all began, and, in patriotic zeal, some enthusiasts claimed that baseball was undoubtedly an indigenous American game which owed nothing to foreign lands. This assertion was made as early as 1889 at a public dinner at Delmonico's, New York City, arranged to welcome back from a world-tour America's star players and attended by some 300 guests, including Mark Twain. The claim, made by Abraham G. Mills (President of the National League), one of the speakers, was greatly applauded. On the other hand, Henry Chadwick, a former cricketer and English-born, America's first baseball reporter, and a veritable walking encyclopedia on the sport, contributed an article to *Baseball Guide* in 1903 in which he expressed the view that the game was derived from the English 'rounders', which he himself had played 'back home' as a schoolboy. 'After school time we boys would proceed (with balls and sticks) to the nearest field, select a smooth portion of it, and lay out the ground for a contest. This was easily done by placing four stones or posts in position as base stations, and by digging a hole in the ground where the batsman had to stand.'

A heated controversy was the inevitable result of the contradictory claims supported with ardour (and often emotion) by the two schools of thought. To settle the question for all time, Mr Albert G. Spalding, one of the famous nineteenth-century players and co-founder of the sporting goods manufacturing company bearing his name, suggested the appointment of a committee 'to search anywhere that is possible and thus learn the real facts concerning the origin and development of the game'.

The members of the commission chosen were seven men of 'high repute and undoubted knowledge of baseball, including two US Senators'. Abraham G. Mills was the chairman. Their report, published in 1907, certainly bore the signatures of the whole committee (excepting one member who had meanwhile died), but actually it was the sole work of Mills. It clearly stated that baseball was an indigenous American game and had no connection with foreign sports, particularly not the English rounders, and that it was devised by Abner Doubleday, the renowned soldier, as a youth in Cooperstown, NY, in 1839.

Mills wrote: 'In the days when Abner Doubleday attended school in Cooperstown, it was a common thing for two dozen or more of schoolboys to join in a game of ball.' Doubtless collisions between players trying to catch the batted ball were a frequent occurrence, and together with the practice of putting out the runner by hitting him with the ball, injured the players. He could therefore well understand 'how the orderly mind of the embryo West Pointer would devise a scheme for limiting the contestants on each side and allotting them to field positions each with a certain amount of territory; also substituting the existing method of putting out the base runner for the old one of plugging him with the ball'.

Mills said that Abner had played the first game of this type in Cooperstown on a summer's day in 1839. Arranging it, he had invented the diamond, indicating the positions for the players. However, Mills's only proof was 'a circumstantial statement by a reputable gentleman' — Abner Graves, a one-time resident of Cooperstown — who claimed that he could recollect the fact, sixty-eight years after the event!

Perhaps it is of more than casual interest that Doubleday had been a close friend of Mills. As a Major General, he had been in command of the Union Army at the close of the first day's fight in the battle of Gettysburg, and his remains were interred at Arlington. A famous soldier thus had been made by Mills an idol of sport as well.

Even Spalding himself, as the initiator of the search, was far from satisfied. Nowhere could he trace data that substantiated Mill's story. (And yet, when in 1910 he published a book on *The National Game*, out of loyalty to the commission, he still refrained from reopening the case and thereby rousing new controversy.) Nothing further happened in the sifting of the evidence, which was considered factual and final.

No one could have been happier with the report than the people of Cooperstown. Sincere in their belief that its version of events was correct, they grasped its implications for their own village and acted upon them. Those discovered 'facts' could change their bucolic hamlet into a very focus of American pride — a sanctuary of their country's national game.

Obviously, the first thing to do was to seek out the original field (then a mere cow pasture) and give it proper status. They leased it in 1919 and, in the following year, established it as a permanent national monument, naming it 'The Doubleday Field'. (A New York Supreme Court Order in 1923 made the field the property of the village.) As time passed, the project was ever further advanced until eventually the former grazing paddock had become an exhibition field for Major League matches, with flawless turf and a steel and concrete stadium.

An accidental discovery in 1935 led to a significant development in the baseball saga. In a garret of a home at Fly Creek, a ball was found in a trunk. It was believed this ball had belonged to Abner Graves and no doubt had therefore been handled by Doubleday himself. As soon as the news reached Cooperstown, one of its people rushed to Fly Creek to acquire this relic (for $5).

By now, Cooperstown people were most anxious to promote in any way possible their town's baseball attraction. They were not unmindful, of course, that this would improve business. Could there be anything better than the 'original' ball, a relic linked with the very beginning of the national game, to lure thousands of visitors? The 'find' prompted Cooperstonians to start a baseball museum 'for the purpose of collecting and preserving pictures and relics reflecting the development of the National Game from the time of its inception, through the ingenuity of Major General Abner Doubleday, in 1839, to the present'.

The idea caught on at once, and prized possessions were gathered from all over the country to be displayed at the new shrine. Babe Ruth sent his bat, uniform, and home run balls. Earliest newspaper articles on the sport, pictures of the first games, and cups won by the most famous players were among hundreds of treasured exhibits in the museum. The wide publicity given to the venture really put Cooperstown on the map and made an unknown site, 'way up there in the woods', one of America's most beloved landmarks.

Certainly, no one interested in baseball and its promotion could ignore the opportunity which now offered itself: the approaching centenary of the game — at least according to Mills's chronology — due in 1939. Its nation-wide celebration, if properly organized on a grand scale, would make history. All efforts of Cooperstown (and of other interested parties) now centred on this event.

To the national Baseball Museum was added The Hall

of Fame, solemnly dedicated on 12 June 1939. Bronze plaques on its walls paid homage to the immortals of the game, while above a fireplace an oil painting of Doubleday was hung. The climax of the anniversary celebrations was a pageant portraying the historical highlights of the game, and an all-star contest between teams composed of the greatest players, on the original Doubleday Field.

Everything went according to plan. President Franklin D. Roosevelt himself gave official sanction to the celebration, and thereby recognition to the myth. In a message, he clearly stated that 'we should all be grateful to Abner Doubleday. Little did he or the group that was with him in Cooperstown, NY, in 1839, realize the boon they were giving the nation in devising baseball'. The State of New York placed an official marker at the entrance to the original field to indicate for all time 'the birthplace of baseball'. The US government issued a baseball centenary postage stamp, but wisely omitted Doubleday's picture.

The story of baseball presents a striking example of the pitfalls in recorded history and of the danger of taking for fact even the most widely accepted tradition. It started with one man's undoubtedly sincere but misguided conviction. This was seized upon in all good faith by a few citizens. Fired by enthusiasm and supreme love of the game (and their village), they built up on the unsubstantiated claim a fantastic, monumental complex, all the time supported by the Major Leagues. Duly publicized and utilized, the legend caught the imagination of an entire nation and led it to celebrate and perpetuate a man, a site, and a date for reasons which were unreal. By men's wish to believe, fiction had conquered fact.

However, even while the preparations for the centenary celebrations were in progress, Robert W. Henderson, of the New York Public Library, presented data which proved that all the claims made were spurious. Baseball, after all, *could* be traced to rounders, an English game with similar rules and features. The earliest illustration of baseball (a woodcut showing boys playing it on Boston Common), and its first printed rules, had appeared in *The Book of Sports* published by Robin Carver in 1834. The author himself had remarked on the change of the game's name from 'rounders' to 'baseball' because it was the name 'generally adopted in our country'. However, even more significant was the fact that Carver's rules were an exact copy of the rules of rounders as they had been published in *The Boys' Own Book*, written by William Clerke in London in 1829 and reprinted in the United States that same year. There was no doubt about the fatherhood of American baseball.

Henderson also pointed out that there was clear evidence that years before Doubleday's birth a primitive sort of baseball had been played in at least a dozen places, though Cooperstown was not one of them! Even Doubleday's presence in the hamlet in 1839 could be doubted. On his retirement from the army, he had taken up writing but not once had he made a single reference to baseball. This would be more than surprising on the part of a man alleged to have been its originator.

The earliest stages of baseball's forerunner (no matter which it was) can easily be imagined. A boy would pass his time with a ball and a bat. (The ball, perhaps, was a cast-off cricket ball, or one made by the lad himself of tightly wound yarn without any covering. The bat was a stout, round stick or a discarded cricket bat.) A friend joined him and the two improvised a game with a ball, a bat, and a base (in the form of a stake or a stone). The batter tried to hit the ball far enough to give himself time to run to the stake (or stone) and back, without being hit ('plugged' or 'soaked'). As other boys joined in the fun, they added more bases, until eventually the field of play had assumed a square shape, with a base at each corner. Gradually other features, demanding greater skill, were added. Once the batter had hit the ball, he ran the bases as far as he could get at first, and until 1839, in a clockwise direction. He was 'out' if he missed the ball three times, if the ball was caught in flight or after the first bounce, or if he was hit while trying to reach a base. When each player of one side had been put out, the other took over.

Sometimes the runners collided heavily with the stakes and injured themselves. To avoid this, the stakes were eventually replaced by flat stones. However, when these proved far from an ideal solution, they were superseded by sacks filled with sand. To prevent them from being moved, either accidentally in the heat of a game or deliberately so as to increase the distance the runner had to cover, they were secured to a small peg. The type of game thus arrived at revealed the features of rudimentary cricket and of rounders. Following this evolution of bases, terminology changed and, instead of 'running to the stake', the players began to speak of 'running to the base'. As a natural consequence, it became customary also to describe the game as base ball, eventually to be fused into one word.

Undoubtedly all these games were improvised, and 'rules' were agreed upon on the spur of the moment, depending on the lie of the ground and the number and type of players. A significant difference from later baseball was that a batter was 'out' when hit by a thrown ball. This necessitated the use of a ball that was not too hard. It was made, therefore, of cotton or wool. Its texture, of course, restricted the distance it would travel and its bounce.

All these popular games with bat and ball were merely variations on the same theme. They were really recreations, and not organized sports. Most prominent among them were 'one old cat', 'two old cat' etc., rounders, and town ball. They differed only in minor ways.

In its most primitive form, the game of 'old cat', as played in England, at first used a wooden cat in the shape of a spindle, which was hit by a stick. It then grew into a pastime with a batter, a pitcher, and two bases. A boy, after batting the ball from one base, ran to the other and back. He was 'out' if a rival caught the ball either while it was in flight or after it had bounced. The number of boys taking part in the game determined the number of bases, and according to their number, the game was called 'one old cat', or 'two old cat', and so on.

In rounders, played by schoolboys in medieval England, the field was marked by posts or stones. As in 'old cat', the number of players was not fixed and any number of lads could take part. They divided themselves into two teams of equal size. There was no specified position for those taking the field, except for the pitcher (known as the packer or feeder) and the batter (referred to as the striker).

Town ball actually was only another name for rounders, and possibly it was introduced through games played by village boys on the occasion of town meetings.

Out of those diverse versions of a game with a bat and a ball evolved baseball. It was not born suddenly, but grew slowly and steadily. Baseball, indeed, is the American adaptation of the much older English rounders, though it differs from it as much as draughts from chess. Both are played on a chequered board, yet they are worlds apart in intricacy and the skill they require.

In search of references to some earliest types of American baseball, some significant dates have been found in journals and autobiographical works. Pride of place belongs to the diary of a revolutionary soldier. It recorded a game of 'base' in which he had taken part at Valley Forge in 1778. A Princeton student in his journal referred to a game of 'baste ball' he had played on his university campus in 1786. Another source, an autobiography, speaks of an actual baseball club that existed in Rochester, NY, in 1825. It counted fifty members whose ages ranged from eighteen to forty years.

In the 1820s a rudimentary form of baseball had become (under various names) an enjoyable pastime for groups of people in several places. Yet it experienced no dramatic growth and the game was pursued rather haphazardly. Town ball was an early, popular pursuit in New England and certainly was modelled on rounders. It was introduced into Pennsylvania in 1831, and the

Olympic Town Ball Club was established in Philadelphia in 1833. The 'New York Game' first came under notice only in 1842.

There was no uniformity of rules. Rival captains merely agreed on each occasion on the size of the field, the distance between bases, and the number of players. In the 1830s it had become customary to limit a team to eleven or twelve men, as the batsman rightly felt that to drive a ball through a larger number was hardly possible. There was a continuous exchange of ideas and all the time players improved their game by adopting better features from others. Still, there were marked differences between various cities, though all versions of the game had taken over from rounders the four post base stations and the rule that base runners were put out by being hit with the ball.

In 1842, a group of young men in New York, keen on promoting 'health, recreation and social enjoyment', began to meet in Lower Manhattan. On Sunday afternoons they played baseball on a vacant lot there, the future site of the original Madison Square Garden. To start with, everything was informal. In 1845, they organized themselves into a social and baseball club, which they call the Knickerbockers. One of its charter members, Alexander Joy Cartwright, then pointed out that the time had come to organize and standardize the game, and for this purpose he was asked by Duncan F. Curry, the president, to chair a committee. When they had drawn up rules, they submitted them to the club for due consideration. Baseball owes its modern, significant features to their proposals. In fact, the committee established the fundamental rules that still prevail.

A team was limited to nine men. Each player was allotted a definite place (almost identical with the present-day practice). The committee did not forget, either, to position the scorer and umpire. For the first time it was ruled 'that in no instance is a ball to be thrown at a player'. This was the final break with rounders. The ball was now thrown to a baseman, but no longer at a base runner.

Most importantly, Cartwright himself drew up the blueprint of the diamond, fixing the distance between the bases at ninety feet (27 m). Its modern version is an exact replica of his design. The adoption of the diamond was due to a practical consideration. Players on the home run experienced difficulties in turning the corners of the square, and to streamline their progress the diamond shape was chosen. This enabled them to move almost in a circle.

The Knickerbockers were the very first regular baseball team to be formed. Another similar group started at the same time called itself the New York Club. It was a foregone conclusion that the Knickerbockers, who so far had only played among themselves, would challenge the new club. This happened on 19 June 1846 — an historic date in the history of baseball. The Knicks invited the New Yorks to a match at their new home at Elysian Field, Hoboken, NJ, 'one of the most picturesque and delightful places imaginable', fronting on the Hudson River. The five-acre (2 hectares) property was easily accessible from New York by ferry. The match took place on the Knickerbockers' permanent playing field there, on which they had laid out the first regulation diamond. (A plaque erected in 1946 on its very site commemorates the auspicious occasion, adding the legend that 'it is generally conceded that until this time the game was not seriously regarded'. Of course, the implication here was a protest against the fictitious claims of Cooperstown, and an intention to put history right.)

It did not really matter that the challenger, the Knickerbockers, were slaughtered by 23 to 1 'aces' (the original term for runs). Another historic 'first' of the occasion was the fine (of six cents) one of the Knickerbockers had to pay for — swearing. Unfortunately, his actual words (and what caused them) have not been recorded, though the name of the offender (J. W. Davis) is preserved. In fact, this very first club worked out a whole schedule of penalties. This fixed a fine of fifty cents for disobeying the instructions of one's captain, and of half the amount for disputing the umpire's decision or even anticipating it by voicing one's own opinion.

A few years later (in 1849), Cartwright's group pioneered the earliest baseball uniform: straw hats, white flannel shirts, and blue woolen trousers.

Baseball, indeed, had arrived. All that was to follow merely evolved what the Knickerbockers had started. They certainly could not restrict its practice to any exclusive class. All amateur clubs in the New York district, which were created soon afterwards, adopted their rules. New and exciting techniques were added and the first stars appeared.

In 1857 amateur clubs joined together in the National Association of Baseball Players, which produced the first uniform rules. They stipulated that a batsman was out when a batted ball was caught either in the air or on the first bounce. The length of a game was fixed at nine innings.

In 1869, Harry Wright organized the first professional baseball team in which regular salaries were paid to the players. This was certainly a revolutionary — and ardently criticized — step at the time. In 1871, the National Association of Professional Baseball Players was established in New York. It was also on Wright's instructions that the first knee-length uniforms were designed by a local dressmaker for the Cincinnati Red Stockings. A mask was worn for the first time in 1875. To John Montgomery Ward belongs the courageous innovation (he ignored possible public ridicule of what was a novel fashion) of wearing a glove on the fielding hand.

No one, it seemed, could escape the fascination of playing baseball or watching it being played, not even the future President Abraham Lincoln. It is said that when a delegation of politicians called on him to inform him of his nomination for the Presidency, he was engaged in a game himself and kept the men waiting until he had had another chance to make a base hit.

Baseball became more and more an integral part of

the American way of life. Its vivid slang and terminology entered everyday speech. This even includes the 'giving (or taking) of a rain cheque'. It originated, so it is said, in the custom of issuing spectators with a ticket for another game if the baseball match for which they had paid was interrupted or cancelled because of rain.

Indicative of the magnetism of the sport that no one could resist was this poem, printed in the *Official Base Ball Record* of 1886:

> 'In court', says the card on the lawyer's door,
> 'Back in ten minutes', on many more;
> 'Gone to hospital', on the doctor's slate,
> On another, 'Sit down and wait',
> 'Gone to the bank', on the notary's sign;
> 'Arbitration', that young clerk of mine.
> 'Back soon', on the broker's book;
> 'Collecting rents', on my agent's hook.
> They were all too busy, a matter quite new.
> Very sorry was I, I had nothing to do.
> Then I hied me hands to the baseball ground,
> And every man on the grand stand found.

Henry Chadwick, whose view had been so prominent in the controversy on the origin of the sport, became known as 'the father of baseball'. He originated the box score, and his extensive knowledge of baseball and his unsurpassed love of it made him the most reliable source of information and an apostle of the American game.

The origins of many sports can be traced back to early religious rites or magic. Baseball, however, presents almost a picture in reverse. Started in the streets and on the greens of hamlets and towns as a pastime of young lads, it became almost a cult, with all the paraphernalia of devout religion. It created its own myth and a gospel which, though proven wrong, is still believed by many and fervently quoted. It built a shrine to which thousands of people make a pilgrimage to gaze reverently at numerous relics, assembled and preserved almost with awe. Its heroes are not only lionized but idolized, in the original and not merely metaphorical meaning of the word. Like the saints of old, the heroes are 'enshrined' and worshipped as immortals of a game which is played and watched with a devotion and zest experienced elsewhere only in the realm of religious faith.

Chapter 5

BASKETBALL

Devised by a clergyman, basketball has the distinction of being the only major competitive sport which began on American soil. All other so-called new games were mere adaptations of established sports. Basketball presented something completely original; it was deliberately created as an American game.

It was first played within the precincts of the Young Men's Christian Association in Springfield, Massachusetts, in early December 1891.

Dr James A. Naismith, a Canadian by birth, a graduate of McGill University, and a Presbyterian minister, was also a good athlete. In 1890 he enrolled as a student of physical education at Springfield's International YMCA training school.

His exceptional qualities soon caught the attention of Dr Luther Gulick, head of the athletic department. Most likely it was due to his persuasion that, on completion of the course, Naismith decided to remain at the school as an instructor. An incident at a rugby game had convinced the young clergyman that 'there might be more effective ways of doing good besides preaching'.

He certainly did not believe in the orthodox ways of life, whether in theology or sport. He felt that whenever the exigencies of the times demanded it, a 'new look', a reform, was necessary.

At that period the youth of the country was unsettled and could not find a proper use for leisure hours. Sport was an obvious outlet, and at the YMCA especially, everything possible was done to attract youngsters and get them to play traditional games.

Somehow none of the sports adopted from England, Germany, Sweden, and France proved successful. After a little while, the young people became bored and looked for something new, and membership of the YMCA grew ever smaller.

It was essential to find a sport that could hold the youngsters' attention. At Springfield, the problem was regarded as a national one, and Dr Gulick asked all tutors to devise or suggest an exciting type of game which could be played indoors, day and night, and especially in winter, when baseball was impossible on account of snow or the hardness of the ground.

Naismith carefully studied all the existing sports, listing their distinctive features. He then asked himself which characteristics should be embodied in the new game he was determined to introduce. He was convinced it had to be a team game, easily learned and enjoyed by average men and women. The emphasis was to be not on the players' strength or weight, but on the skill and speed of both the individual and the team. The game had to be exciting both to watch and to play.

Naismith considered that perhaps just a ball should be used, certainly neither sticks nor bats. A large and light ball, easy to handle but difficult to conceal, seemed ideal. To keep the game moving freely and safely, all tackling was to be banned and rough conduct prohibited. The ball should be touched by the hands alone.

All that was left to determine was the game's final objective. Naismith decided that the winning team had to score a maximum number of throws of the ball into a basket, and to encourage individual skill and initiative the number of players in each team was restricted.

Having logically developed the elements of his new game, Naismith lost no time in arranging a match in the gymnasium of the YMCA. A peach-basket was suspended from each end of its balcony, and it was those baskets which gave the game its name.

Earlier, Naismith had worked out rules. To encourage

individual initiative and skill, he restricted the number
of players belonging to each team. Basic provisions were
that:

- the ball must never be kicked but thrown in the air;
- the only way of moving it on was by passing it to
  another player or by dribbling it — bouncing it with
  one hand while running;
- in no circumstances should a player run while holding
  the ball;
- the goal had to be above the players' heads and
  horizontal;
- as a non-contact game, any kind of rough play
  brought disqualification and a penalty.

The rules were displayed on the school's notice board.
Unfortunately, one of the students souvenired them and
with it the only existing copy.

Basketball immediately became popular. At nearby
Buckingham Grade School, the women instructors
wanted to try it out themselves. They were granted
permission but with the one proviso that they did so
in private. The result was that not only did they become
enthusiastic fans of the sport but one of them — Maude
— attracted Dr Naismith's attention so much that they
were married soon afterwards.

The new game caught on throughout America and
then spread throughout the world. Naismith's original
thirteen rules were constantly changed and not until 1934
were they finally standardized.

Each team originally had seven players but in the
course of time the number was changed to five, eight,
nine, and eleven. On one occasion, at Cornell University,
there were fifty students on each side.

The peach-basket was replaced by a metal one and
in 1906 by open loops fixed on a pole or board, ten
feet (3 m) above the ground. This dispensed with the
ladder that had been necessary until then to retrieve
the ball from the basket.

At times, over-enthusiastic spectators tried to do their bit to make their side win. Taking their seat on the balcony as close to the basket as they could get, they used their hands, sticks, or even unbrellas to push the ball on its flight either into the basket or away from it — depending on the team they favoured.

To make such unsportsmanlike interference impossible, backboards were introduced. At first, they were of wire mesh. This soon proved unsuitable. It gave an advantage to the home team, familiar with its peculiarities. Plain wood was then chosen, though in many cases glass also was used so as not to obstruct the spectators' view.

The many benefits of the game soon became apparent. It demanded and fostered alert minds and supple bodies. Decisions had to be made quickly, play had to be neat and nimble. It certainly never grew boring as situations changed all the time, and players had to perfect tricks of sudden stopping, feint-passing, and side-stepping. Furthermore, those anxious to find in sport not only a pastime or a means of character-building but also health-giving exercise, were gratified. The fact that the ball was mostly up in the air, necessitated frequent stretching and jumping on the part of the players. This certainly was most beneficial, particularly for the growing adolescent.

There is no doubt that basketball owes its existence to Naismith. However, it is possible that he was influenced by an indigenous game played thousands of years earlier on American soil by Mayan and Toltec races.

As a student of religion he must have been aware of the exciting discoveries of Mayan and Toltec ballcourts at excavations in Mexico. They had been buried for more than 1500 years under thick jungle. They varied in size. One of the largest is at Chichen Itza. It is in a state of almost perfect preservation.

These ancient races did not play ball to amuse themselves or for the sake of physical culture. For them it was a most serious and solemn fertility rite. The result of the game, they were convinced, determined the life of future generations and the continuation of the cycle of nature — whether there would be rain or drought, fecundity or barrenness.

The playing field was huge — 480 feet by 120 feet (144 m by 36 m) — and surrounded by temples. Two long, high walls flanked it on either side, and, protruding from them, high up at their very centre, were two huge, vertical, stone rings. These were the ancestors of the modern hoops in the game of basketball. The acoustics were so perfect that anyone speaking in an ordinary tone of voice at one end of the court could be heard clearly at the other.

When playing, two teams passed a solid, rubber ball to and fro between them, thereby scoring points. The players, however, were not permitted to touch the ball with their hands. They had to strike it either with the knee, elbow, or hip, for which protectors were worn.

The object was to get the ball through one of the rings. This was most difficult to achieve. When accomplished, it marked the end of the game — and of the losing side's captain. Immediately afterwards, he was beheaded by the captain of the winning team!

The spectators did not go scot-free, either. Fortunately, they were apt to lose only their belongings: clothes and jewelry which they forfeited to the player who had shot the winning goal. No wonder that they tried to escape the moment this happened. But friends of the goal-shooter pursued them to exact the tribute due to him.

Chapter 6

BILLIARDS AND SNOOKER

BILLIARDS

Of many suggestions as to how billiards began, the least likely but most amusing is linked with a sixteenth-century London pawnbroker, William Kew. On rainy days when business was slack, he used to remove the three balls of his trade emblem from outside his shop. At first, he possibly did so merely to preserve their sheen. Bored by inactivity, he soon found that he could use the spheres in a sort of game, pushing them around with his yard-stick. Thus '*Bill*' with his *yard*-measure and three balls created *bill-yard*.

According to this version, a minor change in the spelling of his surname, created the term for the indispensable tool of all billiard games — the *cue*.

An equally fantastic claim is made for the origin of the marker. One of the early players, it is said, was so enthusiastic that he neglected all other duties. His wife certainly did not relish his playing and, well aware of this, he left instructions with the man at the door to watch and '*mark her*'!

However plausible these stories sound, they are based on mere folk etymology. Yet, they add some flavour to the many unconfirmed, unfounded, if not indeed altogether false tales told about the date, the place, and the circumstances of the birth of billiards and its nomenclature.

The history of billiards links fact and fiction, winding its way from the green lawns of early bowling to the green baize cloth of a table, no doubt a reminder of its 'natural' roots. The game's development owes much to the ingenious mind of a French political prisoner and the smart business brain of an Englishman.

No wonder that the complex past of billiards confused early writers, among them Charles Cotton, the friend of Izaak Walton. His was the first English description of billiards. Tracing this 'most genteel, cleanly and ingenious game' in his *Compleat Gamester*, in 1674, Cotton wrote that billiards was first played by the Italians, but then, strangely, also says that Spain was its birthplace:

> Billiards from Spain at first derived its name,
> Both an ingenious and a cleanly game.
> One gamester leads (the table green as grass)
> And each, like warriors, strive to gain the Pass.

Other authorities suggested that in the first place billards was an Oriental sport pursued out-of-doors. The Crusaders had brought it from the East to England, where it had been changed into 'lawn-bowls on tables'.

Frequently cited as the oldest reference to billiards is a passage dealing with Anacharsis, a mythical Scythian prince of the sixth century BC and a contemporary of Solon. On one of his journeys through Greece he is said to have watched players engaged in a pastime very much like modern billiards. Actually, similarities to the game have been pointed out in a great variety of Roman, Greek, and later, French sports.

Another tradition asserts that Catkire More, second-century Irish king and ruler of Leinster, engaged in billiards. He bequeathed, it is told, '55 billiard balls of brass with pools and cues of the same material' to a certain Drimoth. However, this claim, made by Abbe McGeoghegan in his *History of Ireland*, cannot be true. The very wording of the legacy proves it unreal, as in the second century neither term — billiard or cue — existed.

Shakespeare, the source of so many quotations, has been equally cited as an authority on billiards. Indeed, he does mention the game but, unfortunately, in a rather misleading way. In *Antony and Cleopatra* (Act II, scene 5), written in 1607, the Queen of Egypt invites Charmian, her attendant: 'Come, let us to billiards . . . ' This passage has been quoted as evidence that 2000 years ago, in Cleopatra's days, billiards must have been a common pastime. All it proves, of course, is merely that the sport was established in Shakespearean England, so that the poet could expect his audience to understand what he was talking about.

All these various and contradictory claims show that no one really knows exactly where and when billiards originated. We can only reconstruct, hypothetically, how it all started, taking our 'cue' from reliable evidence at hand.

Most likely the game developed out of an early version of lawn bowls. When inclement weather too frequently interfered, the frustrated players went indoors. There, the restricted space led to an adjustment. Instead of shoving stone balls toward the cone, players began to knock them first with a wooden pole, and then a mace, shaped very much like an elongated Indian war club.

Some players soon felt that the new fashion lacked excitement. It was far too easy and needed some features to tax their skill. For that purpose, a number of hazards was introduced, adopted from another, then popular game. Old prints have preserved its main features. Players had to drive a ball through some obstacles and around others, without knocking them down. The 'battleground' thus presented a variety of objects, such as hoops and ivory pegs. In one version, known as the fortification game, the hazards were miniature forts and military equipment.

Such arrangements made the indoor game more exciting, but experience taught that they did not create the ideal sport. When players knocked the balls too hard, they rolled too far. Moreover, stout men could not enjoy a game that called for frequent stooping and bending.

It was almost an obvious step to raise the game on to a platform — the billiard table. In recollection of the original outside lawn (and to give the table a suitable surface), this was eventually covered with a green cloth.

The table further restricted the playing area and this, in turn, demanded a more intimate style and new rules. The balls now had to be pushed, not knocked. This could not easily be done by the former method of using the thick end of the club. The natural thing was to apply the thin end (then broad with a slight curve at the end and pointed) to propel the ball. This was the beginning of the modern cue.

It was now realized that passing the ball through and around many hoops and arches was much too cumbersome. In the course of time these were replaced by holes cut into the sides of the table and known at first as hazards. It is a name preserved to this day in one type of shot, though the hazard itself was eventually superseded by the modern pocket. The changes, of course, made the cone used in the old game redundant.

The game was now played with two balls — one to shoot and the other as a target to be hit and directed so that it would fall into a pocket. The player who could do so with the least number of shots, won. At first, two pockets were fixed, one at each end of the table. Then their number was doubled. When, finally, the table was of an oblong shape, two additional pockets — midway — increased the number to six.

All other developments in equipment, accessories, and style really were mere improvements. The balls, originally round pebbles, were shaped out of lignum vitae, then of brass, and eventually ivory. The sticks which developed from the original club grew lighter and smaller.

By the fourteenth and fifteenth centuries, billiards had been adopted as a pastime both in England and France. Its name is French and is derived from *billiart*, a word describing a little staff or stick. It is the diminutive of *bille*, which means 'log'.

The earliest actual code of rules, framed about 1517, is attributed to Henrique Devigne (also spelled De Vigne), a French artist who lived during the reign of Charles IX. He also designed billiard tables. It was these traditions that led some authorities to regard him as the real father of the game.

King Louis XIV was most instrumental in popularizing billiards. In 1694 his health was indifferent, and his doctor felt it essential for him to take regular exercises after meals. The doctor himself had played billiards in England and was convinced that it was the game for the king to take up.

Louis soon became an enthusiastic and expert player. Eventually only one man could beat him. He was M. de Chamillart. In acknowledgment of his superiority, so the story goes, the king made him a minister of the crown. It must be the only appointment to cabinet rank ever made that was due to skill in billiards! A seventeenth-century illustration (included in Cotton's *Compleat Gamester*) shows the king at play. He is using a shovel-shaped stick to propel the ball on an oblong table. Billiards became a vogue because of the king's interest.

It was well established when Captain Mingaud, one of Napoleon's officers, was imprisoned in the Bastille. While there he somehow managed to have a billiard table installed in his cell, which must have been rather spacious. Experimentation to improve the game occupied him daily, so much that when the time for his release came, he asked permission to stay on to continue his tests for a better style. Billiards owes him a tremendous debt for his inventions.

Through the years, the stick, or mast, further developed and eventually reached its tapering shape, which explains its name, cue, derived from the French word for 'tail', spelled *queue*. About 1790 Mingaud devised a new cue that was adopted universally. With a file — rather an unusual instrument in the hands of a prisoner — he rounded the square end of the stick and created the modern tip. By this simple operation, he could make shots which far surpassed any ever seen before.

Having completed the task, he left prison and spent most of his free time displaying his new skill and his cue wherever billiards was played in Paris. His splendid shots with the novel stick aroused great enthusiasm among spectators, and billiards became the rage. In 1807, he further improved the cue by fixing a leather tip to its end.

The next move to advance the game came from England. John ('Jack') Carr, a most astute man, was a lover of the game. Indeed, he was to become the world's first billiard champion. He also liked money and was well aware that an aura of the uncanny was good for business promotion. And knowing the psychology of crowds, he was able to amass a fortune — through billiards!

In 1820 he was employed as a marker by a Mr Bartley at Bath, and soon excelled in bringing off apparently impossible shots with ease and assurance. His speciality was a side-twist or, as it came to be known later, the screw-stroke. No one else could achieve it, and each time he used it he did so with great ceremonial.

When people asked him how he did it, he confided gravely that it was all due to a magic powder he had invented and applied to the tip of his cue. Of course, its composition was his secret. However, anxious to help other players, he was quite prepared to supply them with his 'twisting chalk' — for a price. He sold his chalk in small pillboxes, at half a crown each, in those days a big amount.

All went exceedingly well for Carr, until one day a customer, who had used up his supply of expensive magic, was unable to buy more and decided to use ordinary chalk. He found it had the same result. Soon he broadcast his discovery and Carr's lucrative business in chalk ended. Carr's stroke became part of billiards and is still referred to as putting 'English' on the ball.

Carr used the money he gained to travel to France and Spain, where he zealously spread his novel style. Wherever he went, his new, dexterous shot and chalked cue tip made him a hero. Eventually, his triumphant tour came to an end, and he returned to England almost in rags. His love of gambling had cost him his fortune. But he had not yet lost his skill or astuteness. Going to a billiard saloon looking very unlike a world champion, he was unrecognized. He challenged a player who in no time lost £70 to him.

Carr left at once to buy himself the finest outfit obtainable, including a blue coat, yellow waistcoat, and top boots. Nobly clad, he returned to the saloon next day and (as indeed 'clothes maketh the man') he appeared to be a different person. He challenged his rival of the previous day who did not recognize him. They agreed on a wager, and Carr won.

When Carr had collected his winnings, the loser remarked how truly unfortunate he had been. On two succeeding days he had met two persons capable of giving him a severe beating. Carr then made himself known, thanked the loser politely, and took his leave.

Because of intemperate living, Carr never enjoyed the money he made. Indeed, when about to meet the famous Edwin Kentfield in a match, he became ill and the match did not come off. Kentfield became champion and kept a 'subscription room' in Brighton. In 1829 he published a book called *The Game of Billiards — Scientifically Explained and Practically Set Forth in a Series of Novel and Extraordinary, but Equally Practical Strokes.*

Tables, so far, had been built entirely of wood. Even the surface had been of timber, though experience had taught makers to construct it using small panels, to allow for expansion and avoid buckling. Marble beds had been tried, but found wanting. In hot weather the marble started sweating. In 1827 slate replaced the wood and marble and, covered with smooth cloth, provided a perfect bed, enabling greater accuracy and giving a smoother run.

The table's edges were soon padded with felt. Next came the introduction of rubber cushions. These gave the ball a much better rebound but otherwise proved inadequate. They were subject to changes in temperature, especially in the English winter. Finally, in 1865, vulcanized rubber, resistant to any weather, was adopted.

The philosopher Herbert Spencer, one of England's greatest thinkers, became passionately fond of billiards. Until his health began to wane, he daily went to the

Athenaeum Club to enjoy a game. He could be seen with his coat off, as intent on scoring a victory on the billiard table as he was known to wrestle with a controversialist in the philosophical arena.

The first public billiard room in Britain was opened at the Piazza, Covent Garden, London, early in the nineteenth century. The Royal House did not lag far behind the enthusiasm shown for the game by ordinary people. At Queen Victoria's request, a billiard table was set up in Windsor Castle.

A general code for the game was adopted by the Billiards Association in 1885, and in 1919 the Control Council was formed to organize championships.

THE CANNON

Rather puzzling, if not intriguing, is the term used in billiards, when the cue ball hits two balls in succession. Called a cannon, people have wondered why.

The most obvious explanations coming first to mind, are incorrect. This cannon has nothing to do with shooting — straight or otherwise. Another wrong suggestion made was that a member of the Church, a Canon, was the first to accomplish this feat. In reality, the term derives from the French for the 'red ball', *carram bule*. This contracted into *carombole*, finally to be distorted into the present-day cannon.

SNOOKER

Snooker comes from India. It was evolved there in 1875 by British army personnel stationed in the country. Its name is English. In fact, it is a term originally applied to first-year cadets at the Royal Military College in Woolwich. The game's inventor, tradition has it, was Neville Bowles Chamberlain (later General Sir Neville) who distinguished himself in several campaigns in the sub-continent.

To pass their time during the rainy season, officers of a Devonshire regiment posted at Jubbulpore, played what was known as black pool. This was a development of life pool, which also used black, so-called Rover balls. Neville, a young subaltern at the time, then suggested adding a pink ball to make the game more interesting. After some experimentation, and the introduction of further colors, the various balls were allotted definite positions. That is how eventually snooker came into existance.

Snooker reached England around 1885, possibly through John Roberts, Jnr., who, on a visit to India, was taught the game by Neville himself. The first snooker rules were issued by the English Billiard Association in 1903. Amateurs became its first enthusiasts. The final popularity of snooker undoubtedly was due to its liveliness.

BEHIND THE 8 BALL

Whoever is said to be 'behind the 8 ball' is in a fix. The expression comes from a certain type of pool game which is played with fifteen numbered vari-coloured balls. These have to be pocketed in the sequence of their number — except the (black) 8 ball, which must come last. A player is in real trouble, when the ball next to be 'dropped' is 'behind the 8 ball'. From pool the phrase found its way as a telling metaphor for an awkward situation into the game of life.

Chapter 7

BOXING

The hands are man's most natural means of defence and attack. There is no doubt that they were his earliest weapons and that they were used against man and beast alike. It is not surprising, therefore, that boxing is one of the most ancient sports. Indeed, it goes back to prehistoric times, many centuries before Greek and Roman days when pugilist contests were common and popular.

Stone representations from the fifth millennium BC were excavated in the Middle East, near Baghdad, unmistakably depicting pugilist tactics, men joined in battle with their fists. And at that early stage, in this first portrayal of the sport, it can be clearly recognized that the fighters' hands were swathed in wrappings.

Some primitive tribes used thick padding of string to protect their hands. Others (on the Mortlock Islands) turned them into most dangerous weapons by arming the fists with sharp shark's teeth. In Hawaii, a sort of umpire separated contestants with a stick if he considered the fight unfair or too prolonged. On the Tonga Islands, boxing matches were held as regular performances commanded by the king.

In earliest times, boxing knew no rules, ring, or rounds. Two men pummelled each other ruthlessly, while moving about over a wide area. Footwork as such was non-existent. Close combat was rare. The use of thongs and gloves did not permit wrestling tactics. Classification according to weight, of course, was completely unknown. Each bout was a fight to the finish. The match was over only when one of the contestants was beaten, no matter how long this took.

The first development of the sport concerned principally the method of protecting and reinforcing the fists. Until 400 BC fighters usually wound soft strips of leather around their hands and arms. These shielded the knuckles and added to the force of their blows. Then gloves replaced thongs. They were made of hard pieces of leather with cutting edges and resembled a knuckle-duster. A more brutal development was the Roman *cestus*. The word generally described a belt or girdle. The *cestus* was weighted with pieces of iron and had metal spikes fixed over the knuckles.

Greek legend associated the introduction of boxing as a national sport with Theseus, its Athenian hero. Passionately he loved mortal fights, and to see blood flow quickened his pulse. Prowess of body and indomitable courage were his ideal. He conscripted the youth of his country. They had to serve in combat, and to be able to excel at this, had to maintain physical fitness.

One means of doing this was by fights with their fists, for which Theseus laid down rules. The contestants had to sit on flat stones, closely facing each other. On a signal they had to start battering each other without mercy. Their fists were enclosed in leather gloves. The fight went on without interruption. Only the death of an antagonist was considered victory for his opponent. A story is told that Theseus eventually found it too tiring and boring to watch prolonged fights and to get quicker results he invented murderous spiked gloves. In fact, it is known that this gruesome weapon was not used until after the Romans had conquered Greece.

Pugilistic bouts became a most popular feature of Greek and Roman holidays, and were also arranged at burial services. It was believed that the spirit of the departed would be so interested in and absorbed by the contest that he would forget all about haunting the living. A new stipulation demanded that fighters had to confront each other standing and they were not permitted to move out of a prescribed area — the first ring!

Boxing matches degenerated into murderous gladiatorial combats. Eventually use of the *cestus* was banned and, during the first century BC, boxing itself was prohibited. For hundreds of years the 'sport' almost completely vanished, to be revived only in the seventeenth century — in England — when it was again considered a thrilling pastime, an invigorating exercise, and a most welcome form of public amusement. Schools of duelling and swordsmanship came to include lessons in pugilism in their curriculum. At first taught merely as a sideline, it was made the main pursuit, once the carrying of weapons had become outmoded among the gentry. Again, displays of boxing became savage spectacles. Often the victims were badly maimed, blinded, or even killed. As was only to be expected, it was then a sport that appealed to the most cruel streak in man and to those crowds who relished watching people hammering each other into insensibility and death.

Modern boxing was introduced into England by Jim Figg. He was not only the acknowledged authority of the ring but also a celebrated fencer and duelist. One of his admirers, Captain Godfrey, left a vivid account of Figg's unsurpassed strength: 'I chose mostly to go to Figg and exercise with him; partly I knew him to be the ablest master, and partly, as the man was of a rugged temper, and would spare no man, high or low, who took up a stick against him'.

In 1719 Figg became the first bare-knuckle champion of Britain. Though his boxing was more a kind of fencing with fists, he developed it into a true art. Godfrey described his mastery in the ring: 'Strength, resolution, and unparalleled judgment, conspired to form a matchless master. There was a majesty shone in his countenance, and blazed in all his actions, beyond all I ever saw. His right leg bold and firm and his left, which could hardly ever be disturbed, give him the surprising advantage already proved, and struck his adversary with despair and panic'.

Through Figg's enthusiasm the new sport soon became a popular entertainment and drew big crowds. These further increased when fights were arranged — illegally — for money. This was the birth of the prize fight.

Jack Broughton's London amphitheatre, situated near Tottenham Court Road, became the centre of boxing. Regulations he issued in 1743, known ever since as the Broughton Rules, introduced 'science and humanity' into the sport, making it respectable and clean. It was really due to his efforts that boxing changed from a coarse and obnoxious combat, enjoyed only by the crude masses, to a well-organized fistic encounter, truly meriting the name of sport. Boxing was now patronized by nobility and royalty. The Duke of Cumberland, the king's second son, regularly attended Broughton's 'booth'.

One of Broughton's fans stated that 'the code promulgated by this Fistic Napoleon whose law making was very much like that of his great successor, had a much longer duration than the "Code Napoleon" — for it lasted in perfect integrity' from the date of its inception until 1838. Broughton was so highly regarded that it was said of him that 'by the moral effects [his teachings] inculcated, more has been done to establish the high character of Englishmen for honour and fair play, than by the eloquence of the pulpit or the senate'.

One of the many problems Broughton had to solve was the common experience during a fight that whenever one of the contestants weakened, his supporters entered the ring to assist their man in every possible way. To stop this malpractice, Broughton decreed that the stage had to be raised six feet from the ground. This has been strictly adhered to ever since. It was introduced, therefore, not, as may be imagined, for the sake of spectators, to enable them to view the fight all the better, but for the protection of the (winning) fighter and to prevent others from participating in a contest meant to take place between two men alone.

There were still no rounds. Bouts went on until one man fell. If he could not take up a fighting position within thirty seconds, he was declared to be 'knocked out of time', and beaten. Some prize fights lasted for hours, others ended within minutes. As the fighters hammered each other with their bare fists, they usually first bathed them in a solution of soda to toughen them.

Broughton invented the modern boxing glove — but this was then worn only for sparring and not for serious contests. He also introduced a chalked square-yard at the centre of the ring. Each of the fighters had to toe the line on opposite sides of the square before beginning a bout. Footwork was not as free as in modern matches, and, as turf was underfoot, the men frequently wore shoes with spikes or studs.

Although Broughton's rules had a tremendous effect on the sport, there was still much room for improvement. In 1867, the Marquis of Queensberry reviewed all aspects of boxing as then known and drew up his twelve famous rules which, only slightly modified, have been observed throughout the world ever since. His innovations provided for the use of padded gloves, canvas, and three-minute rounds with a one-minute interval. Among other things, he also ruled that

- fighting had to be a fair, stand-up match in a twenty-four-foot ring, or as near that size as practicable;
- should a glove burst or come off, it must be replaced to the referee's satisfaction;
- a man on one knee should be considered down and, should he be struck, entitled to the stakes.

Boxing, which had always been a combat for the fittest, demanding vigorous exercise, endurance, and skill, now far removed from its earliest fearful beginnings, had graduated to a noble sport, commanding respect and being regarded with well deserved deference.

That for centuries the art of boxing was known as *pugilism* is easily explained. In a most descriptive manner, the word recalls (from the Latin *pugnus*) one who fights with his 'fists'. However, the term *boxing* is something of a mystery.

Henry Downes Miles in his *Pugilistica* oddly derives the word from the Greek *puxos* (the origin of our modern 'box' as a receptacle and also of the 'pyx' in church, the vessel in which the consecrated bread is kept) for the 'closed hand' or 'clenched fingers', the Greek synonym for anything 'in the shape of a closed box'.

The most likely explanation is that it was first applied by Bernardino, a thirteenth-century Italian priest, later raised to sainthood. In an age of frequent combats, he was horrified by the injuries and fatalities that resulted from use of weapons. Eventually he persuaded fighters to use their bare fists only and this merely for the purpose of defence. Describing the method, he referred to it as 'the art of *boxing up* an opponent'.

The *ring* recalls the early days of the sport when bouts were held in the huge circle of ancient arenas, without ropes or restrictive space. Another theory is that the reference is to the *circle* formed by spectators.

Boxing has left its traces in most unexpected ways. Those who 'throw in the sponge', unknowingly bring back the early days of the sport when it was most crude, uncontrolled, and gory. Professional gamblers then sponsored no-rules bouts held in barns and improvised rings. Opponents fought to the bitter end. Blood flowed freely and to wipe it off between rounds, 'seconds' were given sponges. When a man was so battered that he could not stand up for another round, his second threw the blood-soaked sponge into the air or into the ring. It was the sign of surrender. Ever since, to 'throw in the sponge' has become a vivid expression of admitting defeat and giving up the fight.

Another relic (so to speak) from early bouts is the well-known phrase 'to come up to scratch'. An actual such 'scratch' existed as a mark at the centre of the 'ring' in early prize fights. A boxer who had been knocked down was permitted a breathing spell of half a minute in his corner. Then, within eight seconds — counted out aloud — he had to make his way to the line. Should he be unable to 'come up to [the] scratch', he had lost the fight.

The German breed of dog known as boxer rather merits its name. This square, short-haired species was specially raised for the purpose of fighting and, no one can deny, very successfully so. If for nothing else, it deserves its pugilistic name by the very technique it employs in combat. The (canine) boxer, when fighting, uses its front paws very much like its human prototype his fists, though it might be difficult to determine who was the teacher.

BANTAM WEIGHT

For a boxer to be compared with a chicken appears at first rather uncomplimentary, and yet, the bantam weight boxer (with his maximum weight of 54 kg) has been so called in admiration.

His description usurps the name of a famous fowl once bred in Bantam, a district in the north-west of Java. A bird of small size, the bantam fowl was known for its courage and fighting qualities. Without fear, the bantam rooster would face others of any size. Because of its stamina and fortitude it was said of this rooster that it had 'a great soul in a small body'. The bantam weight boxer thus bears a chicken's name of which he can be justly proud.

Chapter 8

BULLFIGHTING

Bullfighting has roused man's emotions either in enthusiasm or revulsion. Some have decried it as the most callous of sports; others have praised it as an art. However there is no division in its appeal all over Spain, Portugal, and Latin American countries, where thousands of people flock weekly into the plazas to watch bullfights.

Bullfighting or, as it is properly called, the *Corrido de Toros,* meaning 'a running of bulls', began as a religious rite all over the Mediterranean world, and far beyond. In pre-Christian days it was known in countries as far apart as Egypt, Crete, Greece, Rome, Korea, and China.

Man's greatest need was to find sufficient food; in his search for it, he soon realized his dependence on the forces of nature. In his primitive reasoning, he felt that it was necessary to do everything possible to propitiate those powers.

The earliest cattle-breeders knew of the fertility of the bull and it became for them a natural emblem of the generative force. So it was that ancient races worshipped the bull as a sacred beast. The Israelites in the desert at the very foot of Mount Sinai were tempted to revert to its adoration and frantically danced around 'the golden calf'. That we continue to call a constellation of stars Taurus ('the bull'), first so named in far-off Babylonian days, recalls the animal's original, sacred character.

All over the world, thousands of years ago, the bull was venerated as a god itself. It was sacrificed, and its blood was drunk or poured on the ground to be soaked up by the soil. The blood was believed to imbue the earth and man with new life. At times, even the bull's testicles were eaten and its flesh fed to boys.

Egyptians who thus deified the bull, made the animal their symbol of the warrior king. Strong and unbeatable, with death-dealing horns, it was the god of strength. The Persians paid homage to it. The University Museum of Philadelphia treasures a terra cotta plaque that was unearthed in Mesopotamia. Made by the ancient Sumerians in the third millennium BC, it strikingly depicts the bull. Fiery darts shoot from its four legs, while its human, bearded face is lit up by an angelic smile. All these are symbolic of the generative force that fertilizes the earth.

Other classical representations found in the eastern Mediterranean show a slain bull with vegetation springing from its flesh.

One of the main features of the ancient, sacred ritual of Mithra, the god of light and truth, was the sacrifice of a bull. This took place inside a cave, where the animal's blood was applied to the initiate, thereby admitting him into the faith's secret circle. The slaying of a bull was part also of the sacred solemnization of the death and resurrection of the mythical Attis, held in spring. The baptism of the devotee of this cult has been described in James G. Frazer's *Golden Bough*.

Crowned with gold and wreathed, he descended into a pit. Its opening was then covered with a wooden grating, on to which a bull was driven, adorned with a garland of flowers and its forehead glittering with goldleaf. Stabbed to death with a consecrated spear, its blood poured through the apertures of the grid and covered the worshipper underneath. He finally emerged from the pit drenched in blood. His ascension was regarded as his resurrection from the grave and worshippers, who had been waiting for that moment, paid homage to him. He was the one reborn to eternal life and washed clean from all sins by the blood of the bull!

Similar cults conducted a ceremony in Rome at the sanctuary of the Phrygian goddess on Vatican Hill, almost on the very site where St Peter's now stands. When early in the seventeenth century, the cathedral was enlarged, inscriptions were discovered which referred to the ceremony. From the Vatican Hill, the ritual spread as far as Gaul and Germany.

In man's mind the shedding of the bull's blood became not merely a symbolic act, but a magic means for promoting and ensuring fertility and hastening the new birth of vegetation.

Well-known is the Cretan myth of the monstrous Minotaur (literally meaning 'the Minos bull'), killed by the hero Theseus. Eventually, the Minotaur too was deified and its slaying dramatically reenacted annually. It was the same, age-old, agrarian ritual of the god-king, of life enduring in death. The bulls were ceremoniously killed in a ring, with a priestly matador dealing the final blow.

In modern days to become virile, African Zulus carried out a similar custom. They killed the bulls with their bare hands, and warriors then drank the gall while youths ate the flesh.

All these ancient rituals and mystic plays obviously were variations on the identical theme and the basis of the modern bullfight. Other factors came to reinforce and, finally, secularize this originally religious act. Savage cattle lived in the primeval forests and early man soon found it necessary to hunt them. Also realizing that the very ferocity of the bull could serve him in his own battle for survival, he made use of it in warfare. In 229 BC the defenders of besieged Ilici (the modern Elche in Valencia, Spain) herded the wild beasts, hitched them to chariots, and drove them with burning torches fastened to their horns into the Carthaginian army, routing it.

People engaged in religious rites and cruel combats experienced a thrill in dealing with and fighting fierce bulls, and, eventually, bloodthirsty contests came to be held solely as exciting adventures. Men delighted in

pitting their strength and agility in a life-and-death struggle against the vicious bull. They gloried in proving their
superiority, and thousands of spectators relished the
encounters. That is how, in the end, a religious rite
became a popular entertainment: a primitive sport, in
every sense of the word. It was influenced and further
fostered by the gladiatorial games of pagan society,
especially the Roman circus, which also pandered to
the lowest instincts. When the decaying empire wished
to entertain the masses to distract them from revolutionary ideas, the authorities arranged just that type of
fight.

Psychologists have examined the question of why men
like fighting bulls, and have suggested several reasons.
The fight gave man a feeling of pride and achievement,
and a sense of glory. Man instinctively longed for thrills,
a desire certainly gratified when facing the possibility
of death in its most elemental form by confronting the
frightening crescent of the needle-sharp horns of an
enraged bull.

Every modern arena has a chapel, in which, before
the fight, the matador prays for divine protection. An
up-to-date operating room is prepared for any emergency. Some matadors never eat anything solid before
the *corrida* to make, if necessary, the surgeon's task less
difficult. Even a priest is attached to every bull ring,
in case of need to administer extreme unction.

Psychoanalysts have traced the love of fighting and
mastering a bull to hidden, unconscious sources of homosexuality, and the transference to an animal of thwarted,
infantile desires of patricide.

The matador's pleasure in fighting a bull and proving
himself its superior, psychiatrists have claimed, resolved
the perpetual problem of every man: whether he is able
to overcome a situation that could overwhelm him with
desperate fear. Bullfighting represented also the belated
conquest of an unmastered anxiety.

A German writer, Gerhard Nebel, compared the bullfighting arena to a giant bath for the cleansing of man's
soul. Watching the contest, man purged himself of all

malice, anger, and resentments that poisoned his being. They were soaked up in the sands next to the carcass of the slain beast which, after the bullfight, made spectators return home purified.

Freudian psychologists saw in the bullfight a vivid portrayal of the three divisions of human personality. The bull, obviously, represents the *id*, or the untamed beast in man. The matador takes the place of the *ego*, that is, the *id* curbed ('half-tamed') by the influence of the outer world. The spectators are the *super-ego* — the critic and conscience, approving or condemning. According to this interpretation, man's inner fight is dramatized in the arena: his perpetual conflict between pleasure and duty, his primitive, elementary urges and his highest concepts and ideals, his wish to indulge and his task to obey.

Modern lovers of the sport, rationalizing its meaning, found in it a symbolic dramatization of man's quest for knowledge. They interpreted the various stages of the fight as phases in man's intellectual progress and evolution. When, before the commencement of the fight, the bull is kept confined in darkness, it represented man's original lack of knowledge and understanding. The animal's entry into the ring was like man's first confrontation with reality. Both are perplexed and perturbed, yet in their probing of the surroundings reveal individual characteristics, reactions, and attitudes. The following stages, when the picador and the banderilleros thrust their lances and darts into the bull, portrayed man's assault on his ignorance. Like the matador, he was trying to gain mastery (over his passions and instincts) by his own hand (his higher nature), ultimately, if he followed the rules and remained strong, to prevail. Not by accident, it is claimed, has the climax been described as 'the moment of truth'.

Even the 'suit of light' (*traje de luces*), the popular description of the matador's embroidered costume, has been linked with this explanation and tradition. Light, personified by the bullfighter, was attacking darkness, represented by the bull, eventually to conquer it.

Further improvement of the sport, its growth in 'refinements' and intricacies, ritual and rules, resulted from various factors. These included national predilections, royal and papal attitudes, climatic and economic conditions, and, last but not least, the influence of individual, outstanding matadors whose innovations were adopted throughout the bullfighting world.

Several explanations have been given as to how the sport first came to Spain, its true mother country, whose soldiers and colonizers carried it wherever they went. Some have suggested that bullfighting was introduced by the Roman conqueror who well knew how to fight a bull. Julius Caesar, it is said, if not giving it a try himself, certainly encouraged others. However, most authorities believe that the Moors brought bullfighting to Spain. Nevertheless, it might have been indigenous to the country, where it evolved out of an early vegetation rite. Tradition has it that the Cid, who drove the Moors from Spain, indulged in bullfighting as his favourite pastime. He was the very first to organize it in an enclosed area — the first 'ring' — and in the presence of spectators. Dexterously guiding his horse to protect himself and his mount from injury, he killed a savage bull with a lance.

Irrespective of the historicity of these traditions, bullfighting soon captured the imagination of the Spanish people. Initially, the principal participants in the sport were members of the noble class. A knight or a nobleman, mounted on his precious steed, chased the bull around the arena to tire it out and then, awaiting its charge, threw a spear to kill it. (In fact, this is the origin of the present-day banderilla, now used solely to weaken the bull and force it to keep its head down.) A lance eventually replaced the early dart. The noble's servants, all on foot, were engaged, whenever the need arose, to divert the bull's attention by movements with a cloak.

No definite records exist about the initial procedure. Certainly, there were no hard and fast rules. We do know that during at least 600 years, the *torero* (a Spanish title meaning 'bullfighter') fought the bull on horseback.

It is equally certain, and testified by early accounts, that for a long time fights were far from orderly, the ring presenting a scene of utter confusion with bulls, dogs, mounted nobles and their footmen servants getting in each other's way.

Only slowly (and not before the twelfth century) were fights properly organized. They became the highlight of state occasions. No feast, indeed, was complete without its 'running of bulls'. Bullfights also served to promote proficiency in the use of arms. The fights were held in the plaza (the city square), and that is why up to this day a bull ring is so called, though in reality the name no longer applies, and *corridas* mostly take place far away from the city centre.

Meanwhile another development, totally divorced from the arena, took place. In the course of time it was to give bullfighting a completely different style. Some of the *torero's* helpers began to give their own, separate performances. Too poor to own horses, they did so on foot at country fairs, competing with other sideshows. Unable, of course, to buy a new bull for each occasion, they used the same animal time and again. Often they did this at their own expense — and in a much more costly way. The bulls soon learned to anticipate the 'no killing' tactics, and the gorings and the death rate at those fairs rose frighteningly.

It was no wonder, therefore, that in 1567 Pope Pius felt the need to ban bullfighting, threatening with excommunication both spectators and participants. He decried such occasions as 'fitting for demons and not for men'. Yet the papal edict did not have the desired effect, and Pope Gregory XIII felt compelled to recognize that bullfighting could not be stopped. In a new and far more lenient decree, he reserved excommunication for the higher clerical orders, also stipulating that each bull could fight only once.

Then history intervened. When Philip V, the first Bourbon to rule Spain, ascended the throne, he left no doubt in his courtiers' minds (possibly because of his French background) how much he loathed the cruel sport which he deemed unworthy of noblemen. They could not but obey their master's wish that they should relinquish it. It was the third (and last) stage in the history of the sport. Once a primitive ceremonial, then an aristocratic pursuit, it was now — around 1700 — 'democratized', becoming the pastime of the common people. So far they had merely served their masters in the ring, as footmen following their orders. Now they themselves began to fight and kill the bull (as some of them already had learned at fairs).

Thus the man on foot emerged as the central figure. Because of his proud misson to kill the bull, he was appropriately called matador, a title combining the Spanish words *matar* (to kill) and *tor* (bull). (Those who call him *torero* do so in error. Similarly, the term toreador never belonged to the bull ring. A toreador is a baritone in an opera, and was introduced to the world through Bizet's *Carmen*!)

On the other hand, since the noblemen no longer had a part in the fight, the horsemen were now the poor and lowly, acting as mere assistants. Theirs was a subordinate role: to enrage and weaken the bull by sticking a lance — the pica — into its neck muscles. This accounts for the name by which they have been known ever since — picadors.

All this development, of course, was gradual. Francisco Romero, born around 1700, is credited with having perfected the new style and is rightly considered the pioneer of the modern bullfight. Trained to be a carpenter, he became the founder of a great dynasty of bullfighters who dominated the ring for a hundred years. With unprecedented skill he employed every part of his body in subduing the bull, and fearlessly stood his ground against the attacks of the ferocious beast. More efficiently to manoeuvre and 'play' the bull around the ring — to tire it out and prepare it for the kill — he invented the muleta, which now is so much part of the equipment of every matador. It supplanted the former loose cloth or cape that fighters had used for the identical purpose. Francisco well realized its great disadvantage: unsupported it could not be managed easily. By draping it over a stick, it became a much more pliable accoutrement.

In addition to the picador, the matador now also engaged as helpers the banderilleros. Their duty was to plant banderillos — barbed darts — into the bull's neck, to weaken the animal even further, to enable the foot-fighters to get close. (The coloured streamers decorating the darts explain their name, literally meaning 'little flags'.)

Matadors on foot needed much practice for their dangerous task, but through the years they became the most qualified fighters — a profession of their own. It was their individual style that exerted the greatest influence on the further development of the sport which was now regulated by definite rules. Successive measures civilized bullfighting ever more.

No individual has done more to give bullfighting a 'new face' than Juan Belmonte, one of the most famous modern matadors. Indicative of his untiring pursuit of the art is the fact that in one season alone (in 1919) he fought 109 *corridas*. Due to his efforts (really motivated by his own physical handicap of being of slight stature and bow-legged) the emphasis in the fight was shifted from the killing of the bull to manoeuvring it dexterously by the skilful use of the cape and muleta. He showed to a supreme degree how to master and dominate the creature. This, and not the actual death of the bull, became the *corrida's* real thrill and greatest attraction. Belmonte's new style has been described as a revolution in the ring.

On each of the sport's features hangs a tale. An example is the muleta, now a small piece of red cloth attached to a stick and used by the matador during the final stages of a bullfight. Originally, the muleta was white. Then, because matadors imagined that each bull had its favourite hue (at that time no one realized that the animal was actually colour-blind and short-sighted), they equipped themselves with an assortment of coloured muletas. There were at least three — red, yellow, and blue. During their first passes they changed cloths to discover the bull's preference. Only in 1870 were the muleta's shape and red colour finally standardized. The phrase 'as a red rag to a bull' is completely unreal. It is not the colour, but the cloth's movement that enrages the beast. A bull will always rather charge at a moving object than a still one.

The earliest fighters wore ordinary clothes. They could ill afford anything else. It did not take them long to appreciate the need to protect the body and, at the same time, create their own kind of uniform. For this purpose, they wound a long sash around their body (sometimes three times). Thus equipped they confrontd their opponent well padded! Through the centuries the original 'armour' grew smaller, eventually becoming the present-day narrow ribbon, worn merely as an adornment. The matador's suit of lights, his proud costume, very largely retains a style suggested by the conspicuous dress of eighteenth-century dandies, further embellished by later additions, such as the frilled shirt and the tassels.

The *coleta* (pigtail) is considered the matador's emblem, which goes back to the time when he grew his hair shoulder-length and, during the combat, held it back in a net. Next, he used a ring to secure it. Then he plaited his hair into a pigtail. Eventually, he tied this into a small bun behind his head to protect it should the bull toss him. Nowadays, the pigtail is artificial. Yet it is still part of the language of every matador who, when retiring from fighting, says he is 'cutting the pigtail'.

Actions with the heavy cape, the way it is held and swung, are known as passes. They are calculated to guide the animal's charge and bring it into the desired position. The manoeuvring can be done in numerous ways and through the years has developed into a graceful art. No other excitement is said to equal that of making a bull *pass* by. Outstanding matadors invented new moves in this most dangerous art, whose stylized movements have been likened to a ballet. Critics laud or deplore the matador on the basis of his passes.

Each type of pass has its name. The *Veronica*, for instance, recalls the Gospel story of the woman who held a cloth to Christ to wipe the sweat off his brow, in the very same manner as the matador holds his cape to the bull.

With the passing of time, bullfighting became ever more standardized and controlled. Early in the nineteenth century *corridas*, which once had taken all day, were limited to the afternoon. To supervise the training of matadors, a royal bullfighting school was opened in Seville in 1838. The king, at his own request, appointed Pedro Romero as its director. He was then seventy-six years old and had been retired from the ring for thirty years. In eight maxims he summed up the philosophy of bullfighting. These he had painted in large letters on the walls of the school. They told the pupil that a coward was not a man and that only a man could fight bulls. They reminded him that more tosses were caused by fear than by the bull. They impressed on him that a matador's honour was upheld by never running away from a bull, but, with the sword and the muleta in his hands, to stand his ground.

When in 1930 the Spanish government legislated that the picador's horse had to be properly protected against goring with a heavy mattress (of thick cloth stuffed with cotton), another of the cruel elements of the sport was eliminated. However, so far, it is only in Portugal that the bull is not killed.

Step by step, thus, bullfighting grew from early mystery cults and propitiation rites into today's mass entertainment and the art of *tauromachy*. It has never lost its appeal to the Latin people, and continues to draw enormous crowds. It also remains one of the most controversial of all public spectacles.

Spaniards consider it an essential part of a gentleman's life. One of their proverbs says that to begin to be a whole person, a man must write a book, have a son, plant a tree, and — fight a bull.

It may be that even the apotheosis of the steak among men is a vestige from the bullfight.

Chapter 9

COCK-FIGHTING

For cocks to fight each other is a natural instinct to attain dominance, to rule the roost. For people to watch the mortal combat of the male rivals — and to enjoy it — made cock-fighting one of the earliest spectator sports. For man to take sides and make a certain cock his favorite was almost an inevitable further step in the evolution of cock-fighting. To lay bets on the outcome of the fight added to its excitement, and was the final stage in the establishment of cock-fighting as a popular attraction in many parts of the world.

Cocks were available in great number (and before the breeding of precious gamesters, at a relatively cheap price), and it was easy to pit two birds against each other in a hollow (the 'cockpit'): the sport appealed to the poor therefore as well as the rich.

Another feature that made the sport so acceptable was that it offered little opportunity for abuse by crooks, a fact that made people who were anxious to see 'fair play' admire it as a 'clean' sport and 'absolutely on the level'.

All these circumstances explain how cock-fighting, through many centuries, even millennia, of its existence, possibly had more followers in the world than any other sport, and how so many of its terms to this day — without most people realizing it — belong to our everyday vocabulary and the idioms of our speech.

Like so many sports, cock-fighting probably evolved from religion and a ritual. It could well have grown from a magical rite, watched with awe, to ensure fertility, the casting out of evil spirits, and the bringing of victory to man in his continual battle against natural and supernatural foes. The cock was (and, in some primitive societies, still is) regarded as a sacred bird. Several of the bird's characteristics (its shrill crow at dawn, its pugnacity, and its salaciousness) already in ancient days gave people this notion, a fact that is documented by early religious literature and later writings.

The cock's place is especially prominent in Persian mythology in which this 'herald of dawn' was the strong ally of the forces of light in their battle against the powers of darkness. Its Greek name — though in a doubtful folk etymology — has been explained to mean 'ward off' and 'protect'. A cock's crow ushered in the new day and its shrill cry was considered to put to flight the evil spirits of the night that could not tolerate the sound.

The New Testament preserves traces of this tradition when it relates how Peter denied knowing Jesus: three times before the cock crowed twice (Mark XIV:72). Commentators explained that the mentioning of the cock's crow was not merely an indication of the early hour of the day and Peter's disloyalty so soon after his master's arrest. Its significance went much deeper. In fact, it was the very cause of the disciple's realization of his treachery. The devil had urged him to deny his master and was keeping him in his power. But at the cock's repeated crow, the 'evil one' was forced to flee. That is how Peter suddenly came to himself and bitterly repented what he had done.

Even the placing of the figure of a cock on top of church steeples can be traced (like the ringing of bells) to the belief that it would scare away demons. Later, its more rational purpose was to serve as an innocuous weather vane.

This background prompted the introduction of an early Hebrew prayer in the Jews' morning worship, praising God, the Lord of the universe, for having given the cock the 'understanding to distinguish between the night and the day'. Arabs believed that cocks crowed whenever they became conscious of the presence of demons, and peasants kept a cock inside the home to keep out the devil.

Sacrifice of the bird became a powerful means of warding off disease and obtaining forgiveness of sin. Greeks, who called the cock also 'the Persian bird', offered it to the goddess Maia, and in mystery rites initiates did not eat chicken. Particularly, Greeks sacrificed the bird to Asklepios, the god of healing; even Socrates, when about to take his life by drinking the cup of hemlock, still remembered that he owed a cock to Asklepios.

Scots were known to have buried live cocks under the bed of an epileptic to cure him of his 'possession', and the bird's blood was mixed with flour to bake cakes for invalids. Jews offered a cock as a means of atonement before the beginning of their most sacred holy day, the Day of Atonement. The 'scape-cock' served them in a similar role to that of the scapegoat in biblical days.

To sacrifice cocks assumed an even deeper meaning. Cocks came to be considered protectors of the souls of the departed, and as such were needed in the 'underworld' to keep away hostile demons from their charges. Russians are known to have strangled cocks as an offering to the dead. By the common association of opposites, the cock was also used in perverse rites of black magic as an evil bird.

From earliest days, cocks were known too for their virility, and became a symbol of fecundity. They were employed — magically, and at the cost of their lives — whenever and wherever people wished to ensure the fertility of the soil and of man. They also have their place in primitive marriage ceremonial and in the harvesting and sowing of the fields. Sir James Frazer quotes many examples of European customs in which cocks were associated with the bringing in of the last sheaf, and being identified with the spirit of the corn.

A cock was tied up in the last sheaf, and killed. Its feathers were kept until the following spring to be scattered with the seed magically to quicken and fertilize the new life in the soil. Thus the cock became an emblem of immortality and appeared in Christian catacomb paintings as a resurrection symbol: just as this bird announced the dawn after the darkest of nights, so the Christian faith proclaimed the life of the world beyond at the time of spiritual obscurity.

A sacred bird from which demons fled (both in this world and the next), a bringer of fertility whose own death ensured life, the cock also served for divination. It has long been held that chickens were first domesticated not for food, but for this purpose. The cock's intestines and liver were thought to foretell the future. Who else faced death so bravely and even invited it so that he could prove himself the better bird? Even the destiny of a nation was considered to be linked up with the cocks' contest!

Cock-fighting thus was not a cheap amusement at first, but exciting in a completely different way from mere sporting events: it concerned not just the life (and death) of a bird, but the immediate and ultimate future of man.

Records show the significant function cock-fighting fulfilled in primitive religious cults. It is told that in Sumatra, for instance, an annex of a temple was reserved for the keeping of fighting cocks. These were pitted against each other in solemn battles watched by the congregation and presided over by a specially chosen priest qualified as a cocker, astronomer, and philosopher. The victorious cock was at once offered to the deity. Its slain victim, however, was burnt with gum and spices on an altar and its ashes subsequently placed — for perpetuity — in a golden urn. In a concluding sermon the priest exhorted the congregation to apply to their lives the 'lesson' — not read from a volume of holy scripture but the drama staged by the birds. This would render them invincible and create in them a firm and stable state of mind.

Through the years, cock-fights have been staged to promote courage, calling on men (and especially on soldiers) to emulate the birds. Christian, King of Denmark, is reported to have said that were he to lead an army against the 'infidel of Constantinople', he would choose none but cockers for his commanders, and none but lovers of the sport for soldiers.

Cock-fighting was enjoyed in southern and southeastern Asia at least 3000 years ago. In earliest combats grey or red jungle fowl (the ancestor of the game cock and our domesticated chicken) were used. If those were lacking, partridges and quails took their place. From India the sport spread into Persia and thence to Greece.

Its introduction into Europe has been linked with martial endeavour and a general's wish to make his soldiers triumph in battle. A tradition tells that the Athenian statesman and commander Themistocles (528-462 BC), while leading his army against the Persians, had his attention drawn to the indomitable bravery of two cocks joined in a fight. Realizing that their example could inspire his men, he stopped them and invited them to watch the contest. Addressing the soldiers, he said that those cocks fought to the death for the most selfless reasons, not 'for glory, for liberty, or the safety of their children, but only because the one will not give way to the other'. And it was the birds' courage and resolute heroism they should now imitate: 'to be firm and unshakable in the midst of danger, nay in death itself'.

Thus encouraged, his troops with unsurpassed valour locked in battle with the Persians and defeated them. In celebration of the victory, Athenians made cock-fighting an annual feature in their city, as a sacred and patriotic event. Of course, people soon took it up merely for their own enjoyment.

From Greece the sport was carried to the entire Mediterranean world. Initially, Romans frowned on this cheap 'Greek diversion' but then became such devotees of it that a first-century writer expressed his concern over people wasting all they had on bets on cocks. In fact, Romans were the first to hold organized cock-fights.

Colonizers from Rome then brought the pastime to western Europe, and in England (which, according to some sources, had held cock-fights even earlier) it attained immense popularity among all classes and all ages from the twelfth century onward.

Cock-fighting had its dangerous features for the onlooker. Cocks trained to fight, in the heat of battle, would pursue each other into the crowd and, with their deadly spurs, could easily inflict serious injuries to any one in their way. To protect spectators, promoters in the early development of the sport learned to dig round pits to contain the ferocious fighters. This was the origin of the cockpit which soon belonged to almost every village. Cock-fights were arranged also in churchyards and even inside churches and in schools!

William Fitzstephen, in his twelfth-century chronicle, records how the teachers themselves directed the match (called a 'main') and did so not without some personal interest. The dead birds became their property.

The annual climax of all English cock-fighting was reached on Shrove Tuesday (so called because in olden times, Christians making their confession then were 'shriven'). It offered a last opportunity to people to enjoy themselves before the long fast of Lent, as well as to eat meat, most likely supplied in huge quantities by the fallen feathered warriors. On that day pupils brought cocks to school and the entire morning was given over to the fights. Parents, for their part, were expected to subscribe to their children's 'entertainment'. Their annual contribution was known as 'cock-pence' and was used for the purchase and training of the birds.

English monarchs made cock-fighting a 'royal sport'. Henry VIII favoured it so much that he added a cockpit to his palace at Westminster. It was equally enjoyed and enthusiastically promoted by Kings James I and Charles II. And, naturally, the royal example was copied by the kings' subjects, the nobility and the commoners.

Detailed instruction on how to arrange a fight (including the choice, the breeding, diet, and training of the birds) were contained in a treatise published in 1614 dealing with *Pleasures for Princes*. Attempts by the Church to ban cock-fighting were short-lived and even

Oliver Cromwell's outlawing of the 'diversion' by an Act of Parliament in 1654 ended with the Restoration of King Charles II, when the national pastime was revived also. Only in 1849 did the British Parliament declare the sport illegal.

Throughout the years decadent tastes were pandered to by sadistic refinements in the cock-fights, and various versions were developed in this most popular of amusements which also served as a model to the first (eighteenth-century) rules of prizefighting.

Only the best of fowls were considered good enough to enter the arena, and the breeding of fighting roosters became a consuming passion which, it was hoped, would pay dividends on the day the fighters were let loose. Pedigreed birds became prized possessions. No effort was spared to prepare them for the confrontation. Sometimes, for thirty to fifty days before the main, the bird was trained and properly conditioned. To toughen its body it was given daily baths and massaged with a mixture of alcohol and ammonia. To increase its fighting stamina and pugnacity it was fed a special diet, often of a secret composition. To make its attack more deadly, its spurs, beak, and claws were filed and sharpened. The ancient Greeks had invented metal spurs to fortify the birds' natural ones. This cruel practice was also adopted to give both contestants an equal chance, as the cocks' own spurs varied greatly in different breeds.

Wagering on the birds made the fights an even more breathtaking experience, as this involved the spectators personally. To begin with, the owner of the winning game cock received awards in money, and a prize. It did not take long, however, for the onlookers to put money on their favourites. Enormous sums were won and lost in the cockpit, which provided the most common opportunity to gamble. This, not least, was responsible for the cock-fights' unsurpassed popularity.

Pepys, watching a cock-fight for the first time in his life (on 21 December 1663 at a new pit in Shoe Lane, London) not only remarked in his journal that 'I soon had enough of it'; he added 'one thing more: It is strange to see how people of this poor rank, that look as if they had not bread to put in their mouth, still bet [so much] and lose it.'

Most exciting of all tournaments was the 'battle royal'. In fact, it is from the cockpit that this term entered our language as a metaphor for a general squabble. In its original, cock-fighting connotation, it referred to the bloody elimination contest between a maximum number of birds (eventually fixed at sixteen), dropped simultaneously into the pit, each finding its 'match'. With the first round over, the eight surviving cocks were then pitted against each other and had to fight it out until just two remained. Their confrontation determined the ultimate winner. This 'perfected' form of mass combat shocked even hardened men.

From Spain, where cock-fighting was introduced by the Romans and became a major sport, it was carried across the ocean to the Spanish possessions in the New World, which explains why in some Latin American countries it is still practised. The English brought the sport to North America, where it was even patronized by Presidents Washington and Jefferson.

Cock-fighting is no longer a favoured sport and is banned in most parts of the world. Yet, the legacy of its popularity in former times lives on as an integral part of our speech.

For the combat the birds were dropped into a pit and 'pitted' together fought their bloody battle. And so we still speak of teams and opponents being 'pitted' against each other.

The fact that cockpits were restricted in space made people apply the term figuratively to other small enclosures. Seventeenth-century warships used the word to describe the quarters of junior officers. To call these 'cockpits' was the more appropriate because they served also as first-aid posts for those wounded in combat and, therefore, at times presented a bloody spectacle. Airmen in World War 1, adopting naval tradition, feeling rather confined in their flying cabin, began to call this a cockpit, as well. From its initial, temporary, improvised stage of a mere hollow in the ground, the real cockpit developed as a permanent feature. Circular in shape, to give all the spectators the best possible chance to watch the fight 'in the round', the matted stage was guarded by a barrier to prevent birds from falling off. And just as 'cockpits' became the site for England's performances of dramatic art, present-day theatres still recall this early 'stage' by describing the lowest part of the auditorium as 'a pit'.

The effect of cock-fighting also extends to terms relating to weapons and to concepts such as cowardice and bravery. 'Crestfallen', indeed, was the bird that gave up fighting. Standing listlessly with its crest drooping, it waited for the death blow. When a game cock was so intimidated by its opponent that it decided to give up the fight, it announced the fact by lifting its hackle and, in doing so, revealed white feathers under the hackle. To 'show the white feather' thus became identified with faint-heartedness and proving oneself a coward. Patriotic women during World War I presented men staying away from the fighting front with a white feather — and everyone knew what it meant. Another theory suggests a different origin of the 'white feather'. The best fighting cocks were of a pure breed and had coats of black and red feathers. Inferior birds, which lacked courage, were of mixed blood. This could be recognized by a white feather in the tail. No matter which explanation is right, both agree that the white feather as a symbol of weakness and lack of daring comes from the cockpit.

The bird's self-assurance created the term 'cocksure'. Its courage, pugnaciousness, and (in most cases) determination to fight to the death became a symbol of valour and aggression. This has left its trace in the history of the gun. In its earlier forms, the powder, placed in the pan, was fired by dropping into it a lighted match (a cord impregnated with saltpeter), held in the hand. In the late fifteenth century a movable arm was invented into which the burning match (or wick) was placed and, by means of a trigger, released into the firing pan situated below. Appropriate to its 'aggressive' function, the novel match lock was shaped like a cock. Even when flint and hammer had supplanted the cock, people continued to 'cock' their weapon (in the manner of speaking) when readying it for discharge.

A study in itself are the pros and cons regarding cock-fighting. They are revealing of human nature and the devious working of the human mind. Those stressing the cruelty of the sport nevertheless sometimes admitted that, at least, it diverted men from slaughtering each other. Sponsors of the contests (like lovers of bullfights) gave numerous reasons for holding the fights. They claimed that they promoted bravery in man, and self-lessness, by the birds' example of carrying on the combat against any odds — to complete exhaustion and the bitter end. Cocks could not be enticed to fight but did so only by their own 'free will'. It was their inherent disposition, and therefore no cockfight could ever be arranged without the birds' cooperation. All that a cocker did was to let the rooster live (and die) according to the plans of nature.

The very motive-power of the fight was the cocks' innate pugnacity, and not any feelings of fear. In fact, they relished the battle and, after all, prior to it they led a 'luxurious' kind of life in which everything was done to keep them happy and in comfort. The excitement of the actual combat was so immense that the contestants certainly were unaware of any injuries or pain inflicted. Death came so quickly that the mortally wounded bird was spared agony. As for the use of artificial spurs, often in the form of razor-sharp knives, these were far from cruel. On the contrary, they expedited the final, mortal blow and thereby prevented drawn-out battles, with possible unnecessary suffering.

Cock-fighting was also seen as greatly fostering the breeding of the best of birds, which profited not only nature lovers but — very substantially — the poultry farmer and through him the diner's table!

Those opposing cock-fighting pointed out how most

of the 'pro' arguments proffered were spurious and mere rationalizations. Was it not obvious, they asked, that even admitting the birds' innate pugnacity, the cockers greatly fostered it by providing circumstances that brought out something merely latent that otherwise might never be manifested?

The betting associated with all fights, opponents declared, was demoralizing. It was not merely cruelty towards the birds that had to be prevented. Worse was the fights' brutalizing effect on the spectators, in whom they roused the lowest and ugliest traits of human nature. Finally, to amuse oneself at the expense of any creature was unworthy of people calling themselves civilized.

Chapter 10

CRICKET

For many enthusiasts, cricket today is a way of life. Anything that is 'not cricket' is considered unworthy of an Englishman.

Its beginnings are obscure. Like all bat-and-ball games, cricket evolved gradually from various sources. It is related to an early Scottish sport known as 'cat and dog', a thirteenth-century pastime called 'hand-in-and-hand-out' (*handyn and handoute*), and a similar French game.

Some suggest that cricket was first 'properly' played in the forests, where tree stumps offered a natural mark for attack. The word 'stump' may recall early forest matches where the uprights were rooted in the soil.

Cricket is related closely to 'stool ball', a game played particularly at Easter, which was then a season of courtship. Both men and women took part. One player threw a ball at an upturned, three-legged stool which was defended — with his outstretched hand — by another player. Subsequently, a second stool was added. That is how the two wickets came into existence.

Other authorities have contended that stumps of any kind were unknown at first; that players simply cut two circular holes in the ground. The player guarding the hole was armed with a bat (the 'dog') with which he tried to keep out of the hole a small piece of wood (the 'cat'), aimed at it by his opponent. The batsman was 'out' when the ball was bowled into the hole. Naturally, the target was no easy one, which rendered the game rather slow and cautious.

The great need was to make the hole more conspicuous and the most obvious means of doing this was to indicate its position with a stick. Soon players began to aim at the stick, instead of at the hole, and a rule was introduced which put a batsman out if the stump was knocked down by the ball.

By 1700, two upright stumps had taken the place of the original single stick. They were then one foot (30 cm) high and two feet (60 cm) apart, with a third stick (or bail) stretching across and beyond both of them. This arrangement soon proved inadequate as the ball went between the stumps without touching either of them. To remedy this, a third stump was added.

Yet another hypothesis traces the introduction of the third stump to a different cause. Early in the evolution of the game, the striker, in making the run, had to thrust the end of his bat into the hole which was then situated between the two sticks. The wicket keeper, on the other hand, tried his utmost to anticipate him by getting the ball into the hole. In attempting to do so, his hand was often seriously injured by the batsman's bat. To avoid this, it was decided to abolish the hole between the stumps and to replace it by the middle stump.

Whatever the real reason, the third stump came into existence around 1775, when the bail was stretched across all three. At that time the pitch was twenty-two yards (19.80 m) long and the wicket twenty-two inches (55.80 cm) high and six inches (15.24 cm) broad. No rule then governed the size of the bat, which often was very long, and bent.

Various claims have been made (and disputed) regarding the first mention of cricket and its earliest pictorial illustration. In some documents cited, and pictures discovered, it really is not certain whether a game called *creag*, or 'club and ball', was actually cricket.

The account of the Royal Household for the twenty-eighth year of the reign of King Edward I (1300) itemized the expenditure of a hundred shillings for the king's son, the Prince of Wales (then sixteen years old) for 'the Prince's playing at *creag* and other sports at West-minster'. It is interesting to note that though the entry is in Latin, the word taken to mean cricket, having no Latin equivalent, appears in Saxon, as *creag*.

A fourteenth-century illustration produced in England in a document issued under Papal authority, depicts a boy with a club and ball, and his tutor, who unmistakably is demonstrating a game very much like cricket.

The oldest description of the sport has been attributed to a poem by William Goldwin, of King's College, Cambridge, published in 1706. The first preserved cricket score and earliest code of laws date back to 1744. They relate to a match between Kent and All England played at the Artillery Ground, Finsbury, London, and won by Kent by one wicket. Nevertheless, it was not until the second half of the seventeenth century that cricket became a generally adopted sport. It gained popularity among the higher classes, the noble and wealthy, in the following century.

To add tragedy to the sport, it is also known that in 1751 Frederick, the Prince of Wales who greatly enjoyed the game, was killed by being hit with a cricket ball. Even this misfortune could not stem the Englishmen's enthusiasm for the sport. The Hambledon Club had been founded just prior and was to play a significant part in the evolution of the game. It was superseded by the Marylebone Cricket Club. With its headquarters at Lord's, London (called after Thomas Lord), this was to become the world authority on the sport and its sanctuary.

Just as the game has a fascinating history, so its terms have a colorful background.

The original *bat* was a primitive club, used for attack and defence. In an early translation of Holy Scripture, John Wycliffe equips a crowd of men with 'swerdies and battis' while smugglers in southern England who moved about armed with cudgels were referred to as 'the Sussex batsmen'.

Bats greatly varied in shape, length, and weight. The

earliest bats gave *cricket* its name. They were just branches broken off a tree, and slightly curved. The linguistic root of cricket is *cricce*, from the Anglo-Saxon. The word has survived in a great variety of things and terms which all share the same underlying meaning — 'something that is not quite straight', something that has a curve or a twist. Thus, a bishop's or a shepherd's crook is really a looped stick: a creek is a winding rivulet, and a painful crick in the neck the result of a twist.

Similarly, cricket as a sport recalls the *crooked* club (resembling the modern hockey stick) with which it was once played. Indeed, some authorities claim that the first to join in the game were sons of shepherds who used broken-off parts of their father's crooks as bats. (One hypothesis sees a direct link between cricket and the French *criquet*, using it as a 'confirmation' of the French origin of the game! Others, going even further, have discovered an affinity with croquet.)

The *wicket* certainly goes back to pastoral life and sheep-pens, whose entrance usually was a small hurdle consisting of two uprights and a movable crossbar — a bail.

It was this gate into the pen that was first called a wicket, a word also derived from Anglo-Saxon and meaning, very appropriately, 'to yield', or 'to offer a way through'. Early theological treatises used the term in this very sense. When in 1545, for instance, Wycliffe's tract on Transubstantiation was published, it was known as 'Wycliffe's Wicket', presenting, as it were, 'a narrow opening to Salvation'.

THE DUCK

Players who have not scored at all, have a '0' placed next to their name on the board. The figure is reminiscent of a duck's egg. Hence we continue to speak (in the case of any failure) of 'laying an egg' and cricketers still use the shortened form of 'a duck' for nil.

Americans seem to prefer geese, and in their game a no score thus appears as a 'goose egg'.

A MAIDEN

To speak of a maiden nowadays sounds rather old-fashioned. An unmarried girl, she was innocent and 'unspoiled'. To speak of a 'maiden over' in cricket therefore was a very appropriate choice of term for an 'over' during which the batsmen have been unable to score any runs.

THE HAT TRICK

For a bowler to take three wickets with three successive balls is known as a 'hat trick'. Meaningless now, the expression goes back to the days of elegance, when a player who achieved this feat was entitled to receive from his club a new top-hat!

THE ASHES

Most famous of all cricket terms is 'the Ashes'. Its origin goes back to an historical match between England and Australia played at the Oval in London in 1882. The Englishmen were thoroughly beaten and, in fact, the test had been so exciting that one of the spectators dropped dead. On the following morning the *Sporting Times* published an obituary note: not on the victim but on English cricket. It read:

IN AFFECTIONATE REMEMBRANCE
of
ENGLISH CRICKET,
Which died at the Oval
29th August 1882.
Deeply lamented by a large circle
of Sorrowing Friends and
Acquaintances.
RIP
NB — The body will be cremated,
and the ashes taken to Australia.

When, in the following year, an English team went to Australia, its captain, the Hon. Ivo Bligh, was asked to bring back 'the ashes'. Taking the request literally, the Australians, when beaten, burned a bail and put its ashes into an urn which they presented to their victorious visitors. This urn, 'the Ashes', now rests as a treasured possession at Lord's, and Australians and Englishmen have battled — in the traditional phrase — for them ever since.

Chapter 11

CROQUET

Monuments honour battles, discoveries, and national heroes of all kinds. So it is with many streets. Few, however, would guess that a famous thoroughfare in the fashionable quarter of one of the world's greatest capitals recalls a game once enthusiastically practised there by the aristocracy, but now completely forgotten; a game which was really the forerunner of modern croquet.

London's Pall Mall is so called because the game of palle malle was once played there. The word derives from the French *pallemaile* and traces also to the Italian *pallamaglio*, as the game was introduced into Britain from Italy by way of France in the seventeenth century during the reign of Charles II.

The basic idea of the game was to drive a ball (*palla*) with a mallet (*maglio*) through raised iron rings, or hoops, along an alley. That is how it received its name. The London street in which palle malle was first played by the king and his court was initially called Catherine Street, in honour of Catherine of Braganza. Because the game was played there, the street acquired its present name.

In an old house in Pall Mall illustrations were found of a mallet actually used then. It shows a mallet of rough workmanship and was circled by iron rings to prevent it from splitting. Its shape was 'irregularly oval and slightly curved'. Its head was of oak and its handle (of which the top was covered with white, soft leather, to ensure a firm grip) was of ash.

Samuel Pepys recorded in his diary for May 1663 how he walked 'in the Park, discoursing with the keeper of Pell Mell, who was sweeping of it; who told me of what the earth is mixed that do floor the mall, and that overall there is cockle-shells powdered'.

Palle malle then is the father of croquet. How palle malle itself came into being is still shrouded in mystery. However, it is clear that it goes back, like other ball games, to man's ancient, intuitive wish to hit a stone with a stick and then to propel it through a single or multiple goals.

Some suggest that the game developed straight from field hockey. One writer, in a lengthy (but unconvincing) treatise, has traced its rise to the ancient Greek sport of *chicane*.

There is evidence that palle malle was played in the old French province of Languedoc in the thirteenth century. A book published in Paris in 1717 gave a detailed description of the implements used, though it is very vague about the actual manner in which the game was played. A picture shows a player about to hit a ball approximately the size of a billiard ball through an arch.

English political exiles, no doubt, became enthusiastic about palle malle while in France. Thus, when Charles II and his retinue returned to England, they brought back with them as well as other sports palle malle. And so the Stuart king introduced and himself enjoyed the game in Britain, where it soon became the rage.

It was played on level, sand courts or tracks covered with the powdered cockle-shells referred to by Pepys. Long-handled wooden hammers served as mallets to drive boxwood balls through suspended metal rings almost one foot (30 cm) in diameter. Then palle malle suddenly petered out and had become almost forgotten by the eighteenth century. It was to be revived under a new name — croquet — early in the 1850s.

Once again, the reborn game reached Britain from France. The use of the distinctive mallet, shaped very much like a hockey stick, now led people to describe the entire game as croquet, a name which is derived from the French word *croc*, meaning a hook or a crook (also known from the hooked crochet needle). The croc in its primitive form, as used by French peasants, had a simple broomstick for its handle. A knotty piece of hard wood was fitted into one end of the handle, through a hole, to serve as a striker. The earliest hoops were fashioned of willow rods.

From France the sport spread to Ireland, where it was played in 1852. From there it soon reached England. Some accounts credit a Miss Macpherson with having reintroduced the game to England under its new name, from the Emerald Isle. Others accord the honour to Mr Jaques, of Hatton Gardens. He had watched the game in Ireland and was so taken by it that he not only promoted its appeal in England but at an early stage began to manufacture the necessary equipment. A long poem acclaimed him as the game's great pioneer, although it also indicated the mystery of its origin in its opening stanza:

> Whence Croquet sprang to benefit the earth,
> What happy garden gave the pastime birth,
> What cunning craftsman carved its graceful tools,
> Whose oral teachings fixed its equal rules,
> Sing, Jaques, then apostle of the game!
> If dissylabic is thy famous name
> Or if, as Frenchified, it is but one,
> By saying, 'Sing, John Jaques!' the trick is done.
> Mysterious Croquet! like my 'Little Star'
> Of infancy, 'I wonder what you are?'
> Owning new parent, yet here in no shame,
> Where all the honour would so gladly claim.

Soon, as formerly, croquet became a national pastime for men and women. A serene game which did not depend on muscular strength, it had its dramatic ups and downs. Croquet made many friends, and matches were played in numerous country centres. However, rules, if they existed, were most inadequate and often there was chaos on the lawn.

LLYFRGELL COLEG MENAI LIBRARY

Determined to organize the game properly, Walter James Whitmore zealously set to work and came to be regarded as the true father of croquet. He roused the spirit of competition and in 1867 challenged other players to meet him at Moreton on Marsh. He beat them all and became the world's first Croquet Open Champion. He then devised a real system of play which he published in 1868 in his book on *Croquet Tactics*. At the time, hoops were still nine inches (22.86 cm) wide — as compared with the eventual standard size of a mere 3¾ inches (9.52 cm). Whitmore considered any narrower gauge as 'absolute lunacy'! Ten hoops were used (instead of the later six) and there was a 'turning peg' and a 'winning peg' (instead of the single one of the modern game, introduced only in 1922).

Considering a governing body essential, Whitmore convened a meeting in 1868 at the office of the English weekly *The Field*. The result was the formation of the All England Croquet Club, meant to be 'analogous to, and perhaps of similar benefit to croquet as the Marylebone Club is to cricket'.

In 1870 it acquired four acres (1.60 hectares) of grassy land at Wimbledon for the laying out of proper courts in terraces. A first championship meeting was held and all seemed to go exceedingly well. Indeed, croquet became so popular that its appeal was surpassed only by that of cricket. For some difficult shots, its addicts did not disdain to lie flat on the ground and use the mallet's handle, sometimes rubber-tipped, like a billiards cue, a practice that eventually was banned.

Then suddenly, Major Wingfield's invention of lawn tennis caused a revolution. Lawn tennis courts became an indispensable adjunct to country houses and quickly began first to supplement and then to replace the croquet lawns. The attraction of the new game of tennis proved all-potent; even the croquet club's committee reluctantly felt compelled to admit tennis into its precincts at Wimbledon and lent one of its courts to players of the new sport.

The consequences were disastrous. Within seven years

of its foundation, the croquet association's title was extended to read 'The All-England Croquet and Lawn Tennis Club'. Within another five years, croquet had so lost its lustre that no longer was it felt worthwhile to buy a new challenge cup, and the word croquet was deleted from the club's name. The deletion underscored the game's decline.

Croquet, indeed, soon became the butt of jokes. It was said that the game was suitable only for elderly ladies and the vicar. Thirteen years later, croquet made some kind of comeback. Significantly it had to take second place to lawn tennis and the name of the famous club, though readmitting the sport, put it into its 'proper' — subservient — place. It called itself now the All-England Lawn Tennis and Croquet Club. In 1897 the Croquet Association was founded, but three years later its headquarters were moved from Wimbledon to Roehampton and finally to Hurlingham and its original site was wholly taken over by tennis. (More than half a century passed until in 1957 Wimbledon invited croquet back, supplying its players with a court. History seemed to repeat itself, but in reverse.)

Meanwhile, and for many years afterwards, croquet, played with wide hoops, became the garden-party variety, enjoyed by the leisured class and especially ladies. In 1903 the *Graphic* described the pastime. 'Croquet,' it wrote, 'has a wonderful hold . . . It is even more popular than golf, and suits equally well the active old lady, or the dashing young girl. It is now generally accepted as a game of skill and the "shop" talked by croquet players has grown to be as unintelligible to outsiders and as keen and earnest as that of any other sport.'

Croquet's development continued to be one of change and of decline, particularly during the two great wars. However, to make it more attractive and interesting for everyone, and again a serious game, its rules were altered and became ever more intricate. Now, indeed, it needed the strategy of a good chess player and the delicacy of touch of a billiards expert. Reconstructed, croquet revived. So simple outwardly, yet when properly played it demanded skill, resource, and utmost accuracy.

Croquet enthusiasts say that the game has enriched English idiom. They contend that the expression 'to ring a bell' — to recall some faint memory — comes straight from the croquet lawn of former days. At one time, a player in making the winning stroke actually caused a bell to ring. The game was completed when the winner hit, not the stick used now, but a combination of two hoops which crossed each other at right angles forming a dome from which a bell was suspended. The game was over when the player drove the ball through the hoops and thereby rang the bell.

The bell eventually was replaced by two sticks, officially called pegs. Then, in 1922, to make the game more difficult, one of the pegs was removed from the play and the other moved into the centre, a practice claimed first to have been introduced in Australia. The winning hit had to touch the peg. The game was finished, and one 'pegged out'. The term was then transferred (so croquet lovers assert) from their lawn to life (or rather death). When the 'game' is over, you 'peg out'.

Chapter 12

CURLING

Scotland, that beautiful country of heather, lochs, and staunch men, had another grim winter. As usual, all the crofters' work had come to a stop. The fields were as hard as rock, and many a plough was frozen to the furrow. The lochs, tarns, ponds, and streams were covered with ice. Everything was at a standstill.

The men were at a loss what to do with themselves when, on the spur of the moment, an ingenious fellow loosened a rock from a river bank (or was it out of a field?) and casually hurled it across the icy surface of the stream. He was so delighted when it slid along fast and smoothly that he repeated the performance. Others who had watched him soon began to imitate his throws. The innate spirit of competition then made them try to out-distance each other in throwing stones along the frozen surface. Eventually, they put on the ice a distant mark that they tried to hit with the stone, or 'draw' as near as possible to it. Some players managed to propel their stone in such a dexterous manner that it either knocked an opponent's stone out of its position or 'promoted' (i.e., knocked into a better position) a stone belonging to his own team.

Further to advance their game, the players improved the rough rocks with which nature had provided them, by chipping these into better shape and polishing their bases. All that was needed now for the game to develop was an agreement on rules.

An unplanned pastime thus evolved into a new sport.

Friends formed regular teams that met in contest and then, joining together, challenged a neighbouring hamlet in hurling missiles of granite across the ice.

That is how, with a little imagination, the beginnings of curling could (and, indeed, have been) reconstructed, more so as there is no historical evidence of its origin.

Curling has been described (to the indignation of curlers themselves) as 'lawn bowling on ice'. Some authorities claim that it arose out of that summer game which had already been popular for centuries among the Scots. Undoubtedly, man's need of exercise in cold weather led to the sport's inception. The sight of thick layers of ice, his innate love of hurling stones and pleasure in seeing them slide along a smooth surface were all contributing factors.

Curling is the Scots' national game and wherever they went — climate permitting — they introduced the pastime. However, their anger has been aroused by a suggestion that curling was not indigenous to their country but imported either from the north (Iceland) or from the south (the Netherlands), where 450 years ago games very similar to the earliest forms of curling (which were akin to quoit-pitching) did exist. It was asserted that either Flemish migrants had brought it to Scotland some time during the sixteenth century or Scottish travellers themselves had brought it back on their return from visits to the Low Countries (or Iceland).

The only testimony offered in support was the vocabulary of the sport. The majority of its terms, it was pointed out, were foreign — mostly Dutch or German. The word curl itself, it was claimed, was derived from the German *Kurzweil*, denoting a pastime and amusement. Therefore, curling merely meant — very generally — to play for pleasure. Equally, kuting (also spelled coiting or quoiting), an early alternative term for the sport in Scotland, came, it was said, from the Teutonic *kluyten* and referred to a contest with quoits (lumps or balls) on a frozen plain. The word *Bonspiel*, describing a curling match, was obviously foreign and made up of the French *bon* (good) and the German *Spiel* (play).

Some critics were adamant that the solitary fact of the existence of foreign words proved nothing, and that such etymological evidence was as slippery a game as curling itself. Although in fact similar kinds of ice sports were played in the Low Countries four and a half centuries ago (in Iceland, people then enjoyed a game played on ice with 'bowls'), there was no proof whatsoever, these critics said, that either was the father of the game which for at least 400 years had been played in Scotland. However, they acceded that only during the middle of the eighteenth century did it become the country's truly national game.

To make an effective shot, curlers learned to deliver the stone with a certain twist which made it rotate, swerve, and curl. It was this twisting, undulating motion of the stone which most probably was responsible for the sport's name.

James IV (1473–1513) was the first Scottish king linked with the sport but no literary mention appears of the game in that country before 1600. Tradition relates that he had ordered a silver curling stone for which men were to play annually. Although there is no historical evidence to support the assertion, a toast proposed in 1844 at a meeting of the Jacobite Society in honour of the then Prince of Wales suggests that James VI of Scotland (who became James I of England) was 'a keen, keen curler who knew how to keep his own side of the rink and to sweep'.

The proposer of the toast suggested that the Royal Grand Club should take the young prince in hand to make him follow his illustrious ancestor's example and 'thoroughly initiate him into all the mysteries of that health-giving, strength-renovating, nerve-bracing, blue-devil-expelling, incomparable game of curling'. To neglect this responsibility would certainly contribute to royal degeneracy and entirely 'bungle the Prince's education'.

There are no historical facts to prove that James VI really was proficient in the game. Nevertheless, the toast highlights the place curling had come to occupy in Scotland's life in the middle of the last century.

Clergymen, particularly, must have enjoyed curling from earliest days. They were even accused of curling on the sacred Sabbath. Presbyterians at the Glasgow Assembly in 1638 indicted the Bishop of Orkney of the Episcopal church of the offence, though the charge was dismissed. Clergymen were the authors of classical treatises on the sport. The earliest historical account of it in existence is that of the Rev. John Ramsay. It was published in Edinburgh in 1811. The most monumental work on curling was written by the Rev. John Kerr in 1890.

William Guthrie, another minister of the same century, was such an expert curler that his admirers expressed the prayerful wish that 'his memory live for ever among us, for a worthier than he never lifted the channel stane'. A further reference to the game at that time was made by J. Wallace, also a clergyman, at Kirkwell. He gave his flock helpful information about sites where 'excellent stones for the game . . . could be found in great plentie'.

Through the centuries curling conquered more and more Scottish hearts, helping to lighten Scotland's grim winter and warming frozen limbs.

The Highlanders have always been renowned for their love of feats of strength. As they knew how to throw the hammer and toss the caber, so they learned to curl. In winter it was only natural for them to transfer their contests of strength and skill to the icy surface of tarns and lochs.

Moreover, curling was democratic and excluded professionalism. It was played solely for the love of the game. Its excitement and exhilaration were sufficient to ban nefarious practices often associated with other games. Gambling and betting were strictly outlawed. A modern guide to the game, issued from Winnipeg, its Canadian centre, affirms an ancient tradition when it declares that 'the heart of curling is its incomparable spirit. Without that spirit, curling is just another pastime. Played in' that spirit, it is the king of all games. The spirit of curling is reflected in its most cherished traditions. Curlers play the games to win, but not to humble their opponents. Every curling game ends with a hearty handclasp of friendship and good will to both teammates and opponents'.

The Scots' love of curling was freely expressed. Hundreds of songs and poems have been written in its honour, and clubs, becoming close fraternities, developed their 'courts', with mystical initiation rites, secret 'grips', and whispered passwords. Scotsmen came to believe in a mystical, unseen queen of curling on whom they called for guidance. No one really knows whether it was mere fun, or a sacred, religious pursuit. Certainly, even sermons have been preached on curling, praising it as 'a splendid sport for man to indulge'.

There is a tradition of the existence of a curling club as far back as 1668 and one of the earliest recorded clubs was that of Muthill, of Perth, founded in 1739. Apart from the fact that only one stone was then played by each man, little is known of the club's actual methods of play. However, regulations were very definite as to proper behaviour 'during the time of game': 'that there shall be no wagers, cursing or swearing'. Those contravening the regulations had to pay a penalty of two shillings Scots per oath, while wagers were declared null and void.

The most famous and oldest club in existence is The Duddingston, named after a small loch. It was founded in 1795. Members were renowned for 'their scientific knowledge, wealth, respectability and worth'. In a special resolution they stipulated that 'the sole object of this institution is the enjoyment of the game of curling which, while it adds vigour to the body, contributes to vivacity of mind and the promotion of the social and generous feelings', in short, to *bonhomie*.

Each parish, however, evolved its own methods of play, which differed as much as the size, weight, and condition of the stones. That was all right as long as the clubs did not meet. But when that inevitable moment came with the increasing popularity of this 'auld Scottish game', much difficulty was experienced and there were heated arguments over arrangements. A general wish

LLYFRGELL COLEG MENAI LIBRARY

to standardize the game resulted, in 1834, in the formation of the Amateur Curling Club of Scotland. It ceased to function four years later.

In the same year, an advertisement in the *North British Advertiser* of 26 May 1838, addressed 'To Curlers' in Scotland, invited them to meet in the Edinburgh Waterloo Hotel on a Wednesday of the following month at eleven o'clock 'for the purpose of making the mysteries more uniform in future, and if requisite to form a Grand Court to which all provincial ones are subject, and to elect a Grand President with other office bearers'.

Adding to the 'mysteries', the announcement was not signed, and when a couple of interested players called at the newspaper office to identify the advertiser, the only information available was that a gentleman had handed in the notice and paid ten shillings and six pence for it in advance but had given neither his name nor address.

Nevertheless, on the specified date, 20 June, about a dozen curlers gathered at the hotel. It soon became evident that the anonymous author of the advertisement was not among them. They waited for some considerable time, not knowing what to do. Suddenly the door opened and a stranger entered, carrying some books under his arm. Throwing them on the table, he introduced himself as 'Mr Cairnie of Curling Hall'. The volumes he had brought were copies of his work on curling. No doubt, he was the anonymous convener of the meeting. It was almost a foregone conclusion that those present elected him, by acclamation, president of the new Society which was officially established (with an initial membership of twenty-eight clubs) at a subsequent meeting. Known as the Grand Caledonian Curling Club, it duly drew up rules and regulations and fixed the maximum weight of the stone, including handle and bolt, at 44 lbs (19.80 kg).

When, four years after the formation of the club, Queen Victoria and her Consort, Prince Albert, visited Scotland, members took due advantage of the occasion. They invited the royal couple to a contest, which the

Queen highly praised, and presented Prince Albert with a pair of exquisite curling stones. Subsequently the club was honoured with the Royal Patronage and received permission to change its name to the Royal Caledonian Curling Club (RCCC). Ever since, it has been the ruling body of the sport throughout the world.

John Cairnie occupies the most illustrious place in the history of curling. Born in Renfrewshire, Scotland, in 1769, he graduated as a surgeon from Edinburgh University. After visiting China and serving in India, he settled at Largs, forty-three miles (68.80 km) from Glasgow, where he introduced curling. In his passionate love of the game he called the home he built there 'Curling Hall'.

Determined to pursue the game as soon as possible, even when the ice on lochs and streams was of insufficient thickness to support the players and heavy stones, he pioneered the artificial rink. Its idea, he related, was based on a boyhood memory when, with other lads — and to everyone else's annoyance and peril — he used to pour water on pavements that soon became covered with ice.

He himself began to construct the first artificial pond at Largs. However, as curlers were few in number in this part of the country and none of these was willing to help him meet the comparatively high cost, Cairnie did not complete his project. Instead, he passed the plan on to the famous Duddingston Curling Club.

Yet he was not prepared to see his own dream unrealized and in 1828 — this time at his own expense — he completed a clay pond for curling. After a good frost he and a party of eight friends inaugurated this new stepping stone in the sport. He was highly gratified to find that the first artificial curling rink in the world was equal to the best nature provided.

As soon as the ice was suitable, Cairnie hoisted a flag at Curling Hall to summon his friends to a game. When he died in 1842 (at seventy-three years of age), the world mourned not only the founder of the ruling body, but the greatest curler. An elegy written by his close friend, Captain Paterson, expressed the sorrow of all at his passing:

> Why droops the banner half-mast high,
> And curlers heave the bitter sigh?
> Why throughout Largs the tearful eye,
>   So blear'd and red?
> Oh! Listen to the pour man's cry!
>   John Cairnie's dead!
>
>   . . . .
> Cairnie! Thy name by land or seas
>   Shall never die.

From Scotland curling reached Canada and the United States and spread to other parts of the world: to Sweden, Norway, Switzerland, New Zealand and even Russia.

The earliest stones were natural boulders, taken from a stream. They were irregular and square-edged. A very primitive type was the loofie. It was as flat as the human hand, which gave it its name — from the Scottish *loof*, for a hand. However, players soon realized that to fling the stone efficiently they needed a firmer hold on it, so they cut into it, on opposite sides, holds or hollows in which they could insert the fingers and thumb. This innovation is thought to have been made around 1500.

After a period of approximately 150 years, these kuting stones, as they were called, were replaced by channel stanes. They received their name from the rock-strewn channels of rivers or brooks from which they were taken. Nature had smoothed them through the centuries with water and ice. An iron handle wedged or pounded into the rock provided the curler with a much firmer grip and enabled him to lift and throw the missile more easily. To fix the handle properly a thicker stone was needed to furnish the essential depth and, this, in turn, led to an increase in weight. At this stage the handle was fitted permanently and the stones certainly were of all sizes, weights, and shapes: triangular, square, oval, and round.

An early description refers to 'some three-cornered [stones] like those equilateral cocked hats which our divines wore . . . others like ducks, others flat as a frying pan'. The handles, also, were 'clumsy and unelegant, being malconstructed resemblances of that hook-necked bird, the goose'.

Individual stones became famous and a few are still treasured by the Royal Caledonian Club. They bore distinctive names, often linked with some conspicuous (or imagined) feature, such as 'The Horse', 'The Hen', 'The Saddle', 'The Barn', and 'The Kirk'. Opinions differed as to the reason for the naming of yet another stone 'The Bible'. Some pointed to its square appearance as being 'bookish' and, of course, to the pious Scot, 'the Book' was the Bible. Others felt that a stone so named would have extra, mysterious power, since it was called after Holy Scripture.

Those early stones were individually marked, which helped to prove the antiquity of the game and gave special encouragement to those engaged in digging up the past. Specimens of giant stones, weighing 117 lbs (52.65 kg) have been discovered. One, of blue whinstone bears the inscription 'A GIFT' in Roman capitals and the date — 1511 — and is considered the oldest preserved curling stone in the world so far unearthed.

The stone with its fixed handle was not the ultimate product. Other stones evolved. No longer rough boulders, as supplied and moulded by nature, they were the result of skilled handiwork. By 1800 stones were both round and polished.

A problem that beset curling enthusiasts arriving in far-off settlements was the absence of the right kind of stone. Reluctant to forgo their pastime, they searched for a substitute for granite, which was far too costly to import. The Royal Montreal Club, for instance, (established in 1807 and the earliest recorded in Canada) curled with 'irons'.

The story is told that after Quebec had been captured by Wolfe's army, soldiers (most probably the convalescent wounded and sick) were keen to curl, but were unable to obtain granite. So an ingenious infantry man melted down iron cannon balls and forged copies of the genuine curling stones. There was no limit to the weight of the 'irons', which ranged from 45 to 115 lbs (20.25 kg to 51.75 kg). In Ontario, however, where Scottish settlers were able to obtain granite from river beds, players soon realized that the poor-quality local stone made it unfit for the game. They thus began to mould their own hardwood 'stones' which they ringed with iron to make them heavy enough.

For many years the game was played in different parts of the world with a great variety of stones — granite, timber, and iron — until finally the modern, standard curling stone was adopted everywhere. It weighed 44 lbs (19.80 kg) and was completely circular and had a detachable handle. Yet it introduced another feature: it could be used either side up, one side being rough and the other smooth, and the player chose the side which best suited to the condition of the ice.

The rock island of Ailsa Craig, at the mouth of the Firth of Clyde, was the most famous source of the best granite, which was exported across the seas for making curling stones. A legend told that whenever the last of Ailsa Craig's granite had been used up, the end of the world would have come. However, even legends have a way of becoming obsolete and the manufacture of synthetic, composite stones, with all the properties essential for curling, assures that life will go on — just as curling will — even when Ailsa Craig is no more.

THE BROOM

An important item in curling, and one which has given rise to controversy as to its usefulness and real purpose, is the broom or *besom*. While one member of the team delivers his stone, his team mates are poised with their brooms ready to sweep (*soop*) or scrub the ice ahead of the moving stone until it reaches its target, should the skip (the name of the captain) consider the stone is moving too slowly.

The broom's first use, obviously, was merely to clear the surface of the frozen loch, or pond, of leaves and refuse blown on to the ice by the wind, or of newly fallen snow that might obstruct the path of the stones. Players quickly realized that proper sweeping smoothed the ice, and it became a practice for partners, 'before beginning to play', to use the broom. Laws were made and then rescinded, to be replaced again by others, as to who should undertake the sweeping, at what stage of the game, and in what manner.

The earliest reason for the practice eventually was forgotten and sweeping the ice became a solemn and even exciting part of the game. Players firmly believed that no one who had not learned to smooth the ice could excel in curling.

Opinions still differ as to the present purpose of sweeping. Some think that, by removing dust, ice, or snow, sweeping adds to the distance a stone will travel. Tests proved, in fact, that proper and effective sweeping made a stone move up to fifteen feet (4.50 m) further. Others believe that sweeping in front of the stone produces a partial vacuum that gives the stone extra power. A third explanation assumes that vigorous 'sooping' melts the ice slightly and thereby lessens friction. Those unconvinced that there is any direct purpose in sweeping have to admit that in cold weather it offers good exercise and that energetic sweeping keeps the players warm (and awake!). Sweeping, too, has a psychological effect on both players and the game. Indeed, to observe curlers keenly 'sooping', with grace and rhythm of movement, is like watching a unique ballet on ice.

Almost a mystical quality came to adhere to the 'besom' and it was not surprising that players, joined in contest, called themselves 'the brethren of the broom'.

The broom itself, once merely a long-stemmed bush, came to be manufactured in definite measurements, suited to the individual player. Lighter in weight than an ordinary broom, its bristles were longer, but its handle thicker, and it was made of soft wood. Curlers became truly fond of the broom. A poem by W. A. Peterkin, published in the *Annual* of the Grand Caledonian Curling Club more than a hundred years ago, reflected this affection towards 'My Bonny Broomy Kowe', of which this stanza is typical:

> You've been my friend at ilka spiel,
>   You've polished up the howe,
> You've mony a stane brocht owre the hog,
>   My bonny broomy kowe.
> As mem'ry noo recalls the past,
>   My heart is set alowe,
> Wi' moistened e'en I gaze on thee,
>   My bonny broomy kowe.

Players used the broom for other purposes also. Some curlers, instead of tossing a coin to determine which side should play first, placed their hands alternately along the stick. The last player able to find room to do so would be the first to curl.

The broom also served to convey the skip's instructions, and saved him from having to bawl them out. The signal of a horizontally held broom, for instance, reminded the player to restrict his speed, and thereby the distance curled. Held in a vertical position, it indicated a stone belonging to one's team. Inverted, it pointed to an opponent's rock.

THE TEE

The aim of the game also passed through several stages of evolution. At first, players simply tried to slide the heavy stone farthest. Then a target was placed on the ice (rules up to this day do not specify its actual nature). The mark was initially known as a *toesee*, or *cock*, later to become the modern *tee*. Most probably it originally was just another stone put on the ice. This was replaced by a wooden pin, standing a foot (30 cm) high, so as to be clearly seen from the other side of the 'rink'. Then, going to the other extreme, some curlers preferred to use as their aim a small coin or a button. The tee may also be a small iron plate, fixed by a protruding spike underneath, or merely a depression cut into the ice.

Eventually, the tee was surrounded by a circle scratched into the ice and its area referred to as 'the house'. Its purpose was to help players in determining the exact distance of shots from the tee.

THE TEAMS

Each team, consisting of four men, is known as a *rink*. This term has been derived either from the ancient Saxon *hrink*, meaning 'a strong man' or more probably from the Anglo-Saxon *hring*, describing a circle and ring. The rink is captained by a skip, who gives detailed instructions to the player about to cast the stone. Nothing excels in importance the right way of 'delivering' or throwing it. What the golf swing is to the golfer, the 'delivery swing' is to the curler. In achieving it, the proper grip of the handle is an essential factor, but no one can curl successfully without a firm stance and to ensure this curlers created another, minor accessory. In its oldest form this was known as the *crampit*. It was a thin plate of iron or steel with small spikes underneath to grip the ice, and straps on top to fasten it to the curler's feet.

'Almost barbarous,' according to famous Dr Cairnie, was its 'improved' version, the Currie crampit, which employed screwbolts to hold the feet tightly. He invented foot irons which in time were called after him and eventually took the place of the crampit. A modern development was the *hack*, consisting of a brass or cast-iron frame with a central ridge. It is called after the original 'hack' (or groove) in the ice, into which the curler used to put his foot to stand firm. The invention of felt and rubber-soled boots rendered all these types obsolete.

Chapter 13

CYCLING

The history of cycling as a sport reflects the story of the cycle itself. A bicycle is a fusion of parts, just as its name joins Latin and Greek. It is a 'two-wheeler', from the Latin prefix *bi*, meaning 'two', and the Greek word *kyklos*, a 'circle'.

Before the adoption of this simple term, pointing to its main feature, the 'two-wheeler' was known by a variety of descriptions, derived from the experience of the rider, his 'super-pedestrian' speed, and other aspects of cycling. It is an impressive and thought-provoking list, not lacking in humour.

In one part of the world the bicycle became known as a *draisine,* clearly referring to one of its early inventors, the Baron Drais. It is an example of the many occasions when a name became a word to honour the person who first introduced or designed the object it came to describe.

A *pedestrian curricle,* another early name, had its root in the Latin verb *currere*, 'to run'; the same root can be found in a *current* of water and even the *curriculum* of a school.

Celeripede and *velocipede* (abbreviated often into *velo*), both stressed 'swiftness of foot'.

The *boneshaker* recalled what early riders must have felt while travelling along uneven, bumpy, and stony streets on their unsprung, uncushioned machines.

The *penny-farthing* emphasized the conspicuous difference in size of front and rear wheels of later models which were popular for a time.

These words, and others, are part of the history of the cycle. They show the long way it has travelled in a relatively short time to its modern design whose name colloquially contracts its two wheels into the bike.

Man has always sought to cover distance at a pace faster than walking. Once he had invented the wheel, he thought of rolling his weight along, instead of carrying it on his own two feet. The idea of propelling himself by means of wheels must have entered man's mind early. In fact, cycling enthusiasts of last century were convinced that some crude form of 'cycling' existed in ancient days, and in 1895 Luther H. Porter wrote:

> When we consider the inferior means of locomotion possessed by man, the dissatisfaction he has always felt with the limitations of his own gait, the vast importance to him of means of rapid progression . . . it is impossible not to believe that he long ago endeavoured to discover means of propelling himself rapidly by the aid of some simple mechanical contrivance.

Early Babylonian and Egyptian representations as well as frescoes excavated at Pompeii, seemed to confirm this opinion. Most frequently referred to is a stained glass window, dated 1642, in a church at Stoke Poges, Buckinghamshire, England (twenty miles — 32 km — from London), the village immortalized by its church-yard, which had suggested to the poet Thomas Gray his famous 'Elegy'. This 'cycle window', as it came to be called, depicts a cherub seated on a two-wheeled chariot! How it moved about was left to the viewers' imagination by the Italian artist who made it. It may be that the cherub used some supernatural motive power, or, as others have claimed, advanced by the rider pushing his feet against the ground.

The first really known attempt to ride a sort of cycle dates to 1690, when a Frenchman, the Chevalier M. de Sivrac, contrived a machine consisting of two wooden wheels with upright posts on their sides, which were connected by a backbone. The people of Paris could well stare. The *célérifère*, as it was called, could not be steered, and hence had to follow a straight course with the rider sitting very uncomfortably astride the crossbar, pushing himself along with his feet striking the ground alternately, in a manner somewhat akin to skating. No wonder, this 'bike' was doomed to failure and soon disappeared.

After others had made several attempts at improvement, all of them short-lived, a Frenchman and a German both became renowned as the true fathers of the modern bicycle. Each claimed 'the child' as his very own and there was an acrimonious controversy between their two nations. Quite likely, it was all a matter of coincidence. It is not uncommon in the history of invention that two men, unknown to each other, have conceived the same idea, on occasion at the same time.

The Frenchman's claim goes back to 1816. M. Niepce was a pioneer of photography. Possibly with Sivrac's contraption in mind, he built a machine that, because of its speed, he called a celeripede. It was a simple device of two equal-sized wooden wheels connected by a bar upon which the rider sat and pushed himself forward by 'walking'. The new machine differed from Sivrac's significantly: it could be steered! In the artistic tradition of France and in keeping with her people's love of ornamentation, the inventor carved on the connecting bar of his machine likenesses of animals and snakes. Frequently, he chose the figure of a horse, and thus, this early model of the cycle became known as a *hobby horse*.

In Germany, Baron Karl von Drais, almost simultaneously constructed a cycle which also could be steered by means of a handle and a pivot incorporated in the front wheel.

Drais was a forest warden, employed by the Duke of Baden. His hobby was making all kinds of gadgets, which led his friends to nickname him the 'professor of mechanics'. His chief duty, of course, was to inspect the woods, a task which, because of their extent, became tedious. As he had not the means to own a horse, his love of gadgetry and his fertile mind combined to move in mysterious ways in a quest for mechanical transport. He asked himself whether it was not possible to accelerate, and thereby shorten, his patrols by inventing a man-made 'horse' — some wheeled contraption suitable for bridle paths. That is how, tradition says, he came to build his steerable 'hobby horse'.

He joined two small carriage wheels in tandem to a wooden spine, adding a saddle with a back-rest for comfort. His system of locomotion broke no new ground — he struck his feet alternately forward, but, in between, he was able to 'coast' along. His scientific bent soon impelled him to publish comparative figures, pointing out, for instance, that whereas it might take four hours to cover a certain distance on foot, he could complete the journey on his machine in one hour.

Drais' chubby figure was frequently seen on his machine in the streets. He wore a green, military coat with gold buttons, and perspiration often ran down his red face as he pushed his bike. People were greatly intrigued by the invention, but it did not take them long to raise objections. In fact, they demanded its removal from the thoroughfares of their city, pointing out that events had unfortunately proved that the new-fangled monstrosity threatened them in life and limb. The machine subsequently entered the history of the cycle as the draisine, being called after its inventor.

The Baron was no fool and knew its value, for all that the people resented it at the time. On 12 January 1818, he obtained from his ducal lord and master a patent protecting his rights. This read:

> We, by the Grace of God, Grand Duke of Baden ... grant to Karl, Baron von Drais, for his invention of the tread machine an invention patent for ten years' duration: that nobody may copy or have copied in the land of the Grand Duchy, or shall use this on public streets or places without having first agreed on it with the inventor and to have received proof of this transaction from him.

In the very year that Drais took out his patent in Germany, Dennis Johnson, of Long Acre, a coachmaker, introduced the bicycle from France into England. In London, he established a school to teach people how to ride the new 'pedestrian curricle'. The cost of the machine was far beyond the reach of ordinary men and women. Dandies, however, took great delight in showing off their 'hobby horse', which led to pedestrians calling it a *dandy horse*. Eventually riding one became almost a mania and Johnson's business began to flourish.

Then, suddenly, it flagged. There were two reasons for this. It was thought that the continuous pushing action caused varicose veins! However, it was public ridicule that really 'punctured' the new sport. But not for long. Cyclists again were awheel, although they had no reason to take pleasure in the tiring 'scooting' method of propulsion. They sought something better. One of the first devices to mechanize the bicycle's movement was a type of gear attached to the front wheel and pulled by a rope. This system was in fact cumbersome and exhausting and often led to the rider falling off the bike. Some completely different idea was needed. It was the ingenious Kirkpatrick Macmillan, a Scottish blacksmith of Dumfries, who supplied the solution, and he was the first to adopt crank-driving.

In 1840 he built a cycle with pedals, for the first time enabling cyclists to ride with both their feet continuously off the ground. Another new feature of his machine was a kind of mudguard, though most probably the inventor designed it to safeguard the rider against getting dangerously involved with the driving wheel.

Macmillan rode his machine to Glasgow in two days — a distance of eighty miles (128 km). Its prototype can be seen at the South Kensington Museum in London. He was able to attain speeds up to 14 mph (22.40 km/h) and, to the dismay of drivers and passengers, on many occasions he overtook the local stagecoach. Enthralled by his invention, he indulged in all sorts of tricks, such as coasting downhill, standing in the saddle, and while steering with one hand, holding a girl on his shoulder with the other. Not infrequently, his many experimental and promotional rides led him into conflict with the police, who prosecuted him for 'furious driving on the road'. Once he knocked down a girl, was duly arrested and fined five shillings. On another occasion, he was stopped by a constable for riding on the footpath. Being a canny Scot, he won the policeman over by treating him to a display of fancy riding, with the result that he was let off and got away — scot-free!

Further advance in the evolution of the cycle was made, once again, in France, when E. Michaux, of Paris, began to construct the original 'boneshaker' in 1865. This was designed by Pierre Lallement, a mechanic employed by Michaux's firm. Its main feature was that the front wheel (larger than the rear wheel) was driven by a crank, fixed on its axle. The wheels themselves were still made of wood, but had iron tyres. When Lallement migrated to the United States, he patented his model there.

In England at about this time, the Coventry Sewing Machine Company began to manufacture the Michaux type of machine. Most of their products were exported to France, but when the outbreak of the Franco-Prussian War made further delivery impossible, and in fact, stopped all orders, the firm, then trading under the name of the Swift Cycle Company Ltd, was forced to seek a home market. These circumstances established the industry in Britain and the English became truly bicycle-conscious.

Further improvements in the machine were to come. These included the introduction of wire-spoked wheels and the substitution of India rubber for the iron tyres. The remaining wooden parts were dispensed with and the entire frame, wheels, and spokes were made of iron. Tubular frames were adopted to reduce the weight of the machine. For the first time a chain and gears made their appearance. However, they were fixed to the front wheel.

To gain greater velocity without increasing the pedalling speed, the front wheel was gradually enlarged, with the size of the back wheel diminishing proportionally. This difference in circumferences eventually reached record dimensions. One rider, it is said, even suggested that the front wheel should be fifty-two inches high, while the rear one should be as low as six inches! This type of bike has always been known as the *penny-farthing.*

In 1871, Harry J. Lawson, of Brighton, made the first rear-chain-driven 'safety' cycle. The pedal now moved the back wheel by means of a chain on sprockets.

It would not have been surprising if, of all names for their machines, the early cyclists considered that of 'boneshaker' most appropriate. A ride certainly shook them up. Even the solid-rubber tyre was not a sufficient cushion on the rough, ill-made roads. It was his own experience of such bone shakings, as well as his ten-year-old son's complaints at the discomfort, that led John Boyd Dunlop to develop the pneumatic tyre. He himself was the first to apply the word *pneumatic*, in this new sense, adding it to the world's vocabulary. The word is derived from *pneuma*, the Greek for 'wind' and 'air'.

Dunlop also was a Scot. He practised as a veterinary surgeon in Belfast, Ireland. Of medium height and with a full beard, he moved about rather ponderously. He was somewhat of a hypochondriac. Ever since he had been told that his mother had given birth to him two months prematurely, he imagined that this had impaired his health, with the result that he always avoided unnecessary exertion. However, it should be noted that when he died in 1921, he was aged eighty-two!

His son, Johnnie, loved riding his bike, although it was not always a pleasure on the cobbled streets of the city. The boy told his father that he had set his heart on outdistancing his friends, all of whom were cycling enthusiasts. To help his son get both a smoother ride and greater speed, Dunlop (then aged forty-eight years) set to work in his back yard. He was convinced that a hollow tube filled with air under pressure, and attached to the rim of the wheel, would act as a cushion and achieve both his aims at the same time. There are two versions of the story of how he did so.

One tells how he went straight to a chemist to purchase a rubber tube. He filled this with air and then, with strips of canvas, fixed it round a wooden wheel. Trained in exact research, he now felt compelled to test his idea by comparing the two types of tyre. He did so in a simple experiment. He sent a wheel with the inflated tyre and another with a solid tyre spinning across the yard of his home. The result confirmed all he had thought. The solid-tyred wheel toppled over half-way across. The newly 'attired' wheel went not only all the way but bounded wonderfully on striking the wall!

More anecdotal is the second report. This relates how Dunlop, deep in thought, was pacing his garden. While doing so, he suddenly caught sight of a length of water hose. At once he grasped its import for the problem he wished to solve. Picking it up, he inflated and fixed it to Johnnie's cycle, with remarkable results. He patented his invention in 1881. So it was that an inventive father's love for his son and desire to please him gave the world of locomotion one of its great advances, still recalled by the trademark of 'Dunlop'. One of the original wheels with the Dunlop tyre is in the Royal Science Museum in Edinburgh. It is said that it had covered 3000 miles (4800 km) before being 'retired'.

Just as in the case of 'Niepce vs. Drais', Dunlop also was accused of plagiarism. It was said that ten years before his invention a one-time cycling champion had conceived the idea, but lack of money had prevented his implementing and patenting it.

At all events, in principle the modern bicycle had now arrived. All innovations that were to be added were mere refinements, such as the free wheel and variable-speed gears.

Cycling certainly revolutionized road transport, but it was quickly discovered to be an invigorating and exciting recreation as well. First, there was the joy of touring the country. Manufacturers stressed the democratic, economical, and healthy nature of cycling, which was taken up by royalty, Cabinet ministers, and ordinary men and women alike. Class distinctions on the bike just did not exist.

Verses in a magazine in 1887, point to the popularity of going awheel:

> Though some perhaps will me despise,
> Others my charms will highly prize,
> Yet, nevertheless, think themselves wise.
> Sometimes, 'tis true, I am a toy,
> Contrived to please some active boy:
> But I amuse each Jack O'Dandy;
> E'en great men sometimes have me handy.
> Who, when on me they get astride,
> Think that on Pegasus they ride.

On numerous occasions, enthusiasts of cycling (supported by medical testimony) stressed its many physiological and psychological benefits. Fat people took to the cycle to lose weight, and lean men to increase their appetite. In 1895, Luther H. Porter expounded the many advantages of cycling in a book he entitled *Cycling for Health and Pleasure*. A representative of the New Jersey League of Wheelmen, he had owned and ridden both the 'old-fashioned' two-wheeled velocipede and, what he called, 'the modern high bicycle'. He did not ride simply for pleasure, he explained, but because cycling had proved to him that it was 'the only means of maintaining health'. He was further convinced that it was 'not too much to claim that cycling meets all the conditions of a perfect exercise in a degree approached by nothing else. . . '

Cycling laid up in the rider a store of health-giving oxygen, and stimulated circulation of the blood. It did not overdevelop one set of muscles (as other sports did) but many, 'simultaneously, gently and beneficently'. The constant change of scenery seen by the cyclist on tour avoided the monotony of indoor exercise and stimulated the mind, thereby creating a happy and vigorous disposition. Indeed, cycling was a boon for people of every station in life.

The Pickwick Bicycle Club of London, founded in 1870, was the first cyclists' club in the world. The League of American Wheelmen was established ten years later.

Meanwhile, a Bicycle Touring Club had been formed in England in 1878 and its membership soon embraced many countries in Europe, and the New World. It aimed at improving facilities for cyclists and defending their rights on the road, which were then still widely denied. Among its various publications were a monthly gazette and numerous handbooks and guides. The club also protected cyclists in the case of collisions, injuries, and damage.

Cycling made an impact on everyday life in most unexpected ways. In 1897, Gilbert Floyd drew his readers' attention to the multiple 'Humour of Cycling'. It had introduced totally new terms and topics in conversation. Tabletalk now frequently was preoccupied with 'punctures, handlebars, and speed gears'. According to one cycle enthusiast who quoted statistics, the sport had even been responsible for stopping the declining marriage rate in Britain! It had led to friendships, courtships, and subsequently, weddings.

People interested in the occult and 'outside' influences discovered a new magic possessed by objects in or near the path of the cyclist. They seemed to hold an irresistible, magnetic force of attraction!

Many cashed in on the new cycle mania — by fair means and foul. Manufacturers rightly collected their due. Dishonest men, ready to take advantage of any situation, learned to use riders for their own enrichment.

A story was told by one cyclist that, when riding through a certain hamlet in England, a duck suddenly got in his way. He tried hard to take evasive action, but was unable to do so. He was stopped by an irate owner who displayed a flattened bird and permitted him to proceed only after having paid damages.

About a week later, the cyclist again passed that way. Strangely he was involved in an identical accident, at the same spot. The man who not long before had proffered a dead duck as evidence of negligent driving, showed the cyclist an exhibit that he quickly noted had a striking resemblance to the bird in the previous accident. In fact, it was no newly killed bird, but a well-prepared fake victim that had served many times over!

Americans astutely commercialized cycling even in the realm of religion. Japanese Buddhists use the traditonal prayer wheel in their worship. Its underlying principle is the mechanization of man's petitions. The text of them is attached to a wheel, whose every rotation is counted as one prayer. The more often it is 'said' (i.e., wheeled around), the more it gains the god's favour. American manufacturers, keen to conquer the Japanese market, cleverly produced cycles that had prayer strips fixed around the tyres. This gave the pious Japanese a double advantage: they could 'say' a maximum number of prayers ('pray while you wheel') and enjoy additional safety as the strip protected their tyres against splitting!

Almost from the very beginning of cycling, people in many countries realized the cycle's great potentialities for racing. Early competitions were very informal and, naturally, aimed at covering a distance in record time. The formation of clubs stimulated the sport. In France, for instance, contests were held every Sunday.

The first official cycling race on record took place at Hendon, England, in 1868. France did not lag far behind. In the same year, a French manufacturer organized a 1200 metre race. In 1869, an International Road Race, open to all, extended from Paris to Rouen, starting at the Arc de Triomphe. Its rules make interesting reading: riders were not permitted to change machines during the race, but could employ any type — with rubber tyres, crank or gears, and wheels of all dimensions. However, competitors were not permitted 'to be trailed by a dog or use sails'!

A rider's credential was an officially signed map, which he had to collect between 6 and 7 a.m. on the day of the race, at the sponsoring firm's office. The first prize was 1000 francs. Of 323 cyclists who entered, 200 started

Shooting at butts, c. 1340—from the Toutrell Psalter

Battledore and shuttlecock, 1743 (after Hayman)

The earliest illustration of the game of baseball—old English woodcut, 1744

The opening game of the Boston Baseball Club, 1889

BOSTON BASE-BALL CLUB.

Ancient Mayan ball court excavated at Chichen Itza, Mexico. Note the stone rings on either side

From the first English description of billiards by Charles Cotton, 1674

THE COMPLEATE GAMSTER.

Billiards at Versailles, 1694—engraving by Antoine Trouvain

Early boxing gloves—detail, Roman statue of a pugilist wearing the 'cestus'

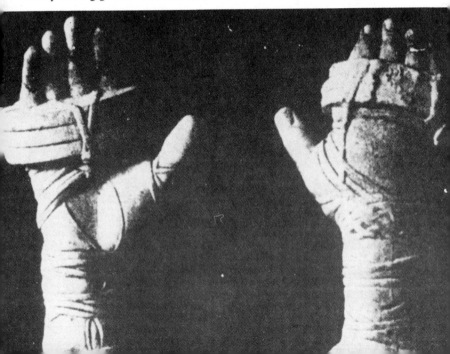

Club Ball (early cricket)—13th-century engraving

Cricket near London in 1743

Final Test match—Australia *v.* England, August 1882, at the Oval (origin of the 'Ashes' legend)

Croquet—engraving from *Laws and Regulations of the Game*, John Jaques, 1865

The 'Hobby-horse' Cycling School—from an 1820 print

Cycling in 1889

Salukis in Egypt used for hunting, 4th millennium BC—carved on a slate tablet known as the Oxford Palette, c. 3200

Sword play (fencing)—13th-century engraving

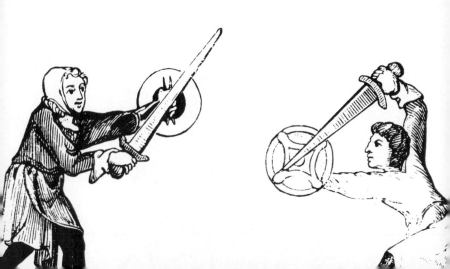

Football in the 14th century—from the *Gloucester misericord*

Mr Angelo's Fencing Academy (English Rosenberg after T. Rowlandson)

Football at Rugby, 1870

Australian footballers—opening match *v.* Devon 1908

Marble tablet, Rugby College, Warwickshire, England

THIS STONE
COMMEMORATES THE EXPLOIT OF
WILLIAM WEBB ELLIS,
WHO WITH A FINE DISREGARD FOR THE RULES OF FOOTBALL
AS PLAYED IN HIS TIME
FIRST TOOK THE BALL IN HIS ARMS AND RAN WITH IT
THUS ORIGINATING THE DISTINCTIVE FEATURE OF
THE RUGBY GAME
A.D. 1823

Golf or Bandy-ball (from a 14th-century manuscript)
The ancient top hat filled with feathers—the amount of feathers which went into a featherie golf ball

An early form of hockey

First totalizator in New Zealand, 1891; authorized by a New Zealand Act of Parliament

Saxon chieftain with huntsman and hounds, pursuing wild swine—from a 9th-century manuscript

Hunting—15th century

Player of the 17th-century Dutch game of *Kalv*—engraving by Romein de Hooghe

St Lidwina's accident, 1396—earliest known skating print (15th century)

A Samurai

Two celebrated warriors, Kawadsu-no-Saburo and Matano-no-Goro, retainers
of Yoritomo

in the race which was staggered, because of the great number of competitors. The English cyclist James Moore (pronounced by the French as Jimmie Meere) was the winner. His machine had been manufactured in a French jail just outside Paris!

It was to promote the sport even further and to add to its excitement (as well as to make it a more profitable source of income) that the famous six-day race was devised. It was inaugurated at Madison Square Garden, New York, in 1891. It was run over 142 hours, with 'Pugger Bill' the winner.

In England the National Cyclists' Union (established in 1878, under the name of the Bicycle Union) was the first association to put up danger boards and issue regulations to control cycle traffic. It held annual championships and became the controlling body of all forms of cycle racing, including record breaking on the roads and the tracks. Eventually, it was recognized by the International Cycling Union, the world body of the sport. This had been formed in 1900 with its headquarters in Paris, to become generally known by the abbreviaton of its French name as the UCI.

That is how, through the years, the various types of racing evolved, with men either riding against the clock or against each other.

Chapter 14

DOG-RACING

The dog is man's oldest companion and friend. Beautiful legends seek to explain that it all started with the dog's own choice.

When God had created the world and all the beasts in it, He wished to crown His work with a masterpiece. So He made man, but He soon realized that he was far from perfect. Therefore, He caused a chasm to open up between man and all other creatures.

The dog, standing among his animal brethren, watched man across the ever widening gap. Taking pity on him, he jumped across the canyon on a sudden impulse, to become man's loyal companion, which he has remained ever since.

Another myth tells how the snake devoured Adam and Eve on the first night after their creation. When God made them all over again, the serpent swallowed up the second couple as well. So for the third time, God had to fashion man and woman. Determined to preserve their lives, He created the dog, to serve as their guardian. When, after the setting of the sun, the snake once again appeared, ready to devour Adam and Eve, the dog chased it away by barking. To protect man's life, the dog has never left his side, and that also is why, the legend claims, a dog howls whenever a man dies.

No one really knows the origin of the dog's domestication. It has been suggested that in earliest days wild dogs used to gather outside caves and wait for scraps to be thrown to them. Eventually, man took some of those uninvited guests 'indoors'. Another theory claims that, when hunting and roaming the country side, man came across a litter of young dogs and ate most of its members. However, he felt pity for one of the puppies and took it home to rear it. That is how, one way or another, man befriended the dog and soon came to realize its usefulness to him.

There is no doubt that from prehistoric times dogs proved their value in helping man chase his quarry and provide him with food. All over the world, man came to appreciate the dog, to utilize and even to venerate it. Myths of dogs belong to the lore of numerous races in every continent.

Cerberus, with its many heads, was believed to guard the gate to the infernal region of Hades, while in Borneo a fiery dog was thought to watch the entrance to paradise.

Many ancient monuments, some dating back to 5000 BC, have been unearthed, telling in picture or word the story of man's love for his dog, and the part it already played in his life in that early period.

Long before the building of the pyramids, Egyptians had adopted the dog. They called it by individual names, and early hieroglyphic signs refer to it by the syllables *b* and *w* which anticipated by thousands of years the children's custom of speaking of the dog as a *bow wow*. Egyptian reliefs portrayed dogs as companions of their master at home and in the field. Mummified bodies of dogs were found in Egyptian graves, showing how, at the dawn of history, man venerated the canine species.

Dogs were also pictured on the friezes of Assyrian kings, on Greek terra cotta vases, and on numerous artifacts of the Romans. Mayan civilization lacked all domestic animals — except the dog. The Incas kept it, both as a pet and a scavenger, while the Mochica race raised dogs that had no bark, and their artists immortalized the dog's shape in exquisite, unrivalled pottery.

Andean tribes around Peru used to eat dogs, a custom that was condemned by the royal Incas. Aztecs sacrificed dogs, particulary so on the passing of a king, to accompany his body across a mystical river. On the other hand, Persians loved the animal so much that anyone killing a dog was severely punished.

Never throughout history did the dog lose its prominent place. Loyally he guarded his master's property and his flocks. When, in the twenty-third Psalm (which compared God's care for man with that of a shepherd for his sheep) the last verse speaks of 'goodness and mercy' that 'shall follow me all the days of my life', some commentators have pointed out that, in fact, 'Goodness' and 'Mercy' were the names of two sheepdogs.

The dog served as a scavenger not only among the Incas but all over the ancient world — as it continues to do in some Eastern lands. It could be trained as guide and carrier in peace and war. Its sensitivity in hearing and smelling proved far superior to that of man. Many lost people and wounded soldiers owed their survival solely to a dog. Moving and beautiful were the words of a blind man who, so truly, could say of his guide dog that 'my eyes have a cold nose'. In Arctic zones, to this very day, dogs pull man's burdens.

Above all, dogs have proved themselves effective in the hunt. Their pursuit of game, including gazelles, deer, and hares, dates back to antiquity. The dog most favoured in coursing almost from the very beginning was the greyhound. It is remarkable that its breed has hardly changed any of its main features for the last 7000 years. Its characteristics have always been a slender body and long legs but, above all, superlative vision, an acute sense of hearing, and swiftness. These attributes made the greyhound the ideal hunter, unsurpassed in ability to track game and catch up with it. The greyhound followed the quarry not by scent but by sight, which differentiates it from most other dogs. The meaning of its name is not certain and has been explained variously, though all agree that the prefix 'grey' (of which the etymology is doubtful) does not refer to the dog's colour. Hound, of course, is an ancient description of a dog, preserved in the German *Hund*. Some saw in the word greyhound a corruption of 'Greek hound'.

Dr Cayus, Queen Elizabeth's court physician, in his book on dogs, suggested that the syllable 'grey' had evolved from a word signifying 'degree', as this breed was of 'the highest degree'. His book was the first ever to be written exclusively on the subject in England, though in Latin. His opinion, even if incorrect, certainly must have been influenced by the royal bearing, proud stance, and beautiful lines of the breed. No wonder that the greyhound became a living symbol of grace and nobility.

All over the world, the greyhound has been employed as the most reliable and efficient chaser among dogs. Neolithic man used it as such. A species of the greyhound — the saluki — is clearly distinguishable on Egyptian friezes portraying hunting scenes. It appears too in Mesopotamian art, being depicted straining at the leash or racing after the quarry. Excavated artifacts from the Greek world, now displayed in the British Museum, London, also picture the greyhound, identical in all its features with the modern breed.

A stone relief which has survived from Thessaly in the fourth century BC shows a greyhound watching the goddess Hecate, whose sacred animal he was, crowning a horse. The occasion can only be guessed but, most probably, it was the winning of a race. Conspicuous is the greyhound's almost haughty expression. This has been interpreted as the artist's attempt to convey its proud awareness of being an even faster runner than the horse.

The Latin poet Ovid (first century BC), a descendant of an ancient equestrian family, in a vivid description, of the chase of Daphne by Apollo, compares it to the pursuit of a hare by a greyhound.

Dogs rate regrettably low in most of the some forty places in which the Bible mentions them. In the Middle East, a dog was not a domestic pet but ran wild in the streets and was feared for its bite, most likely because of rabies. Contempt for it became so great that the very word dog was used as a term of abuse.

Nevertheless, in one passage (in the book of Proverbs,

XXX:31) — according to most translations of the Hebrew original, a tradition also adopted by the Revised Version — the greyhound is praised as one of four stately beings, majestic as 'makers good of step'. Literally, the Hebrew term means 'girt of loins' and it is only fair to record that other renderings of the phrase saw in it a reference not to the dog, but to the cock or the war horse.

An Arab saying vividly pictured the greyhound's superlative speed by stating that it was so swift that seeing from afar a gazelle biting off a blade of grass, it would reach it even before it had time to swallow it.

The first extensive treatise on coursing was written as early as the middle of the second century by the Greek historian and philosopher Arrian who, on adopting Roman citizenship, called himself Flavius. By its description of coursing as it was practised then, the work shows this sport to be one of the few in the world that has not changed in its principal elements through the millennia. The rules and views set out by Arrian are almost identical with those of modern times.

He wrote that the object of the sport was not the catching of the animal but the enjoyment of a contest in swiftness. Coursers, in fact, he pointed out, were glad if the hare made its escape. Should the animal hide in a thicket, or be found trembling with fear, coursers should call off their dogs, because to continue the chase then was no longer 'sport'.

Arrian relates how, when following a course on horseback, he himself frequently had ridden up to the hare as soon as it was caught and, to save its life, had taken away his dog and tied it up, so that the hare could gain its freedom.

When dogs were no longer used to catch prey to supply their owner with food, coursing came into its own as an independent, legitimate sport. The means to an end had become an end in itself.

Only two dogs at a time were permitted to chase the animal, which had to be given a fair start. Arrian also advises the courser to pet his dog after the chase and to praise it so that it will feel its owner's appreciation.

That sports-loving England would adopt and cherish coursing was a foregone conclusion. It is believed that the greyhound was imported to the country by the Cretans around 500 BC. A perfect specimen became a prized possession in the Middle Ages. Popular was a rhyme (often quoted in after years) attributed to Juliana Berners, who was said to have been the Abbess of Sopwell nunnery. It appears in *The Booke of St Albans*, a tract on hunting, reputedly written by her in 1486:

> If you will have a good sike,
> Of which there are few like,
> He must be headed like a snake,
> Necked like a drake,
> Backed like a beam,
> Sided like a bream,
> Tailed like a rat,
> And footed like a cat.

English monarchs and the nobility patronized coursing and maintained large kennels of greyhounds. King John treasured the animal so much that he gladly agreed to accept greyhounds instead of money in the payment of fines or the renewal of grants. Henry VIII expressed the view that the acquiring of proper skill in every aspect of coursing was part of the education of a gentleman. An intriguing appointment by the Crown under his reign was that of a 'Keeper Chaste of the King's Grey Houndes'. As the title suggests, his duty implied the preservation of the pure, thoroughbred breed.

Queen Elizabeth I liked coursing so much that she commanded Thomas, the fourth Duke of Norfolk, to formulate the first code of rules. She was thus responsible for the beginning of properly regulated coursing in England.

No doubt adopting Arrian's ideas, the rules forbade the coursing of the hare by more than a brace of greyhounds; the hare had to be given a headstart of 240 yards (218.40 m). The code also made the important point that the race was not necessarily won by the dog that made the kill, but by the one most instrumental in achieving it.

Even Oliver Cromwell, who otherwise certainly did not favour amusements, was a lover of greyhounds and showed a keen interest in coursing events. From a pursuit in private, coursing grew into a national sport. The first public trials took place at the time of King Charles I.

Its popularity increased ever more and all classes of people were attracted to it. Those who could not afford to own a greyhound used their fastest mongrel. On the other hand, class-conscious England at times strictly confined the possession of greyhounds, and even the practice of the sport, to society's upper strata.

Modern coursing owes its sound organization to the history-making establishment by the then Duke of Norfolk, Lord Orford, of the first known club at Swaffham in 1776. He was not only a patron of the sport and its zealous promoter, but the owner and breeder of racing dogs. His experimentation in crossing breeds led to a further improvement of the greyhound's stamina.

The club itself was distinguished by several odd features. The number of its members was limited to that of the letters in the alphabet — twenty-six. Each member was given a letter, in addition to a separate colour. Of course, the chief activity of the club was the holding of races, for which each dog owner appointed a judge. Jointly, they chose a referee to act as an arbitrator in any conflict of opinion.

Lord Orford's death has even been linked to his insatiable enjoyment of coursing. Although sick, he was determined to watch his favourite bitch, Czarina, win yet another race (for the forty-seventh time 'running'). Straight from his sickbed, he followed the greyhounds on horseback. When, as expected, Czarina once again proved the winner, Orford's excitement was too much. He collapsed, fell from his horse, and died. There is another version of his death in 1791. It was due, the story goes, to a broken heart over the sudden passing of the girl he loved.

Other clubs were soon formed throughout the British Isles and some of them made valuable contributions to the further advance of the sport. The Ashdown Park Meeting first introduced the idea of a proper enclosure for the coursing field. Not the first in time, but the first in social importance and in its influence on the sport was the Altcar Club, founded by the Earl of Sefton near Liverpool in 1825. To be elected a member of this amounted almost to an accolade. However nothing surpassed the prestige of the Waterloo Cup, which became the 'Derby' of coursing. It was named after the Waterloo Hotel at Liverpool as its proprietor, Mr Lynn, had first suggested the race. Himself a lover of greyhounds, in 1836 he submitted to Lord Molyneux a plan to run a contest of an eight-dog stake (at a sovereign each), also asking permission to use the grounds of the Altcar Club.

The nobleman agreed to both propositions and, enthusiastic about the idea, entered one of his own dogs, Milanie, which — rather deservedly so — won the race. In additon to the stake, the winner was presented with a trophy, a silver snuff box.

The sweepstake's success was so great that another meeting was arranged the following year, when nominations of dogs were increased to sixteen. On the next occasion, a year later again, this number was doubled, and from then the race became the most important annual event in the world of dog-racing. Since 1857 sixty-four dogs have participated in each race and the Waterloo Cup has come to be regarded as 'the blue ribbon of the leash'.

All that was further required was a generally accepted code of rules and a strict supervision of the greyhounds entered to prevent substitutions. The establishment of the National Coursing Club in 1858 met both needs. It became the controlling body and from 1882 onward published a Greyhound Stud Book for the registration of the dogs, their pedigree, and history.

A principal feature of coursing eventually led to its decline and to the creation of the modern sport of greyhound-racing. People no longer approved of creatures suffering for the sake of their own enjoyment, not even the rabbit, however much it was considered a pest as it is in Australia. Coursing came to a dead end as it were.

A drastic change was clearly needed to revive it. The problem was to find a satisfactory substitute for a hare. In seeking one, enthusiasts well remembered that, fortunately, greyhounds pursued their quarry by sight and sound, and not by scent. It was reasoned that an inanimate dummy, moving along noisily, would therefore excite the dogs as much as a live bunny. English sportsmen conceived the idea of using an object that was mechanically propelled but, nevertheless, would make greyhounds chase after it as if it were a living quarry.

A first attempt was made in 1876 on a field near the Welsh Harp, Hendon. The promoters of the race for the first time used a mechanical hare. Mounted on a rail, it was pulled along by means of a rope wound around a wheel.

The experiment failed for two reasons. The course was the traditonal straight track of 450 yards (409.50 m). Chased hares, or rabbits, moved erratically, taxing a greyhound's agility and sagacity. A mechanical hare mounted on a rail never wavered. It progressed in a straight line. Knowing the individual greyhound's approximate speed, and the fact that it almost invariably runs true to form, the result of the race could be accurately forecast and bets were no longer exciting or profitable. Secondly, on the traditional straight track, it was impossible to see the start and finish of a race equally well, which greatly reduced its appeal.

These faults could only be remedied by changing the shape of the course and providing a circular or oval track so that the race not only could be followed easily from beginning to end but no longer would it go merely to the fastest runner. The dog which knew best how to negotiate the curves and take advantage of opportunities in running would be the winner. And so the modern dog-racing track came into being. First envisaged by an Englishman in 1890, its construction died prematurely through lack of funds. Where the English failed, the Americans succeeded. Modern greyhound racing was born in the United States.

The first races were held in Massachusetts in the eighteenth century. The dogs were released from the arms of 'slippers' on a gunshot. They raced towards a cloth waved by a 'handler' who stood approximately twenty feet (6 m) beyond the finishing line. A live hare released into a circular arena replaced the waved cloth, and the winner was the dog who caught it.

However it did not take long for animal lovers to condemn the sport as inhumane and it was prohibited.

Owen Patrick Smith of Oklahoma, prosecuted for ignoring the ban, felt that an efficient replacement for the live rabbit was all that was needed. After years of trial and error he was able to produce an ideal mechanical hare which was run along an electrified rail around an oval track. It was a resounding success and the mechanical hare was eventually adopted all over the world.

In 1925, Charles Munn, an American sportsman and lover of greyhound racing, took the idea to Britain. The conservative British at first gave him the cold shoulder but, undaunted, Munn persisted, to succeed at last in rousing interest and in getting support from General A. C. Critchley. Together, they organized the first experimental track at Belle Vue, Manchester, in 1926. The choice of that Lancashire town had its special reason. The men were convinced, it is said, that if Manchester liked greyhound racing, the whole of England would too. At all events, the new sport caught on and the two men founded the Greyhound Racing Association of Britain.

Greyhound racing, streamlined as the greyhound itself, has thus become the dignified and humanized heir of coursing.

Chapter 15

FENCING

A perfect example of a sport created by warfare is fencing. Its name is an abbreviated form of 'defence'.

A feeling of insecurity has always been with man. Throughout many centuries when an encounter with a stranger could prove fatal, to leave one's sword at home was to invite trouble. So the carrying of a sword became the custom of a 'gentleman'.

With this background in mind it can be easily understood how fencing evolved out of the training for the not uncommon sword fights. Battles were not always determined by the clash of two tribes, or two armies, but by individual encounters between selected representatives of warring groups. To refrain from the practice of fencing would endanger not only a man's life but possibly the very existence of his people. Unprepared for mortal combat, one could become an easy victim of an aggressor. Even more so, neglect of practice in swordsmanship would be tantamount to evading national duty to be prepared for the defence of the clan, tribe, or country.

An Egyptian relief from the time of Pharaoh Ramses III (1190 BC) depicts a fencing bout, not an actual martial fight but a practice match. The carving, excavated in a temple near Luxor, shows the points of the swords covered. The fencers wear masks and are watched by a motley group of spectators, while the fight is supervised by judges. Accompanying hieroglyphic passages quote a proud fencer's request to admire what his valiant hand would do, and the crowd's vociferous urging on of the victor in his superb and praiseworthy fight.

All ancient races had learned to master the sword and records of early bouts from almost every part of the world have been preserved. Swords belong to man's earliest relics. The Japanese treasure as a sacred possession a 'divine sword' which a legendary prince is said to have used to mow down burning shrubs threatening to envelop him, and to defeat the foe. Indian tradition credits Brahma himself with having invented swordsmanship and with having taught it and other mysterious sciences to the initiates of his cult. The supremacy of the sword caused it to become the official symbol of power. To this very day, the English monarch bestows the honour of knighthood by touching the recipient's shoulder with a sword.

Another source of swordsmanship is the duel. Long before it attained its formalized pattern and, to our modern minds, the odd purpose of defending one's honour, it had deep religious implications that alone explain its existence. Fundamentalist believers in the literal truth of the Bible regarded Cain's slaying of Abel as the first duel in history. The scriptural words 'and Cain spoke unto Abel his brother', had been the first challenge given and accepted.

Divine judgment was expressed in the result of the fight that therefore did not depend on the contestants' own strength, but involved supernatural power. That is how David had beaten Goliath; victory had proved the justice of his cause. Some theologians in fact believed that their confrontation divinely introduced the judicial duel.

The duel itself is closely linked with the institution of the ordeal. This assumed that divine intervention established the guilt or innocence of a party. Trials by ordeal were manifold and one form of ordeal was the duel between two men. Not their skill or strength determined the outcome, but the justice of their cause. In this 'trial by battle', might was right.

At first, there were several systems of combat. Opponents might use their bare hands alone, or their fists or wooden sticks of various lengths. They could confront each other with swords and the first who drew blood was proved — by God — to be the innocent party, whose cause was just. In the extreme case, only the death of one of the adversaries would reveal the divine judgment.

Duels were fought almost all over the world and were regarded as the fairest possible way to settle a dispute. There was certainly no possibility of an appeal. However, Roman civilization frowned on it and decried it as a barbarian practice.

The combat is known to have been reinstituted by the Burgundian King Gundobald in AD 501, to take the place of the oath and other ordeals which at the time were equally regarded as the judgment of God. Only women, invalids, and men over sixty (and eventually also priests) were exempt for the trial in which plaintiff and defendant agreed to submit their cause to the judgment of heaven 'by dint of the sword'.

The revived duel was soon accepted all over western Europe as part of the judicial system. It can well be imagined that people felt it necessary to be prepared for any such 'court action' by learning to be good swordsmen and thus be able to prove the justice of their case, should ever the need arise. This fostered greatly the practice of fencing which, no doubt, must have given people a love of it for its own sake. Even when through the invention of firearms the sword was relegated to the arsenal of obsolete weapons, it continued to be employed in the duel.

The original swords were very heavy, as they had to pierce the armour which was also traditionally worn. To wield the sword successfully needed more strength than skill.

In the 1500s the invention of gunpowder and firearms made the bow and arrow redundant. Heavy armour was now useless as it could easily be penetrated by the novel bullet. As an immediate result swords — still necessary for individual combat — were changed. They could (and had to) be much lighter now. Lack of defensive armour meant that the heavy, double-edged, unwieldy weapon was no longer needed. On the other hand, the absence of the weighty mail shirt permitted men to move so much more quickly and deftly. This demanded a weapon that could be easily managed and enabled a man to tackle dexterously an ever more evasive foe. That is how gradually the long, slim rapier came into existence. Its lightness permitted greater speed, which made its use all the more deadly.

When wearing a suit of armour, a warrior had been well protected and thus had used the sword only for attack. But now man had to learn to employ it for defence as well, and skill in swordsmanship became indispensable. Even when open, individual warfare was no longer practised, travellers were frequently threatened by attacks from bandits and, with no police force in existence, had to look after their own safety.

These various factors combined to make an all-round knowledge of swordsmanship almost a matter of life and death. Enterprising and imaginative fencing masters immediately grasped the opportunity and began to promote their art. The first fencing schools and guilds of fencing masters were established. In their own way, and for the new purpose, the schools further evolved the instruments of fencing and its craft. Teachers jealously guarded their particular styles and personal techniques, just as modern nations do with their secret weapons, and all tuition was given in strict privacy.

Spaniards made fencing a highly scientific pursuit. Gonzalo de Cordoba (d. 1515), known as 'the Great Captain', is credited with having invented the hand guard. His sword is still displayed in a Madrid museum.

Italians, however, were without doubt the most prominent promoters of fencing as a science, teaching that not force but skill and speed were of prime importance, and emphasizing use of the point of the sword, not of its edge. Until then, methods of fencing had been crude and rough. Even features from wrestling had been borrowed. The development and refinements in fencing that the Italians prompted caused them to be regarded as the originators of true swordsmanship. Significantly, the Italians called the art by the word *scherma*, which, derived from the German *schirmen*, means to 'defend' and to 'guard'.

Italian fencing masters, having perfected technique, were in great demand. To begin with, both hands of a fencer were occupied. While handling the offensive weapon with his right hand, he used the left for defence, holding a dagger, a gauntlet, or his cloak to throw over his attacker's sword.

Henry VIII, himself a vigorous athlete in his younger years and an enthusiastic fencer, by a Letter Patent of 1540 incorporated professors of fencing in his realm to teach the noble science of defence. The professors enjoyed this right as a privilege and a monopoly. Scholars graduated to become Provosts of Defence.

In 1599, George Silver published *Paradoxes of Defence*, the first book of its kind in English. Writing with an unmistakable anti-Italian bias, he called on his countrymen not to be inveigled into replacing their trustworthy, traditional broadsword (so much more natural for Englishmen), with the new-fangled, unreliable, Italian-fostered rapier: 'I George Silver, hauing the perfect knowledge of all maner of weapons, and being experienced in all maner of fights . . . admonish the noble ancient, victorious, valiant, and most braue nation of Englishmen to take heed how they submit themselves into the hands of Italian teachers of Defence . . .' In spite of Silver's strongly worded advocacy, he fought a hopeless battle, and his book could not stem the adoption of the fashionable rapier.

A change in men's fashion during the reign of King Louis XIV of France was responsible for the creation of the French fencing style, which revolutionized the art. The new elegance of the Sun King's era, with its novel form of dress, no longer permitted the carrying of the long, trailing rapier. A short, light court sword took its place. Gentlemen were expected to carry it in constant readiness for the defence of their honour. More significant than its stylishness were its many advantages. Not only could it be handled with much greater ease, but it was effective both for offence (by the thrust of its point) and defence (by the employment of its blade). Consequently, the use of the dagger, gauntlet, and cloak became obsolete, and the swordsman's left arm was freed.

From this French weapon the modern fencing foil and the *épée de combat* were derived. *Épée*, of course, is the French for 'sword'. The origin of the word foil is uncertain. It has been suggested that it conveys the fact that the point of the sword was foiled, or blunted, as was its edge. Another explanation is that the term stems from the use of the foil to 'foil', i.e., to beat off an attack — in short, to parry.

Until the late eighteenth century the only real protection for practising fencers was to have the swords buttoned. Odd to note is the fact that although in the earliest Egyptian pictures of a fencing bout the fighters wore a mask, its use apparently had been completely forgotten. It was reintroduced by the French fencing master La Boëssière who, in 1780, recommended it as a wise safeguard. Initially however, fencers disregarded it as unmanly and undignified. In additon, the first modern masks made of solid metal did not guard what needed most protection — the eyes. These were exposed to attack through a horizontal slit. As if to highlight this omission, George Robert Fitzgerald (nicknamed 'Fighting Fitzgerald'), a famous but villainous fencer, is said to have poked out one eye of an opponent, not by accident but by design.

The eventual adoption, around 1800, of the wire-mesh mask changed the whole pattern of fencing. With the face now fully protected, completely new methods of defence and attack could be employed.

The sabre, with its slightly curved, wide blade, was introduced in the mid-nineteenth century. Its ancestor is the Asian, crescent-shaped sword, known as the scimitar. It was brought into Europe by the Hungarian cavalry. Horsemen of other armies adopted it and from the martial field it found its way into fencing.

Single combats with the sword now belonged to the far-distant past of primitive warfare, and not duels but courts of law determined the right or wrong of a case. But fencing has survived and through the centuries of its evolution and the ingenuity of fencing enthusiasts has become a highly disciplined, scientific sport and an accomplished art. Notwithstanding the etymology of its name with its defensive implication (and no matter whether using the foil, the *épée*, or the sabre), its main principle still is to hit, and not to be hit.

When the Olympic Games were revived in 1896, their first agenda included fencing as a recognized sporting event. A once deadly method of combat had grown into a highly organized sport of civilized man, 'a conversation with foils', demanding supreme mental and physical fitness, an alert mind and a supple, controlled body. Is it not the wish of all people to see one day a comparable metamorphosis of all warfare into a peaceful and happy pursuit in which men seek not to destroy each other but to add to the thrills of life, sublimating aggressive instinct into constructive aspirations and activities that bring out the best in man?

Chapter 16

FOOTBALL

Most people finding a pebble or stone in front of them are tempted to nudge or kick it. So even if there were no records, we could assume that some kind of football was part of man's life in primitive days. A gruesome tradition has it that in historical times some races used their enemies' severed heads as footballs. An early record from Britain relates how the head of a captured Danish invader was used thus.

We know from numerous sources the ancient popularity of the game. Even the Bible takes it for granted. The prophet Isaiah (XXII:18) speaks of God who will *turn and toss* a state official to whose obnoxious policy he objected, 'like a ball into a large city'. Classical literature also contains explicit references to the sport and detailed accounts of how it was played. Among the early Greeks, for instance, there was a game in which the players tried to carry a small ball, similar to the modern football, across a line defended by the other side.

A game very much like it was played in Rome. Its aim was to drop the ball behind the opposition's base line. It appears that players passed the ball to one another but did not kick it. There was, however, plenty of 'tackling', running, and throwing of the ball. This was confirmed by Galen, a second-century physician and philosophical writer and much-sought-after doctor in Rome. He pointed out how the various functions of the players increased stamina and contributed to their health.

The Romans are said to have fostered football as part of their military training. It is generally assumed that Roman soldiers brought the game to Britain. Indeed, there are (unauthenticated) reports that relate that the people of Derby played football in AD 217 to celebrate a victory against those very Romans.

Football was enjoyed in China in the second century. The Chinese cleverly used both their feet and their bodies to propel the ball but never handled it. An aristocratic version was known as kick ball, which became a feature in the celebration of the ruler's birthday. In front of his palace players erected a unique kind of goal. It consisted of a silken net with a central circular hole (of approximately one foot — 30 cm — in diameter), which they fixed between two long bamboo sticks, adorned with streamers. Teams vied with one another to score goals by kicking the ball through the opening. The prize was a silver cup, filled to the brim with either fruit or wine. The losing team did not get off scot-free. It was 'awarded' a thorough beating of the most literal kind.

Balls once owned and used by the Pharaohs were preserved in Egyptian graves thousands of years old. The British Museum in London has such specimens. Made of soft leather or fine linen, they were stuffed with cut reed or straw. Other similar balls of man's earliest civilizations, in which two hemispherically shaped skins were sewn together, were filled with earth, grain, plant fibres, corn husks, or even pieces of metal. The Mayas, on the other hand, had balls of solid rubber.

The term 'football' did not originally have its present meaning. What it was meant to convey at first was that the ball game was played 'on foot' and not, like other games, such as polo, by men mounted on horses. The word 'football' actually is of comparatively recent coinage. The first document in which it appears dates only from 1486 in England. Until then, the game was referred to as 'a ball play' or 'playing at ball'.

Football belongs to the category of primitive fertility rites. The ball represented the sun. In many parts of the world representations of its shining disc were used in magic ceremonies to fructify the soil and all growing things. The discs were hung on trees and dug into the ground. People threw a round stone or some other type of globular body (replicas of the sun) to each other.

Tribes divided themselves into teams, and engaged in a contest that they believed would have cosmic consequences. Imitating the course of the sun, they played 'ball' in the very direction in which the heavenly body was known to move, from east to west.

In some early instances of the game, the players dipped a ball into water (magically) to ensure rain. In general, the 'playing at ball' reflected primitive man's conviction that the success of his crops depended on the way he tossed the symbolic sun.

Obvious traces of this fertility rite survived for more than a thousand years. In Devon, England, peasants who had planted potatoes on Good Friday ceremoniously kicked a ball across the fields. This was the season when the sun was most needed. At Whitby, it was believed that a young man who failed in the football game on Shrove Tuesday would experience disaster at the next harvest. Indians in Oklahoma played a football game to celebrate the gathering in of their crop. On certain days Irish villagers carefully carried around a gold and a silver ball, symbolic of the sun and the moon.

In some cases, the goal was a tree, a symbol of growing things. To hit it with a ball meant the impregnation of all that grew with the source of warmth and life. Another custom required the player to sink the ball into a hole in the ground. This brought the 'sun' into closest contact with the soil, ensuring a rich harvest.

There was an early division of players into opposing teams: either of bachelors versus married men, or virgins versus married women. They believed that the to-and-fro throwing between them of the symbol of fertility would bring virility and fruitfulness to those who needed it.

Another theory suggests that the modern football did not evolve out of a replica of the sun, but the head of an animal that had been sacrificed. Players of rival teams anxiously tried to get hold of it to bury it in their own ground and to promote growth of their crops. The game thus represented a vital combat, with the fertility of the winning team's field as the coveted prize.

Some authorities believe that not the Romans but the Normans introduced the game into the British Isles. Their opinion is supported by the fact that reliable references to football occur only after the Norman Conquest in 1066. The Normans are said to have developed the game from the rites of the Roman saturnalia, a feast much concerned with fertility.

The first extensive description of English football goes back to the London of 1175. It is a vivid account by William Fitzstephen of how, on Shrove Tuesday of that year, all the youth of the city spent part of the day cock-fighting 'and in other boyish pursuits'. After dinner, they went:

> . . . to a local piece of ground and just outside the city for the famous game of ball . The students of every branch of study have their own ball and those who practise the different trades of the city have theirs too. The older men, the fathers and the men of property, come on horseback to watch the contests of their juniors, and in their own way share the sport of the young men; and these elders seem to have aroused in them a natural excitement, at seeing so much vigorous exercise and participating in the pleasure of unrestrained youth.

Obviously by that time the game had caught on and the centuries that followed saw its popularity increase among the masses. Even a carol linked it with the boy Jesus. It sang of how

> Our Saviour asked leave of His Mother Mary
> If He might go play at ball.

The earliest mention of the game in English literature belongs to the once widely popular ballad *The Jew's*

Daughter or *Sir Hugh of Lincoln* (quoted by Thomas Percy in his *Reliques of Ancient English Poetry* and possibly going back to the thirteenth century). This actually begins with a football game, during which the ball is kicked into the Jew's home. Typical are the stanzas found in one of the ballad's many versions:

> He toss'd the ball so high,
>   He toss'd the ball so low;
> He toss'd the ball in the Jew's garden,
>   And the Jews were all below.
>
> Oh! then out came the Jew's daughter,
>   She was dressed all in green:
> 'Come hither, come hither, my sweet pretty fellow,
>   And fetch your ball again.'

Soon authorities came to view the game as a nuisance and, as in the case of other sports, a danger to national security on the grounds that it interfered with the country's defence, in which efficiency with bows and arrows was most essential.

The only documentation of English football during this period is contained in many and repeated accusations and prohibitions:

> Every able-bodied man of the . . . city on feast days when he has leisure shall in his sports use bows and arrows or pellets and bolts, forbidding them under pain of imprisonment to meddle in football and other vain games of no value.

There were other grounds as well on which the authorities based their opposition to football. Games had become very rough, often ending in brawls.

Most of the people loved football. Everyone could take it up. It was simple and had no rules. All that was needed was a ball. It was the lack of a code that caused the game to degenerate often into a riotous, running battle. Not alone on Shrove Tuesday was it known as 'mob football'.

The entire length of the town became the field, with the goals at opposite ends. The number of players could well exceed 500. The game might last all day, and it was not out of order to kick an opponent's shins or to trip him. In fact, everything could be done to get and keep the ball. Small wonder that the result included innumerable broken windows and fractured legs and, at times, even deaths. No wonder that monarchs began strongly to condemn the sport on this count also. In 1314, King Edward II issued an edict forbidding football:

> Forasmuch as there is great noice in the city, caused by hustling over large balls from which many evils might arise which God forbid, we commend and forbid, on behalf of the King, on pain of imprisonment, such game to be used in the city in future.

Another declaration referred to

> Footeballe, wherein is nothing but beastlie furie and exteme violence, wherefore it is to be put in perpetuall silence.

Yet it seems that occasionally not even clerics could resist the game. This apparently necessitated an order that 'if any minister or deacon shall go into the feelde to play at football, he shall forthwith be banished from the Universities'.

Indeed, all efforts to obstruct or ban it permanently were of no avail though, inevitably, it suffered a decline. This went on till 1603 when, on the coronation of King James I, football was again publicly recognized and the people were even encouraged to take it up. By then, the main reason for its prohibition no longer applied: archery had become redundant with the introduction of fire arms. Oliver Cromwell was a keen player and frequently mentioned the game in his letters.

Football evolved out of confusion into the modern disciplined game. The process was gradual and was not completed before the nineteenth century, when the game was popular everywhere.

SOCCER

Soccer, as played today, could be considered the final offshoot and the purest modern form of man's primitive kicking games. In turn, it became the basic source of Rugby, American football, and Australian Rules, all of which could be classed as its derivatives.

From 1820 onward clubs were formed. Apprentices played football in city streets and young farming lads did so in the fields or on the village common. Of necessity, through the diversity of their playgrounds, their methods differed. As a result, several kinds of football slowly developed. When the game eventually was introduced into the Public Schools, it received a new social standing. These schools naturally created their own style which depended much on the size and shape of the playing ground. In country schools with wide, open spaces, 'handling' and 'hacking' became the rule; players in the city of London, restricted in territory, had to play on cobblestones between walls and soon favoured 'dribbling' and 'passing' the ball.

When pupils of the various schools entered university, they had their separate ideas of how football was to be played. In the end, however, this proved a blessing as it led to the first attempt, at Cambridge in 1848, to unify the game by drawing up a general code of rules. Though the draft of the laws then suggested has been lost, a letter of one of the men who participated in drawing them up, survives. Written by N. C. Malden of Godalming, it vividly recalls the occasion:

> I went up to Trinity College, Cambridge. In the following year an attempt was made to get up some football in preference to the hockey then in vogue. I remember how the Eton men howled at the Rugby men for handling the ball. So it was agreed that two men should be chosen to represent each of the Public Schools, and two who were not Public School men, for the 'varsity. I wish I could remember the others.
>
> We were 14 in all, I believe Harrow, Eton, Rugby, Winchester and Shrewsbury were represented. We met

in my rooms after Hall, which in those days was at 4 p.m., anticipating a long meeting. I cleared the tables and provided pens, ink and paper. Several asked me on coming in whether an exam was on! Every man brought a copy of his school rules, or knew them by heart, and our progress in framing new rules was slow.

On several occasions Salt and I, being unprejudiced, carried or struck out a rule when voting was equal. We broke up five minutes before midnight.

The new rule was printed as 'Cambridge Rules', copies were distributed and pasted up on Parker's Piece, and very satisfactorily they worked, for it is right to add that they were loyally kept and I never heard of any Public School man who gave up playing from not liking the rules.

Nevertheless, this first effort to unify the game proved abortive. Many years later, in 1862, it was Cambridge once again which started the ball rolling in the battle for a generally accepted code. J. C. Thring then published 'Ten Rules' for what he called 'The Simplest Game'. This led, within a year, to the 'Cambridge University Football Rules'.

By this time various clubs had been established and they were experiencing a real boom. The oldest among them was the Sheffield Club. Its founder members were mostly graduates of Harrow, who brought with them their old school's football traditions. These strictly banned handling the ball. To ensure the adoption of their code by other players, they sometimes used an ingenious method. When playing a team of villagers, for example, they presented to each of them a pair of white gloves and a silver florin which, throughout the game, they were made to hold tightly. This, of course, prevented the men from using their hands.

And yet, other footballers relished catching, handling, and carrying the ball and no one could deny the urgent need somehow to combine the various forms of football. For this purpose a meeting was convened at the Old Freemasons' Tavern in London, in October 1863, a date every footballer should cherish. Those taking part came from eleven London and suburban clubs, one Public School, and the rest represented no one in particular. A motion to form 'The Football Association' was adopted and any club of at least a year's standing was invited to join at an annual subscription of one guinea.

This was the birth of modern football and its unified code. Its further development and growth was the result of many years of debates, trial and error experiments, and the eventual resolution of conflicts and controversies by typical British compromise.

That is how Association Football came into existence in its final form. From the term Association, students' slang created the modern term soccer, using the letters *S, O,* and *C* as a base.

Wherever Englishmen went, whether as soldiers, traders, teachers, or even as missionaries, they took football with them. It never took long for the new country to adopt enthusiastically the game which now is played all over the world.

RUGBY UNION

There is nothing obscure about the origin of Rugby or, as university slang came to call it, Rugger. It is known who started it, and where and when he did so. Its name perpetuates the place of birth, Rugby School in Warwickshire, England, famous both for scholarship and sport.

Rugby began quite accidentally. One afternoon in 1823, William Webb Ellis, a student at the college, was participating in an inter class football match, then played according to traditional soccer rules, which permitted only kicking and bouncing.

He became bored with the tedium of the game and on the spur of the moment bent down, picked up the ball, and ran like mad, carrying it down the field. The move was so unexpected and contrary to the rules that some spectators even imagined that the boy wanted to steal the ball.

His action caused much consternation. His captain,

deeply embarrassed, apologized for the lad's unsportsmanlike act and breach of rules. Ellis certainly was sharply criticized, but there is no record that he was ever punished. Reports of his escapade became the topic of much discussion not only at Rugby but at other schools. Some players began to speculate that running with the ball would give the game new verve and improve its appeal. Other players went further than talking and tried running with the ball.

It was only natural that Ellis's unorthodox behaviour was identified with the name of his school. In 1839, Arthur Pell, a student at Cambridge University, suggested to friends that they 'have a go at that game at Rugby'. The name stuck and Rugby football became famous in the world of sport.

When Cambridge players, urged on by Pell, experimented with the different type of game, they enjoyed it so much that they decided to retain it. They adopted the rule that a player could run with a ball if he caught it on the fly or on the first bounce.

Curiously enough, the boys at Rugby School itself continued to play the traditional soccer version, carefully avoiding any repetition of Ellis' offence. Rugby did not return to Rugby College as an accepted part of the official football code until 1841, eighteen years after Ellis' spurt.

It was not long before the new game spread to other schools. In 1848, a meeting was held to standardize the rules for the game, which then was still strictly confined to schools. In 1862, the Old Blackheathens became the first club to adopt Rugger, and their example was soon followed elsewhere. Within a year, the first recorded inter-club game was held between Blackheath and Richmond.

In 1872, in London, twenty-one clubs combined and formed the Rugby Union, a strictly amateur organization. The same year also saw the first international game. It was played between England and Scotland and was won by Scotland. The teams then still consisted of twenty players each side. They were reduced to fifteen players a side for the first time in 1875. This figure was generally adopted in 1877, when the practice of deliberate hacking (kicking the shin of an opponent) was abolished.

Other countries came to love the game. Frenchmen adopted it as early as 1870. Soon afterward it was taken up by students in Montreal, Canada, whence it found its way to the United States. Rugby spread to all parts of the British Empire where it became a force to be reckoned with in sport. Names that speak for themselves are New Zealand's *All Blacks*, South Africa's *Springboks*, and Australia's *Wallabies*.

At first balls were not of standard size. They were made of inflated pig-bladders, and it was really the animal's size that determined their volume. The early pig-bladder balls were round and comparatively large which favoured the practice of dribbling and drop-kicking. It has been suggested that it was the wish to obtain a ball that was easier to catch and carry than the round ball which was responsible for the introduction of the India rubber bladder and the ball's elliptical shape.

Early Rubgy matches, up until 1875, were decided by goals alone. Then tries were added and, in 1887, a system of scoring by points was introduced. This counted a try as one point and a goal as three. Then came the creation of penalty goals. Through the years, the point value of the various kicks was changed — at times increased, at other times decreased.

Scrummage, known equally well by its abbreviated form scrum, is one of the features of Rugby. To start with, it lived up to the word's original meaning, which was 'skirmish'. Indeed, it was a confused, rough struggle between tough men. One mass of players tried by brute force to drive the ball toward the opposite goal through a similar group of tough opponents.

With the development of the game, the scrummage grew into an ordered formation. It was brought together on the referee's order to restart the game, when and where it had been temporarily stopped for some minor infringement of rules. In the words of the Oxford Dictionary, it is then that 'the two sets of forwards pack themselves together with their heads down and endea-

LLYFRGELL COLEG MENAI LIBRARY

vour by pushing to work their opponents off the ball
and break away with it or heel it out'.

Rugby gained world fame and became popular in
many places. As so often in life, the man actually responsible for it all was hardly remembered. The authorities
of Rugby School eventually felt the need to give him
credit and erected a marble tablet on the campus of
the school. It bears the inscription:

THIS STONE
COMMEMORATES THE EXPLOIT OF
WILLIAM WEBB ELLIS
WHO WITH A FINE DESREGARD FOR THE
RULES OF FOOTBALL,
AS PLAYED IN HIS TIME,
FIRST TOOK THE BALL IN HIS ARMS AND
RAN WITH IT,
THUS ORIGINATING THE DISTINCTIVE
FEATURE OF THE RUGBY GAME
A.D. 1823

RUGBY LEAGUE

A question of money created Rugby League. It started
in the early 1890s in the industrial northern counties
of England.

Football enthusiasts there were mostly miners and
mill-workers. They were keen to play for their country,
county, or club, but they could ill afford to do so as
they would miss work and thereby lose pay.

Naturally they demanded that, at least, they be given
expenses to cover loss of wages. As soon as Rugby Union
officials heard of the claim they were aghast. To them,
this was a most ominous threat to the future of the
game. In no time, they believed, it would open the door
to professionalism, an idea which horrified them. Meanwhile, the payment of 'expenses', though not openly
admitted, became the practice of the northern clubs.
Rumours even had it that, apart from defraying hotel
bills and the fares of players, moneys paid out included
what may be termed a retaining fee and bonuses for

LIVERPOOL COLLEGE NAL LIBRARY

goals scored and matches won.

An impasse was reached. It was as if the irresistible force had met the immovable object. Neither side was prepared to give in, though it must be recorded each party was motivated by nothing but the love of the game.

On 20 September 1893, when the annual meeting of the Rugby Union was held in London, the inevitable clash occurred. Two representatives from Yorkshire moved that 'players are to be allowed compensation for bona fide loss of time'. The motion was defeated. However, of 418 votes cast, 136 favoured the innovation.

This gave new confidence to the northern clubs and, far from submitting to the majority's opinion, they remained as determined as ever to persevere in their quest. They met privately many times. At last they felt that the time was ripe to take public action. They convened a special meeting, to which they invited all interested clubs.

The historic gathering took place at Huddersfield on 29 August 1895, and was attended by delegates of twenty-two clubs. These decided to resign forthwith from the Rugby Union and establish their own *Northern Union*, which would permit payment of legitimate expenses for all players. Remuneration, it was laid down, should not exceed six shillings a day. It was the final split. There was no turning back.

The new Union lost no time in arranging matches. The first of these were held within little more than a week of the establishment of the new body (on 7 September) and, very pointedly, on the Saturday before the official start of the Rugby Union season.

The mother body took a dim view of all that had happened. At once, it barred all its members from participating in any way in matches played by the Northern Union. It reaffirmed its resolute stand against even the slightest trace of professionalism and envisaged more stringent rules against any type of monetary compensation.

Soon after the Northern Union's inception, its administrators agreed that there was need for some change in the rules of the game in order to give the new form of Rugby a distinctive character and to improve style.

Variations were introduced in 1897 by which time some eighty clubs had joined the break-away union. The new measures agreed upon aimed at a more orderly game with greater discipline. Late starts carried a heavy fine. A simplified system of scoring equalized the point value of all goals, now to be fixed at two. Progress was the watchword.

Pure amateurism was declared obsolete. However, it was also decreed that each player must follow a legitimate occupation. Penalties were provided for disregard of this rule.

What had been feared in London, happened. Compensation payments did not stop at the comparatively small, fixed sum. They grew out of all proportion to the players' actual loss of wages. Even worse, the buying and selling of good footballers became an almost obnoxious practice. In 1897 the *Badminton Magazine* castigated such type of 'slave trading', to which it amounted. It spoke of a player's transfer papers being prepared 'with all the detailed care and accuracy of the title deeds of a property' and described the procedure under which prominent football players were bought, sold, and manipulated as surpassing the evils of the Roman gladiatorial system.

As the game began to draw tremendous crowds, professionalism became accepted. This was officially adopted as part of the Northern Union Code in 1898. Yet, it was still stipulated that no player should make a living entirely from football. He was to have a full-time occupation as well. In spite of warnings, professionals tried to defeat the clause by accepting bogus jobs. To end such deception, club officials were authorized to investigate each player's occupation and to register it in lists issued weekly and duly signed. Nevertheless, everything possible was done to gain and keep expert players. Possibly strongly biased reports circulated at the time spoke of 'ingenious devices, of money dropped into men's boots or slipped into the hand in lavatories by seeming virtuous officials, of tons of coal arriving from nowhere and stopping at football players' houses'.

There was a continuous increase in attendance figures and play-registration. The Northern Union was firmly entrenched. At the annual meeting in 1899, it was felt that the Union had expanded to such an extent that applications for new membership could not be considered.

The break-away Union now had status, a maximum number of members, huge funds, and, not least, the pick of the players. Its teams now consisted of only thirteen, instead of the fifteen in Rugby Union. Games were both spectacular and fast. The Union certainly had outgrown its geographical description, restricting it to the north of England. When the clubs met in 1922, the majority agreed that a change of name had become imperative. They adopted Rugby League as the new title.

AMERICAN FOOTBALL

Controversy, as was experienced in such vehement form about the fatherhood of baseball, never arose regarding the antecedents of American football. No one ever denied its English ancestry, though it was to become so typical an American game that it well merits its description.

American football is a modified combination of Rugby and soccer. It was not invented at any specific place or date or by any one person or group of people but evolved gradually, by a method of give and take, of compromise between players who knew and delighted in either Rugby or soccer.

Some sort of football was played on American soil from early colonial days. To kick a ball around a 'field' (a paddock or a village green) was a natural type of amusement taken up by the pioneer settlers. It can well be imagined how colonists brought their football with them from Britain and, if not the ball itself, the enjoyment of the game.

In the first part of the nineteenth century (just as had

been the case in England), schools and colleges had organized games on their campuses. Play, however, was so rough and wild that eventually the authorities (both at Yale and Harvard) felt compelled to ban football altogether. They were able to do so only for a short while and could not prevent its revival.

The inevitable happened: two colleges — Rutgers and Princeton — agreed to play against each other. It was the first intercollegiate game and an historical date in the story of American football. The match took place at New Brunswick, New Jersey, on 6 November 1869.

There were twenty-five players on each side and the rules followed were — more or less — those of soccer, as laid down by the London Football Association. The inflated rubber ball could be kicked or batted with the head, but no one was permitted to carry or run with it. Many of the Rutgers students, to distinguish their team, donned scarlet jerseys or caps, the forerunners of the 'uniform'. Two hundred spectators watched the memorable game which was engaged in with so much excitement that two players, while running after the ball, crashed into a fence, smashing it. Rutgers won by six goals to four. The local newspaper *Targum* commented that a 'seventh goal probably would have been added to our score but for one of our players, who, in his ardour, forgot which way he was kicking, a mistake which he fully atoned for afterward'.

Yet another 'first' distinguished the game. To encourage their side, Princeton students introduced the first 'cheer'. They adopted this yell from soldiers of the Civil War. Tradition has it that a member of the Seventh Regiment of New York, while passing through Princeton on his way to the battlefield in 1861, had been heard raising it.

The next significant stepping stone in the growth of American football dates to May 1874. It added the Rugby ingredients to the game. Rugby was then most popular back in England but it was still unknown in the United States. Canadians, however, had adopted it and through them it was brought to the American playing field. It was the result of American courtesy and of a true gentlemanly compromise.

Harvard had invited a team from McGill University, Montreal. When watching their guests in a practice run on their field at Cambridge, they were greatly astonished by the completely different type of play of the Canadians, particularly the players' running with the ball and not solely kicking it.

To pay due respect to either party and to give each an equal chance, the teams then agreed to play the first half of the game according to Harvard's soccer tradition and the second according to McGill's Rugby rules. Though the game resulted in a scoreless tie, Harvard could not help but become enthusiastic about Rugby. That is how the synthesis of both games was started, and with ever more revisions, innovations, and variations American football came into existence.

No individual contributed more to its evolution than Walter Camp who rightly has been called 'the father of American football'. He introduced some of its most distinctive features, including the eleven-man team and the scrimmage line. The rules he laid down revolutionized American football. He wrote (in 1891) the first book ever to be published on the game in the States.

American football grew through the years into the vital and exciting game it is now. With its many American characteristics, its highly efficient organization, padded and armored players, and fervent partisanship, it is a game pursued with deadly earnestness and unsurpassed zeal.

AUSTRALIAN RULES

Australian Rules football, once called the 'Victorian Game', has become part of the Australian way of life. Its roots have been traced to Irish migrants, gold diggers of the 1840s. In their spare time they improvised the wildest of games which they based on whatever they remembered of hurling and Gaelic football at home. And Australian Rules, it has been said, evolved as the refined and civilized version of those early rough battles.

Australian Rules football is played at a tremendous pace, demanding great skill, supreme control, and strength. Yet it is a strange paradox that this game was first introduced for the sake of cricket. Equally intriguing is the fact that the man who developed this specifically Victorian sport, originally came from New South Wales.

Thomas Wentworth Wills was born near Canberra in 1835. He went for his schooling to Rugby in England where he soon proved himself an outstanding all-round athlete, becoming the school's captain and playing cricket for Kent. On his return to Australia in 1856, he settled in Melbourne, Victoria, and played for the Victorian cricket team against Sydney, New South Wales, but was dismally disappointed at the Victorian Eleven's lack of stamina which deservedly lost them the match.

Wills was convinced that the cause of the Victorians' weakness was the absence of practice during the winter months. He believed they must find a sport they could play during that period of the year to keep them in good trim and ready for the cricket season. From that idea the stage was set for the invention of Australian Rules football.

He discussed the problem with H. C. Harrison, his cousin and future brother-in-law, and, as was only to be expected, the first sport that came into their mind was Rugby. It is recorded that they also agreed that 'the ordinary Rugby is unsuitable for grown men engaged in making a living. Let us together evolve a new code which is a little less strenuous'.

About this time a master at Scotch College, Melbourne, who also had been trained at Rugby, had six footballs sent out from England and encouraged his pupils to play with them. Both Wills and Harrison watched their game. After some practice the boys felt ready to challenge others to a match. For this, they approached Melbourne Church of England Grammar School which accepted the invitation. The 'grand football match', as it was advertised, took place near the Melbourne Cricket Ground on 7 August 1858. It is considered the first ever to have been played according to what finally became known as Australian Rules though, in fact, hardly any rules were observed.

The playing field was an undefined area of huge dimensions with goal posts a mile apart. Each team consisted of forty players and teachers and boys joined in what developed into a drawn-out battle. Both teams agreed that the side which first scored two goals should be the winner.

It took three hours for Scotch to kick one goal. Nothing else happened before darkness interrupted the match. It was decided to continue it on the following Saturday but someone must have misunderstood the arrangements for Melbourne Grammar did not turn up. Subsequently they published an explanation, if not an apology, in *The Melbourne Argus*, suggesting that the game be resumed a week later, to which Scotch agreed.

The next step was the formation of the Melbourne Football Club in 1859. The games played continued to be a mixture of soccer, Rugby, Gaelic football, and Rafferty's Rules, and matches lasted several days. The ball used was round and, altogether, this earliest version of Australian football was a 'go-as-you-please' affair. What rules there may have been were made up as the game progressed with frequent breaks during which the players quenched their thirst.

Umpiring was crude. No whistle was used, free kicks were given only if the players appealed for them by, simultaneously, calling out 'Umpire' and raising their arms. This practice sometimes created further complications, and not a little amusement, as in the case of the man who felt impelled to take advantage of his 'appealing' opponent's raised arms to pull his jersey over his head. There was no gate money either, the game being strictly amateur. Not even the umpire was paid.

Wills was convinced a code of rules was essential and to develop these he joined forces again with Harrison who, in later years and not quite correctly, became known as 'the father of Australian football'. They drew up eleven fundamental rules, the first set of laws for the Australian game. Its main points were that —

- the throwing of the ball was not permitted;
- tripping and hacking were strictly banned;
- the side losing the toss was to begin the game by kicking off from the centre; and
- there had to be fixed boundary lines and a maximum size of the field.

With the passing of years, further developments took place. Rugby School's idea of running with the ball was adopted, but modified by stipulating that the player had to strike it against the ground every five or six yards. Other features revealed traces of cricket, such as the oval shape of the field. This goes back to the early days when the game was played on cricket grounds and controlled by cricket clubs.

By 1867 the oval ball was in universal use and eventually exact measurements were specified for it. In 1869 the rule that the winning team was the one which scored the first two goals was replaced by a new law giving victory to the team with the highest score at a fixed time.

Ever more innovations were added. They included the office of an umpire (previously the captains had been the sole arbitrators in all vital decisions), the introduction of uniforms (caps had been used until then as the only means of identification), and rules governing the number of players (eventually eighteen a team), and all measurements, such as the size of the field, the distance of goal posts, etc. In order to be prepared for all eventualities, each team was augmented by two further players; they were reserves to replace any casualities.

Step by step, Australian Rules football grew into one of the fastest and most spectacular codes. It demanded toughness and great exertion on the part of each player. No wonder that a former middleweight boxing champion confessed that no fight in the ring ever left him as sore as a hard bout of Australian Rules Football.

The Melbourne Football Club, founded in 1859, was followed soon by other clubs.

Australian Rules continues to be a most thrilling game, both to watch and to play. The late Conan Doyle once wrote: 'I have played both Rugby and soccer and I have seen the American Game at its best, but I consider that the "Victorian" system has some points which make it the best of all — certainly from the spectacular point of view'.

RAFFERTY'S RULES

Rafferty's rules is the Australian (slang) description for extemely rough play, in which no rules are observed at all. It is not certain what accounts for the odd 'naming' and there is a choice of two explanations.

A great proportion of the population in the early European settlement of the Australian (penal) colony was of Irish descent. The Irish were renowned for their wildness. They could fight like Kilkenny cats, without rules or restraint. Rafferty was an Irishman's name and thus Rafferty's rules was a reflection on his countrymen.

Others, exonerating the Irish, deny that there had ever been an actual person of that name in the phrase. Originally this had referred to the unmanageable situation in a game as 'refractory' or 'raffatory', but not knowing the English word, Australians misunderstood it and imagined that the expression recalled a (Mr) Rafferty's unruliness.

BARRACKING

To the sports-minded Australian, barracking certainly is not a strange word. Nowadays it is mostly a vivid description of the vociferous demonstration of one's partisanship, particularly so in football.

To start with, however, spectators 'barracked' not so much to cheer the team they supported as to jeer at, and hurl abuse at the opposing side. People have wondered whether this was not a cunning manoeuvre to unsettle and ruffle its players, to make them lose control of themselves and thereby the match. Such interpretation has been strongly denied as not being in the English tradition of 'playing the game'.

The etymology of the term itself is uncertain. Some authorities believe that it was a cockney word migrants brought from England. It described 'a jumble of sounds' and 'inarticulate chatter'. Others traced barracking, at least partially, to a French source in which *baragouin* meant 'gibberish'. A third team (of scholars) credits the Irish with the introduction of barracking. In fact, 'barking' had been the original word used for the loud bragging of men about their strength and verve. But pronounced in the Irish brogue, the barking sounded very much like barracking. Truly indigenous is the further suggestion that the term came from the Aboriginal-derived Australian slang phrase in which the making of fun of anyone was expressed as 'poking *borak* at him'.

Least complicated and far-fetched is yet another explanation which links the Australians' barracking with the early history of white settlement. In Melbourne (some believe in Sydney as well) football games were then played on a field that was adjacent to the military barracks. It was only natural for the soldiers stationed there to enjoy taking part in this type of battle. If they did not actually join in the match as part of a team, they participated in it vocally by raucously voicing their approval or displeasure.

Soon they and their shouts became identified with the barracks from which — like from a grandstand — they watched the game. These quarters were demolished long ago. Nevertheless, they survive in the peculiar and expressive term of barracking.

Such is the multitude of views on the origin of the simple term. It is up to the reader finally to decide for which of them to barrack.

Chapter 17

GOLF

No one knows for certain how golf began. Most scholars assume that the name came from the German or Dutch word for club, *Kolbe* or *Kolf*, and that some form of the game was played in prehistoric times with a branch and a pebble. Hitting stones with a stick seems to be instinctive to man, and that, it is thought, is what shepherds did in ancient days.

Sir W. G. Simpson has similarly explained the beginnings of golf in Scotland. On a sheep pasture in Fifeshire, later to become the Royal and Ancient Golf Club of St Andrews, a shepherd, to pass the time, was idly sending pebbles flying through the air with his crook until one fell by chance into a rabbit hole. When he tried to repeat the shot, a friend who was watching challenged him; the first golf match in the land of the heather resulted, each player trying to sink his pebble in the rabbit hole.

It is an historical fact that a sport popular among the ancient Romans, known as *paganica*, was a forerunner of modern golf. This 'game of the countrymen' was played with a bent stick and a leather ball stuffed with feathers. It is most likely that as the Roman legions marched across Europe they carried the game with them, and it was adopted by the conquered nations.

There are many other suggestions about the introduction of golf to Scotland. Through similarities some also trace it to *hurley*, that ancient Celtic ancestor of hockey.

Most frequently, the Dutch have been credited with being the ancestors of golf. Their game of *Kolven* certainly had some of golf's features. It was played either on the ice of frozen lakes or canals, or on a court. This latter was mostly paved and was known as *Kolf Bann*. Contestants tried to hit, with a minimum of strokes, two sticks placed at opposite ends of the court. However, the ball used was the size of a grapefruit and weighed 2 lbs (0.90 kg), and the many paintings (among them an etching by Rembrandt) on which the claim is based, stem from a time at least 200 years after golf had definitely been established in Scotland.

Yet another theory sees in golf an adaptation of the Flemish game of *Chole*, known to have been played as early as 1353. This was a cross-country pursuit, in which both sides played the same ball with a mallet, taking turns to make three strokes each. The goal, sometimes as far as a mile away, was some conspicuous landmark, such as a tree or a gateway.

Though all these games resembled golf in some ways, they obviously were not exactly like it. Golf is unique and, no doubt, the result of a natural evolution of some of these early sports. Records show that a kind of golf was played in Scotland during the fifteenth century, and it has been pointed out many times that the game reveals characteristics in keeping with the Scots' reserve, caution, and meticulous care. Only a Scot, it has been contended, could have created a contest that combined such features as hitting a small ball across rough country to a hole in the ground, without his opponent having the right to interfere in any way.

The earliest existing reference to the game speaks mainly against it. In 1457, the Scottish Parliament voiced the opinion that the playing of golf was interfering with the more important pursuit of archery and ordained that golf be 'utterly cryit doun, and nocht usit'. When, instead of training for their country's defence, men wasted their time in hitting small balls for their own pleasure, the government had to step in and declare the game illegal. James II of Scotland forbade it entirely.

Apparently such prohibitions were only for a limited period. At all events golf became increasingly popular and, eventually, royalty not only gave the sport their blessing but began to enjoy it themselves. Records to the Lord Treasurer for 1503–06 show use of the Crown's money for golf balls.

Both Charles I and James II of England loved the game. Mary, Queen of Scots, the first woman golfer, played several rounds only a few days after the murder of her husband. During her reign (about 1552), St Andrews of Scotland was established — the most famous of all golf courses. No wonder that the Scotsman could speak of 'the Royal and Ancient Game of Golf'.

Inevitably the game spread to England, where the first clubs were formed in the eighteenth century. These made use of public land, meeting at inns before and after their rounds. The world's first golf tournament took place in 1860 at Prestwick, Scotland. The winner received a belt for his trophy and this remained his permanent property. In 1882 the first rules were laid down, as was only to be expected, by the St Andrews Club. They were intended to be adopted universally.

THE CLUB

Golf actually means a club. At first, the sticks were sturdy branches cut from a tree or a bush and, of course, they had no separate heads. They were all of one piece. Their striking end was slightly curved and, at times, studded with flints. Such clubs were crude and clumsy, and the need for improvement urged on man's inventive spirit, and step followed step in the creation of our modern clubs.

Separate wooden heads were introduced, spliced or bound to the shaft. Their original size, extending to six inches (15 cm) in length, was then reduced and the first truly lofted clubs made (known as spoons or baffies). The replacement of the wooden head by an iron one came next. This was fixed to a hickory shaft. And then a whole variety of clubs were produced, differing in loft, weight, and extent of the striking surface.

A shortage of hickory wood and an ever greater public demand for golf equipment created new problems. Manufacturers experimented with other materials, such as bamboo and steel. In the 1920s, American golfers chose tubular steel for their shafts instead of hickory. At first this shaft was outlawed, as it was felt it would increase greatly the distance of a drive thereby necessitating expensive lengthening of most courses. However, in 1926, the new metal club was officially accepted. There was an ample supply of steel, and steel sticks could be produced much more quickly and in far greater numbers. The new type of club soon became so popular that, in spite of initial objections from Scotland's conservative St Andrews which considered the introduction of the steel shaft 'detrimental to the professional trade in the country', it was adopted all over the world within ten years.

THE BAG

At first clubs were carried loosely under the arm. The introduction of the golf bag goes back to the 1870s and the thoughtfulness of a retired sail maker who was employed at the famous links of the Royal North Devon Club at Westward Ho, England. Still endowed with memories of his former trade and, no doubt, also with some of its raw materials, it occurred to him (most probably on a rainy day) that a piece of canvas would keep the sticks' grips dry. From his protective covering the modern bag evolved.

THE BALL

Golf's most important accoutrement is the ball. So small in itself, the number of rules that govern its treatment by far exceed those relating to any other feature of the game. The ball's dimensions have even drawn a dividing line between the English-speaking peoples: its American girth is slightly, though noticeably, larger than that of its British counterpart. The official English ball measures

1.62 inches (4.11 cm) in diameter and the American 1.68 inches (4.26 cm).

Keeping our eye on the history of the ball we can follow an interesting development. There is no doubt that, as in similar sports of those days, at an early date balls were made of turned boxwood. This is confirmed by a document of 1363 which describes a game of 'a crooked stick or curved club or playing mallet with which a small wooden ball was propelled forward'. However, the most popular ball then, like its Roman prototype, was made of feathers. Its production demanded much care and time.

Small thin segments of leather (usually three in number) were sewn together to form a bag. Its opening was used to invert the 'ball' so that the stitches would not be outside. Then boiled goose feathers were pushed through the hole tightly into the bag. This done, the hole was stitched up and the finished ball rubbed with white paint. Meanwhile, the feathers expanded (originally the amount required per ball was sufficient to fill the crown of a beaver hat!) and thereby created a pressure that added to the ball's liveliness.

Obviously its quality much depended on how tightly the feathers had been packed. Altogether making a ball was a job for experts, and those early hand-made missiles were greatly treasured and highly priced.

It was soon realized that the *featherie*, as the ball was called, was far from perfect. In rainy weather it quickly became sodden and heavy. It rarely retained its round shape and repeated hits with the iron caused it to burst. Worst of all, it would not travel any great distance.

Players began to experiment with other types, aiming at finding a ball that was weather-resistant, could take punishment, and, not least, was cheaper. Success came in 1848. A solid ball was moulded from *gutta-percha*, that rubbery juice of Malayan trees, at that time used mainly for purposes of insulation. The story is told that the first such ball was made by a clergyman who used wrappings of a statue of the Indian god Vishnu.

This *guttie* soon showed several faults. Its flight was unpredictable and after it had travelled some distance it dropped like a dead bird. No wonder that the featherie-makers, feeling their livelihood threatened, took hold of such incidents to ridicule the novel ball and point out that after all their product was still much superior.

They did not laugh for long. A professional player, disappointed with the new balls, gave them to his caddie. One day, watching him at play, he was more than surprised to note that the balls, although by then well battered, could be hit much more efficiently than his own featheries. It seemed that the more hacked the gutties were, the better they flew. The fact was that the dents and cuts, either from the club or the impact of stones and trees, had improved the guttie's flight. No longer erratic, it followed its predestined course much more reliably.

Damaged balls, so to speak, were thus at a premium. But why wait for a ball to become battered to be able to play a good game? Would it not be far easier to produce a ball without a smooth surface by artificially notching it? Such a ball was then made, a guttie systematically nicked by hand. It was the birth of the modern pattern of our golf ball. Eventually, in 1880, someone got the idea of streamlining the whole process, and instead of hand-hammering each individual ball, put the pitted markings on its surface by means of a 'pock-marked mould'.

The early guttie broke up after rough handling, but the various pieces could easily be melted down and remoulded into a completely new ball.

The invention of the guttie revolutionized the game. Whereas the featherie was costly and took a long time to make, the new ball could be fabricated cheaply in vast quantities. Golf was thereby no longer restricted to the wealthy classes. Until the coming of the guttie no definite rules existed about the weight and size of the ball. The new manufacturing process changed that as well and led to the standardization of the ball's measurements. Gutties were used until the turn of the century, when the rubber-core ball, invented by Americans, replaced it.

THE 'PUTT'

There are still doubts about the original meaning of 'putt'. Some suggest that the word is derived from the Dutch *putten*, meaning 'to place in a hole'. However, Robert H. K. Browning relates the term to the Highland sport of 'putting the weight' and asserts that the putt once described any shot that started a ball off on a low trajectory.

THE TEE

Equal controversy concerns the first 'tee'. This has been traced to both Gaelic and Dutch. The Gaelic word *tigh* literally meant 'a house', but in sport referred to the marked spot on which players of the ancient Scot's game of curling tried to hurl large rounded stones. The Dutch *tuitse* (pronounced toytse), on the other hand, was the little mound of sand from which Dutchmen used to shoot the ball and which, in fact, was the earliest earth-made tee.

Originally, the teeing ground was very small and situated within a club's length of the hole. Indeed, players often shaped their tees from sand that they took from the hole itself. Actually, tee-pegs were preceded by all kinds of props, including beer bottles. The general rules still adhered to merely demanded that 'the ball may be placed on the ground or on sand or other substance to raise it off the ground'. It was a much later development that divided putting greens from the teeing ground which, as a separate entity, was mentioned for the first time in 1875.

Later on, golf links provided 'tee boxes'. These contained not tees but sand and had next to them a bucket of water. The rest was left to the golfer who moulded the sand tee each time he hit off.

Although George F. Grant of Boston, Mass., had

invented a peg of sorts (with a flexible shoulder) in 1899, it was not until 1920 that an American dentist from New Jersey, Dr William Lowell, patented the simple little wooden peg. His only reason was not to dirty his hands by using wet sand. Good at promotion and possibly as a sales gimmick, he called it the Reddy Tee. Everyone would remember his tee — by its spelling!

Nevertheless, his invention did not catch on right away. It was left to the American Walter Hagen, the winner of the British Open Championship in 1922, to popularize the tee. He did so whilst playing in exhibitions all over the United States. Conspicuously, he had a tee stuck behind one of his ears! Ever since, golf has come a long way — even tee-wise.

'THE CUP'

At first, holes had no standard measure. Their diameter of 4¼ inches (10.79 cm) was introduced quite by chance. Two golfers on the St Andrews links found that one hole was so badly worn that they could not use it. Much of its sand had been removed by previous players for building tees. Anxious to repair the damage and continue their game, they looked around and discovered nearby part of an old drain pipe. They inserted this in the hole. It was the first 'cup', and because it happened to measure 4¼ inches (10.79 cm) across, all cups are now that size.

THE 18 HOLES

Much care is now given to laying out and keeping up of golf courses. During the earlier periods of the game the players chose the most suitable grass-covered stretches of land, which were called links. This explains the application of that term for a golf course ever since.

Gullies and shrubs were the earliest hazards, and nature itself looked after the course. Rabbits cropped the grass, birds' droppings fertilized the ground, while sheep and other stray animals contributed their part in manure as well as the creation of bunkers.

The course the players followed was not predetermined but selected each time rather haphazardly. There were no fixed tees. Golfers simply picked the most convenient clear patch from which to drive the ball toward one of five or six holes. With the development of the game these became more numerous. Sometimes there were as many as twenty holes.

Even the present traditional number of eighteen holes is completely accidental and certainly not the result of a deliberate choice. It merely shows the power of fashion and man's imitative urge.

The Honorable Company of Edinburgh Golfers, established in 1744, was soon regarded the top club, and anything it chose to do set a fashion. All clubs were proud when they could point out that they were following Edinburgh's example. At first, its course had a mere five holes and each fairway was between 400 and 500 yards (364 m and 455 m) long. The official round then consisted of playing the holes three times, fifteen holes all told.

When the links of Blackheath were established, it was not surprising that they adopted the identical number and kind of play. Significantly, as soon as Edinburgh extended its course to seven holes, Blackheath did likewise. Had Edinburgh preserved its leading place in the world of golf, probably no one would ever have dreamed of eighteen holes.

Yet a mere name, however famous, is not sufficient to retain leadership. Because Edinburgh's links were not the best, slowly but surely St Andrews took over leadership, and eventually clubs everywhere based their rules on those of St Andrews.

Originally St Andrews had twelve holes. These were arranged not as nowadays to cause the player to return to the 'club house' but leading ever farther away from it. Furthermore, he hit off his first ball from a tee that was next to the home hole.

Keen golfers did the obvious thing: after having played all of the (remaining) eleven holes on the way out, they repeated the performance on the way back, merely reversing the direction of play. This added up to twenty-two holes. But when in 1764 the members of St Andrews reduced the first four holes to two (probably to increase the distance), the first eighteen-hole golf course had come into existence. What had been done at St Andrews was soon noted, and the playing of eighteen holes became the fashion and later the standard.

Of course, the actual number of holes was still only nine. Much later St Andrews realized that playing in opposite directions over the same nine holes for a 'round' of eighteen holes was far from satisfactory. Thus it introduced separate fairways and greens for the second nine holes and removed much danger, inconvenience, and waste of time in waiting.

THE BUNKER

'Bunkers', too, were created accidentally. They were the result of wear and tear assisted by the forces of nature. Even expert golfers could not help but damage the turf with their old-fashioned lifting irons. The continuous trampling by players caused bald patches. The wind blew away the light soil and left a sandy depression which increased in size. This process was specially noticeable on links near the sea. Eventually, golfers tried to confine these hollows with discarded railway sleepers and other timber, to which they nailed planks for shoring.

Contestants quickly discovered that the damaged parts of the link made the game more exciting by adding new challenges. The 'bunkers', at first deplored, were now heartily welcomed.

Clubs with courses laid out on firmer ground and away from the windswept dune country along the sea, began to imitate the bunker and to build it artificially. When Tom Dunn, famous golf course architect, adopted the novel hazard, it became so popular that ever since the artificial bunker has been a standard feature of every course.

THE CADDIE

That the 'caddie' has travelled a long distance is not surprising. In his case there is no doubt of ancestry though, as is so typical of life, he has come down very much from his aristocratic beginnings.

His home was France, where at the time he was far removed from games and golf. The word caddie is derived from the French *cadet*, meaning a 'diminutive chief' or 'a little head' (itself rooted in the Latin *caput*). The title was mostly used for the younger sons of the upper class. Mary, Queen of Scots, introduced it into Scotland where it soon assumed a derogatory connotation. In fact, the noble word deteriorated so much that it was used to describe messengers and pages waiting around for an odd job. Eventually, 'caddie' was further reduced to refer specifically to those hanging around golf courses to carry sticks.

It was also their job to clean the sticks with emery paper during and after the game. Still carrying on the Scottish queen's French pronunciation, cad-day, the Scots began to spell it their own way, and that is how the cadet changed into the caddie.

Later his task extended far beyond transportation and cleaning of clubs. Before the introduction of tee-pegs, making tees belonged to his duties as well. He did so mostly by taking a handful of sand out of the hole or the tee-box (which also deteriorated in value and changed into the present-day refuse receptacle) and putting it on to the turf, shaping it into a small cone on top of which he placed the ball.

THE FLAGSTICK

Links originally were not reserved for golfers. They also served other purposes such as horse racing, cricket, children's games, grazing for cows and sheep and a drying ground for laundry which housewives had washed in nearby creeks.

A golfer needed a guide to avoid those many obstacles, and at first it was the caddie's job to lead the way and point out the hole which he did with a broken-off branch or by sticking a feather into it, creating the forerunner of the modern 'flagstick'. Indeed, caddies developed an elaborate code of signals to indicate to their employer the best course to follow. Eventually, the caddie became an expert adviser, who told his master not only which way to go, but which club to use. Perhaps he, most of all, learned to appreciate the finer points of the game of golf and was its best critic and most ardent enthusiast.

'FORE!'

'Fore' is the warning call of a golfer to those playing in front — be*fore* him — that his ball might hit them.

Though sounding the same, this 'fore' has nothing whatsoever to do with the numeral '4' (four). It was chosen as a warning cry because its sound could be quickly and loudly produced. It carried far and could not be ignored or mistaken by those 'in front', to the fore.

THE BIRDIE

The first 'birdie' was a mere fluke, in a manner of speaking. It appeared, as it were, out of the air; metaphorically, quite unexpectedly.

It all happened on a beautiful day in 1903 in Atlantic City, USA. A.B. ('Ab') Smith enjoyed a good game of golf, but he also knew that there was room for improvement. Therefore, when on that morning he made a shot that enabled him to sink his ball into the hole with a score of 'one under par', he was rightly overjoyed.

Giving expression to his feelings, spontaneously he called out at the top of his voice, 'That's a *bird* of a shot!' And the bird caught on. In the course of time, players learned fondly to refer to it as a 'birdie'.

The eagle and the albatross were an almost logical sequence. To attain 'two under par', of course, is much

less frequent, just as to see an eagle is not so common.
To encounter an albatross on land was as rare an event
as scoring 'three under par'.

Chapter 18

HOCKEY

Today, the term hockey describes differing games in various parts of the world. In North America it refers to 'ice hockey', elsewhere to what Americans call 'field hockey'. The earliest mention of the present-day name dates back only to 1527, when the Galway Statutes included *hockie* — 'the horlinge of litill balle with ... stickes or staves' — in a list of prohibited games.

The name itself depicts the hooked shape of the stick which is an integral part of the game. Some believe it is an Anglicized version of the Old French *hoquet* meaning 'shepherd's crook'. Others claim that hockey is a diminutive form of the hook. A least likely theory quotes an early alternate name, *hackie,* and suggests that not the bat's shape but its use to hack at players' feet or shins to get the ball was responsible for the ultimate 'hockey'.

Hockey is one of the many sports derived from prehistoric man's delight in stick and ball games which gave the world such varied pursuits as the English cricket, American baseball, Persian polo, and Canadian lacrosse. All of these share the same ancestor and are the result of both man's instinctive urge to hit an object with a 'bat' and his primitive belief in the efficacy of a ball game as a religious rite. Hockey was therefore played, initially and primarily, too, not as a mere pastime but as a solemn ritual of magic and cosmic significance. The flight of the ball and the outcome of the contest, it was thought, would determine the course of nature, the rising of the sun (symbolized by the ball), and the fertility of the fields.

It can only be conjectured how at first a man tore off a branch from a tree, or used the slightly curved leg or antler of a deer, to hit a pebble or a stone as far as he possibly could. That must have been the beginning of hockey, thousands of years ago. Its birthplace was Asia and authorities credit Persia with having devised it about 2000 BC. A people who perfected the game of polo must have known 'hockey on the ground' long before they took up 'hockey on horseback'.

The Asiatic origin of the game might also explain the favourite place it has occupied in the life of the American Indians, who are themselves thought to have made their way into the 'New World' from Asia. No doubt, these Indians, too, engaged in the sport at first as part of their ritual. An Aztec code pictures the gods of light and darkness playing ball. A creation myth among Wichita Indians tells how the first 'hockey' was played as the result of the earliest surgical operation. It relates how out of his own body primeval man had produced the implements for the game. From his left side he removed a ball and from his right a stick with which he immediately started to knock the ball about. Other men, created soon afterwards, learned the art from him and, dividing themselves into two groups (the earliest hockey teams), they joined in the first match.

Sioux Indians played hockey with a soft ball made of elk or moose hair and covered with buckskin. Their sticks were short and had a sharp hook at one end. The Mapuche Indians of Chile, on the other hand, employed hard balls, of stone or heavy wood, which eventually they covered with hide. That the Makah Indians engaged in hockey specifically during the whaling season suggests that the game was a magical rite to ensure good hunting.

Nebraska Indians evolved perhaps one of the fairest methods of choosing teams. They made all players place their individually marked sticks on one heap. A blindfolded outsider was then invited to pick them all up, two at a time. On each occasion he was to put one to his left side and the other to his right. When he had exhausted the store of sticks, he had most impartially allocated each player to a team.

The Indians' hockey games were really rough and the players, completely unprotected, used their sticks pitilessly against any contestant obstructing their way in the chase of the ball. Not infrequently, play turned into a riotous battle with plenty of bruises and injuries. Yet the moment it was over, the players threw off partisanship and, transformed as it were into one fellowship, celebrated the conclusion of the game with a happy feast.

Pursuits very similar to hockey existed in ancient Greece and no doubt were introduced there from Persia. In fact, the earliest pictorial presentation of the game stems from Athens and was found, quite by chance, when in 1922 workmen were repairing the ancient wall built by Themistocles nearly 2500 years earlier, to guard the city from the sea. The relief then discovered showed young men engaged in some sort of hockey game. They hold curved sticks and a central pair can be seen crossing sticks above a ball, very much in the manner of a 'bully' being played. The old Olympian and Isthmian Games included a sporting event in which the contestants hit a ball with a hooked stick.

The Greeks handed the 'stick game' over to the Romans, who must have carried it, like so much of their civilization, to the outposts of their empire and into the countries they invaded.

Modern hockey, as created in England, resembles most closely games once popular in the British Isles and, no doubt, hockey's immediate forerunners: the Scottish *shinty*, the English and Welsh *bandy*, and the Irish *hurling*.

Shinty was a favourite sport of the Scottish Highlanders, in which the players propelled a ball at extraordinary speed with a curved, broad-bladed stick (called in Gaelic a *caman*), either along the ground or through the air. Soldiers thus amused themselves in a combat of great violence, but of a nevertheless friendly nature.

The name shinty may be derived from the same root as shindy, meaning a commotion and a brawl. As among the American Indians, the hockey game concluded with a feast. A keg of whisky, presented to the winning team, actually was shared by all.

It is generally assumed however, that the true ancestor of hockey was hurling. The national game of the Irish, it goes back to the dim past of their history and appears even in their early legends. It was played in the Emerald Isle, so tradition relates, in pre-Christian times, long before the coming of St Patrick. Cuchullian, chief of the Irish heroes, is said to have been a champion hurler. On one occasion, when on his way to the annual athletic feast at Tara, the seat of the high kings of Ireland, he carried the ball on his hurling stick over a distance of nine miles, repeatedly throwing it into the air and catching it, without once letting it fall to the ground.

The original Gaelic name of the game was *ioman,* a word depicting a thrusting action (like that of a rocket), a vigorous forward drive. The forceful 'hurling' of the ball obviously gave the sport its English name.

An early record speaks of a lethal hurling match (with nine hurlers on each side) in which the losing team also lost their lives. Another ancient account tells of balls made of brass and a game played by 150 boys against one solitary lad who, holding the goal with his stick, won the day. However, in consequence of his victory, his opponents turned on him as a pack and took away his stick. In self-defence, he then slew one third of them with his bare hands. But finally, he himself was killed. His head was severed with his own stick. Certainly, even ignoring such legendary traditions, hurling was the most savage, spectacular game—as Irish as the shamrock. For player and onlooker alike nothing could compare with a hurler hitting the ball a great distance through the air, to the stick of a team mate ready to catch it, or toward the far-off goal.

No doubt, hurling crossed the sea from Erin to England, to be assimilated into the English way of life and, eventually, to become hockey. Initially, one of its most favoured versions was known as bandy ball, bandy being merely an alternate (and descriptive) term for the hockey, the bent stick. Obviously the forerunner of hockey, bandy ball was rather a simple game in which the ball, struck by the horn or metal-capped end of a curved stick, was driven either from one post to another farther off, or aimed at a goal.

A passage from Fitzstephen's *Chronicle* has been frequently quoted as the earliest mention of hockey in England, although it is not definite that it really refers to this particular game. It describes how in 1174, London schoolboys were amusing themselves after dinner with a *Balle Playe*. For the purpose, they went into a field with their own balls and sticks. The latter, it has been suggested, were hockeys or bandies.

The image of 'hockey players' (youths with curved bats and a ball) appeared even in early sanctuaries. They are shown on a 1333 silver altar flask, now owned by the National Museum in Copenhagen, and in a stained glass window of 1360 at Gloucester Cathedral.

Hockey became another of the games so enthusiastically taken up that the government became perturbed that it would interfere with men's national service as archers. Hockey was therefore included in a ban, issued by King Edward III in 1365, which is the first definite record of the existence of the game in Britain. It was then still called bandy ball. The king pointed out to his sheriffs that 'by the people pleasing themselves with divers games such as handball, bandy-ball, football ... the realm is likely, in a short time, to be destitute of archers'. Landowners who nevertheless permitted playing of the game on their property faced a fine of £20 and three years' imprisonment.

The love of hockey must have been stronger than fear of prosecution, as the ban had to be repeated several times. Implements used in the forbidden sport were not only to be confiscated but, to prevent their further (ab)use, had to be destroyed.

Views and laws are time-conditioned and eventually, when with the invention of firearms archery became obsolete, there was no longer any harm in taking up hockey. For many years it continued to be played very ruggedly and dangerously, in keeping with its hurling ancestry. A seventeenth-century manuscript spoke of players who were 'plying their hockey vigorously'.

Contestants did what they liked on the field of play as their game was uninhibited by any rules. The positions of the players, and their number, varied greatly. To get hold of the ball, men were not reluctant to belabour an opponent with the stick. They were determined to win at all costs. Anyone joining in the fray did so at his own peril.

Very slowly and gradually the game became more civilized and its roughness, if not totally eliminated, was lessened. Among the earliest refinements introduced was the prohibition on raising the head of the stick above shoulder level, and the immediate suspension of any player who struck his opponent either with the stick or his hand. A wild, dangerous, and uncontrolled game which had been more a brawl than a sport, matured.

The foundation of the Blackheath Club around 1840 (the exact date can only be assumed as records of the time no longer exist) led to the drafting of a first code of rules. Nevertheless, the new clubs that were formed played hockey in their own individual way. The game was finally standardized by the Wimbledon Hockey Club in 1883. Its regulations (adopted in 1886 by the Hockey Association) thoroughly modernized the sport, making it highly scientific and skilful and thereby putting it on the sports map of the world. From then on it spread from England to other countries. In the United States it was played first in 1890.

The first international match was held in 1895— between England and Ireland. In 1908 hockey was included in the modern Olympic Games. It had come a long way from its appearance in the ancient Olympics. Perhaps the most extraordinary aspect of its evolution is that a game once so rough and unruly, was adopted by women (for the first time at Molesey, England, in 1887). They took it up with at least as much fervour and proficiency as the male sex. This development is indicative of the devious route a sport can take. Hockey, which makes the claim of being one of man's first games—in its original form as a solemn, life-giving magic—certainly gave no early inkling of its final destination.

Chapter 19

HORSE-RACING

Philip—from the Greek *phil-hippos*—means 'horse-lover'. All over the world and in every tongue man has cherished the horse.

The horse has been in existence for perhaps millions of years, but even this is still uncertain. Initially, its height did not exceed that of the fox, and amounted to less than a foot (30cm). With the donkey and zebra, it shares the distinction of having a single hoof.

The horse was domesticated in prehistoric times and has served man ever since in diverse ways. At first of course he ate its flesh and used its hide to clothe himself. Eventually, to own this noble and precious creature was a high ambition, though only Caligula (AD 37-41 Roman emperor) went as far as to appoint a horse a senator.

The dog alone can equal the horse as man's companion from earliest days.

The horse, it is thought, was even responsible for the invention of men's trousers. Asiatic riders realized that when they were clad in leggings, their movement was much less impeded than when they were wrapped in their traditional flowing garment.

The Asian steppes were the home of the horse. Here, nomadic tribes were the first to learn to ride it once it had been bred tall and strong enough. The vast expanse of tundra and steppe greatly favoured the art of horse-riding which was not possible in the more restricted and often mountainous regions elsewhere. The nomads took to the horse so completely that whole populations were trained almost to live on the back of the horse. In Asia Minor archaeologists discovered Hittite cuneiform clay tablets from the fourteenth century BC with elaborate instructions for an entire course of horse training. The breeding of horses was practised in Central Asia as early as the fifth pre-Christian millennium.

Assyrians and Babylonians were expert horsemen and made good use of the animal in hunting. A stone carving from Nimrod's palace at Nineveh, now displayed in the British Museum, London, shows the king sitting secure on his galloping horse and, notwithstanding its tremendous speed, shooting an arrow at the prey. Mounted servants are seen following him, carrying a supply of spare arrows and his lance.

A most formidable factor in battle, the horse helped to win wars and, on several occasions, has changed the course of history. On horseback, mighty powers—the Hittites, Huns, Mongols, and the Spanish Conquistadores—swept across entire countries and conquered them. With the invention of the wheel, man learned to build chariots, and, tethering his horses to them, entered the fray of battle on this new war machine with disastrous effect to the foe.

The Parthians were supreme in the mastery of the horse. From the galloping horse, in ruthless, highly mobile, and ever-renewed attacks, they were able to aim their arrows at the enemy with deadly accuracy.

From antiquity onward, horses served to maintain lines of communication over vast distances. In amazement, Herodotus wrote of the swiftness of Roman mounted messengers who at great speed linked the outposts of the empire. If anything, they were even surpassed by the Mongols of Ghenghis Khan who, according to tradition, employed 300,000 horses, stationed at 10,000 posts. They were kept in constant readiness for couriers who, riding through day and night, could sleep and eat in the saddle. Bells attached to the horses announced their approach from afar, so that nothing should stop them (a practice anticipating by thousands of years that of our own ambulances and fire engines).

No wonder that such traditions in warfare, hunting, and communication caused man to produce ever better horses, both in speed and endurance, by selective breeding.

An animal which belonged so much to everyday existence must have induced people early on (soon after its domestication) to think of it also as a means of diversion. Watching two horses running side by side, no doubt, gave them the first idea of a race. This they took up eagerly, impelled by an innate desire to prove supremacy. To out-distance each other on horseback became an early pastime of man, and racing contests with horses date back to prehistoric times.

However, it has also been suggested that first races were run as part of a sacred fertility rite.

Sir James Frazer tells how in the ancient world, the horse was regarded as an embodiment of the corn spirit, whose task it was to hasten the growing of grain. Romans sacrificed the horse to Mars, whom they worshipped not only as a war god, but as the guardian of the fields. In fact, Mars was originally a deity of vegetation. The right-hand horse of a winning team in a sacred race was offered to the god. Its severed head was crowned with a string of loaves and its blood applied to the young crop in spring to ensure its growth and fertility.

That the word race goes back to an old English root describing a 'rush' or a 'hurry', is very appropriate. Few people, however, would imagine that—literally—Chaucer's *Canterbury Tales* have given the horse its canter. But that is exactly the origin of the term. The mounted pilgrims' ambling gait along the Old Kent Road, on their way to the shrine of Thomas à Becket at Canterbury, led people mockingly to call their leisurely progress 'the Canterbury pace'. Eventually, they dropped most of the phrase and retained only half of *Canter*bury. To canter in this way became a fitting word-picture for a horse's slow gallop.

A method all its own is maintained in the measuring of the height of a horse and the distance of a race. One of the most primitive measuring rods of man was his hand. He has abandoned it everywhere except in connection with the equine species. A hand spans four inches (10.16 cm). The bovine world has given equestrian contests of speed their measure of distance. The furlong (today 220 yards — 200.20 m) has been said to derive from the length of a furrow an ox could plough without having to stop for rest. Another, and more likely, explanation is that the furlong (a combination of two old English words for *fur*row and *long*) is based on the extent of the original furrow determined by the once customary size of a field—a ten-acre (4 hectares) square.

From Central Asia, no doubt, at first through invading or marauding forces, the horse and its manifold uses reached Egypt and the western world. The breeding of famous thoroughbreds in the North African region goes back at least to 2000 BC.

To begin with, only Asian races had acquired the art and appreciation of horseback-riding. To Western eyes, a man on a horse initially was such an amazing sight that it filled him with awe. Some have even surmised that the legendary figure of the centaur, so prominent in Greek mythology, originated from the appearance of foreign riders. Half beast, half man, its lower body was equine and its upper torso and head human. A man mounted on a horse seemed a combination which could only be supernatural.

During the Spanish conquest of Mexico the Aztecs and other Indian tribes were so struck with horror at the sight of Cortes' mounted soldiers that, believing they were confronted with divine creatures, they felt it futile to resist them. Pizarro's riders, in like manner, created panic among the Incas of Peru. When one of the Spanish cavalrymen fell from his horse, the Indians imagined that the supernatural creature had broken into two. Going to the other extreme, Attila's Huns, crouching over their horses while racing along, were regarded as cripples who, because of their malformation, could not walk but had to be carried on horseback, safely secured in their saddles!

Even when the riding of a horse no longer appeared

unnatural, it continued to be regarded as undignified. Both Asian and Egyptian nobles preferred to be carried in a chariot, delegating horseback-riding to the scout and courier. Pharaoh Thutmosis included entire units of war charioteers in his army.

The earliest extensive account of an actual chariot race belongs to Book XXIII of Homer's *Iliad* (c.850 BC). It shows how well established the sport was at that ancient date, which suggests a long previous history. Positions in the race were determined by the casting of lots. Apart from a tripod, the first prize offered was a woman, highly skilled in domestic duties . . .

Horse-racing became a favourite Greek sport. By the time of the Pan-Hellenic festivals and the Olympic Games it had become so popular that it was featured in races first of driven and then also of ridden horses. However, at the thirty-third Olympiad in 624 BC., the four-horse chariot still predominated.

The oldest treatise on horse-riding goes back to Xenophon (430-354 BC), the famous Greek soldier and author. His twelve-chapter manual *On Horsemanship* was a comprehensive study of the horse, containing most modern ideas. It deals with the training of a horse, tells how to break it in and to teach it to jump ditches. Xenophon reminds his readers to pay proper regard to the horse's sensitive nature. A trainer should on no account lose his temper. Should the animal be frightened by any object, and refuse to go near it, the trainer should make it feel that it had nothing to fear by approaching the object himself, and touching it. The use of a whip on such an occasion was the worst thing to do, as the mind of the horse would associate the pain suffered with the very object it tried to avoid. A horse of fiery nature was affected by everything it saw, heard, or felt. Hence nothing should be done to it without due warning. Yet another work by Xenophon deals, in a more specialized way, with the duty of cavalry commanders and, in fact, was addressed to a man who was about to assume such a position.

To foster horse-racing the Greeks built hippodromes.

LLYFRGELL COLEG MENAI LIBRARY

These were 600-yards-long, (546 m), rectangular structures, with pillars at either end around which the chariots had to turn. These were light, two-wheeled carts with a platform for the driver, who was protected from falling off by rails in front and on the sides. He was dressed in a long, white tunic which he fastened around his waist. In one hand he held the whip and in the other the reins. Sometimes as many as forty teams competed in a race, run over a distance of almost nine miles (14.40 km).

The Romans inherited the Greek races which they continued to hold, chiefly with chariots drawn by two to four horses. At the very centre of the city the Romans built a vast race-course at which a day's full program comprised twenty-four events. The driver now donned a short tunic, had the reins tied around his body and, to be able to cut them in an emergency, carried a knife in his girdle.

Promoters of racing formed companies ('syndicates'). These had their own stables whose horses and charioteers vied with each other on the course. They identified themselves and their property by certain colours which also were worn by the drivers. Originally there were four syndicates, eventually to be reduced to two—'blue' and 'green'. Spectators (who in the fourth century AD numbered up to 200,000) displayed their favourite colour on which they put their wagers. Races roused tremendous enthusiasm which at times deteriorated into riots. Successful riders were idolized.

The Romans carried horse-racing with them in their conquests and introduced their best stock into the invaded countries. The building of hippodromes also was part of Roman world civilization.

Modern organized horse-racing is primarily of English origin. When, in 55 BC, Caesar invaded Britain, his forces encountered among the tribes highly trained charioteers using native horses. During the Roman occupation, Queen Boadicea and her people, the tribe of Iceni, resided on Newmarket Heath (the future famous site of horse-racing). Significantly, their coins of gold and silver carried on the reverse side the effigy of a horse.

The earliest horse-race recorded in England took place at Netherby, Yorkshire, in AD 210. Organized by the Roman soldiers, it was a contest between Arabian steeds, imported into the country by Emperor Severus Septimus.

Racing among the English evolved by an almost natural, inevitable chain of events. Royalty heard of the exquisite Arabian horses which could travel at such great speeds. Soon they wished to own some themselves, and Henry I is known to have bought a stallion in 1110 to mate with native mares. Other Moroccan and Arabian horses were acquired and proudly designated 'royal horses'. It did not take long for noblemen to copy the king's example and crossbreds of the finest quality gave the English a new type of horse.

The various owners praised their mounts and their own ability to master them. To demonstrate the truth of their claims and to show their superiority, they arranged friendly contests. Thus, the first races were run. For the purpose, the riders chose any ground which seemed suitable for the occasion. They fixed the distance of the race at four miles (6.40 km), once the standard route of the chariot race at the Olympic Games. Of course, these were purely private meetings; the first public races on English soil were part of horse fairs.

The earliest description of such an English horse-race goes back to the time of Henry II. It was run in 1174 at Smithfield, outside the gates of London during the weekly (Friday) horse fair, where the gentry used to purchase their steeds. A field was cleared for the occasion and 'a multitude of citizens' watched the exciting event, generally regarded as the first organized racing of its kind. The example soon caught on and holders of fairs elsewhere included races as a main feature of their program.

Race meetings continued to be held sporadically. However, during the reign of Richard I they became a favourite pastime of knights. It is known that one Whitsuntide, knights held a contest (the first formal race for a money prize) over a three-mile (4.80 km) course for a purse of £40 in 'ready gold'. King John, who ascended the throne after Richard, was the first king to keep 'running horses' in his stables.

For a long time, those participating in the contests did so mostly for the love of it, and for no specific awards. The knowledge of being first was enough. The first racing trophy was offered in 1512 by the promoters of the Chester Fair who presented the fastest racer with a wooden ball adorned with flowers. This rather inexpensive trophy was replaced, in following years, first by a silver ball and then by a golden shell.

The practice of presenting three prizes for a race owes its origin to the unsatisfactory workmanship of a silversmith and thus, like so many of our institutions, started accidentally.

The Sheriff of Chester generously had agreed to donate the trophy (in the form of a silver ball) for the 1609 race in his city. Accordingly, he asked a local craftsman to make it. On its delivery, the Sheriff found it was not up to expectation. The artisan thereupon produced a second ball. However this did not please the customer either. 'Third time lucky', at last the silversmith was able to 'deliver the goods'. On race day the Sheriff thus had not one but three prizes. To use just one—the best— would be a waste. He therefore decided to present all three in their proper order, according to merit and value. That is how our present-day first, second, and third prizes came into existence.

Charles I established regular meetings at Newmarket, where the Gold Cup was first run in 1634. After a temporary banning of the sport during the time of the Commonwealth, it soon flourished again after the Restoration, when Charles II made Newmarket the headquarters of the turf, which it has remained ever since. The king himself rode his own horse to the winning post on 14 October 1671. His favourite mount, 'Old Rowley', became so famous that people began to call the king by its name. Odd names, indeed, were given then to race-horses. Typical were 'Tickle-me-quickly', 'Louse', and 'Kill-'em-and-Eat-'em'.

During his reign, too, England's greatest contribution

to the sport—the breeding of the thoroughbred—began. Today, every race-horse in the world can trace its line back on the male side to those early sires. The word 'thoroughbred', sometimes misunderstood, really means carefully and scientifically bred, and not, as is often mistakenly assumed (and adopted in its French and Italian translations), pure-blooded.

To improve the native breed, England imported oriental horses, mainly Arabian, Barbs, Turks, and Persians. The earliest record in existence dates back to 1685, when, for the purpose of better breeding, the stallion 'Byerly Turk' was brought to England. Opinions differ as to whether it was captured from the Turks or purchased in the east.

It was one of the three great 'foundation' stallions. The second, also a Syrian or Turkish sire, was imported as a four-year-old by Thomas Darley and, therefore, is referred to as Darley Arabian. The Earl of Godolphin acquired the 'Godolphin Arabian' which, the story goes, was saved from the menial task of pulling a water cart in the streets of Paris.

Continued royal patronage made racing the 'sport of kings'. Monarchs, of course, included queens as well. In fact, Queen Anne of England was one of the sport's greatest promoters. She introduced proper methods in the breeding of horses which up to her time had still been rather haphazard. She also originated the first sweepstake in 1714 when, apart from donating a gold cup (as she had done several times before), she stipulated that the owners of each of the eleven starters put up a fee of ten guineas, the winner to take all. And it was only fitting that *Star*, her own horse, won the first cash prize ever awarded in a race.

A favourite of the queen was Tregonwell Frampton who has been called 'the father of the English turf'. Already under William III he had been appointed 'Keeper of the Running Horses of His Sacred Majesty', a position he continued to hold under Queen Anne and the first two Georges. For a period of almost fifty years he dominated the Newmarket scene and from 1700 onward received an annual stipend of £1000, which he drew until his death, to look after the ten royal horses. Frampton, no doubt, could be described as the first professional horse-trainer in the world.

He was an odd sort of man who, in spite of his friendship with the queen, hated women. He was always dressed the same way and had a shabby, unwashed appearance. But he had a tremendous love for the horse and was addicted to racing. The steeds he bred he sold at an enormous price. Because in one of the races in which he had an interest vast sums of money changed hands, Parliament passed an Act prohibiting the recovery of bets in excess of £10, 'in order to put a stop to such ruinous proceedings'.

Around 1750 enthusiasts of the sport and owners of horses began to meet—very informally—at Newmarket. At first it was little more than a dining club for gentlemen keen on horses. They discussed future races and the rules and conduct that should govern the sport. Eventually, they agreed to form themselves into a group, which they called The Jockey Club. (This was to grow into the most powerful organization controlling horse-racing. It became the arbiter in all disputes and was not afraid to interfere. In 1791 it even demanded of the Prince Regent that he dismiss his favourite jockey who was suspected of having rigged races. 'Their actions became precedents, their advice grew into law.')

Interest in racing had grown to such an extent that to supply all possible information on horses, the *English Racing Calendar* was established in 1773 as an annual account of all the 'places, matches and sweepstakes run in Britain and Ireland', with their winners and prizes. It has been published regularly ever since.

The 'sport of kings' found ever greater favour and drew bigger and bigger crowds. Through the years a number of innovations by ardent patrons became historical landmarks.

Colonel Anthony St Leger felt that the traditional practice of racing at his time demanded too much of a horse. Frequently, five-year-olds had to run eight, if not twelve, miles in one afternoon. In 1776 he therefore introduced at Park Hill, near Doncaster, a race for three-year-old colts over two miles (3.20 km), with one heat to decide. Within two years, people had started to call it after him, the 'St Leger'. And so this racing classic was born.

Fame is attained in the most unexpected ways. A man might spend his life in the service of an ideal, but this is completely forgotten. And yet, one feature, least expected, might immortalize him.

The Stanleys were one of England's most aristocratic families. They were descended from one of William the Conqueror's companions and had served their country well for many generations and in countless causes: as Lieutenant Governors of Ireland, Privy Counsellors, Chief Justices, and famous soldiers holding command on many a battlefield. In the fifteenth century they were presented with the Earldom of Derby. Nevertheless, few would know of them nowadays had not the 12th Earl of Derby been a lover of horses.

He was concerned about three-year-old fillies which did not qualify for the St Leger. In 1779, to provide a feature race exclusively for them, he inaugurated a race on his property, the Oaks, in Epsom. It was to be a race over a distance of a mile and a half (2.40 km), again with 'one heat to decide'. Just as had happened with the St Leger at Doncaster, it did not take long for people to give the race its name. This time they called it not after the founder himself, but his estate—'the Oaks'.

The Earl made a second contribution to the sport of kings which was to link his name for all times with one of the chief events of horse-racing. In pursuit of his hobby, the 12th Earl of Derby in 1780 added to 'the Oaks' yet another race, also over a mile and a half, but this time open for three-year-old horses of both sexes. Run annually at Epsom Downs, it became 'the blue ribbon of the turf'. That it was called 'the Derby', some say, was the obvious thing to do. However, a tradition has it that the choice of name was due to mere chance.

At a dinner party at his homestead, the Earl discussed, it is told, the future race with his friend, Sir Charles Bunbury, who in no small measure was responsible as well for its inauguration. Having resolved to start the race, they also agreed to call it after one of them—either 'Derby' or 'Bunbury'—but leave the final decision to the tossing of a coin. The coin came down on the Derby side. And 'the Derby' it has been ever since.

There is another version of its origin, linked with wagers made at *Tattersall's*, which is another name written large in the racing world.

Tattersall's is called after its founder, Richard Tattersall, whose own story and place in the sport has hardly an equal. A Yorkshire farmer, he had taken up the buying and selling of horses. Soon his reputation in this field had become so great that people said he was the first honest horse dealer in the world. The Prince of Wales (the future King George IV) made him his personal adviser on horses.

In 1766, Tattersall had expanded his trade so much that he opened up premises at Hyde Park Corner, London, to auction there in its courtyard, the finest horses he could gather in from any part of Europe. For this purpose he had his agents travel far and wide.

The extent of his property was so great that it could accommodate 150 animals with their grooms and handlers. He also set aside a fifteen-acre (6 hectares) paddock to have the animals exercised.

Anxious to serve his customers in every way and to give them a congenial meeting place, he purchased the adjacent Turf Inn and completely rebuilt it. He included a 'subscription room' in which his clients could place and settle bets. In fact, the proper organization of this part of racing, which became so important to the sport, was his great ambition and under his supervision the first rules of wagering were drafted. *Tattersall's* became a name renowned among all patrons of the turf in almost every English-speaking country.

Horse owners and race-lovers gathered regularly in the establishment on Monday nights for a convivial dinner with plenty of wine. Naturally, they discussed across the table the various horses and argued about their relative merits. On one such evening, early in 1780, the topic of conversation was three-year-old gallopers owned by some of the men. The owners could not speak highly enough of the horses' superb qualities, but others disagreed and a heated controversy ensued.

To settle the issue, someone suggested what was really the most obvious solution: to test the horses in action. To do so they arranged to hold a special race in May of that year, at Epsom Downs. As the event should have a name all agreed there was none more appropriate than that of one of the best-known experts on horses at the time—the Earl of Derby, whom they could thus honour as well. That is how, according to this story, the 'Derby Stakes' were launched.

It is interesting to note that the original distances set down for the races at Doncaster and Epsom were never adopted. An initial error in measuring was responsible for their having been slightly changed from the very beginning.

Meanwhile, The Jockey Club had become England's recognized leader in the sport and its organization served as an example to the whole world of the turf. It controls the *Stud Book,* yet another history-making institution of racing—first published by Messrs Weatherby in 1791. In Volume I of 'The Book', they included all records at their disposal of thoroughbred pedigrees in the previous fifty-four years. It contained the names of approximately a hundred brood mares and an equal number of sires which were authenticated parents of winners. A rule of 1913 stipulated that only those horses could be described as thoroughbred whose lineage could be traced back to ancestors recorded in either the first volume or, in the case of some mares, the second volume of 'The Book'.

THE JOCKEY

The *jockey* (as a word) is really a diminutive form of

Jack (which is merely coincidental with the fact that jockeys usually are short and slight). At some time all horse-traders were addressed in a rather familiar sort of way as Jock or Jack. There was no great distance from trading in horses to riding them. That boys first did so would easily explain Jock's becoming jockey.

The jockey's cap goes back a long time to the head-covering of Roman charioteers. Their skull-protecting caps were made of bronze and they were identical both in shape and purpose with the modern cloth cap. Like twentieth-century astronauts, the charioteers had to safe-guard themselves against potential dangers. Their fast motion along the racing track, with its repeated turns around the pillars at either end, in itself could cause vertigo. In addition, the rays of the burning sun reflected by the sands of the arena could easily blind them. To avoid this, and therefore for merely utilitarian reasons, the Romans ingeniously added to their bronze head cover the peak. It was this peaked cap which became the modern jockey's headgear (just as its shape was also adopted as part of the English school uniform).

THE SADDLE

It is generally conceded that horse-riding owes the saddle, bridle, and spurs to the Asian nomads who, in their invasion of Europe, introduced them there.

Long before using a saddle, riders had learned to throw some kind of cover on to the horse's back, a custom thought of most probably at various places independently and known early in Egypt and Greece. Riders at first did so not for the sake of comfort, about which toughened men did not care. They soon realized that while riding at a gallop, a saddle would seat them more securely and give them better balance.

Animal skins, or some crude type of fabric, fastened under the horse's belly, served as the earliest covers. Some of the sculptured horses in the Parthenon, Athens, distinctly show such saddle cloths.

However, the proper type of saddle, fitted to the

horse's back, is of a much later date and, no doubt, was copied from the barbarian Asiatic horsemen. This saddle was known to the fourth-century Byzantines who, in their clash with forces coming from the east, had adopted it from them. In combat, the saddle enabled the warrior to throw the spear or to shoot the arrow so much better. The saddle can be discerned upon the frieze of the column erected at Constantinople in honour of the Roman Emperor Theodosius who, in an edict of AD 385, had limited the weight of a saddle to 60 lbs (27kg).

The Gauls employed a different sort of saddle, reminiscent of the howdah used by Arabs and Indians when riding the camel and the elephant, but also already known to the Chinese of the Han dynasty, which came into power in the second century BC. The horsemen were well aware that the contraption raised them higher, thereby giving them an advantage over the foe.

Considerations of combat as well contributed to further developments in the shape of the saddle used by the medieval knights. Obviously they needed a firm support in tournaments but once these were no longer held, the saddle's weight became ever lighter and eventually it evolved into the so-called English saddle of the nineteenth and twentieth centuries.

Americans gave to the world of racing the short stirrups and the 'monkey crouch' which replaced everywhere the traditional English seat. It is only fair to state that Australians claim to have pioneered the 'monkey seat' almost simultaneously and, certainly, independently.

SPURS AND STIRRUPS

The earliest spurs were bone splinters.

A problem for any rider was how to mount his steed the fastest way. To begin with, he leaped on to it by using his spear or a pole. The employment of 'mounting blocks' (of one kind or another) was an alternate, obvious, and simple way. In search of a better method, man eventually invented the stirrup. This, however, was not added to the Roman saddle until the fifth century, when hordes of Huns brought it to Europe. Nevertheless, it has been doubted whether they themselves had devised this refinement. Much more likely is the suggestion that they had merely adopted it from the Chinese, their eastern neighbour. Most probably, however, the first stirrup was conceived by the Indians toward the end of the second century BC. Suitable for barefoot riders, it was of the 'big toe' variety. Wherever Indian culture spread, it carried also the stirrup. Thus it arrived in China. As the colder climate there made it necessary for riders to wear boots, in the fifth century AD they enlarged the one-toe stirrup sufficiently to hold the entire foot.

The most primitive sort of stirrup was a loop in a rope that hung from the saddle. It was the combination of its purpose and material that actually created the word from the Old English. *Stirrup* is a fusion of *stige*—'to climb', and *rap*—'a rope'.

THE BRIDLE

The word bridle is derived also from an Old English root, meaning 'to pull', and the most primitive contrivance to pull or direct the horse the right way goes back to earliest times and to the East. Man then used a raw hide strap or a thong which he pulled through the animal's mouth and tied up under its jaw. Its loose ends served as reins to restrain and guide the horse. Archaeological finds have proved the existence of this method in 2000 BC. Bones, horn, wood, and eventually metal replaced the thong. To start with, a single bar was used to which was fixed at either end a ring to hold the reins.

Medieval knights attached sharp spikes to the bit. They did so not to hurt their steed and perhaps thereby spur it to obey commands, but to prevent the foe in man to man combat from grasping his opponent's mount by means of the bridle.

THE HORSESHOE

Horseshoes were generally adopted on the continent of Europe as late as the tenth century and introduced into England by William the Conqueror. The earliest use of the horseshoe has been the subject of much controversy and confusing conjecture.

Ancient Greek records have been quoted and then rejected as misleading on the ground that they were based either on a misunderstanding or a wrong translation of the original text. Homer's reference to 'brass hoofs', for instance, was not a description of early horseshoes (it was said) but merely a figure of speech to picture the prancing advance of the horse and the firmness of its hoofs.

A passage, often cited in the past, mentioned a kind of stocking or sandal, tied to the horse's feet by means of a strap to enable the animal to advance more easily over difficult territory and great distances. Xenophon tells of little bags put around the horse's feet in the depth of winter, so that it should not sink into the snow.

However, on examination of the texts, other authorities pointed out that the so-called protective covers were only adopted as dressings by early veterinary medicine, and were not the forerunner of the metal shoe. Aristotle's is the only authentic reference to leather shoes. These were put on camels to avoid foot soreness.

Not one of the many Greek sculptures in existence, featuring the horse in most detailed form, reveals the use of 'shoes'. The Bible did not know them either. It was only in the way of a metaphor also when it spoke in Deborah's song (Judges V:22) of the foe's horses in flight with their stamping hoofs, or in Isaiah's prophecy (V:28) of the enemy's advance with chariots as swift as the whirlwind and the horses' hoofs as hard as flint.

Only an abundance of iron could lead to its use for hoof protection. Bronze was too soft and would have worn down speedily. That is why the introduction of horseshoes was of a relatively late date. Man's trend to specialization is well exemplified by the fact that the production of horseshoes and the nails necessary to fix them, created a specialized craft. Farriers were very conscious of their skilled vocation and considered themselves (as one of them expressed it in a treatise devoted to the craft) the aristocrats of the nail trade.

THE HEAT

Heats now are the preliminary contests to a sporting event, to eliminate competitors. The term goes back to the horse track. Prior to a race a horse was exercised to *heat* it up. A record of 1577 suggests, 'walke him to chafe him, and put him in a heate'.

HORSE BELLS AND BRASSES

Superstitious beliefs have been attached to the horse, not least to its hoof, as the universally accepted lucky horseshoe shows. An emblem of fertility, usually linked with the moon's crescent, it has also been oddly explained to owe its sexual meaning to its imagined rough resemblance to the vulva.

A piebald horse was regarded almost as a walking, magical medicine chest. A hair from its side, or merely the smell of its stable, were thought to possess curative properties. Eventually, these were transferred to its owner. Advice he gave for the treatment of sickness, solely through his association with the piebald, would effect a cure. On the other hand, Yorkshiremen regarded an encounter with a white horse on leaving home as an omen of misfortune. The only possible antidote was to spit on the ground, preferably three times. A horse with white-stockinged forelegs generally was taken to mean good luck.

Many fables and legends have credited the horse with clairvoyance, giving its master timely warning of things to come. It is not surprising therefore that Carl Jung, the famous Swiss psychologist, saw in the horse the symbol of man's intuitive understanding, his magical side, 'the mother within us'.

The introduction of horse bells and brasses was due to superstitious notions. A horse was considered specially vulnerable to the attacks of mischievous forces, particularly the evil eye that, it was thought, by an invisible ray could inflict worse harm than the most poisonous arrow. The origin of the belief may be based on the not infrequent irrational behaviour of a horse. Man was bewildered by its refusal to go on and its breaking out into sweat or stumbling, on occasions when human eyes or mind could not see any apparent reason.

To protect the horse against such invidious, unaccountable forces, its owner provided it with an amulet. Plates of metal or bells were attached to the animal, by their noise to frighten off the evil forces. Another 'devil repellent' was an object of bright and shining colour fixed to the forehead of the horse. A red piece of cloth, a red coral, or a magical silver hand served for the purpose. Most effective of all, it was considered, was a brass disk. It assumed a variety of forms, all regarded as of sacred potency, such as a cross, an eight-pointed star, the horseshoe, the lunar crescent, or the solar wheel. What appears nowadays a mere ornament and decoration thus can be traced to early religious beliefs and magic.

THE BOWLER AND THE DERBY

Fashionable Englishmen at the Derby wore a stiff felt hat, known as a bowler. Its origin has been—at least by some—associated also with riding.

It is told that around 1850 a Norfolk horseman had experienced great annoyance while wearing the then customary tall hat, as this was apt to be swept off the head by overhanging branches. Anxious to keep his hat on, he had contacted his personal hatter, a Mr Beaulieu (the most outstanding representative of the trade at the time), and asked him to design a more practical model. The result was a lower-crowned, hard felt hat, called after its manufacturer, in the Anglicized version of his name, a 'bowler'.

Another theory traces this hat to a more English-sounding William Bowler, a specialist in riding outfits. He first fashioned the hat for clients who were steeplechase riders and often suffered head injuries when, in making a jump, they not only lost their hat but fell to the ground. Obviously, the hard crown and stiff brim would afford them at least some protection.

Other authorities quote an item from the London *Daily News* (of 8 August 1868) which related that a 'Mr Bowler, of 15 St Swithin's Lane, has, by a very simple contrivance, invented a hat that is completely ventilated whilst, at the same time, the head is relieved of the pressure experienced in wearing hats of the ordinary description'.

A fourth claim associates the word not with the name of a hatter (whether French or English-sounding) but with a simple basin—a bowl. Being of round shape and stiff construction, it could easily be 'bowled' along.

Going even further, in both space and time, others have seen in the bowler a resemblance to a Persian, melon-shaped hat, known as *kolah* which, as early as the fifteenth century, was favoured by sportsmen. Somehow, if this hypothesis be correct, English lips must have transformed the *k* into a *b*.

The bowler also proved a safe head cover, yet other writers assert, not merely for those riding horses but also for those riding in English stage coaches at a time when highway robberies were quite common. To frighten travellers, bandits often hit them on the head. To wear some stiff cover was therefore a wise precaution!

Certainly, a source of wonderment are the many genealogies attached to such a comparatively simple hat as the bowler. Whichever its true origin, the fact remains that riders adopted it and soon those who came to watch them did likewise. In the usual way of fashion, the novel style became the vogue, particularly among those who attended the English Derby, that annual red letter day of racing. And from there it spread to the United States.

Traditions again vary and no one really knows whether American horse-lovers attending the English Derby or newspaper reports appearing in the United States made the New World first take notice of the English bowler. No matter how, Americans adopted and adapted the hat for their own use and, in honour of the English, called it the Derby hat.

According to one report, James H. Knapp of South Norwalk, Connecticut, in 1850 manufactured the first consignment of three dozen Americanized bowlers that were sold in a New York store. There, this story also says, one of the clerks actually had first suggested their new name. By 1875 the Derby hat had become fashionable at the Kentucky Derby, modelled on the English event. Thus man owes to equestrian origin not only his pants but even two kinds of hat.

THE STEEPLECHASE

An odd story explains the origin of the steeplechase. Eighteenth-century fox hunters were returning home disappointed because their chase had proved a complete failure. They had been unable to make a single kill.

To compensate for their lack of success one of the men, on the spur of the moment, suggested a different type of chase. He may have conceived the idea when he caught sight of the steeple of their village church in the far distance. Pointing to it, he proposed that they should race in a direct line towards it, no matter what obstructions they had to overcome on the way. The first to touch the steeple with his whip would be the winner.

Thus even the church has found a place in racing, as long as this is across ditches, fences, hedges, and other formidable hazards. Traditionally the earliest race of this type took place in Ireland around 1752 and was run from one church steeple to another over a distance of about four miles (6.40 km). From Erin, the sport spread to England, where its course was extended to more than twenty miles (32 km). An early match is said to have been held between two Lords near Huntington in 1807. Hunters and cavalry-men particularly welcomed and sponsored this adventurous riding.

THE BOOKMAKER

Early bets on horses caused no problem. Races were run among friends and each trusted the other to fulfil his promise. Later, when strangers joined in the gamble, they began to deposit the money wagered with some trustworthy person who eventually came to be known by the obvious description of a 'stake-holder'.

A multiplicity of races, and an ever greater number of competing steeds, made his task so onerous that he could no longer afford the time entailed without compensation. As by then his duties had become an indispensable part of racing, horsemen agreed to pay him five per cent of all takings, an amount he duly deducted when paying winning wagers.

When the public also took up betting, the keeping of accounts became even more complicated. Stake-holders now needed a book to note down the many wagers and the odds, as well as the final settlement. That is how the 'bookmaker' was born as a professional betting man. Familiarity and perhaps his friendliness made people speak of him colloquially as 'the bookie'.

No animal in the world has served man as long and as much as the horse. With its own flesh it has nourished him. Its blood, and not only in the cases of diphtheria and tetanus, helped him to fight disease. In earliest days, its hide clothed him and through thousands of years the horse bore man's burden, fought his battles, chased his quarry, and delivered his messages between far-off places. But the thrills it provided him in the sport of kings surpass all else. Small wonder then that the horse has left numerous marks in man's thoughts and speech.

A 'dark horse' has not revealed its qualities (or their lack) to the general public. Disraeli was the first to use the phrase in this sense in *The Young Duke*. An American anecdote tells about a coal-black horse which looked a very ordinary sort of nag but won its Tennessee owner countless races and bets. His usual procedure was to ride his 'Dusky Pete' into a strange town and create the impression that it was a saddle horse. Local people, not guessing its true quality and past history, were glad to arrange a race—to their later cost.

All horses share the celebration of their birthdays on one day of the year. This may differ between various countries, according to the breeding season. It is 1 January in America and 1 August in Australia. A horse born a single day before the official birthday, within twenty-four hours will already be one year old!

To ascertain the true age of a horse, as almost everyone knows, an examination of its teeth is sufficient. Anyone wishing to gain authentic information, welcomes it, therefore, 'straight from the horse's mouth'. Hence it is not fair to look a gift horse in the mouth, a rule of etiquette suggested by the Romans as early as AD 400.

The exuberance of a horse caused men to describe boisterous behaviour among his own kind as 'horse-play', while the animal's frisky neighing created the 'horse-laugh'.

Self-explanatory are other idioms and sayings shared by many nations and expressed in their various tongues. They ranged from the advice to 'hold your horses' to the lesson, dearly learned, how useless it is to 'lock the stable door after the horse has bolted'. That 'you can take a horse to the water but you cannot make it drink' is as correct an observation as that it is pointless to 'flog a dead horse'.

Horse chestnuts, certainly, are peculiarly named and many people have conjectured on the origin of their equine association. On the loom of language the word 'horse' at times has been used to imply inferior value. One theory thus suggests that horse chestnuts were the most common kind. However, there is also a 1597 veterinary claim that the horse chestnut received its name because of the curative properties of its fruit in treating a horse's cough.

The lauded 'horse sense' possibly has its basis in the physiological fact that, except for the ostrich, no other animal has larger eyes. These are positioned so strategically that, with its head held up, the animal has an all-round view. In fact, the horse need not turn its head (as the jockey might do) to find out what is happening in the rear.

Horse-racing, no doubt, has produced the greatest complex of sporting activities. The world owes to it a maximum of adventure and excitement — whether as riders, spectators, or punters. It has developed industries of the most diverse kind. Enormous amounts of money have been and are gained or lost on the track. The horse itself, however temperamental, knows only good or bad riders, solicitous or neglectful owners. No respecter of person, as Ben Johnson said, 'he will throw a Prince as soon as his groom'. Throughout the millennia and in every clime, from Stone Age man to twentieth-century affluent society, the horse indeed has proved itself both a servant and a friend of man. It has helped to make man what he is today and the 'sport of kings', at least in the eyes of many, is the 'king of sports'.

THE AUTOMATIC TOTALIZATOR

The automatic totalizator which revolutionized racing throughout the world was invented in Australia by Sir George Alfred Julius, the son of an Archbishop and Primate of New Zealand. He himself never became a racing fan. The only times he went to the races, were to see his betting machine in action, and to test its efficiency. That the 'tote' was an aid to the making and winning (or losing) of bets on the relative value of horses, indeed, was never a matter of great interest to the inventor.

George was born in Norwich, England, in 1873. His father, a devout Anglican clergyman, loved gadgetry and was most adept in making tools. He constructed all types of mechanical devices. No wonder that he instilled in his son, from earliest childhood, a special love of tinkering. Julius himself liked to relate how, at the age of five, he worked the lathe treadle for his father in the hobby shed of their Norwich home.

In 1889, the Rev Julius accepted the post of archdeacon to Ballarat, Victoria, and with his family—and his tools—emigrated there. Soon afterwards he was appointed Archbishop of Christchurch and Primate of New Zealand. Conscientious about his ministerial duties, he nevertheless continued his hobby, often making gadgets out of knitting needles and hairpins. Most of all, however, he enjoyed repairing clocks, and he became a real expert in clock mechanics. When people saw him going to church, they could not always tell whether he did so to conduct a service or to repair the clock high up in the tower. Similarly, on his calls to the vicars of his diocese, he not merely discussed their work but improved the working of their watches as well. Many a clergyman anxiously waited for his bishop to put his timepiece right, free of charge.

George inherited his father's delight in gadgetry. After graduation in science at Canterbury College, Christchurch, he accepted an appointment as assistant engineer in the locomotive department of the Western Australian Government Railways. It did not take people long to recognize his brilliant mind. He was promoted to the position of chief draughtsman and then became the engineer in charge of the department's tests. Racing, however, was still the furthest thing from his mind.

Any mechanical problem attracted Julius and, in a peculiar way, it was a dispute on the votes cast at a Western Australian election which became the basis of his future horse-racing fame. He considered that any acrimony and controversy could be avoided by mechanizing both the counting of votes and of preferences. For this purpose he designed a machine which, being far too expensive to construct, has never gone beyond the blueprint stage. After all, elections are not held frequently and no government was prepared to spend the enormous sum it would cost to build the machine.

It was disappointing to the young engineer that apparently all his work and ingenuity (as well as precious time) had been wasted. That is why Julius looked around to find some other application for his invention. It was while discussing his problem with friends that they suggested the 'tote' to him. 'What is a tote?' Julius is said to have innocently asked.

Eventually, he resigned from the Western Australian Railways and, moving to Sydney, established himself there as a consultant engineer. Not forgetting his friends' proposition, he now seriously considered the construction of an electrically operated, fully automatic machine that would record bets and compute dividends.

In his research, he took note of previous attempts, such as had been made in France and New Zealand, but had proved of no great merit. The machines had been hand-operated, too cumbersome, and too long in obtaining results, which were not always correct.

For five long years he struggled with all the difficulties that presented themselves, till in 1912 he gave the world the first totalizator. This was still a huge contraption, with a tangle of piano wires and heavy, leaden weights. Within a year, he sold it to the Auckland Racing Club which installed it, with phenomenal success, at Ellerslie course.

Some people never believed that the invention was really his. They were convinced that his father, the Archbishop, had thought it up but, for obvious reasons, had given the credit to his son who was not encumbered by ecclesiastical proprieties. In fact, the story was told how one day, when the new machine had broken down, race-goers observed their beloved Archbishop rush into the building. They even imagined that he had turned up his coat collar—to hide his clerical garb. Soon afterwards the wheels were turning again. Some pious onlookers suggested that their Primate had blessed the machine. But those of a more prosaic nature bluntly stated that the 'Arch' had repaired his brainchild.

Once the success of the new invention was apparent, Julius established the firm which, though under a different name, continues to supply the world market with the totalizator. Its basic principles, first worked out by Sir George, have remained virtually unchanged. Australia exported the machine to twenty-nine countries which, in addition to the United Kingdom and the United

States, included Nigeria, Malaysia, Eire, India, and Brazil. The automatic totalizator, it is well to remember, was not merely a betting machine. It exerted altogether a lasting effect on the sport of racing.

In recognition of his many outstanding services to the cause of science, Julius was knighted in 1929. Of all his many achievements, none has won him greater fame than his totalizator, one of Australia's great contributions to the world of sport.

Chapter 20

HUNTING

According to one view, man, to begin with, did not eat meat. He lived on the natural products of the soil, such as berries, roots, seeds, and wild fruit. Even the formation of man's teeth, it has been further asserted and cited as a confirmation of this theory, indicated an originally meatless diet. Man's carnivorous habits only developed later, after he had tasted flesh and blood and thereby acquired a liking for them.

The Bible suggests that for the first ten generations man did not eat meat, but was completely herbivorous, and that Noah had introduced the practice only after the deluge. However, the findings of anthropology, archaeology, and anatomy seem to agree that from the very beginning man lived on a multiple sort of diet, eating both the growth of the soil and meat. Therefore, from the start he must have learned to hunt. By partaking of the flesh of some killed foe (either of his own or the animal species), man turned into a carnivorous being and has remained one ever since. But he began hunting in self-defence.

Surrounded and threatened by ferocious, marauding creatures, man had to kill them not to be killed by them. That is why he took up hunting — for self-protection. Using his strong hands, stones, and clubs, he attacked the beast. But he was taught by bitter experience that he was confronted by a being far superior in tooth and claw. In such an unequal fight man was bound to be the loser unless he evolved some technique to compensate for his deficiency. In his battle for survival he was forced to use his mind, and he proved himself a 'tool-making animal'. He became an inventor and, in various stages, devised the spear, the harpoon, the boomerang, the bow and arrow, nets, and the sling. He grasped the value of sharp fragments of flint and rock which he attached to his missiles. Archaeologists have unearthed skeletons of prehistoric creatures with the heads of stone arrows and spears still embedded in the bones.

Once man had acquired the habit of eating meat and had become dependent on it, he experienced another crisis — shortage of food. On occasion, and for long periods, animals did not approach near enough to be bagged. And so the first hunting expeditions were organized. These were communal, and the food the killed beast provided was the property not of the individual hunter, but was shared by his entire group.

Hunting thus began as a dire necessity. In seeking security, food, tools, and clothing (more or less in that order), man had to find prey and, by devious methods, kill it. The hunter developed the art of hurling stones with deadly accuracy; he invented the sling, the spear, and the axe; and, as primitive races continue to do to this day, he ran after the game to tire it out or to drive it into nets or across cliffs to fall to death. In winter, American Indians chased bison into deep snowdrifts where, caught up and unable to escape, they were easily killed. The first representation of the use of skis — on rock carvings discovered in Scandinavia and dating back to 2000 BC — shows hunters gliding along the snow in pursuit of the elk. Already some primitive tribes had reserved the chase to a special class of professional hunters, trained in the art.

Man's genius led to perhaps the greatest of all discoveries, one which has been compared in importance to the invention of the wheel. He found he could make nature work for him. He learned to dig pits and build animal traps which eventually he camouflaged. The prey was caught, as it were, automatically. The trap was the first robot.

The various types of traps ingeniously constructed by early man, revealed his intuitive knowledge of laws discovered only in the scientific age. He took advantage of the force of gravity and wisely employed the principle of leverage and the stored-up energy in a spring, whose equivalent then was a bent tree or twig. A hole dug in the ground was carefully covered up so that the unsuspecting animal would step on the cover and fall into the pit. Heavy stones, to be released by the slightest touch, were cleverly positioned to crush the game. Any contact caused spring-poles to go off and ensnare the wild beast in an attached noose.

Primitive man was deeply conscious of his dependence on superior forces. He felt that alone he could achieve nothing, certainly not bag any quarry. To subdue nature he needed the help of supernatural power. To gain it he evolved magical hunting rites, still practised in modern days by Aboriginal races.

Led by holy men he joined in chanting magical songs on the eve of the hunt. Games were 'played' and dances performed in which a disguised member of the tribe played the role of the game to be hunted. Even painting was utilized as a most significant rite for ensuring the success of the hunt by sympathetic imagery.

The earliest, extant prehistoric drawings of man, discovered in caves and rock shelters (the most famous of all in southern France and north-western Spain), are of animals — mammoths, bison, buffaloes, and reindeer. Preserved for millennia in their glowing colours of red, yellow, brown, and black, they were found far back in the caves which were man's earliest picture gallery. Mystical symbols of geometrical pattern (now understood to depict traps) were added to the most naturalistic protrayal of the beasts. For some time these pictures baffled modern man. There is no longer any doubt. They were part of the hunting magic.

To primitive man, a picture was something real. He who had drawn an animal had already caught an essential portion of its spirit. Similarly, the symbolic spearing of a beast (or the catching of it in a trap), drawn on a wall or traced in the sand, by magical means pre-destined the outcome of the actual chase. Hence, when the hunters went out, perhaps on the following morning, they knew that in reality the principal part of their work had already been done, that they were merely collecting what supernatural powers had prepared for them. The magical drawings were indeed an odd kind of the earliest 'grace before meals': not expressing thanks for the food about to be received, but making sure of obtaining it. They also illustrate the beginnings of art — drawing, painting, dancing, chanting, and drama — not as art for art's sake but as part of man's battle for existence.

Primitive man really did not cherish killing animals. He saw in them creatures like himself, endowed as he was with a soul or a spirit. He believed that taking their lives was highly dangerous, as the slain animal's spirit would try to take revenge. Surviving brethren would also seek to wreak vengeance, to take life for life in a kind of blood feud. Consequently, early man fenced in all his hunting with solemn rites and ceremonies, endeavouring to propitiate the animal's soul and its outraged family, even asking their pardon in advance.

Before the actual hunt man would purge himself, fast for long periods, and offer sacrifices to pay for the crime he was about to commit. Many taboos thus belonged to the hunter's life. Readying himself for the task, he would abstain from certain activities which, he imagined, might impede if not totally spoil the chase. Some tribes, for example, would not wash themselves. They were convinced that if they did so, the wounds they inflicted would prove merely superficial. Only if the hunter him-self, and his weapon, had been properly safeguarded for the chase, would it be successful. Charms of various kinds were employed. They were worn by the hunter or fixed to his hunting tools. He would chew red pepper or blacken his face (not for the purpose of camouflage) with the soot of burnt, fragrant bark. Hunting involved even those staying at home, as any inadvertent action on their part could interfere with its success.

When the chase was over, other taboos and rites were

observed. The hunter would confront his kill and apologize for his deed. When carrying the slain prey home, some tribes carefully avoided taking it through the customary entrance, as this was considered ritually unclean since it was used by women. Bones of the killed beasts were treated with caution, if not reverence. They were burned, or carefully buried.

Hunting as a sport was only the ultimate stage. The powerful kings of the ancient world — in Egypt, Mesopotamia, and Persia — made hunting a royal sport and proudly recorded their successes in bagging enormous numbers of a wide variety of beasts. Their accounts are still preserved on cuneiform tablets and in hieroglyphic inscriptions.

Only occasional references are made in the Bible to hunting. Scripture praises Nimrod as a mighty hunter — 'a hero of the chase' — before the Lord, and his name became proverbial in the description not only of a hunter but generally of a sportsman. Esau is pictured as a skilful hunter who brought venison to his father Isaac. King Solomon's table was enriched with the flesh of harts, gazelles, roebucks, and fowl. Mighty Samson, with his bare hands, rent a young lion he encountered in the vineyards of Timnah, and Benaiah slew the king of the beasts which had been caught in a pit 'in time of snow'.

Hunting was practised among the Hebrews against predatory animals, and for food. In its dietary legislation the book of Deuteronomy included a list of seven varieties of game permitted to be eaten, among them the hart, the gazelle, the roebuck, and the antelope. Yet Isaiah, in his vision of the ideal future, the Messianic Age, foresaw a time when even animals would abandon all carnivorous practice and 'the lion shall eat straw like the ox'.

Many are the stories of the hunting exploits of legendary heroes and mythical figures. Apollo, a son of Zeus by an earthly woman, the 'lord of the silver bow' and 'archer king', slew with his arrow the dragon at Delphi. The Athenian hero Theseus killed the Minotaur, that man-eating creature of human body and bovine head. Well known is the legend of St George, the patron saint of England, who killed, with the power of Christ it is said, the monstrous dragon.

With the advance of civilization man was able to contain and further reduce the beasts of the forest and jungle. He acquired the art of agriculture and domesticated once wild animals. Hunting thus largely lost its original purpose. However, man's hunting instinct, like some of his organs that no longer fulfil an original function, did not disappear but assumed various forms in different parts of the world, especially so among leisured classes. Falconry, big game hunting, fox hunting, and pig sticking are prominent examples.

No doubt it was very early — even when the life-preserving motive of hunting was still valid — that man came to appreciate the sheer enjoyment of the chase. Xenophon spoke of man being 'in love with hunting'. There was nothing as exciting as matching his strength and wits against those of a savage animal and experiencing the triumph of victory. Hunting thus quite naturally, grew into a sport.

Almost equally soon it was realized that hunting was a wonderful aid in training man. It made him strong, promoted his powers of endurance and his courage, all necessary in a different type of fight for survival: not against the dumb beast but against his own flesh and blood. Hunting was a good rehearsal for warfare. Xenophon, therefore, counselled young men not to despise the art of hunting, pointing out that it would make them fit for war and any pursuit that demanded quick thought and action. In the fourth century BC the philosopher Plato praised as standing 'above and surpassing all ... the pursuit of wild animals by the hunter in person'. By racing, fighting, slinging, and chasing, the hunter showed his deep concern with 'the ideals of manhood'. In the fourth century AD the Roman author Flavius Vegetius in a treatise on military science recommended 'hunters of stags and wild boars' as the most 'welcome recruits'.

LLYFRGELL COLEG MENAI LIBRARY

Man also quickly learned, without conflict of conscience, to train animals to help him chase and retrieve the quarry. For this purpose he employed dogs, hyenas, cheetahs, and ferrets. The ancient Egyptians even used lions. Everything that could help man obtain his prey was enlisted, including the birds of the air. That is how falconry developed, and in early times itself grew into a noble sport. Potentates prided themselves on their birds of prey which, with great efficiency, caught the quarry. Hawks were bred and trained thousands of years ago in China and Mesopotamia, long before falconry flourished on the European continent and in Britain.

It has been suggested that this sport has enriched our vocabulary by one word — debonair. From the Old French, *de bon aire* (of good disposition), it now describes an affable person, one of pleasant and genial demeanour. However, according to this theory, it was used at first in medieval France not in reference to a man but by falconers in connection with their best hawks. Fine specimens were highly treasured and proudly displayed and, in fact, their excellence provided a favourite topic of conversation. Everything was done by their owners to care for them. The birds of best appearance and of almost gracious bearing were lauded as being 'of good air'. Debonair hawks in falconry became prized possessions.

That their praiseworthy description was eventually extended to humans is just another example of the influence of the world of birds and beasts on man's phraseology and figures of speech. We speak of people having the hide of an elephant, the industry of an ant, and of being as busy as a bee. When, through the use of firearms in hunting, hawks had become largely an auxiliary in the chase, and — in the seventeenth century — falconry died out as a major sport, 'debonair' became the exclusive property of the human species.

Hunting the wild boar was an early pursuit of man. In Greek days, the boar was feared almost as much as the wild bull. Heracles' third labour was the capture of the Erymanthian boar which he had been ordered to take on his own. According to one tradition, he caught it in a net and then carried it on his shoulders to Eurystheus. It caused such fright that from then onward he was commanded to announce the successful completion of his tasks from outside the city walls.

Some authorities believe that the phrase 'to beat about the bush', which undoubtedly is of hunting origin, was born specifically in relation to the chase of the boar. This ferocious animal often hid in the undergrowth and beaters employed were ordered to go straight in to chase it out. But very much aware — and afraid — of the animal's sharp tusks, they much preferred merely 'to beat about the bush', a practice strongly disapproved of by their masters. Boars no longer threaten us and today are chased only in a few parts of the world, but they survive, if this derivation of the phrase is correct, in every English-speaking country, in the description or reprimand of those who do not come straight to the point.

Many are the phrases and idioms used in present-day conversation that, although now completely divorced from hunting, originated in the employment of animals to track, catch, or retrieve prey. This applies not least to the canines. That is why, up to this day, we speak of 'barking up the wrong tree'. Dogs used in the chase of racoons, chiefly undertaken at night, were trained to indicate the tree in which the animal, running for its life, had taken refuge, by barking at it. But, of course, even dogs can err and at times barked up the wrong tree.

A riot now refers to a crowd's lawlessness and the disturbance of the peace. Those who run riot have thrown off all restraint. In its root meaning, a riot described 'a quarrel', and the word was used first by hunters in reference to a pack of hounds which had become unruly and insubordinate to its leader, or which instead of following the prey on which it had been set, raced off madly — like Lord Ronald's horse, according to Leacock — in all directions.

The modern sleuth in his detective work owes his name

to man's love of hunting. Without derogatory implications, he has been honoured with the shortened description of a canine forebear. *Sleuth*, an Old Norse word,
originally referred to the track or trail of an animal.
The English, as keen hunters, adopted it from the Normans. Animals which they bred (mostly bloodhounds),
and trained to follow the quarry by scent, they appropriately called sleuth hounds. And was not the detective,
in ferreting out evasive criminals, equal to the animal
that had perfected the art of tracking? Thus, in admiration, people came to speak of him as a sleuth, wisely
and kindly dropping the hound.

Mounted on a horse or, in early days, in a chariot, man
followed his prey. Hunting became a favourite pursuit
'to brace the nerves and stir the blood'. It was regarded
'a noble art' and taken up for the excitement it gave
and its precious loot in the form of hides, furs, horn,
and tusks. Once 'the labour of the savage', it grew into
'the amusement of the gentleman'. It took on such proportions that, particularly through ever more efficient
hunting techniques, it so reduced the number of animals
that laws were issued prohibiting hunting altogether or
restricting it to certain seasons, areas, and classes.

Laws strictly defined hunting grounds, protecting not
only the animals but the rights of the king and of those
to whom he granted the privilege of the chase. Royal
forests were patrolled. Killing the king's deer or tres-
passing into his domain was punished with heavy fines
or imprisonment. Commoners were denied the keeping
of large dogs in lands adjacent to those used in hunting.
Poachers could be transported for seven years or, worse
still, lose both eyes, hands, or their life.

There were times when clergy were hunting-mad, a
fact condemned by the Church as well as by poets.
Chaucer, for instance, deplored the fact that priests,
instead of preaching the word of God, spent their time
chasing game. Hunting the fox grew into a popular
pastime for all classes. George Washington enjoyed it
and encouraged it in America. Hunting was also pro-

moted by governments, who regarded it an excellent school in the art of warfare, making for efficient marksmen and soldiers.

Field sports, described as blood sports, eventually became a most controversial subject, rousing vehement opposition. To kill for food was bad enough, but to do so for fun (or funds) was considered not only inhuman but evil. Oscar Wilde's definition of fox hunting became famous. He described it as 'the pursuit of the uneatable by the unspeakable'. Actually, he merely reiterated an earlier description of the sport as 'pursuing with earnestness and hazard something not worth catching'. People decried hunting as a sport 'that owes its pleasures to another's pain'.

No doubt, a passion for hunting, as Charles Dickens wrote, is 'deeply implanted in the human breast'. Its spice of danger, spirit of adventure, and demand for supreme powers of observation, concentration, and endurance have always attracted man and caused it to become a universal sport. However, those condemning the infliction of pain for the sake of pleasure can still hunt, though in a different way. They can go on safari and most adventurous chases. Instead of shooting the animal, they shoot merely its picture, which is at least as permanent (and less bloody) as the traditional trophies of rugs, tusks, and antlers.

Chapter 21

ICE HOCKEY

It is natural enough for the origin of a game that has its roots in the ancient past to be a subject of heated controversy. However, it is more than surprising that a modern, late nineteenth-century sport should fare similarly. But that is precisely what happened in the case of ice hockey. Obviously, the game is a combination of field hockey and skating, played according to rules adapted from football. No one knows who first joined the three together.

Official commissions were appointed and investigations were conducted, but the assertions they made and the findings at which they arrived differed greatly. Maybe their deductions were influenced (even unconsciously) by what they were looking for, and local pride might have led them in the selection of data, thereby rendering the result of their research almost a foregone conclusion.

Certainly, ice hockey originated in Canada. However, when was it first played, where, and by whom? These are the questions. Whoever was its true father must have known shinny, originally a children's game in which youngsters with broomsticks pushed stones along an icy surface.

According to some, English soldiers serving with the Royal Canadian Rifles at Kingston, Ontario, were the first to put hockey on ice. They improvised the game at the rear of their barracks at Tête du Pont, on the iced-up harbour, at Christmas 1855. It seems to have been a veritable potpourri of sports. After sweeping the snow from the ice, the soldiers tied 'runners' to their boots and, with borrowed hockey sticks, played a match with an old lacrosse ball.

Supporters of 'the Kingston claim' brought forward a further argument. The city had once been the site of shinny games, undoubtedly a close relative of ice hockey which indeed was only its modern and adult form. Was it not perfectly clear therefore, that only at Kingston could ice hockey have been evolved — out of shinty?

Another tradition maintains that G. F. Robertson, of McGill University, Montreal, first thought of ice hockey. On a visit to Britain in 1879 he had watched a (field) hockey match and had been greatly intrigued by it. Himself a skilled ice skater, he had wondered if it was possible somehow to combine the two different sports and thereby to create one that was completely new and exciting. On his return home, the story continues, he discussed the idea with a friend. Together, they worked out a synthesis of hockey and skating, adding, for good measure, some football rules. Enjoyment of the game proved so great that, from an initial experimental venture, it soon graduated at their college into an invigorating sport of tremendous speed, leading eventually (in 1880) to the foundation of the McGill University Hockey Club.

However convincing McGill's claim may have sounded, an ex-McGill man is said to have destroyed it. In one of the investigations he was quoted as having said many years earlier that the original idea of the game at McGill had been proposed by J. G. A. Creighton, a student from Halifax! He had also obtained the necessary sticks for the occasion — on loan — from his home town. Therefore, it was contended, Halifax must have preceded Montreal in the sport.

Thus no one knows for certain the originator of the game — whether it was Kingston, Montreal, or Halifax. Maybe it just happened to be played 'first' at various places almost simultaneously, a phenomenon not uncommon in other spheres of life where novel ideas were conceived independently when their time was ripe.

The earliest recorded use of the term ice hockey for a match is linked with a game that took place at the Victoria Skating Rink, Montreal, in 1875.

Canadians' love of ice skating and a knowledge of shinny provided the proper conditions for ice hockey to evolve. Experience of the thrills of field hockey must have been the final spark that fired some sportsman's imagination to think of transferring hockey from turf to ice. Quite conceivably, too, English troops stationed in Canada, anxious to find some pastime to amuse themselves during the long winter months, adapted for this purpose sports they knew from home (namely, hockey, ice skating, and shinny) to the climate and special conditions of Canada. So they became the pioneers of ice hockey.

In the first games — played on frozen ponds, lakes, or rivers, in fact on any icy surface that offered itself — the traditional hockey sticks and a hard rubber ball were used. There was no fixed number of players, as long as each team was of approximately equal size. The goal was a simple line.

It did not take long for keen players to realize how much room there was for improvement. Use of the rubber ball on the slippery ice proved impractical. Propelled with vigour, it was much too erratic and travelled too far, thereby holding up the game. Teams were too unwieldy. The kind of goal used was also unsatisfactory. Most of all, enthusiasts who were anxious to arrange matches with other teams could not do so, because uniform rules were lacking, and each group and centre played ice hockey differently.

Solution of each of these problems led to the final establishment of ice hockey as a sport. McGill University deserves most of the credit for standardizing the game. It fostered the game in its early days and has properly been called 'the cradle of ice hockey'. To promote competition, it produced the first code of rules in 1879.

Gradually, the number of players on each side was reduced, eventually to be fixed at six. The goal line was replaced by a net and the evasive rubber ball scrapped.

It was superseded by the 'puck', a flat rubber disk which is said to have been first cut out by McGill players from the original ball.

Once the 'McGill Rules' had been adopted, matches between the various centres were held and ice hockey quickly gained an ever wider appeal. One of its enthusiastic sponsors was Lord Stanley of Preston, then the Governor General. To encourage further growth of the game, he donated in 1893 a trophy which was called after him. A sterling silver bowl, it was to be awarded annually to the most outstanding team.

Unfortunately, even this prize, like the claims for fatherhood of the game, became a topic of heated controversy. To attract bigger crowds, clubs felt the need to offer spectators the best of ice hockey and for this purpose began to hire players. Immediately opposition arose, debarring a winning team employing 'professionals' from the Stanley Cup. In the ensuing dispute, supporters of the professionals pointed out that the Vice-Regal donor had promised the trophy for award to those best in the game, without discrimination and certainly without regard to their status. Professionals were as much entitled to it as amateurs.

They were right of course in their argument — as far as it went. However, they did not wish to remember that when Lord Stanley created the prize, there were only amateurs and therefore there was no need on his part (or thought in his mind) to qualify the type of player who could compete for the trophy. Eventually, the Stanley Cup became the symbol of world professional supremacy and in compensation as it were, a corresponding trophy presented by Sir Montagu Allen in 1909 was reserved for amateur teams.

Not without initial protest from Montreal and Halifax, the Hockey Hall of Fame at Kingston became the shrine of the sport and paid homage to the 'immortals' of ice hockey, the world's fastest team game, as much a child of Canada as lacrosse (the latter is Canada's national sport). As in the case of ice skating, technical invention greatly advanced ice hockey, and the introduction of artificial ice rinks made this young sport independent of the seasons and weather conditions.

Ice hockey reached the United States in the early 1890s, and became so popular that North Americans came to speak of it simply as hockey.

The International Ice Hockey Federation was organized in 1908 and, Great Britain, where the sport was also first popularized by Canadian teams, formed its national Ice Hockey Association in 1914.

Chapter 22

ICE SKATING

Well-known is the story immortalized by the English essayist Charles Lamb, that roast pork was discovered by the accidental burning down of a Chinese home. An ingenious theory suggests that an accident, of another kind, might also have been the father of skating. From time immemorial men have slipped many times, and not only on banana skins. One of our ancestors living in an ice-bound region might one day have slipped on a piece of bone on the ice, so that he was propelled at considerable speed for some distance before he landed on his bottom. On getting up, he could not fail to remember his experience. However, being an intelligent type, instead of moaning about the mishap and feeling his bruises, he applied what the fall had taught him, and made man's first skates of bone.

Of course, it is not possible ever to determine historically who the very first ice skater was, and in which part of the world the earliest attempts were made thus to course over frozen water. Most probably, as in many other cases, they occurred simultaneously and independently at several places.

Some theorists claim that the original skates in reality were mini-skis and that skating evolved from skiing. As skis initially consisted of large and extensive bones which, because of their cumbersome size, impeded swift progress over the frozen waterways, anyone could have surmised that the easiest way to achieve better mobility and speed was merely to use smaller and less cumbrous bones, resulting in the birth of the *skate*.

However, it is more likely that skates were invented without any skiing forerunners. Their primitive form was the shankbone of an animal (an ox, a reindeer, a sheep or a horse) fastened to the feet by leather thongs. They existed in prehistoric times in Asia and Europe, and archaeologists have unearthed such specimens, shaped very much like the modern skate, both in Central Europe (at the site of modern Hungary) from the Bronze Age, and in Scandinavia from the days of the Vikings. There is no doubt that skating of a kind was practised in Norse countries long before the birth of Christ. Eskimo hunters pioneered another type of skates from walrus which they fastened to their boots when pursuing prey.

The word skate is derived from the Dutch *schaats*, which itself can be traced to earlier roots in Low German and Old French, denoting an animal's shankbone or legbone. It properly indicates the substance of the first skates. In fact, in its ancient usage the original term described a device that, like a stilt, elevated the wearer above the ground and, in Dutch for instance, then acquired the meaning of wooden shoes and clogs.

Early man soon developed small refinements in skates. He split the bone and drilled holes either at one or both ends, through which the thongs could be tied. The rounded side of the bone was used as the skating surface.

As was the case in other pastimes, skating began as a necessity when nomadic tribes in Asia and northern Europe sought some way to travel more quickly over frozen lakes and fjords, whether to escape an enemy, to hunt for food, or merely to move from place to place. Naturally it started as a novel and better method of getting about on the ice in winter. It did not take long, however, for people thus 'skating' to gain enjoyment from their newly acquired art and to practise it for pleasure's sake. It was only a small step to competing with others in speed and distance covered, which led to racing on skates.

The earliest literary reference to skating occurs in the *Edda*, a famous collection of Icelandic *sagas*. According to a traditional translation (sometimes challenged), this describes how the god of winter was speeding over the ice on animal bones.

However, the first mention of the actual sport — and not merely of a myth — is contained in the *Description of the Most Noble City of London* written in Latin (in 1175). This chronicle by William Fitzstephen (included in his *Life of Thomas à Becket*) gives a plain and amusing account of skating at the time. It relates: 'When the great fenne and moor . . is frozen, many young men play upon the yce, . . some tye bones to their feete, and under their heels and shoving themselves by little picked staffe, doe slide as swiftly as a birde flieth in the air or an arrow out of a cross-bow. Sometimes two runne together with poles, and hitting one the other eyther one or both doe fall not without hurt. Some break their armes, some their legs, but youth desirous for glorie, in this sort exerciseth itselfe against the time of war.'

As it appears, the heavy bone skates which did not cut into the ice and grip it properly were not sufficient in themselves to keep the skater moving. To gain momentum, he pushed himself along periodically with a pointed stick or staff, in a manner very reminiscent of the modern use of poles in skiing and punting.

Propelling themselves vigorously, men began to compete in skating races across the ice.

No country invited the use of skates more than the Netherlands, a land criss-crossed by numerous waterways which freeze for many months in winter. The fact that the ice was not covered usually with deep snow — as was the case in more northerly climes — favoured skating. No wonder, therefore, that Netherlanders soon took up skating both for commerce and pleasure.

Skates used then were made no longer of bones, but completely of wood. They had a wide travelling surface and were fastened, not very securely, with straps and buckles to the foot and ankle.

It was the use of iron (probably also initially in Holland) that brought a real advance to skating. To begin with, only iron runners were fixed to a wooden base which in turn was strapped to the foot. It enabled the skater to get a real grip on the slippery surface of the ice which increased both speed and mobility and made the use of poles redundant. Skaters now could gain momentum merely by running, as this allowed them to slide over the ice until the impetus was spent, whereupon they simply repeated the procedure. Iron-bladed wooden skates can clearly be recognized in the earliest illustration of skating — a woodcut printed in Holland in 1498. Apart from being a 'first', it is distinguished by several other features. This oldest portrayal of skating pictures an accident on the ice; it shows, so early in the history of the sport, women enjoying it; its central figure — the victim of the mishap, a girl of fifteen — was to become the patron saint of all skaters, St Lidwina.

Lidwina was born at Schiedam in Holland in 1380, the daughter of a nobleman and a poor country girl. Even as a young child she had revealed a deeply religious bent. She was drawn to the Mother of God whom she worshipped with deep devotion before a miraculous image at a shrine in her home town.

When in the winter of 1395, she went skating with girl friends, she fell on the ice and broke a rib. (It is this accident which the woodcut depicts.) The fracture proved tragic. No medical skill could cure the many complications it caused. In fact, the accident was the beginning of the girl's martyrdom and her future sainthood.

She became a permanent invalid. Pain wracked her body almost constantly, but even in her agony, she never lost faith. If anything, her prayers became more fervent, and she claimed to have divine visions. But people began to suspect her, believing that, after all, she was merely a fake or perhaps possessed by the devil. To test her, her priest brought to her bedside an unconsecrated host. She immediately recognized it as such, and only then did the Church acknowledge her genuineness, and no one any longer doubted Lidwina's nearness to God. Pious and famous scholars came to visit her and brought with them tracts they had specially written for her comfort. Miracles began to occur at her bedside. But what would have been the greatest miracle of all — her cure — never happened. Her suffering did not cease until the moment of her death on Easter Day 1433, after thirty-eight years of pain. She was fifty-three.

A vision of a rosebush in bloom had told her that the end of her suffering had come at last. Soon after her passing, pilgrims from far and wide came to pray at her graveside over which, within a year, a shrine was built. Venerated by the devout for centuries, Lidwina became the patroness of skaters and in 1891 was made a saint by Pope Leo XII.

History shows that a victory in war can certainly be claimed through the employment of skates. In 1572 when the Dutch fleet was ice-bound at Amsterdam, Spanish forces under the command of Don Frederik were about to capture the vessels. But the use of skates by Dutch musketeers enabled them to launch a swift attack on the enemy from the rear. Completely taken by surprise the Spaniards were routed. By then speed skating was an established sport in Holland, pursued both by men and women and drawing many spectators.

King Charles II of England, it is said, learned skating while in exile there and, on his return home, no doubt, brought with him the iron-bladed skate. The English diarist Samuel Pepys tells in his journal how amazed he was on 1 December 1662 when 'it being a great frost', for the first time in his life he watched in a London park 'people sliding with their skeates, which is a very pretty art'. In an entry for the same day John Evelyn in his *Memoirs* also recorded his admiration on seeing 'on the new canal in St James Park ... the strange and wonderful dexterity of the sliders... after the manner of Hollanders' — 'with what swiftness they passe, how suddenly they stop in full carriere upon the ice'.

No longer merely a sport, skating had become also a graceful and elegant art. However, it still lacked proper organization. The credit belongs to Scotland for having established, in Edinburgh in 1742, the first skating club. To qualify as a member early regulations stipulated that applicants had to prove their ability to skate a complete circle and on either foot to jump first over one, then two and, finally, three hats!

Thirty years later the first handbook on figure skating was published in London. Its author, Robert Jones, explained that its principles were 'deduced from many years of experience by which that noble exercise is now reduced to an Art, and may be taught and learned by a regular Method, with both Ease and Safety'. The treatise was illustrated with copper plates, 'representing the attitudes and graces'.

Skating, thus, was not only enjoyed as a pastime and as a racing sport, but people also had become aware of the variety of intricate movements possible on the ice, including an inside and outside edge. Instructions on how to learn them suggested some strange procedures. The learner was advised to weight his pocket with shot and, in addition, to carry a bag of shot and some heavy article in his right hand and then to transfer the ballast to the left side for performing the outside edge.

By 1813 skating had become so well established in Britain that followers of the sport began to publish their own journal, *Frostiana*.

Experimentation with new and improved designs of skates was carried on through the nineteenth century. All earlier models suffered from certain defects. Most obvious was that they either slipped easily off the foot or were strapped to it so tightly that they stopped the circulation of the blood. One major concern was to discover some method to secure the skate more firmly, yet comfortably. The greatest advance from every point of view was the invention of the first all-metal skates (with blades of hard steel) by E. W. Bushnell in Philadelphia in 1848. This type of skate eliminated the cumbersome wooden footplate. To begin with it still used those bothersome straps — at times as many as four. However, eventually Bushnell discarded them and manufactured skates that were fastened to the boot by clamps. He sold his invention at $30 a pair.

Even his skates were not perfect. They frequently became unclamped. A further and most welcome improvement was the introduction of skates that could be screwed firmly to the sole of the boot. One of the first to use these skates was the greatest skating champion of the time, Jackson Haines, a young American from Chicago.

It is not only the technical development of the skates to which ice skating owes its high place in the world of sport. Even more so, it is through the promotion it received from great skaters. First in line, undoubtedly, was Haines. His name is perpetuated in the classic spin he invented after, some say, nine years of arduous practice. His contributions to the sport surpassed by far this single item in the repertoire of every ambitious skater.

Son of a cabinet maker, he spent some time in Europe as a youth but returned at the age of seventeen to the United States, at his father's request, to join the family business. However, his love of the stage was too strong and he embarked on a theatrical career. He specially favoured dancing. Being a perfectionist, he had a large mirror installed in his home to study every movement he made. It was at this time that he learned to skate. Immediately he recognized the tremendous contribution he could make by employing on the ice his masterly art of dancing.

Still a ballet master, he soon began to give, with theatrical flair, spectacular skating exhibitions in many centres along the east coast and in Canada. He further developed his own skates which were much more solid than any previous models. He fixed the blade to the toe and heel plates, which in turn he screwed to the skating boot.

When the American Civil War almost completely stopped his career as a dancer, he decided to go to Europe again. He arrived there in 1864 to go on a tour that was to electrify the Continent and revolutionize skating throughout the world.

At first, however, when in London, he met with no response. Certainly, the British had been among the first to develop skating as an art so much admired by Pepys. Gradually they had perfected what came to be known as the English school. Concentrating on the purity of poise, its style was very rigid. No wonder, therefore, that the conservative English were not impressed by the uninhibited, natural way Haines skated, with even his 'unemployed' arm and leg playing a prominent part. Skating had graduated from a mere drill to a dance. It was not surprising that Haines' performance actually shocked Londoners. They condemned it as being much too fanciful and theatrical.

But on the continent, the enthusiasm Haines aroused knew no bounds. His trip became a triumphant tour. People acclaimed him with frenzy. Vienna, the musical city, most of all took him to heart. Children were christened with his name and ice rinks were called after him.

He never tired of presenting new features, always appearing on his own. To add to the attraction of his entertainment he donned every type of costume. He danced on skates as a fairy prince, or disguised as a lady or a polar bear.

Then, because of failing health, his career came to a sudden end. He retired to Finland where, when only thirty-nine years old, he died in 1879. 'The American Skating King' reads the simple but telling inscription on the stone over his grave. His death did not stop the revolution he had wrought in skating. The rigid British school was now replaced by the scintillating, lively method he had pioneered and which, still the basis of all modern figure skating, has been known ever since as the international style.

Amateurs were still those most prominent in the sport, whether in figure or speed skating. This was changed when Sonja Henie, the 'Norwegian doll' (who had been the first in history to win three Olympic championships) turned professional. By her supreme art on the ice she captured the public's imagination and gave skating a completely new aspect, making it a spectacle second to none and drawing enormous crowds. 'To skate like Sonja Henie' became a world-wide endeavour.

No one should imagine that her rise was easily achieved. Her father 'put her on the ice' at the age of seven and a minimum of eight hours' practice soon became her daily routine. This she continued throughout life. She had every justification therefore to point out in a reply to one of the countless letters she received in later years, soliciting financial support, that had the supplicant worked eight hours a day from the age of seven, prosperity would not have eluded him.

She was one of the few fortunates on earth who always could do what they wanted. Her hobby became her work. In her autobiographical *Wings on My Feet*, she wrote: 'All my life I have wanted to skate and all my life I have skated.'

It is interesting to know that Sonja Henie was the first to introduce the mini-skirt. She did this in 1924 for professional reasons. In the beginning people were shocked, but soon other skaters copied her, realizing the freedom of movement the abbreviated skirt gave.

Skating's final and greatest advance was the modern invention of artificial freezing, first used for the purpose of food refrigeration. This led to the creation of indoor rinks and enabled lovers of skating both as a sport and a spectacle to pursue and watch it on ice rinks everywhere and at all times, no matter what the climate.

The first mechanically refrigerated ice rink was London's Glaciarium, opened in 1876. Constructed in a permanent building, it contained special galleries for spectators and its walls were decorated by a French artist with Swiss alpine and forest scenes. The first artificially frozen rink in the United States was installed in the old Madison Square Garden, New York City, in 1879, and covered an area of 6000 square feet.

Coming down from antiquity and born of necessity, skating has truly conquered the world as a sport and an art. Some of the world's great writers enjoyed and extolled it. William Wordsworth was an ardent skater who is said always to have been the first on the ice and to have been so expert in its art that he could cut his name with skates. Goethe also was a passionate skater. Time spent in its pursuit, he wrote, was never wasted. Skating was not only a magnificent aid to him in producing poetic inspiration but, he was convinced, was most suitable for each and every one 'to keep off stagnant old age'. This 'poetry in motion', he firmly believed, caused 'an awakening of noble thoughts'.

Chapter 23

JAI ALAI (*Pelota*)

Jai alai, pronounced high-a-lie, is Basque, meaning 'a jolly feast' and is one ot the fastest and most vigorous games in the world.

Opinions still differ as to its origin. Some suggest that it is an ancient sport, first devised in Central America by the early Mayas and Aztecs. When Cortez conquered their country in 1519, he watched jai alai played there and carried the idea back to Spain.

Others, however, feel that credit for initiating the game lies with the Basque people of northern Spain, whose national sport jai alai still is. Their contests were mostly held as part of public celebrations and were distinguished by great exuberance. That is how they came to call the game itself jai alai — 'a jolly feast'.

From the Basque country jai alai spread to the rest of Spain and southern France, and then further to Cairo, Latin America (where it was adopted first in Cuba in 1900), and even China. It was introduced into the United States at the World's Fair in St Louis in 1904.

The game is related to ancient Greek ball games and, most likely, was carried to the Basque country by the Romans. It was influenced by seventeenth-century hand-ball and is similar to English 'Fives', so called, according to one explanation, after the five fingers of the hand.

The invention of the lively rubber ball added to the excitement of jai alai. The Basques were anxious to enliven play even more and it was with this aim that they developed by trial and error the modern paraphernalia of jai alai.

First of all, there was the ball itself. In Spanish, this is called *pelota* (a little ball — preserved in the English 'pellet'), and Spaniards to this day know the game by this name.

As the ball had to withstand tremendous impact, the rubber type used soon proved completely inadequate and did not take long to disintegrate under the rough treatment it received. The modern jai alai ball, which meets all the demands of the game, is about three quarters the size of a baseball, harder and heavier than a golf ball (weighing about four ounces — 113 g), and much more lively. Its core consists of hand-wound strands of Brazilian rubber. This is enveloped by linen threads and the whole is encased in two wrappings of hardened goatskins.

In early games, players aimed the ball at an ordinary adobe or brick wall. This, too, it was found, could not take the battering for long, nor cause the ball to rebound at the desired high speed. Concrete walls also proved unsatisfactory against the repeated impact of the stone-hard ball. Finally, huge, granite blocks were chosen.

To add to the thrills of the game, two more walls were introduced. First, a side wall was placed at right angles to the existing wall. Then, during the middle of the eighteenth century, a back wall completed the present-day *fronton*, which is the Spanish description of the jai alai court.

Originally, players used their bare hands to throw and catch the ball, but this method was not entirely satisfactory. The hard ball, caught in mid-air at high speed, inflicted excruciating pain to the hand, and to get greater power to propel the ball, some booster device was needed. Players began using a bowl-shaped glove to cushion the impact of the ball, but this certainly did not help to speed the actual throw. For this purpose players tried flat, wooden bats, approximately two feet (60 cm) long, but this combination did not prove ideal either.

Many experiments followed, resulting at last in the curved wicker-work basket used today and known as *cesta*, from the Spanish *cestero*, 'basket'. Its adoption changed the whole game. The 'basket' is three feet (90 cm) long and is firmly fixed to a leather glove worn by the player and secured tightly to his hand by strong tape strapped around the wrist. Instead of batting the ball, players could now catch and return it with tremendous speed.

Betting soon gripped jai alai, at times causing authorities to ban it. Thus, a temporary ban was imposed in Mexico City in 1934. Nowadays, the excitement of watching skilful, quick-moving contestants catching and throwing the ball without stopping is heightened by the bets that may be made as the game progresses, with the odds changing continuously according to the developing score.

Chapter 24

JUDO

With few exceptions, Western man has always acted on the conviction that force must be opposed by force. To his mind, it would be absurd to suggest that victory against a powerful opponent could be attained by gentleness. But this is the very basis of judo.

Judo means 'the gentle way'. It was created by Professor Jigoro Kano, a great Japanese educationist. To teach it, he established his own school in Tokyo in 1882. It came to be known as the Kodokan Institute. Kodokan means 'lecture hall', but Kano defined it as 'a school for the study of the way'. From an initial enrolment of nine pupils it grew into the headquarters of a sport pursued by countless people all over the world.

Judo is one of the few sports of which the origin is known in definite detail. The story of how it started tells of a remarkable man of inexhaustible energy and imaginative initiative, who was concerned not merely with the introduction of a new sport but with man's way of life. While its immediate forerunner was ju-jitsu, the traditions on which Kano based judo—and without which it could have never come into existence—can be traced back.

However well known the origin of judo is, obscure indeed are the beginnings of ju-jitsu, essentially a combat without weapon. While some assert its indigenous Japanese roots, it is commonly believed that its fundamental concepts were brought to the country, like so much of its civilization, from China. One Japanese dictionary even claimed that the Chinese invented the art as a method of torture which, more than 2000 years ago, the Japanese had transformed into a system of self-defence and physical exercise.

Tradition links its invention with religion. Chinese monks of the twelfth century, living in isolation and having to travel desolate roads, had been threatened by brigands' attacks. As they abstained from the use of weapons, they had to learn to defend themselves without them, skilfully developing the art of unarmed combat.

Centuries later, in 1659, a Chinese priest named Chin Gen Pin, coming to Japan, taught the art of 'kicking and striking' (known in China as *kempo*) to three independent warriors. They immediately grasped its value for their own people, and to train them in its practice, they opened three separate schools. To the imported *kempo* methods of combat, they added specific features of their own invention.

However, it is a fact that before the priest's arrival, Japan already knew forms of barehanded fighting although, no doubt, Chin Gen Pin contributed to their evolution by his instruction in kempo.

The earliest account in Japanese lore of an unarmed struggle is contained in the *Ancient Chronicle (Koji-Ki)*. It tells of a mortal combat between two mythical figures in the presence of the Emperor Suinin (29 BC– AD 70). Their fight (in which the loser was kicked to death) combined elements of wrestling with striking at an opponent, and therefore the combat has been claimed as the origin of Japanese wrestling (called sumo), jujitsu, and karate.

That feats of strength determined the course of Japanese history even in the dim distant past, is the tradition of yet another myth contained in the *Chronicle*. It deals with an early occupation of the country by hostile forces. A national hero and his aide called on their leader and demanded their immediate withdrawal.

Surprisingly, the enemy agreed to do so with the proviso, however, that before giving his final decision, he would discuss the matter with his two sons. He consulted both in the presence of the two men. While one son was prepared to leave Japan at once, the second strongly resented any such suggestion. Taunting the patriot, he said that he would settle the argument by force and was about to attack him with a stone. But the patriotic hero did not waver. Standing his ground, and unarmed, he challenged the invader's son to see what he could do, then caught him by his hand and effortlessly threw him to the ground.

That unarmed combat might have originated among men bereft of weapons is an obvious possibility. Such combat must have started with earliest man who, unarmed, had to fight for his survival, and in self-defence developed skills to subdue any adversary with his bare hands, feet, and body.

Myths of many races tell of early grappling matches. A manuscript discovered in a Tibetan monastery spoke of two gods who kept their followers to the right path by the employment of special 'holds'.

Throughout history examples are many of victorious nations prohibiting the defeated foe from owning any armament and from training their people in pursuits of war. Their subjection, it was considered, should be permanent and no opportunity (or temptation) put in their way to free themselves and again change the balance of power, now in the victor's favour.

Equally frequent were attempts on the part of the loser, one way or another, to circumvent such a ban. If swords could not be used, the vanquished trained their men in the handling of mere sticks—with deadly efficiency. When Germany, after World War I, was prevented from rebuilding her air force, nationalists cleverly promoted gliding. People who want to fight will fight, if necessary with their bare hands. The banning of weapons, of whichever kind, will never prevent war.

As early battles were fought not always between the people themselves or their armies, whether mercenary or conscript, but between representative champions of both sides, it sometimes happened that the weapon of one or both was broken or struck out of the hand. Nevertheless, they were expected to continue the contest to the complete submission of one of them. The men had to go on fighting at close range and unarmed. To be prepared for such an emergency became a matter of life and death.

Living in an aggressive world, people, from earliest times, must have often been concerned with their defence. Strong men could always be confident that by sheer force they could tackle any adversary. But not so the physically weak man. Determined to survive in spite of it, he must have looked for ways and means to outwit his opponent. Countless stories are told in which a David struck down a Goliath.

Perhaps worry about his own inadequacy in traditional combat led a frail person of unknown identity to discover a technique in which even the weakest could overcome the strongest. A Japanese tradition to this effect tells of a doctor from Nagasaki who, it suggests, invented ju-jitsu. He had learned the art of unarmed combat in China, but had found that as practised there it demanded great physical exertion. While his mind was preoccupied with the problem, he witnessed a storm and discovered the answer to his question in its effect: a sturdy cherry tree was uprooted and overturned but a nearby willow tree, by yielding to the gale, resisted it and, unharmed, eventually lifted its bent branches to their original height.

Did not nature thus teach man that only by yielding could he survive? Convinced that this principle could create a totally new approach to life, and taking advantage of his knowledge of anatomy, the doctor worked out techniques of defence which were to become ju-jitsu, and taught them at a school which he called 'the heart of the willow'. Irrespective of the historicity of the tale, it became a most favourite metaphor in the demonstration of the power of gentleness: how with skill and balance the weak could overwhelm the strong.

No one really knows which of the various consid-

LLYFRGELL COLEG MENAI LIBRARY

erations and traditions (singly or combined) actually were responsible for the origin of ju-jitsu. However, there is no doubt that its roots go much deeper. Ju-jitsu, with its teaching of unarmed combat, could never have arisen or flourished without Taoism, one of the great, indigenous faiths of the Chinese people which exerted a deep influence on the Eastern mind. It is not accidental that the very name of Taoism indicated 'the way' or 'the path' (*tao*) man is meant to choose, anticipating by thousands of years the description of judo, meaning 'the gentle way'.

The concept of Tao teaches that by following 'the way' man has the power to transform and perfect everything. But only he who is gentle, humble, frugal, and free from egoism can do so. He will realize how the soft overcomes the hard, the weak the strong, and how he who grasps only loses.

It is essential to keep the mind in a state of perfect balance and to follow nature, taking the line of least resistance. Taoism condemns all weapons of war as 'instruments of ill omen'. All man needs do is to yield. Laotse, the founder of Taoism, frequently applied the simile of water. Water is able to adapt itself instantaneously to every circumstance, yet it always seeks the lowest point. Similarly, man must not try to change, but must learn to accept what life offers. Nothing on earth is as weak and yielding as water, but for breaking down the strong it has no equal. Thus, man in his weakness can conquer the mighty. He ought to wait until things happen to him, and then to respond like an echo.

Taoist concepts became part of the Oriental world view, and principal elements of its philosophy reached Japan from China. Their presence in the ideological background of unarmed conflict is conspicuous. Only a society that accepted and was influenced by the basic teachings of Taoism could develop and perfect ju-jitsu.

During the long and turbulent period of internecine struggle in Japan, the feudal lords kept men specially trained to fight their battles. This led to the creation

LLYFRGELL COLEG MENAI LIBRARY

of a class of warriors—the Samurai. They learned to excel in every type of combat—archery, swordsmanship, and grappling without the aid of any weapon, known then as kumiuchi.

Out of kumiuchi ju-jitsu emerged in the sixteenth century as its improved and refined form. It developed the original crude and violent methods of barehanded fighting into a highly effective system of unarmed combat. The fact that superior force could be overcome without use of any weapon and merely by right techniques resulted in the choice of name—ju-jitsu, usually translated as 'the gentle art'. *Ju* is a term for 'soft' or 'yielding' and *jitsu* describes a 'practice', and 'art', and a 'technique'. One story goes that Samurais first adopted ju-jitsu when they were debarred from using their traditional swords, bows, and arrows. To survive, they learned to perfect the 'gentle art'.

Among the numerous techniques evolved were blows with the hands and kicks with the feet, thrusts, choking, the bending and twisting of arms, and the throwing of the opponent on to his back and keeping him immobilized on the ground. Throughout the sixteenth and seventeenth centuries numerous schools were founded. Each specialized in a particular style and acclaimed its superiority in causing pain and fractures, in crippling or killing an adversary. To prevent others from learning the methods, the various schools guarded them jealously, handing them down in secrecy, only to pupils.

There is a suggestion that, initially, not the Samurai but the common man introduced ju-jitsu. In the feudal period he was not permitted to bear arms and no doubt on many occasions had to ward off attacks with his bare hands. However, no matter who first acquired it, training in ju-jitsu, which grew into a masterly and elaborate art, became almost a monopoly of the Samurai class.

It fitted in perfectly with its code of ethics and honour, known as bushido, itself deeply influenced by the austere discipline and character training of Zen Buddhism, which reached Japan from China in the twelfth century. The 'way of military knights' demanded loyalty, sincerity, and rectitude, as much as unflinching courage. It also taught that bravery had to be tempered by benevolence. Among its chivalrous traditions was an early practice never to permit oneself undue advantage over a foe. For instance, should the latter lose his sword, it would be unfair and dishonourable to go on fighting him, armed. The correct thing to do was to cast the sword away and to grapple the opponent hand to hand. To be ready for such an eventuality, both fighters had to be adept in the art. That is how schools of ju-jitsu came to occupy an ever more prominent place in Japanese life.

Ju-jitsu became a most widespread pursuit among the Samurai and its essential secrets were carefully guarded by this warrior caste. In keen rivalry, masters taught their individual styles, evolved scientifically with increasingly more complicated techniques and not rarely including fearsome, cruel, and vicious features.

The opening up of Japan in 1854 to Western thought and civilization brought ju-jitsu into disfavour and disrepute. The Samurai class ceased to exist and, with it, the promoters of ju-jitsu. In the excitement of the adoption of a totally new way of life, Japan went to extremes to belittle and deplore her own traditions and, with the fervour of a convert, to embrace all that was new. The rejection of ju-jitsu was also due in no small measure to the many rough methods it then employed, methods which were a danger to life and limb.

Ju-jitsu would eventually have died out had it not been for one man, Jigoro Kano. As a frail youth, he had taken up many sports and also ju-jitsu, possibly to increase his strength. He studied it under the finest masters who by then lacked pupils. Early on, the story goes, he had discovered how he himself could improve on the methods taught. At one of the schools he joined, he became an easy victim of its star pupil, a sturdy fellow, by far his superior in strength, stature, and weight. Determined nevertheless to tackle him, Kano ingeniously conceived a new ju-jitsu technique with which he was able to defeat the hitherto invincible opponent.

Possibly encouraged by the feat, he continued to explore the large field of martial, unarmed combat tradition. In doing so he realized the great loss it would mean should ju-jitsu disappear altogether, although he also was convinced that it needed a completely new image and purpose. He elaborated, adapted, and synthesized the best features of all schools, wisely eliminating all those elements which were crude, cruel, and dangerous.

With scientific acumen, he created a completely novel style and transformed what had been a way of fighting into a fine sport. He called it judo, 'the gentle (or yielding) way'. This was not a new term. It had been used for one of the many methods of ju-jitsu, although of a different kind. The choice was deliberate. The inclusion in the name of the word *do* (pronounced dough) had deep significance. From the beginning, Kano wished to make clear that his new system, not being a combative art, was yet more than physical exercise. It was meant to be 'a path to perfection' for the entire man, embracing his body, mind, and spirit. Judo was not only to be practised 'on the mat', but as a way of life. Its fundamental principle was to obtain maximum efficiency in the use of the mind and the body, with minimum effort. The practice of non-resistance—yielding, ultimately to conquer—was merely one of judo's applications.

Quite possibly, too, there was another reason that prompted Kano to give a new designation to what was after all an outgrowth of ju-jitsu. The term ju-jitsu, through abuse, had acquired a low and unworthy connotation, and he knew that anything practised under its name, however different, would be rejected by the mass of the people.

At the time, Kano lived in the compound of the Eishoji Temple and in 1882 (he was then twenty-three years old) he opened his first school in its living room. It provided ten mats. Even in his wildest dreams he could not have guessed that from this simple cradle in a Buddhist shrine would grow a sport of worldwide dimensions. In fact, Kano initially had a hard struggle to keep his 'institute' open and provide his few pupils with sustenance. Lacking funds, he was forced to raise them by working at English translations first thing in the morning and late at night.

People continued to resist his idea. They would have by far preferred to see ju-jitsu in any form (or under any name) never revived. When at first Kano taught his new method, he had to camouflage his class by pretending that the pupils attending it were taking a course in English literature. But Kano persisted and, believing in the supreme value of the new sport, was able to inspire his students with his infectious enthusiasm.

Four years after the establishment of the school, a public match between judo and ju-jitsu experts proved the irrefutable superiority of 'the gentle way' over 'the gentle art'. It was a decisive victory which led to the recognition of judo as an outstanding art.

The government realized its tremendous value in the training of the nation and put Kano in charge of the country's physical education at schools. He made judo an obligatory part of their syllabus. His enthusiasm and perseverance had been worthwhile. However, to reserve judo for Japan was wrong. With almost missionary zeal and with organizational talent, Kano gave practical demonstrations in other countries. On a visit to the United States one of his pupils gave a display at the White House in Washington and inspired in President Theodore Roosevelt a love of the sport.

In recognition of his work, Kano, the creator of judo, became in 1909 the first Japanese to be elected a member of the International Olympic Committee. Unquestionably he had given the world a new sport of great potential benefit.

Perhaps even more significant to the present-day world than its throws, locks, and holds, is the message contained in some of its basic principles. In an epoch of specialization it calls on everyone to be concerned with the entire man: not only his muscles but his intellect and spirit as well. In a permissive age it stresses the essential need for self-discipline and self-control. In an era in which brutal force (or its threat) plays such a significant role, it suggests that the better way to meet and master the problems of the world and of life is the gentle way.

Chapter 25

KARATE

Karate means 'empty hand'. Its name highlights its principal feature: the hand holds no weapon, not even a stone. With sumo, ju-jitsu, and judo, it shares the origin and traditions of weaponless combat. Yet is is vastly different.

Karate is the most outstanding example of how the total ban on weapons led to the introduction of a deadly system of unarmed fighting. Its practice was conceived in deadly earnest for the defence of life and was never intended to become a sport.

Karate was developed early in the seventeenth century in Okinawa, the main island of the Ryukyu group, approximately half way between China and Japan. The circumstances of its birth were expressive of man's undying will not to submit to an enemy, and his irrepressible longing for freedom.

Okinawa had been invaded once again by a most powerful and tyrannical enemy, the Satsuma clan of Japan. To ensure the complete subjugation of the conquered people, the possession of arms was made a capital offence. However, determined to liberate their country and cast out the invader, the islanders took up training their men clandestinely. As they could not use arms of any kind, they employed a unique, secret weapon, so secret that no search party could ever detect it—an empty hand.

Through necessity they discovered that nature had provided them with a potentially most lethal weapon:

their own bodies. By arduous training the fists, elbows, knees, and feet could be developed to such a degree that with the application of proper methods the islanders could maim, smash, and kill any opponent by aiming blows from a safe distance at the most vunerable parts of his body (such as the throat, groin, or temples). That is how karate was created. It was called, briefly, *te*— 'hand'.

Of course, all training had to be done surreptitiously: i:1 the early hours of the morning and under cover of dark, late at night. Only those known to be loyal patriots were allowed to join the force. The circumstances were such that the existence of the underground groups with their newly developed fighting techniques could not be divulged. For that reason early records of the practice of karate are lacking.

Few if any ideas, institutions, and pursuits in life are 'original'. Mostly, they are evolved from earlier concepts and, by adaptation, transformed into something completely new. This was true of the new art of karate. Though developed in Okinawa, its principles were not indigenous to the island but had found their way there from China in the form of kempo and Shaolin boxing. Even these had grown out of other systems that preceded them, going back, step by step, almost to the beginning of history.

Archaeological discoveries and extant pictures supply evidence of the early existence of barehanded combat in Egypt and Mesopotamia. The Greeks 'perfected' the art in the Pancration which—for some time—they made part of the Olympic Games. The Pancration (Greek for 'all powerful') was a most vicious and dangerous contest in which the entire body served as a weapon. The fighters used methods of boxing and wrestling; they hit, strangled, and twisted the limbs of the opponent. To kick the other man in the stomach or to break his fingers was fair. Only gouging and biting were disallowed. No wonder that, realizing the cruelty of the Pancration, the Greeks eventually omitted it from their programs. However, it was revived in another form by the Romans who developed and transformed its practice and created out of it the modern sport of boxing and wrestling.

On his conquest of the East, Alexander the Great may have introduced features of unarmed combat to India. However, it is also known that this country had mastered the art long before the arrival of the Macedonian king. It belonged to Buddhist religious practice and was considered essential for mental and physical health. Some of the stances and postures of the early statues and pictures of Buddha indeed reveal a striking resemblance to those of modern karate. Not surprisingly, then, Buddhist missionaries, wherever they went, introduced not only their faith but armless combat techniques as well.

Tradition tells that the Indian 'fighting technique' was brought to China in AD 520 by the great mystic Bodhidharma, the founder of Zen Buddhism and China's first Buddhist patriarch. He trained the monks of the Shaolin monastery to excel in it, incorporating breathing methods from yoga and Zen. The proficiency of the monks in the art eventually led to the establishment of a whole school, referred to as 'Shaolin boxing'.

No one really knows who first brought its practice (or that of kempo) to Okinawa some time in the fifteenth or sixteenth century. Maybe it was a traveller from the mainland or Okinawans themselves who, on visits to China, had watched it there. One theory even suggests that in earlier days enemy soldiers had introduced kempo to Okinawa and taught it to the people. No matter who it was, almost providentially it existed on the island when it was needed most to inspire the freedom fighters to evolve from it their only means for survival in the very face of the foe, and for liberating their country from its occupation.

Thus karate, the creation of the Okinawans, became, as it were, their property and, though temporarily forgotten, was practised on the island for centuries. From there it spread—first in the nineteenth century—to Japan where, however, it was firmly established only in the 1920s by the demonstrations of the karate master Gichin

Funakoshi. With refinements and applications of ju-jitsu traditions, it eventually grew from a secret, martial art and lethal method of self-defence into a sport, with competitions and tournaments.

Qualities of humility and self-discipline became an essential requirement of all true karate men. Their ability to perform incredible feats of strength with their 'empty hand' (elbow or knee) is fantastic. They can smash strong brick walls, blocks of ice, and stone. To watch a flawless demonstration of karate can give aesthetic pleasure. Born in China, developed in Okinawa, and refined in Japan, it is now practised everywhere. Although it has become a sport, it is incorporated also in the training of military units and police forces.

Chapter 26

LACROSSE

Lacrosse, the national sport of Canada, is the fastest game on foot. In a peculiar way it links American Indians with Jesuit missionaries, and an ancient war game with a bishop's insignia.

The game's name—obviously French—was chosen by an early cleric who went from France to Canada to convert the natives to Christianity. Some authorities say it all happened in 1705 when Pierre François Xavier de Charlevoix arrived in Quebec and saw Algonquin Indians playing the game.

He named it after the hooked stick with which the Indians tried to catch and propel a ball toward a goal. Because, to his clerically trained mind, the stick looked very much like a bishop's crosier, he called the sport 'la crosse'. Quite correctly, the name was spelled at first in two words. Later, these were joined.

It was a rather strange choice of name, as the game called by the symbol of a faith which preached peace and goodwill toward man was practised originally as an exercise for war and training in close combat.

It has been suggested that the game was adopted from early Norse settlers who brought it to Canada from their home in Iceland. There it was a popular pastime in the ninth century and called *Knattleikr*. The few features known of it through writings certainly show a striking resemblance to the Indian's game.

Among the North American Indians lacrosse was known as *baggataway*. It was a roving battle between up to 500 warriors on either side. Indeed, whoever wished to join in the fray was welcome, though the chiefs tried to keep the rival groups at a roughly equal number. Frequently, whole villages pitted their strength against each other. On some occasions it was a bloody encounter between hostile tribes. The men were almost naked. To get them into a frenzy, squaws followed them up and down the lines, hitting them with stout switches.

At times, the men appeared in full regalia, with feathers adorning the head, and paint the face and body. Goals are said to have been twenty feet (6 m) high and the contest extended over many miles. Though each goal counted only one point, the total of goals scored in one game might exceed one hundred!

The occasion was a solemn religious feature of Indian life, with medicine men taking an active part. They lined up as a living goal and when the spirit moved them, wandered around the field. The goal could thus shift in one game by as much as ten miles.

Each side tried to obtain possession of the ball with a stick, and then to hold the ball and carry it across the goal line. The stick had a loop on one end and, to retain the ball, had also a carved hollow or (at a later date) a rawhide bag or sack.

In the beginning, baggataway was a savage chase, men being seriously injured or even killed. Tripping and fouling were quite common. Men jumped over each other's heads and dashed among the opponents with loud war cries. In fact, anything was permitted to score a goal.

The stick was used not only to catch and propel the ball, which then was made of deerskin stuffed with hair, grass, or plant fibres, but as a weapon with which the players belaboured each other, trying to knock out as many opponents as they could.

On the eve of a match, the men gathered and, throughout the night, engaged in a wild, ceremonial dance. This was a ritual invocation to the Great Spirit—for victory. Meanwhile, four medicine men, chosen to act as umpires, sat apart. They prayed, asking for the gift of impartiality but also tried to foretell the outcome of the contest.

Play usually began at 9 o'clock the next day, when young girls covered the men with tokens of affection, such as beads.

Thousands of spectators crowded along the sidelines, well aware that even they were far from safe. When, in the heat of battle, the ball fell among them, the players, without any qualms, carried the combat among the onlookers, not caring what happened to them. Once the game was over, no one bore a grudge.

Lacrosse is probably the only sport in the world associated with a fearful massacre. The game was used as a stratagem by American Indians to wipe out an entire British garrison on Canadian soil, soon after the Treaty of Paris in which the French ceded Canada to the British.

The Indians hated their new masters. Settlers robbed them of the best soil and decimated their finest forests, while fur traders cheated them.

The Indians awaited an opportunity for revenge. This came at the celebration of the birthday of King George III on 4 June 1763. Pontiac, high chief of the Ottawas, a savage and cunning leader, carefully laid his plans. He conspired with the Ojibways, who had made the king's birthday the occasion for a game of baggataway just outside the British garrison at Fort Michillimack-inac. The Indians pretended that they had specially arranged the match to entertain the soldiers on that happy day, and to honour their king.

According to some, the English had received warning of the plot but did not heed it. In fact, the Indians said they had chosen the field close to the garrison so that there would be no need for the soldiers to leave to watch the play.

At first, the gates of the fort remained closed. However, the soldiers and traders inside got so carried away with the game that to get a closer view, they opened up the fortress and came out, standing around in groups. That was exactly what the Indians had hoped would happen. The garrison lay wide open to them.

The Indians carried only their hooked sticks. Their womenfolk sat quietly on the sidelines wrapped in thick blankets, although it was a warm day. No one suspected their unusual garb. It was assumed that this was their way of dressing.

The game had gone on for about an hour when suddenly, on a signal, the men dropped their sticks and the squaws the blankets under which they had hidden tomahawks. These their men quickly grasped. With piercing war-cries they charged the stronghold, mercilessly cutting down all inside it. Only three men are said to have escaped.

Another version tells how in the apparent heat of the battle—though actually according to a prearranged plan—an Indian threw the ball into the fortress. Thus play was transferred into its precincts and the Indians had occupied it before the British soldiers realized what was happening.

In spite of this unhappy association, lacrosse continued to attract the white settlers, and Indians came to delight in giving displays. As they were playing for spectators, they had to limit the field and introduce some rules. That is how the game slowly changed from a wild affair into a strictly ordered sport, from a roving chase to a game confined to a certain area.

The Europeans were anxious to take up the sport themselves, and records tell of early matches arranged between Indians and French Canadians as far back as the 1840s.

The year 1856 saw the establishment of the Montreal Lacrosse Club. The game gained royal acclaim when in 1861 the Prince of Wales watched an exciting encounter between Indians and Canadians, with twenty-five men on each side.

Dr George W. Beers, a Montreal dentist, has been called 'the father of modern lacrosse'. He was instrumental in the drafting of the first definite rules and—in 1867—encouraged a convention of enthusiasts to form the National Lacrosse Association which drew up a proper code. In the same year Parliament formally adopted lacrosse as the national game of Canada.

The old Indian ball of deerskin stuffed with hair was

replaced by a ball of India-rubber sponge. The stick was improved. Instead of the early rawhide sack, it carried at its end a pocket made of thongs. The number of players was limited to twelve on each side and their exact positions on the field were defined. (It was only in 1933 that the teams were further reduced to ten players, the tenth man being the goal keeper.) Playing time was fixed at two periods of forty-five minutes each. There were to be two small, netted goals about eighty yards (72.80 m) apart. The goal opening had to conform to a definite measurement, eventually six feet (1.80 m) square. A circle around the goal, clearly marked in white, became known as the 'crease'.

Soon lacrosse spread beyond Canada. It was pioneered in the United Stated by the Mohawk Club of Troy, New York, in 1868. Even before that date, French Canadians and Indians had given demonstration matches in France and Britain.

In 1876, Indians and Canadians played at Windsor Castle before Queen Victoria who recorded the event in her *Journal* (the extract having been published in her *Letters*). She wrote on 26 June 1876:

> . . . at five, after having tea, drove with Beatrice and Janie E., below the South Terrace, very near the summer house . . . and I watched a game of la crosse played by a team of 14 Canadians and 13 Iroquois Indians . . . The Indians who had most curious names, came up, headed by their Chief, a very tall man, and read a long address in the Iroquois language . . .
>
> They were strangely painted and some were very dark. They wore coloured feathers on their heads and sorts of 'tricots' like acrobats. I gave both Canadians and Indians, each, one of my signed photographs . . .
>
> The game was very pretty to watch . . . It is played with a ball, and there is much running . . .

Lacrosse became popular in England, especially at some schools, which imported sticks from Canada. The game was modified to serve the new purpose and lost all its original, war-like aspects. It was completely civilized and any type of body contact was strictly banned.

Some headmistresses welcomed the sport as most suitable for education. Dame Frances Dove, when introducing lacrosse at her school, said that she valued it because it

> . . . required qualities of obedience, courage and unselfishness for the sake of the side—a player who attempts to keep the ball instead of passing it, being absolutely useless—and is full of interest on account of the various kinds of skill required, fleetness of foot, quickness of eye, strength of wrist, and a great deal of judgment and knack. . . . The game of lacrosse well played is a beautiful sight, the actions of the players being so full of grace and agility. The skill required moreover, is so great that the attempt to acquire it is a splendid training in courage and perseverance.

The first British club was formed in Glasgow and within a decade, the game spread to other parts of England and Ireland.

North of England played the South in 1877 in a match that resulted in the formation of the Northern and Southern Lacrosse Association. The English Lacrosse Union was established in 1892.

Throughout the years play was tightened up, and pads, gloves, and a headguard adopted to protect the players. The game came to demand more brains than brawn.

A unique feature of lacrosse is the confrontation of the opposing teams before the game. Players face each other at the field's centre. Originally, this line-up enabled officials to inspect equipment. In the early days players often used unauthorized sticks and shoes. Nowadays the purpose of the line-up is to give each player an opportunity to meet his opponent. This, too, symbolizes the maturity of a sport that, in spite of its bellicose and bloodthirsty roots, has grown into a most civilized pastime.

Chapter 27

LAWN BOWLING (*Bowls*)

Today's bowlers, in their distinctive cream outfits and carrying their highly polished woods, now made mostly of plastic, are easily recognizable, and the carefully tended greens on which they play are familiar sights in cities, suburbs, and in country towns.

The game of bowls is possibly yet another of man's earliest and simplest sports, its main requirement being to roll or aim an object at a target lying on the ground. It satisfied, and still does, a human instinct that makes man love to throw and hit things.

That is why the first bowlers amused themselves by rolling a round object (perhaps a coconut, a clay ball, or a stone) toward a chosen mark, probably of the same sort. No elaborate equipment was needed; nature supplied everything.

The origin of the game is still a matter of conjecture. Finds in Egyptian tombs, likenesses on ancient painted and sculptured vases, and diverse artifacts of early ages proved the existence 4000 years ago of a game that consisted of rolling balls or other rounded objects as a pastime at the royal courts. From Egypt the sport spread to ancient Greece and Rome. The Caesars knew some type of the game, calling it *boccie,* a term that still survives in Italy.

The Romans probably introduced bowling to northern Europe, where, as records show, the population enjoyed it in the tenth century. It was another 300 years before England adopted it, but it was there that the modern game was born and became a most favoured pastime, at first among kings and noblemen.

Bowling alleys and courts then were privately owned, usually forming part of a royal, or a gentleman's, garden.

Bowling (some prefer to call it bowls) is one of the oldest British national games. It may well be true that when the Spanish Armada approached the English coast in 1588 Sir Francis Drake, who was just then playing in a match with fellow-officers, refused to stop the game, saying there was plenty of time to 'win the match and beat the Spaniards'.

From the beginning, Englishmen called it bowling, a word going back to the Latin *bulla*, 'a bubble', which referred to a bowl's shape.

It was not because people had become fastidious that they began to describe the sport, more explicitly, as 'lawn bowling', but to differentiate the game from skittles (or nine-pins) which, from early times, as still today in the United States, was also called bowling. This duplication of terms may be rather confusing when investigating the past of both sports, as one can never be quite sure which kind of bowling ancient documents are discussing. They could refer either to bowling at pins, to knock them down, or at a jack on the ground to lay the bowl nearest to it.

In a rudimentary sort of way, the game was played in England as early as the thirteenth century. This is proved by a manuscript of that period, now in possession of the Royal Library at Windsor. It depicts two players aiming not at a jack but at a small cone. Another picture of the same century, however, shows players bowling much the way they do today.

In 1299, *bowles* (as it was then spelled) became so popular in the British Isles that a group of enthusiasts formed the first club in Southampton. As the Southampton Town Bowling Club, it is still in existence and its members play on the original green.

The history of the sport was not all smooth running. It had its many ups and downs. Its very popularity almost became its undoing when the 'common people' took up the game, neglecting other pursuits, especially archery which was so essential for the country's defence.

Another development rendered bowling, in the eyes of responsible governments, even more harmful. Somehow it became a game closely associated with gambling. People played it not so much as a pastime but to place wagers and enrich themselves 'the easy way'.

As in the case of other modern methods of gambling, they were bound to lose large sums of money earned by hard work. In 1579 the greens were described as 'moths that eat up the credit of many idle citizens'. Hunger and penury, it was reported at the time, had come to face the families of those who spent their time bowling and gambling away their money.

To make it worse, most greens were attached to inns as a means of encouraging drinking at these places. Thus the game attracted dissolute persons and led to betting, drunkenness, quarrelling, and even duelling.

That is why edicts, as issued by the governments of Edward III and Richard II, made bowling illegal. Even when the introduction of gunpowder and firearms rendered archery obsolete as a means of national defence, the law was not changed, and an Act of 1511 still forbade the playing of bowls to 'artificers, labourers, apprentices, servants and the like—at any time except Christmas and then only in their master's house and presence'.

Other regulations threatened anyone playing bowls outside his own garden or orchard with a fine of £6.8s. Owners of properties whose annual value exceeded £100 could apply for a licence for a private green. But in 1555 Queen Mary again cancelled the permits as the game had become 'an excuse for unlawful assemblies, conventicles, seditions and conspiracies'.

In spite of the discredit into which the game repeatedly fell, a great number of monarchs and noblemen went on playing bowls. Reports speak of their delight in the game (mostly when getting on in years), the bets they laid, and the money they lost.

That is why, all through that period, opinions differed about the sport, some praising it as the finest pastime,

and others condemning it as the most nefarious form
of gambling.

Royal estates were equipped with beautiful greens on
which to play the game. Though Henry VIII prohibited
the game for the masses, he had a fine alley laid out
at Whitehall, so it is said, to amuse himself between
executions. James I actually advised his son to take up
the game. Charles I was an expert bowler who placed
bets on himself and, on one occasion, lost £1000 to a
merchant. It was only in 1845 that the Gaming Act
legalized bowling for all.

The earliest bowls were made of stone; by 1409, the
bowls were wooden. The sixteenth century brought a
further important change; to make the game more difficult, the bowls were biased in several ways. The most
obvious yet least common method was to insert a piece
of metal in one side. Reports say pewter, brass, lead,
and iron were used for that purpose. Almost from the
very beginning, however, another practice was adopted,
and is still retained. The required bias was produced
by the way in which the bowl was shaped.

This ingenious way of creating the bias, it is believed,
goes back to a game popular in 1477 and known as
half-bowls. It was played with a perfect hemisphere and
fifteen conical pins. Twelve of them were arranged in
a circle, the thirteenth was placed at its centre and the
remaining two at its back. The principle of that game
was to knock down the circle of pins by sending the
bowl around the two pins in the rear. It was the strong
bias of the half-bowl that made the feat possible.

The knowledge of how a half-bowl was pulled sideways
suggested the shaping of the modern, biased, round bowl.
Players soon experienced the extra thrill of its use, the
fact that the bias drew it from the direction in which
it was aimed, challenging their skill.

Yet not everyone accepted the innovation, and some
even opposed it. At a tournament in 1857 it was stipulated that 'no loaded bowls' should be employed. But
when in 1892 the Scottish Bowling Association was
established it introduced a minimum standard of bias

that was generally adopted the following year.

Today, it is a requirement wherever the game is played that all bowls used conform to a minimum bias. They are tested and stamped officially as a sign that they fulfil this condition.

All through the centuries, the development of bowling owes much to the Scots who first played the game in the sixteenth century. Its standardization is mainly due to them. Many of the rules they laid down 300 years ago still remain in the modern game. Most influential of all in the governing of the sport were the laws they framed in 1848-1849 under W. W. Mitchell, one of the greatest bowling authorities the world has known.

Chapter 28

MOTORCYCLE SPEEDWAY RACING

Speedway motorcycle racing, or dirt-track racing, is the second sport (the first being Australian Rules Football) which originated in Australia. It was created quite by chance, not as a sport but as entertainment to fill an unexpected gap in programmed features.

It happened at Maitland, New South Wales, in 1925. 'Johnny' S. Hoskins was presenting a diversity of attractions as part of the Agricultural Show which was then being held on the Agricultural Society's grounds. He suddenly realized that a scheduled number could not be staged. He had to decide quickly what should be substituted.

A couple of young, local motorcyclists told him that they were prepared to fill the gap by racing around the show ground's grassy track. On a trial run, however, they found that the surface was much too slippery and caused their bikes to skid dangerously. A firmer course was needed to give the tyres a better grip. A nearby slag-heap was the solution to the problem. Losing no time, the cyclists covered the track with a coat of cinders and all was ready for the world's first dirt-track race on a short circuit.

It was an immediate success. A new sport had been born of an emergency, just one more of the odd coincidences which have enriched life in so many ways. Hoskins certainly realized at once the great potential of the new sport. A man of initiative and drive, he did not let grass grow under his feet on the new cinder track.

At first, dirt-track races were included as novelty events at Sydney's Speedway Royal. The first permanent dirt-track was laid in 1926 at the Sydney Show Ground. Speedway racing soon spread throughout Australia— and far beyond. In 1928 Hoskins himself and A. J. Hunting, a Queenslander, went to England with their teams to establish the sport there and become its successful promoters.

It was yet another mere chance that provided the new sport with one of its finest early exponents who greatly helped to put dirt-track racing on the map of Australia and other countries. He is Lionel Van Praag.

A Sydney-born tailor's son, the world of motor racing soon dubbed him 'the Flying Dutchman' because of his Dutch-sounding name. Motorcycles were his passion. His father did not stand in his way, and without much resistance he agreed to lend his sixteen-year-old son the £50 with which Lionel acquired his first machine. It was an old touring motor bike that he duly 'souped up'. He repaid the loan after his first race, having won a prize large enough even to keep some pocket money for himself.

He went to the speedway, mixing with the riders and befriending them. At the time, Johnny Hoskins offered a special opportunity for adventurous youths. They had to run a hundred yards, then grab a machine, race it to a bucket of flour out of which they had to pick an apple with their teeth, jump back on the cycle, and dash on to deposit the apple in a bin further away. Lionel won the race without much effort.

He took up dirt-track racing seriously, making it his career. Soon he became champion, establishing outstanding records on numerous tracks. Well aware that only a perfectly geared machine could attain victory, he started his own, well-equipped workshop. There he not only carried out all repairs himself, but continually experimented, evolving new, specialized equipment.

The world's first dirt-track championship was held in Wembley, London, in 1936, and was won by Van Praag, the 'master of the cinders', in the presence of 75,000 spectators.

Australian-born speedway racing now has become a spectacular sporting feature in almost every country, with many exciting variations.

Chapter 29

MOUNTAINEERING

Sports are many and diverse. Attempts have been made at various times to classify them. Such groups of specific types differentiated, for instance, between conquest and contest sports, sports pursued singly and in teams, spontaneous and organized sports.

Roger Caillois in a study, *The Structure and Classification of Games,* separated competitive sports from games of chance and pretence, and games 'in which people have deliberately sought out the confusion that a slight giddiness provokes'. He included in the latter class mountaineering—a rather strange explanation of man's love of scaling heights.

At first, mountains were feared and looked upon with awe, if not superstitious dread. Their height, vastness, and remoteness made people shun them. The clouds that enveloped the summit, the mist that shrouded the foothills, the sound of howling wind and the crash of falling rock puzzled and frightened man who, in his imagination, peopled mountain peaks with divine and demonic powers. Typical was Lot's remark when, reluctant to leave the cities of the plain, he declared: 'I cannot escape to the mountain lest evil overtake me and I die.' (Genesis XIX:19)

Mountains were avoided as a stronghold of evil spirits or, as the summit was so close to the sky, as the seat of gods. The fear was universal and applied to the heights of Olympus, Fuji, Everest, and Sinai. The mighty mountain ranges were regarded as a God-made barrier that man must not penetrate and as a defence against hostile forces.

In the Bible there is a close association of mountains with the great moments of revelation, with the early history of the Hebrews, and with the life and death of Elijah and Christ.

Mountains were considered the realm of God, where men could commune with the divine. Their towering elevation could serve as a platform from which to view a country or look out towards the distant horizon. Moses ascended Mount Sinai to receive on its summit—all alone with God—the Ten Commandments. From Mount Nebo he was permitted to see the expanse of the Promised Land he himself could not enter. Solomon built the Temple on the lofty hill of Mount Zion. On Mount Carmel Elijah proved the supremacy of monotheistic faith over the idol worship of Baal. And from the same mountain his servant saw the little cloud—'as small as a man's hand'—approach from the Mediterranean, heralding rain and thereby ending an almost catastrophic drought.

The New Testament tells of the mountains of Temptation and Transfiguration, Jesus' 'Sermon on the Mount', and his crucifixion on Mount Calvary.

The Bible used the mountain as a symbol of everlastingness, of stability, of difficult and dangerous paths in life, and of insurmountable obstacles.

The earliest attempts at climbing mountains certainly were far removed from sport.

The Greek philosopher Empedocles, a follower of Pythagoras, is said to have ascended Mount Etna (10,880 feet—3264 m) in 433 BC merely to throw himself into its crater, so that by his sudden disappearance people would think he was a god. But his plan went awry. The fiery mountain spewed out one of his bronzed sandals, thereby showing that he had been swallowed up and had not been raised to divine status! Another version of the legend tells that Empedocles actually had hoped to survive and therby prove his immortality. However, in anger, the gods had punished him by causing the vulcano's flames to consume his body.

The Roman Emperor Trajan and the Macedonian King Philip V climbed mountains. They did so solely for national and military reasons: to survey territory and devise strategy.

When, many centuries later (in 1335), the Italian poet Petrarch read of Philip's mountaineering, he was so inspired by the account that he decided, out of curiosity, to repeat the feat near his retreat at Vaucluse in the French Maritime Alps. The breathtaking view and the rarity of the air (on a 6430-foot-high—1929 m—peak) dazed him, and in sublime elation he related how the experience made him raise his soul, 'as I had done my body', to higher planes.

Immediately on his return he wrote to his spiritual adviser in a mood of exaltation: 'I have this day ascended the highest mountain in this district for the purpose of seeing the remarkable altitude of the place.' He also spoke of the moral lesson the climb had taught him: 'How steadily must we labour to put under our feet, not a speck of elevated earth but the appetites of our terrestial impulses.' To him, the ascent indeed had proved to be, as it were, a sermon in mountains.

Another difficult climb was the first ascent of Mt Aiguille, near Grenoble, carried out in 1492 by order of King Charles VIII. The very fact that it was done not voluntarily but by royal command disqualifies it from being considered sport.

Apart from these occasional feats of mountaineering, for many centuries people continued to shun mountains and did so out of fear or mere indifference. Some still regarded the forbidding heights as realms of supernatural danger, shrouded not only in clouds but in mystery. God (or the gods) had created them, it was firmly believed, not to be ascended by man, but to be left alone as a divine domain.

However, a more enlightened faith eventually made man take up climbing. He did so not yet for its own sake but to challenge and destroy the taboos and out-dated notions as well as to foster research and to experience the beauty of nature in its most sublime and unspoilt form.

The first such ascent of a mountain—in the Swiss Alps—was made in 1387 by six clergymen. A legend told how, by condemning and crucifying Christ, Pontius Pilate had angered the Roman Emperor Tiberius Caesar. Recalled to Rome, Pilate was imprisoned and sentenced to death. But he anticipated the execution by taking his own life.

This, of course, greatly displeased the emperor who, to save face, pointed out that suicide was the most humiliating kind of death. To show his contempt for Pilate even posthumously, he had his body, weighted down with heavy stones, thrown into the river Tiber. However, this scheme too did not go according to Caesar's plan. The evil spirits living in the river were so exuberant at gaining the company of so bad a man that they stirred up a tempest.

Panic-stricken, the emperor commanded that the body be immediately removed from the Tiber, this time to be cast into the Rhône—far away, but with almost identical result. The local demons' boisterous celebration at having Pilate in their midst frightened the population so much that, before any harm could be done, they retrieved his body from the water and sent it on to Lausanne.

Aware of previous happenings, the Lausanne citizens apprehending trouble for themselves, had the unwelcome body carried all the way up a steep mountain, to be dropped, near its summit, into a marshy lake...

Ever since, people were warned against climbing this mountain which, appropriately, was called after Pilate himself—Pilatus. (In reality, the name has no connection with Pontius Pilate but is derived from *mons pileatus*—'the cloud-capped mountain'.)

Tradition further relates that once every year Pilate was permitted to leave the lake and, wrapped in a scarlet cloak, to relax on a rock. Anyone unfortunate enough to catch sight of him on the occasion was doomed to die within the year. As no one knew the exact date of

Pilate's annual resurrection from his watery grave, it was wise to shun the mountain at all times. If, nevertheless, people dared to climb it, they were never to throw a stone into the lake, as this would rouse Pilate's anger who, in revenge, would stir up tempestuous winds and appear in the neighbouring city of Lucerne on the next Good Friday.

People firmly believed this story. Even the local government acted on the superstition and, to avoid any possible disaster, banned all ascents under threat of punishment.

In spite of it, six ecclesiastics defied the order. They were determined once and for all to destroy the superstitious fear that had kept people in dread for so long a time. They climbed Mt Pilatus and, as they had expected, their venture caused neither tempests nor an avalanche, but only their own imprisonment by the orthodox government of Lucerne. It was a price well worth paying as, after all, they had succeeded in their fight against obscurantism. In their mission, they also became pioneers of mountaineering.

Almost 150 years later (in 1518) yet another minister of religion (of the Reformed Church) and three friends repeated the feat. They even hurled stones into the lake. Apart from temporary ripples, their action roused neither Pilate nor demons. However, the stones killed the last vestiges of superstition linked with the mountain.

Extensive records exist of the history-making mountaineering efforts of two Swiss professors in the middle of the sixteenth century. Their motivation was primarily scientific research.

Professor Conrad Gesner of Zurich was an eminent naturalist who, to further his botanical studies, ascended the nearby Alps. It was an experience he never forgot and which, in fact, spurred him to further exploits. In a letter to a friend in 1541 he spoke of his resolution 'so long as God grants me life, to climb mountains every year, or at least one . . . partly for botanical observation, partly for the proper exercise of the body and the delight of the mind'.

Indeed, Gesner was among the first to realize and

express in so many words the joys and gratification mountaineering could give by gaining new knowledge, invigorating the body, and exhilarating the spirit: 'What must be pleasure, think you . . . to gaze upon the huge mountain masses and, as it were, lift one's head into the clouds? The mind is strangely agitated by the amazing heights and carried away to a contemplation of the great Architect of the Universe.' It was equally wonderful after the climb to recall all its toil and its dangers and to talk of them to one's friends.

Professor Josias Simler, Gesner's successor, continued his predecessor's scientific work as well as his exploration of the mountains. His was the first book ever to be published (in 1574) on the Alps, and his *Commentary* included the first practical advice 'concerning the difficulties of alpine travel and the means by which they may be overcome'. In fact, it is the earliest treatise on the craft of mountaineering. It recorded the experience of crossing glaciers and the use of ropes, the *Alpenstock,* and darkened glasses to protect the eyes against snow blindness. Simler was also the first to mention climbing boots which 'resembling the shoes of horses, with three sharp spikes', enabled mountaineers to counteract the slipperiness of the ice and to stand firmly.

No doubt, the professors' example and enthusiasm inspired their students to take up the craft. They formed themselves into a mountaineering group, adopting the sound ideas explained in their teacher's *Commentary.*

None of those climbing the mountains, for whatever reason, could fail to acquire a love and a longing for mountaineering for its own sake. That is how, eventually, mountaineering became a sport—undertaken just for the love of it.

At first, of course, attempts at conquering peaks were very sporadic. No mountain was then viewed with greater awe than Mont Blanc. In 1760, Horace Benedict de Saussure, a naturalist and physicist of Geneva, offered a reward to the first man to conquer its summit. As no one came forward to make an attempt, he renewed the offer two years later. However, it was only in 1786 that Michel Gabriel Paccard, a country doctor and hunter from Chamonix, succeeded in climbing Mont Blanc. His feat became one of the most important events in the history of mountaineering and led to its becoming a vogue.

The ablest of men took it up, sharing Dr Paccards' view that 'the desire of ascending the highest part of remarkably elevated land is so natural to every man'. What had been an exotic pastime gradually grew into a recognized sport followed without any ulterior motive, not as a means to an end, but for itself alone. The Jungfrau was climbed in 1811 and the Wetterhorn in 1854 by Mr (later Sir) Alfred Wills, a climb which, it is generally held, inaugurated the Golden Age of British mountaineering.

The foundation of the Alpine Club in London in 1857 was the beginning of modern, organized mountaineering. The club's expressed aim was 'the promotion of good fellowship among mountaineers, of mountain climbing and exploration throughout the world, and of better knowledge of mountains through literature, science and art'.

It is an interesting observation that the name (like British postage stamps to this day) omits any mention of the country where the club was formed and had its home. To its (English) founders, there was no need to identify its locality. British mountaineers' world renown made, in their mind, such qualification unnecessary. Everyone would know where and whose the Alpine Club was!

An early controversy concerned conditions for joining the club. At first it was proposed that only candidates who could prove to have climbed to the top of a mountain of a minimum height of 13,000 feet (3900 m) were eligible. Other foundation members strongly objected. They reasoned (and had their view adopted) that the most important feature of mountaineering was not the reaching of certain heights, but the effort expended and the difficulties overcome.

The club's first dinner was held on 3 February 1858

at the Thatched House Tavern, St James Street, London, and was attended by fewer than a dozen members. No one then guessed the eminent part the club was to play in the development of the sport. In the words of William Longman, whose publishing firm was to print almost all of the earliest Alpine Club books, 'it certainly never entered the mind of any of its founders to conceive that it would be the parent of fruitful children, some of them more prolific than itself'.

The English example was soon copied in other countries. The Austrian Alpine Club was formed in 1862; the Swiss Alpine Club came into existence in 1863; and in 1878 the Appalachian Mountain Club became the first Alpine Club to be established across the Atlantic.

Meanwhile, the original club had made a decision that was to have a great effect on mountaineering. It was agreed upon 'that members should be invited to send ... a written account of any of their principal expeditions, with a view to the collection of an interesting set of such documents for the general information of the club'. Within less than a year (in 1859) a first volume was published under the title of *Peaks, Passes and Glaciers*. It proved such a success that reprints became necessary almost at once.

An interesting phenomenon is the prominent part played by clergymen in the creation of mountaineering as a sport, and not just to dispel superstitious notions, as the clerics on Mount Pilatus had done. Many of the scientists who climbed the peaks, such as Professor Simler, had taken holy orders. Clerics comprised more than one quarter of the men who enthusiastically answered the circular that suggested the establishment of the Alpine Club. Ministers of religion eagerly made the climbing of mountains their chief recreation. It has been pointed out that, in fact, hardly any of the classical mountaineering feats in the Victorian Age was without some Christian clergy's support or participation.

All this was not accidental but the result of the clash of science and religion at the time, and the very effect of mountaineering. If anything, the scaling of lofty heights produced even greater satisfaction of the mind than the body. It was a spiritual experience that seemed to give a heightened sense of God and thereby to justify the theologians' belief.

Religious men felt, as Wills had done on Wetterhorn: 'the more immediate presence of Him who had reared this tremendous pinnacle.' That is why mountaineering, they were convinced, by its very nature, disproved those who with the new scientific claims tried to eliminate God from the pattern of life and the evolution of the world. It could make man, once again, realize his puniness, putting him—suddenly so self-assured and almost arrogant—back into his proper place, with a deep sense of humility and moral obligation.

One of the pioneer mountaineers thus could write that 'the deeper we penetrate into the *arcana* of nature, so as to discern "the law within the law," the more clearly do we perceive that above and beyond all law rises the supreme will of the Almighty lawgiver'. No wonder, therefore, that clergymen became enthusiastic and devoted mountaineers and contributed an eminent part to the growth of the new craft.

Mountains that had once terrified man had become a powerful magnet, and mountaineering a recognized sport, the severest test of man's courage, endurance, and resourcefulness.

Remarkable feats were performed, and to many a man, to conquer some of the world's highest peaks became a consuming passion. In 1865 Edward Whymper, then twenty-five years old, on his ninth attempt succeeded, with six companions, in assailing the 14,690-foot-high (4407 m) Swiss Matterhorn. Only a few years earlier it had been pronounced unscalable. However, his victory ended in tragedy when, on the descent, the party's rope broke and four of the seven men fell to their death. The disaster brought the Golden Age of mountain climbing to a sudden close.

Inevitably there was a flood of criticism of the new sport which led Queen Victoria to suggest that it should be prohibited by law. But nothing—and no one—could halt its progress in every part of the world.

In 1868 D. W. Freshfield led a first expedition to the Caucasus. In 1880, E. Whymper climbed the Chimborazo in the South American Andes. The Rev. W. S. Green with two Swiss guides made a first attack on the New Zealand Alps in 1882, reaching the top of Mount Cook. In the following year W. W. Graham made a first successful attempt on the heights of the Himalayas, climbing to an altitude of 24,000 feet (7200 m), a record not to be surpassed for twenty-six years. Mt McKinley in Alaska was climbed in 1913.

Their own fear and nature itself were the climbers' opponents; the lonely, wild mountains their arena. Many a time they failed, but never gave up hope that one day they would succeed. During each try the world followed their progress from afar and jubilantly acclaimed the final victory.

The conquest of the world's highest mountain, Mount Everest (29,028 feet—8708.40 m), at 11.30 a.m. on 29 May 1953 by Edmund P. Hillary of New Zealand and his Sherpa guide Tensing, presented the culmination of man's quest to prove himself master against apparently insuperable odds. Hillary and his team's achievement was duly acknowledged by Queen Elizabeth II who made its leader a knight.

Mountaineering has been described as the purest example of a conquest sport. It gave the successful climber a sense of overcoming and a feeling of unsurpassed gratification. He was convinced, in the words of the very title of a mountaineering account, that *Where There's a Will There's a Way.*

George L. Mallory, who lost his life on Everest in 1924, had stated after a successful, earlier climb: 'Have we vanquished an enemy? None but ourselves. Have we gained a success? That word means nothing here ... We have achieved an ultimate satisfaction.'

To the mountaineer, no risk involved was too great. On the contrary, its very existence was the greatest challenge to him and his love of adventure.

People have wondered frequently about the fundamental motivation of climbing—what it was that made man endure almost unbearable hardships and dangers merely to reach a barren peak. Classical is the answer Mallory gave: 'Because it is there.'

Though it began as an independent sport comparatively late and only incidentally, as a byproduct of other pursuits, mountaineering fulfilled one of man's great cravings: to prove himself master and to subdue the earth. With undaunted courage and restless energy the mountaineer learned to assault and conquer, across frightening chasms, peaks of dizzying height.

How different is such pursuit from that of modern, worried man who burdens his life and mind by mountaineering over molehills.

Chapter 30

POLO

The story is told that polo began in India in the early 1860s. To entertain British army officers stationed in the Punjab, horsemen from Manipur gave a display of fancy riding. This included all kinds of tricks, notably hitting a ball with a stick while the rider raced at a gallop.

One of the officers watching was greatly intrigued by the strange game and he asked one of the players what it was. 'Pulu', was the answer. This was a Tibetan word meaning 'ball'. However, linguistically, *pulu* recalled the root of a willow tree out of which the ball was fashioned.

The soldiers, as was to be expected, were anxious to have a go at the game themselves. Improvising sticks, they obtained one of the balls and, racing their horses across a paddock, they enjoyed immensely, as they called it, 'polo'. This pronunciation has been used the world over ever since to describe both the ball and the game of 'hockey on horseback'.

When the officers played it again, they added sports features known to them at home, such as goal posts and lines. This was the beginning of modern polo.

However convincing this story may sound, records prove that polo is one of the most ancient of games and was merely revived by the British in India in the 1860s. It became their favourite pastime, and there is some justification for calling one of their number, Major Sherer, the father of polo in its modern setting.

No one knows exactly where and by whom polo was

first played. Yet thousands of years of tradition testify that it belonged to far-off days, and started in the East. Legend relates that Attila, king of the Huns and 'the scourge of God', had a polo team accompany him on his conquests. The *Arabian Nights* relate that a wise man invented the game for his king, as a cure for leprosy.

The original purpose of playing polo, as was with almost every ancient sport, was to promote the growth of crops and increase the cattle. Polo thus too, began as a fertility rite, and so was especially practised in the spring, to help with magic the forces of reproduction in the perpetual struggle between summer and winter, growth and decay. This was dramatized ritually by two teams, sometimes with more than 1000 people on each side. The ball itself (representing the sun) was the symbol of fertility.

It has been suggested that the earliest polo was played in Egypt where the ritual was practised on foot. Spreading eastwards, it was adopted by the expert Persian horsemen and thus took on its equestrian form. On pictorial evidence, preserved in the British Museum, Persia is now generally considered to be the true birthplace of polo.

Polo soon lost its original religious meaning and became a secular game. The players used a forked instrument, but how it was employed is not certain.

The authorities encouraged the game as it proved most helpful in teaching horsemanship and developing military qualities. For those reasons officers of the Persian army were commanded to take it up. Persians proudly cited as the three elements of the educational system the training of children to tell the truth, the arts of archery, and—riding.

From Persia, the game of 'horse-ball' spread both west, reaching Constantinople and Cairo, and east, as far as China and Japan. The early Japanese players, however, dribbled the ball and used a stick with an oval-shaped racket attachment at the end, instead of a mallet. At first, polo was reserved for royalty and the court.

Historical records abound with interesting facts about

polo. A polo stick was presented to Alexander the Great on (or prior to) his conquest of the East. Some say he received it as a tribute; others have suggested that it was meant to be a warning: he should play with it rather than make war. Firdusi, the great Persian poet who lived in the eleventh century, mentions the popularity of the game at the court of the famous Sultan Mahmud.

The first fatal polo accident is recalled by a monument still standing in a small sidestreet in the bazaar of Lahore, Pakistan. The memorial was erected on the grave of a sultan who died in 1206 after having been injured in a game.

The sixteenth-century Mogul emperor, Akbar the Great, whose wisdom, vigour, and humanity were unsurpassed in the East, has not only been called 'the guardian of mankind' but also 'the patron of polo', which was played regularly at his court. It was through his initiative that the first set of rules was drawn up for 'horse-ball'.

Tradition says that Akbar was an outstanding player who was able both to hit the ball while it was in the air, and before anyone else. However, cynics have suggested that other players deemed it wise to keep out of their ruler's way.

It was in Persia that the rule was introduced that the ball must be struck only at a gallop. At Isfahan there can still be seen ancient, stone goal posts, eight yards (7.28 m) wide and 300 yards (273 m) from each other, measurements that have survived through the centuries.

Because the manner in which polo was played depended on many factors, including the type of horse and saddle available, the lie of the land and the climate, variations of the game inevitably developed.

In olden days, horsemen in the eastern countries used cumbersome saddles with high fronts and backs, placed on heavy quilting. They were much too heavy for small ponies, whose speed and agility were thus impeded. In China, polo was played on mules and donkeys, and accuracy rather than speed was all-important.

The popularity of the sport underwent several ups and downs. There is no doubt that without the British it would have died out altogether. Historical circumstances combined to cause its revival in India in the middle of the last century. In that country the horse was then one of the main means of transportation, and many people owned saddle-horses which were cheap. As a result, polo was popular.

The game was then played without hard-and-fast rules, and there was no restriction on the number of players in a team. Sometimes even stony, hilly village streets served as playing fields. One of the main centres of polo was the state of Rajputana, whose principal city, Jodhpur, has given its name to riding breeches, which properly pronounced, incidentally, should be *jodpoors,* not *judpurrs.*

In the 1850s British planters in Assam began to participate in the local polo games, and in the 1860s British officers who had watched their first polo game were so taken by it that they started playing themselves. They referred to it at first as 'hockey on horseback'.

Meanwhile, in 1859, the first European polo club— the oldest in the world—had been established. Three years later, for the first time since the dissolution of Akbar's empire, polo was played in public at Calcutta. It was then taken up enthusiastically all over India.

Opinions still differ as to who introduced polo into Britain. Some assert that it was a cavalry regiment that had returned from service in India. Others claim that subalterns of the Tenth Hussars, stationed at Aldershot, who had read of the game, were captivated by its description, and decided to try it out themselves.

Certainly the first recorded game in England was played on Hounslow Heath between the regimental teams of the Royal Horse Guards and the Tenth Hussars. The officers rode their chargers and played with hockey sticks and billiard balls. They soon realized that the horses were too big and the balls too heavy. Ponies and willow root balls were imported from India, and the game was then organized on the original Indian pattern.

In 1873 the Hurlingham Club, London, felt that the newly imported 'hockey on horseback' might serve as a welcome change from their then chief sport of pigeon shooting. The club adopted the game and became the headquarters of English polo and the governing body for the British Commonwealth. Within a year it published the first modern code of rules, reducing the number of players in a team from eight to five. The present number, four, was introduced in 1882.

All over the world, countries began to adopt the British pattern of polo, derived from India. As there was no world governing body, several types of polo developed. Just before the outbreak of World War II, England and the United States agreed to unify the polo code and an International Rules Committee was set up for the purpose.

Originally, British officers had seen Indian players ride their small, native horses. Introducing the game into England, the officers had continued the practice of using mounts limited to a height of fourteen hands. As the play grew ever faster, bigger horses with greater stamina were needed. In 1919 the rule restricting their size was abolished. Today, mounts are full-sized thoroughbreds of great value—and yet we continue to speak of them as ponies!

With the growth of the game it became evident that there had to be a true partnership between horse and rider, and rules were drawn up covering the treatment of mounts, even in the stables. Grooms were reminded that 'a pony hates noise and being shouted at', that the pony always objected to a 'bad-tempered master but will appreciate the good attentions of someone who is considerate and understanding'.

Polo balls underwent little change. They continued to be made from willow wood.

Chapter 31

RACQUETS

Racquets (or rackets) is a very young—and remote—relative of tennis. But while tennis can pride itself on a royal ancestry, racquets, developed in the late eighteenth century, is of the lowest of parentage, which may account for the uncertainty about the correct spelling of its name.

It came out of prison (at least, this is generally assumed). However, in spite of its disreputable cradle, racquets became a most fashionable sport and almost the exclusive property of the rich and educated. Its path led from rags to riches.

It all began in the Fleet Gaol of London, where debtors languished, waiting to be summoned before the judge of the insolvents' court. As they were not hardened criminals, they were given liberties denied to other prisoners and were permitted to exercise in the prison yard. As its area was very restricted, the choice of pastime, of course, was limited. To amuse themselves with a ball was the obvious thing for the debtors to do. It has been suggested that as the inmates of the prison were often gentlemen of high standing, they might have thought at first of court tennis which they had enjoyed before incarceration. However, as there was not enough room to run after the ball they improvised a game by batting a ball against one of the walls that confronted them.

The ball they used was exceedingly hard and to return it with the bare palm of the hand was most painful which rather spoiled the fun of the game. To obviate this they ingeniously got hold of a plank, whittled it down at one end to provide a handle, and used the other part as a striking surface. With this rudimentary sort of racket the men began to play the game called after it.

Experts have disputed the origin of the name. Several of their explanations are imaginative, rather than scientific. Racquets, some said, had obtained its name from noise (the 'racket') that used to accompany the sport or the word could be a diminutive of the (torture) rack, since stretching was 'the essence of racquets'. Alternatively, racquets stemmed from an early root that meant to 'dash against'. And rightly so, it was said. Was not the principle of the game to dash a ball against a wall?

However, the true etymology of the word racket, as in tennis, traces it via the French *raquette* to the Arab *rahat,* a colloquial form of *raha*—the palm of the hand, which certainly was the very first (and natural) racket used.

Charles Dickens in his *Pickwick Papers* has given a description of the game as it was practised and watched in the prison. No doubt it was through his authority as a writer that the origin of the pastime was attributed to prisoners of Fleet Gaol.

According to Dickens the area of the yard, in which Mr Pickwick stood, was 'just wide enough to make a good racket court' and 'one side, of course, [was formed] by the wall itself and the other by that portion of the prison which looked (or rather would have looked, but for the wall) towards St Paul's Cathedral ... Sauntering or sitting about, in every possible attitude of listless idleness, were a great number of debtors ... some were shabby, some were smart, many dirty ... a few clean ... Lolling from the windows which commanded a view of this promenade were a number of persons ... looking on at the racket players, or watching boys as they cried the game'.

Many a 'gentleman' thus acquired a liking for racquets during an enforced stay in the Fleet Gaol and it can be said that he was given ample opportunity to perfect himself in the game with the result that, once out prison, he wanted to continue playing, though in different company, what he had learned so well within the four walls of his confinement. However, his dilemma was that he could not excel in it too much, as people otherwise might rightly surmise where he had undergone his training, which was no recommendation. Nevertheless, the first true champion of racquets, Robert MacKay, of London, who won the title in 1820, did not hide the fact that he had learned the art of the game while domiciled in Fleet Street.

Somehow the game fascinated the most respectable circles, and in 1822 it first became part of the sporting activities of English Public Schools, particularly so at famous Harrow, and then at Cambridge University.

Harrow, which was preeminent in the sport, preserves in its records a detailed account of the racquets courts there, and of some of the outstanding games played on them. Originally one of the schoolyards served as a court. The game played there against an old Elizabethan wall presented great difficulty, as there were many wire-covered windows, corbels, and projections of every sort. This certainly gave the finest training and demanded skill and judgement in placing the ball accurately.

Two proper racquets courts were built in 1850 at a cost of £600 and £250 respectively, the money being raised partly by subscription and the rest by a grant from the Governor. Both courts were uncovered and one had only one side wall. Fourteen year later, a new court was added at a cost of £1600, a sum collected by 'Old Harrovians and others'.

Old Boys then tranferred the game to the precincts of their clubs, and a sport that was first pursued in the dingy, dismal exercise yard of a prison attained a social status of the highest degree. The Prince's Club of London built a court as early as 1853 and the Queen's Club did the same in 1888. The earliest important date in the story of racquets refers to the establishment of the Amateur Championship at the Queen's Club.

Racquets grew ever higher in public esteem, especially

when crack cricketers took it up during the winter months. It reached the peak of its popularity in the Victorian Age.

Of course, in its early stages, hardly any definite rules existed. Racquets was played on courts of any size, with or without side walls. Then, to make the game more exciting and exacting, young men introduced ever more intricate rules which demanded more elaborate courts and equipment.

As racquets became more sophisticated it was played within four walls, instead of against a single one, and hazards were added. Eventually, so that the game could be played in all seasons, the court was roofed. This underscored the paradox in the evolution of racquets. Courts at first were in the open air of a well-guarded and enclosed (prison) yard. The moment the game became the aristocrat's property, the play areas were closed in completely, and the primitive, rough outdoor court became a lavish indoor construction of cement, built at enormous expense.

The balls and rackets, too, became costly. They were manufactured with utmost care to give the maximum of satisfaction in this fast and exhausting game. The handmade balls consisted of tightly wound strips of cloth and were leather-covered; and the racket had to be strong enough to take great punishment from the hard ball which travelled at tremendous speed.

Racquets, played in prison and in taverns, in the Public Schools, universities, and clubs of England, next spread to the (then) colonies, particularly so to India, to find its way via Canada to the United States.

Racquets, the child of an English prison, never conquered the world. Yet it made a significant contribution in the history of sport by giving birth to another more compact and less expensive game—namely, squash.

Chapter 32

ROLLER SKATING

Love of one sport created another. That, in short, is the story of the origin of roller skating. Actually, it took almost a hundred years for the child to cut itself completely loose from the apron strings of its mother.

It is traditionally believed that roller skates were invented early in the eighteenth century by an unknown Dutchman. His love of ice skating, a sport highly popular in his country, was so great that he wished to enjoy it all the year round, even in summer. Artificial ice rinks, of course, were then unknown.

His problem, therefore, was how to transfer the art from the slippery ice to firm ground. For this purpose, it was obvious, he had to adapt the ice skates. He did so by fitting large, wooden spools to the wooden strips (or blades) nailed to the skater's shoes, a method which, in retrospect, looks so simple.

Thus, even when the canals were no longer frozen, Dutchmen could still follow their favourite sport in a different version. Instead of sliding over the ice, they rolled along over the gound.

It was soon realized that skating on rollers demanded its special skill and long training. The earliest models of roller skates were cumbersome and crude, and as a result movement was considerably restricted. Further advance of the new sport therefore depended very much on the evolution of the rollers.

Men in various countries took up the challenge and ingeniously constructed new and better types of skates.

First of all, they replaced the original rollers, or spools, with wheels. In not a few cases this device proved inadequate, if not dangerous, as some of the creators learned to their cost.

A typical example was the 'pair of skaites' (as a contemporary writer spells it) built and demonstrated by Joseph Merlin, a Belgian, He was a musical instrument maker, a violinist, and, not least, it seems, a showman. Actually, he is the first man on record to have made roller skates. When he came to England to settle in 1760, he displayed his skates and tried to promote their use by a gimmick which, alas, ended in disaster.

Invited to a fashionable party, he brought his roller skates with him. Mounted on them, he mixed with the dancers, rolling along and playing his violin at the same time. His strange acrobatics, which attracted the attention of all and sundry, had a most unexpected result. Reaching a dangerous speed, Merlin tried to stop or, at least, to change direction. He was unable to do either and smashed head on into a large, gilded mirror valued at £500. As well as the mirror, he broke his priceless violin, and injured himself seriously. Roller skating with Merlin's skates was just not good enough and, certainly, too costly.

Various types of skates were developed, each with some novel idea thought to be an improvement on earlier models. The *Volito*, for instance, used five wheels, arranged in the fashion of the ice skate blade in a straight line. Another kind had only a single wheel. Yet another inventor used copper rolls. But it was a patent taken out in France in 1829 which became the prototype of the modern roller skate.

Sometimes, a sport, a fad, or a product is promoted in the most unexpected way, not by design, but by mere accident. This, indeed, was the case with roller skating. It was used, though surreptiously, in a completely different setting from sport — in the world of art.

In his opera *The Prophet*, composed and first performed in Paris in 1849, Giacomo Meyerbeer included a skating scene. Since ice skates could not be used on stage, the actors and singers used roller skates. The opera surged to success and the skating scene became its most famous part and, inevitably, roller skates a topic of world-wide discussion.

When, in the same year, Paul Taglioni, choreographer and ballet director of the Royal Theatre in Berlin, staged his ballet *The Skaters*, he also had the dancers use roller skates.

However, none of the skates then in existence was satisfactory enough to make roller skating a success as a sport. The models so far produced were difficult to master. In 1863, an American, James L. Plimpton, of New York, at last was able to construct a pair that presented a real advance. With four small boxwood wheels cushioned by rubber pads, it enabled skaters to take due advantage of the force of gravity and keep a right balance and even perform intricate figures.

Nevertheless, as the wooden spools or wheels often split, throwing the skater to the ground, they certainly did not help to popularize the sport. It could not capture mass imagination. Only the introduction of metal wheels with pin bearings, and of casters, enabled men and women not only to roll along smoothly but to work up speed without having to fear a sudden collapse or collision.

Meanwhile, in 1864, another American, Jackson Haines, the famous ballet master who already had promoted ice skating as an art, had taken up roller skating as well. By his supreme performance on wheels (made possible by the substitution of inclined axles for the fixed axle) he opened up completely new vistas for the sport, introducing to it dance movements from ice skating, and spins, jumps, and figures.

A National Skating Association was formed in Britain in 1879 to foster the sport further (early referred to also as 'rinking'), and London's famous Olympic Hall was built as a roller skating rink. Finally, the invention of ball-bearing wheels, patented by L. M. Richardson in 1884, led to a boom. Roller skating swept America almost as a craze, and then spread to Europe. A promoter staged an historical six-day race at new York's Madison Square Garden where the winner covered 1091 miles. At numerous places new rinks were constructed and people realized the great advantage of roller skating: its complete independence from seasons: it could be pursued both indoors and out and, most of all, without the expense of artificial freezing.

However, in England ice skating and roller skating were jointly controlled for nearly a century. The formation of the United States Federation of American Roller Skaters for the first time made the sport totally independent. The Fédération Internationale de Patinage à Roulettes (FIPR) became the world governing body.

Enthusiasts of the sport developed various exciting competitions on roller skates, concentrating either on speed or on grace of movement. The roller derby, introduced by the United States, was a totally new idea, dreamed up by Leo ('Bromo') Seltzer of Chicago. Gaining widest popularity in the late 1940s, it presented one of the roughest and wildest forms of skating competitions, embodying features of wrestling, football, hockey and, in its early stages, even of six-day bicycle races.

Thus an unknown Dutchman's early dream and first crude device, through periods of trial and error, emerged as a pastime and a sport taken up either singly or in exciting rivalry all over the world.

Chapter 33

ROWING

By its very nature, rowing undoubtedly is one of the most exciting of all water sports. Even without research, it is not difficult to picture how it developed ... Primitive man was challenged by water barriers ... rivers became the earliest traffic lanes ... often they were hazardous ... strength, ingenuity, and keen powers of observation were demanded of the oarsmen-ferrymen.

From earliest times in the various parts of the world men learned to build boats. Although dependent on natural resources, they used almost identical methods. Ancient canoes dug out from the mud of river mouths and portrayed on Egyptian bas reliefs and rock engravings prove that boat building was one of the earliest crafts. It is so ancient that similar words for oars and rowing are common to all Indo-European tongues.

Man saw a drifting log and conceived the idea of using it as a means of transportation, perhaps at first by merely sitting astride it. Soon he began to hollow it out with primitive tools or by burning the wood and patiently chiselling away the charcoal. This was the birth of the first dugouts. The smoothing of the exterior of the craft was another step forward, and its proper shaping a final refinement.

Where the felling of trees was too difficult a task, peeled bark supplied another kind of canoe. North American Indians used this type especially, to navigate forest streams. In some of the bark boats the open ends were filled with clay.

In countries that had little timber (such as Egypt), bound bamboo or reeds were used. Skin-boats were probably constructed in the ancient world as a result of an observant and imaginative person having seen a swollen carcass floating down a river. In some still primitive regions, inflated skins are today employed as a unique kind of river craft. The hunter in remote times learned to sew the skins of killed animals into garments and discovered he could use the hides similarly to make canoes.

No matter which way the first boats were shaped, and which material was used, the next obvious step was to propel them by means of a stick or branch of a tree which eventually evolved into the paddle and oar.

When several boats were crossing a stream, or plying their way along it, it was a natural instinct for the men to try to overtake and outdistance one another. To do so, they applied extra power and, by trial and error, went on to improving their craft so as to give it greater speed. This process led at last to boat races, enjoyed not as a hobby by amateurs, but contested for material reasons by professional men engaged in river traffic.

All further development was merely a matter of time. The dimensions of both the boat and the oars, and their shape, were important areas of early research. In southern Europe a type of craft was evolved which came to be known as 'carvel-built'. Its planks were fixed flush, edge to edge, to a framework. Phoenicians, Greeks, and Romans used this kind of boat. In later years, it was revived and its superiority, in speed at least, proven.

Evidence shows that rowing was practised as a sport in classical times. We owe one of the earliest descriptions of rowing to the poet Virgil who, in his masterpiece, *The Aeneid* (completed in 19 BC), vividly pictured boat-races as part of the funeral games arranged by Aeneas for his father Anchises:

> The waiting crews are crowned with poplar wreaths;
> Their naked shoulders glisten, moist with oil.
> Ranged in a row, their arms stretched to the oars,

All tense the starting signal they await.
Together at the trumpet's thrilling blast
Their bent arms churn the water into foam;
The sea gapes open by the oars up-torn;
With shouts and cheers of eager partisans
The woodlands ring, the sheltered beach rolls up
The sound, the hills re-echo with the din.

In exciting detail the poet relates how the Trojans had organized 'a rivalry of naval speed'. One of the boats competing in this early regatta was the *Chimaera*. It was of

Huge bulk, a city scarce so large
With Darden rowers in triple bank,
The tiers ascending rank o'er rank.

But their coxswain did not know how to lead them, and when, in the heat of the race, the crew's captain became ever more incensed by the steerman's shortcomings, he flung him out of the boat and himself took charge.

Yet, neither leadership nor stamina finally determined victory in the race, but a god's 'helping hand'. Portunus, protector of ports and harbours, was moved by a fervent prayer from Cloanthus, captain of the *Scylla*. In answer to the supplication the god added his divine power to that of the *Scylla's* rowers and supernaturally pushed the boat onward to victory.

Ancient myth thus reported on an early regatta with its aura of the mysterious and its religious fervour. However, translating Virgil's account into modern concepts, we may say that he tried to show the existence of imponderable factors in any race.

Another tradition tells how Ulysses, on his return to Ithaca, was entertained by the islanders' taking part in a spectacular boat race.

However, such myths and legends apart, it is believed that rowing contests belonged to early Greek festivals, such as the Isthmian and Panathenaean Games.

It did not take long for rowing to become generally adopted for transportation in peace as well as in war. Since it was considered unworthy for free men thus to exert themselves, slaves, criminals, and captured foes were conscripted as oarsmen, especially among the Egyptians and Romans. Often the rowers were chained to their seats, which gave rise to the term 'galley slave'. The number of oarsmen varied according to the size of the boat and could range as high as eighty.

Caesar's legions landed on English soil from oar-propelled boats. The Britons, paddling along in their coracles, were no match for the Roman triremes with their three banks of oars. Indeed, the Britons were helpless against the invaders' far superior boats.

It was from their Roman conquerors that the Britons eventually learned the art of rowing. However, instead of using forced labour, they hired men for the task and their boats often were constructed small enough to need only one or two men to operate them.

Wherever it was feasible, boats became an essential means of conveyance for both people and goods. Yet it took many years — in fact not until the beginning of the eighteenth century — for rowing to be revived as a sport. Credit for this goes, as in the case of so many other athletic contests, to the English people, among whom rowing developed at first almost haphazardly and then by natural evolution. It was the English, as well, who first adapted canoes for the specific purpose of racing.

For many centuries rivers were the great natural highways, the Thames the greatest of them all. Bridges were non-existent; boats provided the link from shore to shore. Watermen thus filled a significant place in London's life. At one period their number exceeded 40,000 (in a population of just over six million). As nowadays commuters stand on street footpaths to signal a passing taxi, so wayfarers then from numerous piers used to beckon a bargeman to take them up or down or across the river.

People of social standing, royalty and the wealthy,

had their private boats and employed their own water-men, just as their twentieth-century counterparts were to hire chauffeurs for their private limousines. It was a status symbol to have one's personal waterman. He was liveried in a uniform which gave him an air of distinction.

Members of the nobility whose homes were on the banks of the Thames, 'up the river', almost exclusively made use of barges. These were equipped most luxuriously. In 1454, Sir John Norman, Mayor of London, had his own barge built. It was of impressive dimensions and noble appearance, with silver oars. The Mayoral procession by water to Westminster became an annual festive occasion and attracted large crowds. (It was discontinued only in 1856.)

However, a waterman's life was far from secure. All through the year he had to escape from being 'shang-haied' into the navy, for which he was a most suitable candidate. He was threatened by unemployment during the winter months, when the river was frozen over. No wonder that the coming of 'the great thaw' greatly cheered him, as vividly pictured in verses by an anonymous writer in 1784:

> The Water-men now at all stairs they shall fly.
> 'Next Oars!' — 'Next Sculler!' let this be their cry:
> For now you may see they have changed their notes,
> They pull'd down their tents, and they row in their boats.
> 'Twas the work of the Lord, we may well understand,
> He made mighty rivers as firm as the land.
> > Then let us be thankful, and praise God therefor,
> > For He in good time heard the cry of the Poor.

In spite of its tribulations, a waterman's occupation was much sought after, and an ever increasing demand led many unsuitable individuals to join the ranks of the watermen. These lacked proper skill and training and in many cases were ruffians and persons of low repute. Such newcomers introduced an element of unruliness among bargemen and caused frequent collisions and accidents. During the reign of Henry VIII matters went so out of hand that urgent control measures were needed. For this purpose in 1555, the Watermen's Union was established.

The introductory part of the Act of Parliament that provided for the union to be constituted gives a detailed account of the unfortunate circumstances that necessitated the legislation:

> Whereas heretofor, the lack of good government and due order amongst the wherrymen and watermen, exercising, using and occupying rowing upon the Thames, there have divers misfortunes and mischances happened, and chanced of late years past, to a great number of the King's and Queen's subjects, as well as to the nobility, as to the common people, that have passed and repassed and been carried by water, by reason of the rude, ignorant and unskillful number of watermen, which for the most part have been masterless men and single men, of all kinds of occupations and faculties... and many boys, being of small age, and of little skill... and do for the most part of their time use dicing and carding...

Under the Act, only those registered with the union could offer themselves for service, and unauthorized watermen faced severe terms of imprisonment. The new law also stipulated that anyone seeking employment had first to serve a proper apprenticeship. This also was regulated in every detail. Young men anxious to take up the occupation had to submit to strict rules, extending to their general appearance as well as to their dress, which had to be provided by their master.

Dress had to be simple and inconspicuous, lacking any adornment of silver or silk. The apprentice could wear no rings, nor carry a sword or dagger, but only a knife. Hats were banned within the precincts of the city, and the only headcover allowed was a woollen cap.

Towards the end of the reign of King Henry VIII, more than 3200 watermen had been issued a license, and the number of apprentices was even larger. The new regulations undoubtedly gave the occupation a new

standing and reputation. For a long time watermen
retained their significant position in the life of London.
In a later century — the year 1774 — a poet could
still speak of one such man —

> And did you not hear of a jolly young waterman,
> Who at Blackfriar's Bridge used to ply?
> He feather'd his oars with such skill and dexterity,
> Winning each heart and delighting each eye.
> He look'd so neat and row'd so steadily,
> The maidens all flocked to his boat so readily.
> And he eye'd the young rogues with so charming an
> air,
> That this waterman ne'er was in want of a fare.

Water parties became highlights of royal entertainment.
In fact, tradition has it that, in much later years, Handel
composed his 'Water Music' for one such occasion. Well
known (but often refuted) is the story how he came
to write it. His refusal to settle in the kingdom of Hanover
had incensed George I. To bring about a reconciliation,
one of Handel's friends secretly invited the composer
to join one of the king's water parties, though in a
separate barge, and delight the monarch by writing special airs for this festive event. His boat should follow
so closely that the king should be able to hear every
note.

A newspaper report of the time recorded how thus
a city company's barge was employed 'with fifty instruments of all sorts, who played all the way from Lambeth,
while the barge drove with the tide without rowing'.
It continued to say that 'the finest symphonies, composed
express for this occasion by Mr Hendel' delighted His
Majesty 'so well that he caused it to be played over
three times — going and returning'.

With so many boats plying the river, and the oarsmen
serving different masters, rivalry in oarsmanship grew
quickly, and the rowers strove to prove their superiority.
It may be that it all started with one boat simply trying
to overtake another, but the fact is that races between

watermen soon became a common sight. On some occasions, rich and noble owners themselves took to the oars to engage in a contest. The boats, however, were still not built for racing but for carrying passengers. The seats were fixed and the rowlocks built into the gunwales.

Any crowd likes excitement and the many people along the river banks must have taken a keen interest, as well as sides, in the competitions. It did not take long for them to place bets on their favourite boat. The masters themselves, proud of their watermen, started to offer prizes, among them a new badge and coat. Professional sculling grew from these beginnings, with the rowing matches of later years an inevitable outcome.

Thomas Doggett, a Dublin-born actor (d. 1721), was the first to make an annual event of boat-racing. Tradition has it that he decided to do so on the spur of the moment. He used to enjoy watching impromptu matches between the various oarsmen from the vantage point of the Swan Tavern, an inn on the Thames. One evening, when ready to go home, he could find no bargeman prepared to row him across the river. The tide was too strong, the watermen said as an excuse. However, one young fellow at last came forward and Doggett gladly engaged him. During the trip Doggett learned from the lad that he had only just served his apprenticeship.

Doggett took a liking to this youngest member of the Union and showed his appreciation in the form of a big tip. He also resolved that to encourage such men, he would establish a race for all those 'just out of their time'. On the morning of 1 August of that year (assumed to have been 1715), he put up a poster on London Bridge that announced:

> This being the day of His Majesty's happy accession to the throne, there will be given by Mr. Doggett an Orange Colour Livery with a Badge representing Liberty to be rowed for by six watermen that are out of their time within the year past. They are to row from London Bridge to Chelsea [a distance of 4½ miles]. It will be continued annually on the same day for ever.

The establishment of this historic race for scullers ante-dates the Oxford and Cambridge Universities' annual eight-oared event by more than a hundred years.

Doggett has been described as 'a little, lively and spract man', creative in whatever he did — 'one who borrowed from none though he was imitated by many'. Nothing is remembered of his stagecraft but his name is immortalized in the history of sport by his bequest to those fond of rowing: the Red Ribbon of the River, as it has been called.

In his Last Will and Testament he provided a fund to ensure the regular holding of the race which, ever since, has borne his name, the oldest rowing race in the world still in existence. His wish was that the 'Doggett's Coat and Badge' race should be held annually on 1 August 'for ever', and it has been honoured.

Curiously, he appointed as trustees not the Watermen's Union, which would have seemed the obvious thing to do, but the Fishmongers' Company. At that time the prize to be awarded, apart from the coat and badge, was a sum of money: £10 for the winner and £11 to be shared between those finishing second and third.

Rowing matches for a long time were restricted to 'watermen and persons of the more humble walks of life'. Eventually the great English Public Schools took it up, at first despite the strong disapproval of the authorities. Only at the beginning of the nineteenth century university students conceived the idea of rowing carnivals. They held inter-class regattas, and records show that the earliest college-rowing took place in 1815. The boats were very broad with a gangway along the centre.

It was a foregone conclusion that eventually Oxford and Cambridge would meet. They did so in 1829, at Henley, inaugurating the famous boat-race which almost without interruption has been held annually ever since.

Charles Wordsworth, nephew of the poet, originated the races while a student at Oxford. Previously (in 1827) he had been responsible for the first inter-university cricket match. After having taken up rowing also, and encouraged by the success of the cricket event, he visualized the possibility of arranging a similar competition in rowing. A subsequent correspondence between the two universities resulted, in March 1829, in Cambridge's challenging Oxford 'to row a match at or near London, each in an eight-oared boat during the ensuing Easter vacation'.

The race, the first of its kind, duly took place. The course chosen on the Thames extended from the Hambledon lock to Henley bridge, a distance of two and a quarter miles (3.6 km) against the stream. Oxford won by a hundred yards (91 m) in fourteen and a half minutes.

At first the crews had difficulty in choosing a colour, as the representatives of the various colleges making up each team naturally wished to use their own college colours. Oxford eventually selected dark blue. Cambridge rowed the first race with pink (or scarlet) ties and sashes. However, at the next race they changed their colour to light blue. Why they did so is told in different versions. Some say that it was out of superstition. At the very moment the crews were about to start, a Cambridge man had rushed off and purchased a piece of light blue ribbon in a store nearby. This he attached for luck to the Cambridge boat.

Most famous of all regattas is that at Henley, which started in 1839. It was a colourful occasion, with gay, brightly-coloured uniforms worn by the oarsmen. Henley soon developed into a fashionable social event. The word regatta itself stems from the Italian and was first applied to gondola-races held on the Grand Canal in Venice. It means 'a struggle for mastery'.

The earliest aquatic sport group was the Leander Club. Its actual foundation date is unknown, but it had been firmly established by 1820. It is said to have revived the activities of two earlier clubs, 'The Star' and 'The Arrow'.

All the innovations which led to the advent of the modern racing craft were made in the nineteenth century. The original boats were heavily built and inrigged, meaning that their rowlocks were built into the side of the boat, thereby greatly restricting and impeding the oarsmen's stroke. The first important change was the introduction of the outrigger, which mounted the rowlocks on brackets. Known as early as 1828, it was not until 1844 that Henry Clasper, a well-known Newcastle-on-Tyne boatbuilder, perfected it. The first 'out-rigged' eight in the university race appeared in 1846.

The invention gave a great impetus to racing as it set in motion a whole chain of improvements. A new rowing style was developed. As the outrigger gave oarsmen all the leverage they wanted, it permitted the building of narrow boats. These were lighter, encountered less water resistance, and so were faster. To enable them to carry weight and at the same time maintain buoyancy, the boats had to be lengthened. This gave more room to each man, who had no longer to keep his feet next to or below the seat of the man in front, or come up against his back when reaching forward. All the oarsmen now could use an uninterrupted swing.

The next significant step in the growth of the racing boat was the building by Clasper of the first keelless craft. This had a wholly smooth hull of polished cedar. Oxford used this carvel-built boat for the first time in 1841, instead of the traditional clinker-built (that is with the external planks overlapping like the tiles of a roof). Possibly because of their inexperience with this new type, they lost the race. Certainly, they blamed the new boat for their failure and in the following year again used the clinker design.

Nevertheless, the carvel-boat soon proved its tremendous superiority, It was light and it also greatly reduced friction between water and craft.

Rowing methods were further changed for the better after Matt Taylor's boat had competed at Henley in 1856. Not only did it have the sole keelless hull for its eight rowers but its length had been shortened to fifty-six feet and the broadest beam (or master section) placed well forward, instead of almost midship, as in the older, larger models.

The final, history-making improvement in the sport

came not from England but from the United States. It was the invention of the sliding seat. This had been anticipated in the practice of many oarsmen of greasing or polishing the fixed thwart, enabling them to move more easily back and forth. The first sliding seat was constructed in Chicago in 1857 and used in an American race in 1870. A Mr J. C. Babcock, of the Nassau Boat Club, is said to have been the first to fit the sliding seat in his sculling boat. The earliest of the new seats slid on bone runners, or by means of greased glass or steel grooves or tubes. Eventually, the modern wheels were used exclusively.

As is the case with almost all new inventions, not everybody welcomed the sliding seat. It was described as inelegant and much too noisy. Some people even considered the sight of eight pairs of knees rising simultaneously as uncomely!

Oarsmen competing in the United States were the first Englishmen to see the new seat in use. The story goes that when they returned home and rowed in a race, one of them had his boat fitted with the new seat. He did not tell his rival and won easily. In no time boat builders adopted the invention. Some authorities maintain that the credit for introducing the sliding seat to Britain should go not to the Englishman but to Walter Brown, American champion sculler.

Within less than fifty years a phenomenal growth in the art of rowing had thus taken place. The period witnessed the change from a short, clinker-built, inrigged, keeled boat, with fixed seats, to the design of the modern racing craft: the long, outrigged eight with sliding seats, smooth exterior, and no keel.

Meanwhile, other rowing enthusiasts anxious further to improve its style, approached its problems scientifically. With diagrams and formulae they worked out mathematically ideal methods. Typical was a Swiss mathematician's book published in French under the title *Théorie Complète de la Construction et de la Manoeuvre des Vaisseaux*.

Some concentrated on methods of training. German-born professional strong man Eugene Sandow, whose feats of strength earned him the title of modern Hercules, as an exponent of physical culture, suggested most unorthodox ways. He offered to coach a crew who had never before sat in a boat. They would be permitted to do whatever they liked, without any of the usual training restrictions on eating, drinking, and smoking. All that he would require of them was — under his supervision — a regular, daily, two hours of practice, to gain greater muscular strength.

Steve Fairbairn, an Australian, has become a legendary figure in rowing. His theories revolutionized its style. Previously rowers had assumed that a steady pull with the arms and trunk was essential for speed. Fairbairn taught (and proved by results) that the true basic principle was a powerful thrust of the legs, which gave the greatest possible 'punch' to the start of the stroke. It has been suggested that the adoption of his method by Cambridge enabled it to win an unbroken series of races over Oxford after World War I.

In his exposition of the 'Fairbairn style', he explained, 'I coach for wins, not for show' and then methodically summarized the fundamental rules he had employed in coaching crews and leading them to victory:

> THE A B C OF ROWING
> A is for Action,
>   Which must easily be done,
> B is for Boat,
>   Which smoothly must run.
> C is for Crew,
>   Who together must row.
> D is for Dash,
>   Which makes the boat go.
> E is for Ease,
>   The hallmark of pace.
> F is for Feet, used
>   To make the boat race.
> G is for Gather
>   On your stretcher to strike.

H is for Hand
 To draw as you like.
I is that Idol
 Perfect form ever more.
J is that Joker,
 The "body-form" oar.
K is for Kicking
 The stretcher like Hell.
L is for Listen:
 The boat runs well.
M is the Maxim
 Which lies under all:
  'If you can't do it easy
  You can't do it at all.'
N is for Neatness—
 Not flashiness, nor show.
O is for Oar, which
 You must learn to row.
P is for Poise: the
 Foundation of Time.
Q is for Quickness
 To which you must climb.
R is for Ring
 The bell note sublime.
S is for Spring.
 If elastic, 'twill do.
T is for Timing,
 Must be mechanically true.
U is for Use
 The oar as a friend.
V is for Vigour
 Which to victory will tend.
W is for Water
 One drives with a hit.
X is for Excellence:
 Strive ever for it.
Y is for Years
 Through which you attain
 Perfection by rowing
 Again and again.
Z is for Zebra,
 Whose stripes represented
 By your blade in the water
 Will make you contented.

Chapter 34

SAILING

Long after the era of sailing ships passed, we have continued to speak of the *sailing* of huge ocean liners and even of atomic-powered submarines. This shows not only man's conservatism in his manner of speaking, but equally the significant role that sailing has had in the history of civilization.

Like yachting millennia later, sailing as a pastime and recreation could be classed as a typical example of man's 'natural' sports. It arose almost inevitably out of some of his early essential pursuits: to transport himself (and later, his goods) and to catch fish. How he first began — adventurously — to leave the dry land to move across water can only be guessed, as can be seen in the stories on the origin of how rowing, surfing, and swimming originated.

No doubt man used the first 'boat' on a river, and not on the sea. To get to the other side of the stream, he ferried himself across. In countries such as Egypt where a huge river was the most obvious means of conveyance, either for himself or his chattels, he learned to take advantage of it. There is evidence to show that huge blocks of stone were carried by boat along the Nile for the building of pyramids in 5000 BC.

Possibly before he tried to reach nearby islands, man dared farther out on the water in his battle for survival, in his search for food. When the growth of the soil and the meat of the hunt were insufficient to sustain him, he found that riches were waiting for him out at sea, where thus necessity taught him to fish. He also soon discovered that the denizens of the sea could be found in greater numbers in shoals further out from the coast. To reach them, he might have held on with one hand to a log or, perhaps, to a bundle of reeds. Possibly these were starting points of the raft and the boat.

Always dependent on material near at hand (and his tools), man built his first sailing craft out of reeds, logs, or skins. There were at least four kinds: the dugout canoe, the raft (also developed from a single log), a bundle of reeds (used as a float), and inflated skin 'boats' or coracles. Even catamarans appeared early in the history of man. Two large logs were joined together, side by side. The method is recalled in the catamaran's name which, from the Tamil, is merely a contraction of the two words *kattu* (to 'tie') and *maram* ('wood').

Paintings, drawings, and actual models of ancient boats have been discovered at many excavation sites, including Egyptian tombs. Some most primitive vessels are still employed in isolated parts of the world: for instance, in Polynesian waters, on the Euphrates, and, 13,000 feet (3900 m) above sea level, on the huge South American inland sea, Lake Titicaca in Peru.

The earliest way to propel and steer a boat was by means of a tree branch. From it evolved the punting pole (when the water was shallow), the paddle (for greater depths), and eventually the oar. For a long time no one ever thought to make use of the wind.

Again, it can only be conjectured how the first sail was rigged and what it was that led man to discover that he could harness the wind to carry him across the water. No one knows when and where this happened. Certainly, it took several thousands of years to reach this stage. Most likely, of course, it was not by design but accident that the discovery was made. Possibly, a hide or some reeds joined together, after having been used to catch fish, were hung up on a pole to dry out on the return trip. To his amazement man might then have noticed how, caught in the wind, this primitive 'sail' helped him to propel the boat.

Ingeniously man learned to make sails out of skin, papyrus, and cloth. He hoisted them first on one pole, and then on two or three. These were the original masts. Once he knew how to take advantage of the wind, he realized how this saved him much arduous toil in punting, paddling, and rowing.

We know that Egyptians used sails at least in 4000 BC. Similarly, sails were rigged on Chinese junks and Viking boats in very early years. It was a development, it can be assumed, that occurred not at one place alone, but wherever man ventured on the surface of the water. The first sails were rectangular. Next came the triangular, lateen shape (introduced in the Mediterranean by eighth-century Arabs), to be surpassed by the fore and aft rig, greatly improved by the Dutch. Norsemen poetically called their sail 'the cloak of the wind' and 'the tapestry of the masthead'.

Out of the pursuit of sailing as a means of fishing, commuting, commerce, and warfare, the sport was born naturally. Experiencing the challenge of the wind and the water and all this meant in adventure, excitement, and exhilaration, man must have acquired a love for sailing for its own sake. Boats once used solely for utilitarian purposes, began to serve man for pleasure.

To begin with, and for many centuries, only the high and mighty, royalty and nobility, were able to sail for enjoyment. The ships they used were of the traditional type but reserved (and possibly more luxuriously equipped) for the pastime. These pleasure boats were the forerunners of the yacht.

The Egyptian Pharaohs enjoyed cruising on the waters of the Nile. Its navigation became so important to the country that nautical terms even entered their language. 'To go south' was thus expressed by 'to go upstream'. Most famous of all was Cleopatra's barge, from which the queen watched the battle at Actium. Its sails were of purple silk and its poop was covered with gold. The Viking kings also are thought to have kept pleasure boats.

Sailing as a pastime certainly was known in the British

isles before the advent of the yacht. A 'vessel with purple sails' was the regal gift bestowed in AD 925 by the king of Norway to Athelstan, England's Saxon ruler. King Robert of Scotland is said to have owned his own pleasure craft (in 1326) while Queen Elizabeth I had hers, called the *Rat of Wight*, built at Cowes in 1588. In 1604, Phineas Pett (of the family of renowned English naval architects) constructed at Chatham 'a miniature pleasure ship' for Prince Henry, the eldest son of James I. 'Garnished with painting and carving', the royal family cherished it although inexplicably it bore the ominous name *Disdain.*

Such craft were rare and differed completely from the kind that introduced yachting. These were born in the Netherlands, in the seventeenth century. The Dutch were an outstanding maritime nation, a true sailing race. By the very nature of their country — many of its thoroughfares are waterways — the Dutch had become an amphibious people. They excelled in 'boating' and 'sailing', whether in their own country, on its canals and the Zuider Zee, or in the service of the East India Company. Boats (whether large or small) were not only their most customary means of commuting and transportation, but almost a way of life for them.

Both the word yacht and the sport of yachting come from the Dutch. Possibly, neither would have spread throughout the world without Prince Charles' exile. This shows once again how even misfortune can have its blessings.

The English word yacht is derived from the Dutch *jaght*, meaning 'chase', 'hunt', and 'pursuit'. The word was used in many combinations and not merely in connection with a boat sailing the sea. A *jaght hond*, for instance, was a hunting dog. A hawk was a *jaght vogel*, a hunting bird. A *jaght schip* was thus a hunting boat.

There are several possibilities of how it came to acquire this name. Some believe that it was applied specifically to boats on the Dutch canals that were speeded up by being towed along by horses. Perhaps it was because compared with other boats a *jaght schip* was so much faster — an essential in the hunt. Most likely however is a final explanation that a hunting boat was used at first for the pursuit of marauding pirates and hostile vessels. No doubt it was built not for the transport of cargo, but to give the finest performance in point of speed. No matter what the original connotation, a *jaght schip*, by expansion of its meaning, eventually became a general term for any fast sailing vessel.

Merchants realized that this very same *jaght schip*, so swift in the chase of buccaneers, could serve them as well, and most profitably so, in meeting at sea the large vessels of the East India Company on their homeward voyages. The merchants enjoyed the trips in themselves, so much so that they soon went cruising merely for pleasure, inviting their friends to join them. Sailing became a pastime and 'the thing to do' for the leisured classes. It was a status symbol as much as hunting and horseback riding were in nineteenth-century England.

Almost inevitably, the merchant-yachtsmen began to build and use *jaght schips* for pleasure alone. The frequent use of the name led to its abbreviation. *Schip* was dropped altogether. The remaining *jaght* was finally Anglicized into the present-day yacht.

Highlights of Dutch yachting events of the time were aquatic parades. Vast formations of sailing boats, gaily decorated, advanced in orderly lines. Mock battles climaxed the displays. Descriptive of their type is an account (of a later date) of just such a performance on the occasion of the visit of Peter the Great to Amsterdam in 1697. It tells how 'after the Muscovian Ambassy had seen all that captures the eyes and hearts of foreigners in the famous merchant city ... the worthy Council of the city conceived the idea of presenting to the Ambassy a mock fight, imitating a sea fight, on the river Y'. Notwithstanding the large number of craft participating in the spectacle, it proved an outstanding success so that when at nightfall the battle ended, the visitors 'expressed perfect pleasure at all they had witnessed'.

'Yachting' of that type, indeed, occupied a prominent

place in the life of the Dutch. But, significantly, as a pastime — apart from cruising and parades — it did not include racing of any kind. Nor did the Dutch ever think of forming a yachting club. Both were the great contributions the English made to the sport.

When young Prince Charles fled from England to find temporary refuge in the Netherlands, the country was riding the waves of affluence, and sailing was one of its favoured recreations. The young prince soon took a liking to it and became enthusiastic about those swift boats, so easily manoeuvred and built for so much comfort. No wonder that, at the Restoration of the monarchy, he carried home a love of yachting and established it as a real sport in his kingdom. As if to make sure that the king should never forget the Dutch yachts, the Prince of Orange and the Dutch East India Company presented him with a choice yacht, the *Mary*, which in fact carried him part of the way home, from Breda to Rotterdam. Built in Amsterdam, she was 'beautifully carved and gilded at the stern'. Her keel was fifty-two feet long, her width nineteen feet, and she was manned by a crew of thirty. Samuel Pepys, the future Secretary to the Admiralty, himself went on board this yacht, the first ever to be seen in Britain. In his diary (in the entry for 8 November 1660), he described her as 'one of the finest things that I ever saw for neatness and room in so small a vessel'. Reminiscent of the early military employment of such boats, the *Mary* carried eight guns.

Commissioner Peter Pett who, with Pepys, had inspected the *Mary*, was now called upon (as Pepys also records) 'to make one to outdo [the *Mary*] for the honour of his country', although, as the writer continues, 'I fear he will scarce better'. Taking the Dutch boat as his model Pett built the first yacht ever in England.

In spite of the many new tasks that no doubt occupied the young king's attention on ascending the throne, he did not lose his love of yachting. Just as he introduced into his country many of the customs and refinements he had noted and admired while in exile, he must have been determined to teach his people the admirable qualities of yachting as a recreation. Within less than two years after the Restoration, the young king arranged the first yacht race, against his brother, the Duke of York. Their yachts, called after their wives, *Katherine* and *Anne,* raced on the Thames from Greenwich to Gravesend and back. Writing of the historic event, John Evelyn (another diarist of the time) recalled: 'I sailed this morning with His Majesty in one of his yachts (or pleasure boats), vessels not known among us till the Dutch East India Company presented that curious piece to the King; being very excellent sailing vessels. It was a wager between his other new pleasure-boat, built frigate-like, and one of the Duke of York's — the wager 100 to 1... The King lost it going, the wind being contrary, but saved stakes in returning. There were divers noble persons and Lords on board, His Majesty sometimes steering himself.'

Charles II thus was England's pioneer yachtsman, and as in other sports, the royal example was ardently taken up by the nobles of the land who, by their English predilection for any sport and the additional British love of seafaring, soon learned to develop sailing for pleasure, revolutionizing the original Dutch practice.

The first yacht club in the world was established at Cork, Ireland, in 1720. Originally known as the Water Club of the Harbour of Cork, it was to become the Royal Cork Yacht Club. Some of its rules make odd reading. Apart from introducing fortnightly meetings for sailing and dining during the season, and limiting the number of members to twenty-five, they bestowed on the official steward, who also acted as secretary, the grandiose title of 'The Knight of the Island of Haulbowline', which served as the headquarters of the club. The bylaws further stipulated that no Admiral 'do bring more than two dishes of meat for the members' entertainment' or 'more than two dozen of wine to his treat'. Another rule, initially, banned the wearing of long-tail wigs, large sleeves, or ruffles. Even the talking of shop was restricted; any club member who continued to discuss sailing matters after dinner was liable to be fined, the penalty being a bumper of wine.

A memorable parade of the club's yachting vessels is featured in a 1748 account of *A Tour Through Ireland*, published in London by J. Roberts. It tells of a ceremony 'they have at Cork, very much like that of the Doge of Venice':

> A set of worthy gentlemen, who have formed themselves into a body which they call the 'Water Club', proceed a few leagues out to sea once a year in a number of small vessels, which for painting and gilding exceed the King's yacht at Greenwich and Deptford. Their admiral, who is elected annually and hoists his flag on board his little vessel, leads the van and receives the honours of the flag. The rest of the fleet fall in their proper stations and keep their line in the same manner as the King's ships. The fleet is attended with a prodigious number of boats with their colours flying, drums beating, and trumpets sounding, and forms one of the most agreeable and splendid sights.

Obviously, it was a continuation of the early Dutch tradition, with all its pomp and circumstance.

During the second half of the eighteenth century races began to be sailed frequently in English waters, notably in the Thames estuary. England's first yacht club came into being in 1775 and in honour of its founder and patron, the Duke of Cumberland, was known at first as the Cumberland Fleet. Later it assumed as its new name The Royal Thames Yacht Club.

A notice inserted in the *Advertiser* on 6 June of that year informed the readers that 'a silver cup, the gift of his Royal Highness the Duke of Cumberland' was to be sailed for from Westminster Bridge to Putney Bridge and back 'by Pleasure Sailing Boats, from 2 to 5 tons burthen...' Interested gentlemen were invited to apply for further information.

The inaugural race, the date of which had to be postponed because of bad weather, proved a resounding success. All of the eighteen to twenty contestants agreed to don an aquatic uniform (it was its introduction into yachting). The Duke himself ceremoniously presented the winner, a Mr Parkes, in the *Aurora*, with the trophy which was worth twenty guineas. Earlier, the Duke had drunk Parkes' health in claret from the cup. Mr Parkes duly responded, proposing the health of the Duke and the Duchess to the accompaniment of loud cheers, raucous music, and the booming of guns.

Obviously, yachting at the time was still very much restricted to court circles and the wealthy. It was of great social importance, as the Cork event showed, and linked with much ritual. This was reflected in the early use of a yacht when not engaged in racing. It was defined in a 1771 *Marine Dictionary* as 'a vessel of State, normally employed to convey princes, ambassadors or other great personages from one Kingdom to another'. However, it was merely a matter of time till yachting as a recreation and sport, and without any frills, became the property of all classes and, in cruising and racing, emerged as a truly democratic 'pursuit' in which everything was kept 'shipshape'. No wonder that in modern days Joseph Wechsberg included yachtsmanship in *The Best Things in Life* and regarded a boat as the perfect answer for the man who has everything and wants to get away from everything.

Those tied to the land may see in the sea a great division between people, nations, and continents. To any sailor, inspired by the call of the sea, it is a uniting link, a bond of friendship, a challenge.

THE AMERICA'S CUP

In 1851, only seven years after the foundation of the New York Yacht Club, international yacht racing began with what later came to be known as the America's Cup.

The club's commodore, John C. Stevens, received an invitation from the Earl of Witton, Commodore of the Royal Yacht Squadron, England, to join in a race along a difficult sixty-mile (96 km) course around the Isle of Wight. The immediate occasion was the holding of Britain's Great Exhibition, the first World Fair.

Expressing warmest thanks, Stevens agreed on behalf of his associates 'to avail ourselves of your friendly bidding, and take with a good grace the sound thrashing we are likely to get by venturing our longshore craft on your rough waters'. He added that four or five of his friends were about to launch a schooner that they would like to enter in the race.

This boat was the *America*. She had a low black hull, her bow was 'as sharp as a knife', and her stern 'remarkable broad, wide and full'. In spite of the reservations voiced in the letter, the *America's* builders entertained the most sanguine expectations about her performance. And, 'built to represent a nation', with thirteen men aboard, the *America* duly sailed for England.

She had been modelled after the well-known New York Harbour pilot boats. Of course, the American prediction of defeat by the British, renowned for ruling the waves, made in the original letter of acceptance, had been merely a polite (if not clever) flattery. No forecast could have been further from the mark.

The *America* proved vastly superior and outsailed all of the fifteen contestants, picked vessels of the Royal Yacht Squadron. Apocryphal but telling was the often quoted message said to have been sent by an English signalman to Queen Victoria. Anxiously following the race, she had inquired who was the winner. Supposedly the signal had read: '*America* first, Your Majesty. There is no second.'

The trophy won was The One Hundred Guinea Cup. A typically Victorian, ornate silver ewer, it became a priceless award to be 'preserved as a perpetual Challenge Cup for friendly competition between foreign nations'. Because it was first won by the US schooner *America*, the race and the trophy have been known ever since as the America's Cup.

The triumphant American syndicate who had entered the schooner had one great disappointment. Irrespective of the feelings expressed in the original letter, they themselves had been certain of victory, although they had hoped that it would come as a great surprise to all others.

They had spent an enormous amount of money on the construction of the boat, being convinced that they would more than recoup their outlay in wagers and side bets they expected to be laid on their ship. But, unwisely, the *America,* during her final lap from France to Britain on her trans-Atlantic voyage, had disclosed her mettle. To test the performance of the American challenger, the *Lavrock,* an English cutter of seventy tons and one of the fastest afloat, had sailed from Cowes to meet and to race the visitor. The *Lavrock* had been so easily beaten that even the most adventurous gamblers refrained from placing any bets. In material gain, the *America's* victory thus provided the syndicate with nothing but a mediocre wine jug. (Yet ever since, millions of pounds and dollars have been spent to gain — or retain — it).

Perhaps symbolic was the fact that when finally (in 1857) John C. Stevens (in whose home it had been previously deposited) handed it for safekeeping to the New York Yacht Club, it was fixed firmly by a bolt to an oaken table in the trophy room.

In spite of superlative performances, for 132 years no rival was able to wrest the trophy from its first winner. However, in 1983 Australia achieved the feat and, after a breath-taking race, *Australia II* with its 'mysterious', revolutionary winged keel was the first yacht ever to take the 'Cup' outside the United States.

Many opinions have been proffered on what are the most important requirements for a yacht to win (especially the America's Cup). Philip L. Rhodes, the naval architect, felt that, arranged according to importance, the factors most essential for a yacht to come first in a race were these: the crew (and not least among them the helmsman); the boat's sails, and her hull (in which he included the rig). Sometimes, he added, her owner as well. Rhodes said that, sparing no money, the owner must have the wisdom to leave the conduct of the match completely to those put in charge.

Lacrosse in Canada, 1875

Bowling—from 13th-century manuscript: two small cones placed upright at a distance

Bowling on the terrace, Bramshill, Hants., in the Stuart period
Frank Arthur on his Harley Davidson winning the first Golden Helmet
speedway race at White City in London, 1928

Professor Conrad Gesner of Zurich—an early mountaineering enthusiast

Stick crooking in ancient polo

Skating rink at Prince's Ground, Brompton, 1875

Race for the Doggett Coat and Badge, with a view of the White Swan Inn,
Chelsea (T. Rowlandson)

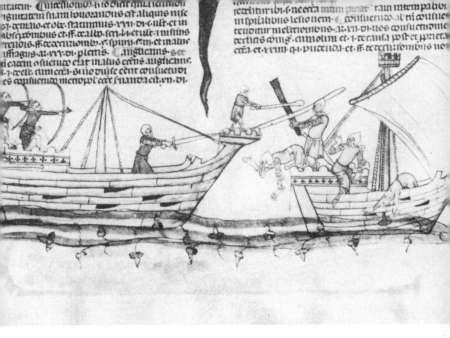

Sailing—from a 14th-century manuscript

Dutch *speeljacht* of the 17th century (S. Savery)

Short and long skis of Lapp skier

Norwegian ski race, 1894

Fives (forerunner of squash), 1878

Surfing, Polynesia, 1831

Assyrian warriors firing on fugitives swimming across a stream (c. 885 BC)
Surfing—pioneers of the life-saving movement, Bondi Life Saving Club, with reel, 1907

Table tennis—V. R. Price *v.* F. W. Last, October 1922

Tennis in 1769—from Diderot's Encyclopaedia

Major Walter Clopton Wingfield, probably the inventor of lawn tennis

Tennis in the time of Henry VII (after A. Forestier)

Dutch aristocracy of the 17th century bowling skittles (Pierre Hooch)

Ten-pin bowling, America, 1890s

Greek racing chariot and horses—from an archaic hydria

Jackey, winner of the Late Aintree Trotting Stakes at Liverpool, 1861

Water polo at Hunter's Quay, Scotland

Water polo match at the Crown Baths, Kennington Oval, 1890

Water Skiing on Lake Ullswater, England

Group of wrestlers from the Egyptian tomb wall painting at Beni Hasan, c. 1900 BC

Old style of Japanese wrestling

Olympic Games, Greece—winner receiving an olive wreath

Members of the international Committee which revived the Olympic Games
(Baron Pierre de Coubertin second from left)
First Olympic Games of the modern series, Athens, 1896

The worldwide pursuit of yachting made its inclusion on the agenda of the first revived Olympic Games in Greece in 1896 almost a foregone conclusion. However, the weather would have none of it, and its inclemency led to the cancellation of the sailing event. It was held during the next meeting, in 1900.

No matter who carries home the 'blue ribbon' of world sailing supremacy or, for that matter, any award in yachting, the true yachtsman, loser or winner, will echo the sentiment once expressed in the paraphrase of the famous tag that 'it is better to have raced and lost, than never to have raced at all'.

The importance of sailing and the part it has played in man's life, are demonstrated by the countless traces it has left, like other sports, in descriptive phrases, idioms, and words. Some are very obvious, others hardly to be recognized.

Coming first to everyone's mind are expressions such as 'plain sailing', 'to sail close to the wind', or 'to take the wind out of one's sails'. We speak of 'riding the crest of a wave', being 'at one's beam's end', 'on the rocks', and 'out of one's depth'. But who would guess that 'to take the gilt off the gingerbread' might have started on boats (and not in their galleys!). Gingerbread cakes used to be made in various forms; often in the shape of men, animals, and birds. Sometimes they were covered with gold leaf and sold at fairs. Eventually, their name came to describe showy and tawdry objects. When in the seventeenth and eighteenth centuries· the sterns of warships were decorated with gilded carvings, these were colloquially referred to as 'gingerbread work'. As this frequently deteriorated because of the water and weather, sailors spoke of 'the gilt being taken off the gingerbread'. And from them, the phrase reached the land...

Even 'to make both ends meet' started at sea — when sailors endeavoured to repair a torn rope. To avoid expensive replacement, they pulled together and spliced its two tangling ends. It certainly took some time 'to know the ropes'! Most likely this phrase also stems from the sailing boat and not, as has been also suggested, from the wise handling of a horse's reins.

Supposedly an acronym, formed of the initial letters of an entire phrase of the maritime world, 'posh' is said to go back to the early days of P & O liners, on the Britain to India run. In order to avoid the burning sun of the Indian Ocean, wealthy passengers reserved for themselves accommodation that was '*P*ort-*O*utward-*S*tarboard-*H*omeward'. Its contraction (on the purser's list) soon came to denote 'posh' travellers, able to afford such luxury.

A combination of the sea, sailors' love of strong drink, and a coarse sort of cloth is the peculiar mixture that supplied grog! The origin of this odd 'cocktail' can be dated to 1740. Some sailors enjoying their generous allowance of neat rum (they received daily a total of half a pint — 0.28 l — in two rations) became raucous, and there were many violent brawls. Admiral Edward Vernon, concerned with naval discipline, was determined to stop such excess. Consequently, he issued an order that henceforth all rum had to be supplied in diluted form. The innovation certainly was not welcomed by the crews who immediately called it by part of the Admiral's nickname — '(Old) Grog'. This had been bestowed on him because of his practice of walking the decks in a cloak made of *grog*ram (from the French *gros grain* — 'coarse grain').

Who would expect even the word 'filibuster' to have been born on the high seas? Yet it is a fact that the word has travelled a long way from the sea before finding its obstructive, delaying function in modern parliamentary procedure. It originated among early pirates who were preying on shipping around the West Indies. These buccaneers were called by the Dutch word *vrijbuiter* (freebooter) which by way of the French *flibustier*, eventually assumed its English version, now completely land-logged and preying merely on politicians' time.

The buccaneer himself, so much once part of the high seas, could be said to have reversed direction, at least in his description. In Haiti, natives largely lived on the cattle and pigs that roamed the island. As salt was in short supply, and therefore costly, they devised their own method of preserving meat. First, they dried it in the sun. Then they smoked it over fire on a wooden grid, known as *boucan*. When the French invaded their country, they soon took over the custom but they also stocked their boats with the dried meat, not only for their own provision but to sell it at a profit. This caused them to be eventually identified with this very meat (or rather the boucan from which it was taken to their ships) and that is how they received as their nickname, buccaneer. As they also, and not least, were pirates, the word finally, far removed from its original meaning, came to refer to any adventurous marauder.

Of course, like other sports, sailing and yachting, too, have created their own vocabularies. Some of their common terms have interesting origins.

The earliest yachts in American waters were either of the sloop or schooner type and, significantly, both names stem from the Dutch. Sloop recalls the *sloepe* rig of seventeenth-century Dutch boats. *Schoon* (like the German *schön*) described anything that was lovely and beautiful. Another school claims that the schooner obtained its name from the word *scoon*, meaning 'to skim' (along the water). The story is told that when the first vessel of its kind had been built by Andrew Robinson at Gloucester, Massachusetts, in 1713, one of the men watching her being launched called out in admiration: 'Oh, how she scoons'. Whereupon Robinson, hearing the remark, decided on the spur of the moment, thus to call the vessel — 'a scooner let her be'.

Starboard, the right-hand side of a ship looking forward, has nothing to do with stellar matters. Its star derives from the Anglo-Saxon *steor* (to steer). Early mariners used to steer the boat with a paddle or oar on that side (*bord*) near the stern. The left side, on the other hand, originally was known as larboard. According to some, this term was a modification of ladeboard, assimilating the d of lad to the r of star. As the rudder projected on the right of the boat, to do the loading (*lade*) sailors pulled their craft in with the left side to the dock. An alternate suggestion traces the name to *leere*, the Old English for 'empty' (still extant in the German *leer*). With the steersman stationed on the right side, the left remained vacant.

Starboard and larboard, however, sounded so much alike that shouted directions of the helmsman could easily be confused. To differentiate clearly between the two, larboard was replaced by port. It was an obvious choice, as this was the side nearer to the wharf or jetty (the port) when in harbour.

The measuring of the capacity and displacement of a ship by tonnage goes back to the old French description of a 'cask of wine' (*tunne*). Boats, particularly those plying for Bordeaux wine merchants, used to carry many tunnes. It was natural and appropriate for the merchants to ascertain how many casks a ship could take. Even when wheat superseded wine in importance as cargo, the original casks stayed on as tonnage, at least in nomenclature.

The diversity of *ballast* carried in ships is reflected in the variety of the word's etymological explanations. These range from a 'bad lading' and 'bare load' to the 'hull's load' and 'belly load'. *Last*, the second syllable of the word, always means, of course, a load or burden.

Preserved for all time is the frequent employment of ships in warfare, when sea battles were fought at close range and boats became floating platforms for infantry combat. The battle continued even when enemy soldiers had boarded them. Fortified superstructures (like castles) were built for this purpose. One of them, the military 'forecastle', now peacefully survives in our present-day, curiously abbreviated fo'c'sle.

Intriguing is the custom of calling a ship 'she'. It is a tradition that is even more paradoxical when 'she' refers to a man of war, a merchantman, or to vessels called after monarchs and presidents. Cynics have pointed out that the feminine gender was well applied as, after all, a ship also needed plenty of paint. Wits reminded the inquisitive seeker for an explanation that boats (also) were attached to b(u)oys.

Its real reason may be traced to one of two facts. The sailor's close and intimate link with his boat made him consider it not just an inanimate object but a person. Who would be dearer to him than a woman? More likely as the cause of the boat becoming a 'she' is an even older tradition. In far-off days every vessel was dedicated to a goddess whose shrine or image it carried. Out of deference to her and to acknowledge her presence, the ship itself took on her gender.

Actually, some authorities claim that the naval custom for officers and men to salute the quarterdeck, and nowadays explained as paying honour to the flag (or, in the British navy to the reigning monarch — as all ships are His or Her Majesty's ships), really originated in that early period when sailors kept the sacred image aboard, to safeguard their passage through dangerous waters. Coming aboard, before doing anything else, they paid homage to the goddess on whom, after all, their lives depended. No wonder some consider sailing a divine pursuit.

Chapter 35

SKIING

What made man first think of skis? No doubt, it was his wish to improve his foot grip on the snow. To achieve this he must have thought initially merely of enlarging the soles of his boots—a method which would explain the early reference to 'snow shoes'. A chance experience might have led him to the next important discovery: that it was so much easier and swifter to glide along the snow than to traverse it step by step. But for this purpose, his novel 'platform' had to be lengthened and narrowed down. Skis then served man in his search for food—in hunting reindeer and elk.

All evidence shows that men have been skiing in northern Europe and Asia from before the dawn of history. The oldest known pair of skis (displayed in the Djurgarden Museum in Stockholm) is thought to be more than 5000 years old. Hundreds of ancient 'snow shoes' have been dug up, mostly from Finnish and Swedish bogs. There are remnants of Neolithic, Bronze Age, and Iron Age skis. Illustrations of skiing were found in the form of rock engravings dating back 4000 years. Skis from early times have been decorated, and carved ornaments on the upper surface have assisted researchers in dating many old specimens.

Throughout the ages, skis have differed in many ways. The world's first skis were probably made from bones of large animals. The earliest skis were made smooth on the running surface, but soft snow got stuck to these and impeded the skiers' progress. Skin of elk, reindeer, and seal was then used to cover the boards to give grip.

Towards the end of the Bronze Age, grooves approximately two inches (5.08 cm) wide were made in the snow shoe and filled with hairy skin — secured by wooden borders. When skiers realized these assisted in keeping a straight course, they abandoned the skin and kept the borders.

Generally the ski was strapped on with leather thongs. Primitive types had a footrest hollowed out of the wood with two wooden tongues holding the foot in position from either side. Thongs were threaded through holes in those side pieces. Some skis had a raised foot-rest.

A great variety of experimentation took place. In the eleventh century skiers used the 'kicking ski' on the right foot and the long 'running ski' on the left, a combination thought to give greater speed. In modern days, Germans and Americans introduced special alloys and plastics to supplant the hard woods, such as ash and hickory, which had replaced the spruce and pine used centuries earlier.

Skiers learned early the advantage of using a stick which, for many centuries, was simply a sturdy branch. Bone points were then fixed to its lower end and a hoop to its top. It was only in 1615 that (from northern Finland) mention was made of the use of two sticks. But there were skiers who never adopted any. They secured themselves by a rope which they tied to the point of each of the skis.

The word 'ski' has a northern European linguistic root describing a splinter cut from a log. It became the Scandinavian term for a shoe, and was pronounced *shee*.

The northern countries of Europe worshipped Skadi, a goddess of skiing, who shot at wild creatures with her bow and arrows while moving across vast stretches of snow on her snow shoes. Icicles were the jewellery that adorned her hair and her clothes.

The god Ull was her male counterpart. He excelled so much as a snow runner — on skis with turned-up tips — that none ever attempted to outdistance him, and his speed was so great that at times he became invisible. A giant in size, he was thought to travel across the snowfields with ships on his feet, though philologists still doubt whether this descriptive phrase really refers to skis and not to a shield. Many skiers believed in his protective care and carried a medal embossed with his image.

The Finnish national epic, *Kalevala* (compiled of numerous folk songs), vividly recalls how one of its heroes chased the elk of the mountain ghost Hiisi, on skis.

> On his back he bound his quiver,
> And his new bow on his shoulder,
> In his hands his pole grasped firmly,
> On the left shoe glided forward,
> And pushed onward with the right one...
> Chased the elk upon his snow shoes,
> Glided o'er the land and marshes,
> O'er the open wastes he glided.
> Fire was crackling from his snow shoes,
> From his staff's end smoke ascending...
> Once again he speeded onward,
> And they could no longer hear him,
> But the third time he rushed onward,
> Then he reached the elk of Hiisi.

Greek authors described primitive skis which travellers had seen in foreign lands as wooden horses, giving rise to the myth of people with horses' hoofs. Pliny, the famous Roman historian, quotes an ancient authority who had claimed that when accompanying Alexander the Great on his conquest of the East, he had met horse-footed men there. Similar reports stem from the first pre-Christian century from China and the Turks also are known to have had skis in far-off days.

It is not surprising that eventually skis were used in war. However, historical records in this regard go back only to the battle of Ilsen (near Oslo) in AD 1200 during which King Sverre, of Sweden, equipped his reconnaissance troops with skis. It is told how six years later, two skiers (referred to as 'birch legs'), loyal supporters of the king, prevented the capture of his two-year-old son by the enemy by carrying the child to safety across vast snow-covered mountain ranges. To recall in perpetuity their valiant achievement, the 'Birch Leg' Race was introduced, a sporting event demanding utmost exertion and agility on part of the skiers, who have to negotiate the most difficult mountainous country over a distance of thirty-five miles (56 km).

During their rebellion against Danish rule in 1521, Swedish soldiers used skis to rescue an injured comrade from the battlefield. They improvised a stretcher, possibly the first of its kind, by *stretching* animal skins between two skis!

Certainly, skis became an established feature in the Scandinavian armies of the sixteenth and seventeenth centuries. Four thousand soldiers, mounted on skis, were employed in the campaign of 1610, ranging as far as Moscow.

It is strange that for a long time no one thought of making use of skiing for relaxation and competition. Skiing as a sport was first practised as late as the eighteenth century by the Norwegians, and then only very spasmodically. Norwegians are the fathers of this modern pastime.

The sport began as part of a military competition held in Oslo (then known as Christiania) in 1767. Soldiers were invited to vie with each other in skiing down a steep slope 'without riding or leaning on their sticks'. Another feature anticipated the modern slalom. Those taking part had to descend 'a moderately steep slope', but had to do so 'between bushes without falling or breaking their skis'.

An early chronicler tells of Austrian peasant skiers crossing the countryside on skis of a mere five-foot length: 'No mountain is too steep, or too overgrown with big trees to prevent them skiing down it; they wind and twist about like a snake. But if the terrain is open they run straight, leaning back on their sticks, firmly and stiffly as if they had no limbs or joints in their bodies.'

However, the real start of skiing as an independent competitive sport dates only from the late 1850s, in Norway, when in the valley of Telemark farmers inaugurated an annual 'meet'.

The first ski jump took place at Huseby Hill, near Christiania, in 1879. A description, given by Crichton Somerville, recalls the occasion:

> The Huseby slope was one which, only a few years previously, had been described as highly dangerous and impossible to descend when snow was fast and in good condition. The leaping competition proved most highly interesting, though in some respects quite comical. Every man, except the Telemarkings, carried a long, stout staff, and on that, so they thought, their lives depended. Starting from the summit, riding their poles, as in former times, like witches on broomsticks, checking the speed with frantic efforts, they slipped downwards to the dreaded platform or 'hop', from which they were supposed to leap, but over which they but trickled, as it were, and landing softly beneath, finally reached the bottom somehow, thankful for their safe escape from the dreaded slide.
>
> But then came the Telemark boys, erect at starting, pliant, confident, without anything but a fir branch in their hands, swooping downwards with ever-increasing impetus, until, with a bound, they were in the air, and seventy-six feet of space was cleared ere, with a resounding smack, their ski touched the slippery slope beneath and they shot onwards to the plain, where suddenly they turned, stopped in a smother of snow-dust and faced the hill they had just descended! That was a sight worth seeing, and one never to be forgotten, even if in after years such performances have been, in a way, totally eclipsed.

No individual has done more to foster the sport than Fridtjof Nansen, the polar explorer. His feat of crossing the frozen wastes of Greenland on skis in 1888 and its description in a book he published subsequently (in 1890) thrilled the world and popularized skiing far and wide.

He wrote: 'Nothing hardens the muscles and makes the body so strong and elastic; nothing steels the will-power and freshens the mind as ski-ing. This is something that develops not only the body but also the soul ...'

The patronage of the Norwegian royal family gave further impetus to the sport and led, in 1892, to the inauguration of the world's most famous skiing 'Derby' — an annual tournament at Holmenkollen, a site distinguished by its exquisite ski run. A small museum just below the ski jump-off treasures some five hundred historic pairs of skis.

All through the decades, Norwegians spread the new and exciting sport into almost every country where it could be practised. Small wonder that its best-known terms are in their language.

The *Christiania* (a swing used to turn or stop short) perpetuates the former name of Norway's capital city. The *Telemark* recalls that region of Norway in which the earliest competitive ski games took place. It denotes an expert manoeuvre in changing direction or stopping short.

Although, like many other ski features, the *slalom* was greatly developed by the British (its modern type is the invention of Arnold Lunn), its name is Scandinavian. It was adopted from the Telemarken dialect into the Norwegian tongue about 1890 and is a combination of two words: *sla,* meaning 'a little slope' and *lom,* describing the track left by something that has been dragged.

Few people realize that Australia introduced skiing as a sport long before it was taken up by Switzerland and Austria. Its birthplace was Kiandra, in the Australian Alps, where the snowfields, in extent, equal those of Switzerland. It was started early in the 1860s by Norwegian gold miners, who, no doubt, had brought their skis with them from their homeland. Locals soon emulated their example by rushing to the nearest fence and requisitioning palings to serve as skis.

Waxes were homemade and known as *moko,* a typical Australian abbreviation derived from the expressive 'more go'. The word was adopted in other countries and is Australia's contribution, in the form of a word, to the world of skiing.

Chapter 36

SQUASH

The Greeks were the first to assert that sport moulded character. They were convinced that only regular exercise could produce a well-rounded personality. It trained them in self-control, promoted a strong physique and physical courage. To the Greeks, athletics was an integral part of the 'good life', and visits to the gymnasium became a daily habit of Greek youths.

Early Greek sculptors portrayed this ideal man of athletic features. The philosopher Plato taught that the ideal state ought to begin in the body of man, which must be made strong by sport. The Greek tradition was succinctly expressed by the Roman adage that spoke of 'the healthy mind in the healthy body' (*mens sana in corpore sano*).

Nineteenth-century England revived and adapted this ancient philosophy of the art of living in its great, exclusive institutions of learning, the Public Schools. (Their name, of course, was rather odd, as in reality these were closed to the general public and reserved for the privileged classes.)

Compulsory organized games became an important feature in their curriculum, which encouraged athleticism as an instrument of education. This aimed at cultivating true 'gentlemen' who had learned to give of their best but to do so unselfishly, in selfmastery and knowing what was 'cricket'. They were trained by sport in the true team spirit. They played for their side, never for themselves. Not winning, but 'playing the game' was all that mattered. A headmaster of Winchester is quoted as having said: 'Give me a boy who is a cricketer. I can make something of him.' Expressive of the very spirit and atmosphere in the life of the English Public School is a verse written by Sir Henry Newbolt, English man of letters and one-time Professor of Poetry at Oxford University:

> There's a breathless hush in the close tonight —
> Ten to make and the match to win —
> A bumping pitch and a blinding light,
> An hour to play and the last man in.
> And it's not for the sake of a ribboned wat,
> Or the selfish hope of a season's fame,
> But his Captain's hand on his shoulder smote —
> 'Play up, play up, and play the game!'

Undoubtedly, the Public Schools, with their love of sport, gave British character some of its distinctive features and social qualities, including the instinct for fair play and sporting demeanour. This explains why it could be said that the battle of Waterloo was won on the playing fields of Eton. Probably recollecting this observation, Adolf Hitler declared during World War II (though with a mocking insinuation) that the fight was between those who had been through the Adolf Hitler schools and those who had been at Eton. It was a challenge Sir Winston Churchill took up when addressing his own former school at Harrow (in December 1940), defiantly saying: 'Hitler has forgotten Harrow . . . '

Harrow, indeed, was and is one of the famous English Public Schools, endowed by a charter of Queen Elizabeth I in 1571. Among other men who had received their schooling there were Sir Robert Peel (the British Prime Minister who inaugurated free trade in England), Lord Byron, and Oliver Goldsmith, the author of *The Vicar of Wakefield*. Racquets was one of the many games played (and, in fact, pioneered) at Harrow in the nineteenth century.

Racquets required a somewhat outsize court and as

only one existed at the school it proved inadequate for all the boys anxious to play. Around 1850 a game was thought out that, though still very similar to racquets, needed much less room. And that is how according to one tradition, squash racquets came into being. Another version claims that Harrow boys devised squash to gain more proficiency in racquets. As it were, they invented the new game as a preliminary 'exercise', in which they could practise the basic strokes on miniature racquets courts. These they easily improvised in the boarding houses in which the boys were billeted, as well as in some of their masters' homes. All that was needed was a wall (and there were plenty of those) and the laying of a sheet of asphalt (which preceded the later wooden floor). Of course, there were many hazards in the form of windows, doors, and pipes but, in reality, this made the game all the more exciting.

Harrow School itself, when building a new racquets court in 1864, recognized squash by constructing four separate courts for it. That their number was further increased in later years (by converting, for instance, three old Fives Courts for squash) testified to how much the game had caught on.

Instead of the traditional, hard racquets ball, the boys used one made of soft India rubber. This, by comparison, appeared rather 'squashy' — in feel and in the sound it made when hitting the wall — and it was this impression which gave the new (practice) game its descriptive name — squash. In fact, it has been suggested that squash is one of the two sports in the world that owe their name to the phenomenon known as echoism or onomatopoeia ('name-making') — the creation of words or names by imitating a sound associated with the object or action to be named, such as 'cuckoo', 'peewit', 'puff-puff', 'sizzle', 'splash', and 'croak'. Squash, in like manner, imitated the sound so typical of the game when its hollow ball hits the wall.

Once the boys had learned their squash, they were ready to master racquets. It did not take long for the new game to become popular on its own merit, particularly as it could be arranged so easily and played at so little cost. Soon other Public Schools took it up, and squash grew into an independent game for adults as well, 'squashing' racquets, which had become much too expensive as a sport, as the building of its courts a lost art.

The fact that the Prince of Wales became an enthusiastic player made the English people follow his example, and thus through royalty squash gained ever more widespread popularity.

It was given additional impetus because its pursuit offered magnificent training to champions of diverse sports. For instance, there is no doubt that it helps to speed up footwork and volleying in tennis. A report claimed that in a handicap lawn tennis match played in Cambridge in June 1875, H. Leaf, Esq., a former Harrow boy, had won as the result of practice at soft (squash) ball racquets at that school. It was possibly the first, but by no means the last, success in other sports owed to proficiency in squash. In more recent times, Harry Hopman, as captain of the Australian Davis Cup team, three times became the Australian squash amateur champion, while training for tennis titles. Peerless batsman Sir Donald Bradman took up squash to keep fit for cricket and in his very first year as a squash player he carried off the South Australian squash championship.

The circumstances of the birth of the new game influenced its early evolution. At first, obviously, it was taken up only by those schools that practised racquets, and at some of their pupils' homes. After graduation, the 'Old Boys' introduced the game into the clubs they joined. Since to begin with, squash was merely a means to an end, no one really cared what the courts were like. These greatly differed in shape, size, and construction, according to the space available.

The greatest handicap in the growth of the sport was its total lack of a unified code, a situation the Tennis and Rackets Association — established in 1907 — tried to overcome by the appointment of a special committee at its very first meeting. This initial governing body was then superseded by the Squash Rackets Association inaugurated at a gathering held at the Royal Automobile Club, London, in 1928. At long last squash racquets was standardized and the possibility of inter-club matches and competitions greatly fostered the sport.

British soldiers and sailors spread the game overseas, wherever they went to serve — in Canada, the Mediterranean, India, the Middle and the Far East.

Squash racquets first reached the United States in the 1880s. A master of St Paul's School, Concord, New Hampshire, the story goes, had specially visited Montreal to bring back from there all necessary information about the 'English game', which subsquently was organized for the first time in his school in 1882.

It was another fifty years, however, before it took proper hold. Developing independently, it also presented a diversity of rules and many types of courts. Thus, the Americans keenly felt the need of a worldwide standardization and consequently approached British players to come to an agreement. But the English (perhaps because of an innate conservatism that likes to hasten slowly) tarried too long for the Americans' liking. Losing patience, they eventually went ahead on their own to lay down final rules. These they based on squash tennis, which meanwhile had grown up in the States as a separate sport. And so it is that squash is still being played differently on either side of the Atlantic.

Yet, no matter what its individual rules of scoring and placing the ball, and the measurements of the ball, racket, and court, wherever it is played it results in the speeding up of reflexes, requires a good eye and strong wrist, and achieves all-round fitness and stamina.

Squash tennis has its own history. It is told that the pupils of St Paul's who early had taken up squash racquets, though liking the game, nevertheless felt that it was not lively enough. To speed it up, while still adhering to its general principles and playing it on the same type of wooden court, the pupils substituted a lawn tennis ball for the more sluggish squash ball and also used different bats, much more similar to the lawn tennis rackets. The new version soon gained its followers and became known, appropriately, as squash tennis.

Chapter 37

SURFING

Nature's challenge to man came not least from the ocean. Tireless in its incessant motion and sonority, its treacherous waters kept man in awe and its mysterious deep demanded countless victims in drowned men and wrecked ships. Its apparently boundless expanse frightened man whose imagination peopled its waters with monsters.

It was precisely those roaring waters, with their mountainous waves pounding shores and breaking on beach and reef, that also gave man a passionate urge to prove himself master. Striving for power over nature and trying to tame its most fearsome element, he took up surfing. To pit his skill against the surging sea, to ride its waves, gave him a feeling of exhilaration, of strength, of supremacy, and even intimations of immortality.

The principal and most elementary source of surfing lay in the very depth of human nature: man's everlasting battle against life's hazards and his innate urge to rise above them as a conqueror. Jack London described this, man's triumph over the rolling waves tumbling shoreward, so mysterious both in their origin and destiny, in a feature that he included as an entire chapter in *The Cruise of the Snark* and entitled 'A Royal Sport'.

Where but the moment before was only the wide desolation and invincible roar, is now a man, erect, full-statured, not struggling frantically in that wild movement, not buried and crushed and buffeted by those mighty monsters, but standing above them all, calm and superb, poised on the giddy summit, his feet buried in the churning foam, the salt smoke rising to his knees, and all the rest of him in the free air and flashing sunlight, and he is flying through the air, flying fast as the surge on which he stands.

Quite likely the thrills of surfing were first realized merely accidentally; perhaps it was an exhausted swimmer being caught up and swept along or a native fisherman in a primitive canoe battling shoreward.

That surfing's first site was the Pacific Ocean is not surprising. Contrary to its peaceful name, its waters can be most violent. Most probably several thousands of years ago the first settlers in the Pacific Islands, possibly coming from India, were the earliest surfers. The word *surf* itself is almost 300 years old and was first used in reference to the Indian coast.

It has rightly been asked why Europeans had never thought of surfing, something which could not be explained merely by the fact that other oceans could not boast of the majestic swell of the Pacific. Was it that Western man lacked the imagination and physical stamina of his 'primitive' and 'savage' brothers? Or, perhaps, was it his fear of the water? It must be realized that in 'civilized' Europe for many hundreds of years men shunned the water and even bathing the body was considered harmful. No wonder that people's bodies reeked and the only method of ensuring 'cleanliness' was to cover up the offensive smell by the application of perfume.

It can be assumed that surfing did not develop in one centre of the Pacific, from where it spread to other islands, by 'diffusion', but that it started independently in various areas. (There is also evidence that it was practised in a minor way on the West African coast of the Atlantic). Through the centuries Polynesians and other related races perfected the art and learned early to exploit the energy of the surf simply by the use of a wooden base, the prototype of the modern surfboard.

When Captain Cook and his crew on their famous voyage reached Hawaii in February 1778, they were amazed to watch men skimming across the water. It was an almost unbelievable sight, and the Hawaiians' mastery of surfing was duly recorded by the explorer:

> Whenever, from stormy weather or any extraordinary swell at sea the impetuosity of the surf is increased to its utmost height, they choose that time for their amusement, which is performed in the following manner: twenty or thirty of the natives, taking each a long narrow board, rounded at the ends, set out together from shore, the first wave they meet, they plunge under, and suffering to roll over them, rise again beyond it, and make the best of their way by swimming, out to sea. The second wave is encountered in the same manner with the first; the great difficulty consisting in seizing the proper moment of diving under it, which, if missed, the person is caught by the surf, and driven back again with great violence; and all his dexterity is then required to prevent himself from being dashed against the rocks. As soon as they have gained, by these repeated efforts, the smooth water beyond the surf, they lay themselves at length on their boards, and prepare for their return.
>
> As the surf consists of a number of waves, on which every third is remarked to be always larger than the others, and to flow higher on the shore, the rest breaking in the immediate space, their first object is to place themselves on the summit of the largest surge, by which they are driven along with amazing rapidity toward the shore.

The popularity and antiquity of the sport, totally unknown elsewhere, but skilfully pursued by the Hawaiians not later than in the tenth century, is attested by numerous legends, sacred chants, and their own rich surfing vocabulary, which gave expression in most detailed form to the various phases and methods of riding the waves. These terms referred, for instance, to the point to which the surfer paddled to catch a breaker (*kulana nalu*), to his sliding at an angle to the swell (*lala*), and to his prone position (*kipapa*).

Class distinctions then demanded different categories of boards. Royalty was privileged to use large and thick boards, called *olo*. They extended to a length of eighteen feet (5.40 m) and, though made of the lightest wood, weighed as much as 150 lbs (67.50 kg). All other men were restricted to 'planks', which were much shorter (seven to twelve feet — 2.10 m by 3.60 m — long), broader, and thinner. They were known as *alaia*. Even the surfing areas were strictly defined by a policy of apartheid. No commoner, on penalty of death, was permitted to surf at places reserved for the royal class. The Polynesian law of taboo thus extended to surfing.

The boards were highly treasured and treated with utmost care. Every time they had been used, they were properly dried and oiled. They were personally owned.

To the Hawaiian islander surfing was not merely a national pastime, but a solemn ritual. This started with the very selection of the tree from which the board was to be carved. Its choice was marked by placing a native red fish at its base. Once the tree had been felled, a hole was dug among its roots into which the fish was put as a sacrificial offering to the gods in payment for the tree, in the prayerful hope that the board would be divinely blessed.

When the board had been properly shaped, polished, and stained, so that it should gleam in the sun, another solemn dedication ceremony was held, preceding the board's first contact with the sea. This was to make sure that the surfboard would ride well.

Of course, successful surfing demanded also the right condition of the sea, which with yet further incantation and magic the faithful Hawaiian now tried to ensure. He did so by joining in hymns, the famous surf chants (many of which are preserved), appealing to the spirits for big surf. As well, priests twirled around their heads vines with which they then beat the surface of the waters. The ceremonial, the surfers were convinced, gained them the gods' favour and, having their minds thus attuned and properly fortified, they were indeed able to attain almost superhuman surfing feats.

Displays and fierce competitions in the riding of the swell soon found a prominent place in Hawaii and contests were made the occasion for betting. Prizes might cost the loser not only all his possessions but the loss of freedom for himself and his family, or even his life. Accounts also tell of more innocuous wagers, for instance the one of sixteen war canoes against 4000 wild pigs. Contests included several heats in a surf race from an outside point to the shore, or a marked buoy near it. The winner was the man who was the first to reach the goal without toppling over.

For many years after their first contact with the white man's culture, Hawaiian men, women, and children continued to enjoy the sport which gave them vigour and health. It was a true expression of their carefree and happy existence. When in 1821 Calvinist missionaries arrived in their country from Boston to teach them a new way of life, they were forced to use *muu-muus* to cover up the nakedness of their body which, it was explained to them, was shameful and sinful. The new puritanical teachings also strongly condemned surfing as a pagan and morally seducing pursuit whose practice was contrary to modesty and the laws of God.

It has been pointed out by those defending the missionaries that in reality it was not surfing itself they opposed but its morally and religiously dangerous 'incidentals': the gambling associated with it, the 'scanty costumes' worn by the surfers and, most of all, the free intermingling of the sexes 'at all times of the day and at all hours of the night'. By decrying and prohibiting these, they rendered the sport so dull and unattractive to the Hawaiians that they lost all interest in surfing which therefore suffered a decline.

The abolition of the traditional faith of the Hawaiians — of which surfing was an integral part — ultimately caused its wane and made the sport almost taboo. Perhaps typical of the revolution wrought was the example on one of the islands, where, to their newly built schoolhouse Hawaiians carried their surfboards to use them no longer for riding on the waves but to sit and to write on them. They transformed them into their school benches and tables!

For almost a century (with one brief exception), surfing was hardly practised in the very isles in which it had been developed to such perfection. It was only at the beginning of this century that the sport was revived — as a tourist attraction on Waikiki Beach — and that the first surf club was formed.

Its pioneer was Alexander Hume Ford, an American from the mainland. When he saw surfing in Waikiki, he immediatley grasped its great potentialities and lost no time in resurrecting and popularizing it, first of all by opening classes in surfing for youngsters. His initiative and enthusiasm made surfboard riding, in Jack London's words, 'the sport of sports': 'There was nothing like it anywhere else in the world. It was one of the island's assets, a drawing card that would fill the hotels and bring them many permanent residents'. Ford's efforts resulted in the foundation in 1908 of the Hawaiian Outrigger Canoe Club for the express purpose of 'preserving surfing on boards and in Hawaiian outrigger canoes'. It was the world's first organization of this kind.

Thus modern surfing came into being, soon once again to flourish on the very shores of its ancient pursuit, not least by the promotion it received by the famous Hawaiian swimmer, Duke Kahanamoku, who excelled in the sport.

Once adopted by Europeans, refinements in the design of surfboards were introduced. These included major considerations such as buoyancy, manoeuvrability, resistance to becoming waterlogged or breaking up, and ease of transport. It was not long either before enthusiastic surfers developed an ever greater variety of styles and stunts. From Hawaii the sport was now carried to other parts of the world.

The pursuit of business was the major factor that brought surfing to the United States. When the Pacific Railroad Company extended its tracks to the Southern California coast in 1907 the route was little patronized and appeared far from becoming a paying proposition.

Anxiously the company's directors looked around for some gimmick, some novel attraction, that would bring thousands to Southern California along its coast route.

Aware of the wonderful surf in that area and people's love of aquatic sports, the directors felt that surfing was the ideal solution. To promote their business, they engaged George Freeth, an Irish Hawaiian and surfing champion, to give demonstrations on Redondo Beach.

Their scheme not only paid dividends to the railroad but made surfing in California a vogue, greatly boosted as well by the nationwide publication of Jack London's *A Royal Sport* and five years later, in 1912, by the visit of Duke Kahanamoku himself, 'the grandfather' of modern Hawaiian surfing. He was on his way to the Olympics.

Thousands of spectators came to watch the sport, this 'novel' and exciting way to ride the waves that was soon to extend to many other centres along the coast.

That is how surfing found its spectacular place in American sporting life, with the United States Surfing Association, established in 1961, controlling and fostering it.

With the ever increasing popularity and growth of surfing, many lurking dangers became apparent. To safeguard against these was one of the reasons for the creation of the first Life Saving Association — in Australia, where the sport had been introduced first by a South Sea Islander in the 1880s.

The actual circumstances have been related by a pioneer of surfing in Australia, George Blackmore Philip (in his *Sixty Years Recollections of Swimming and Surfing in the [Sydney] Eastern Suburbs)*. He wrote:

> The Sunday morning came when the greatest tragedy of the beach occurred, and brought home to us that some practical use must be made of the friendship that had generated from our surfbathing association, when one of my greatest friends, Mr. G. Banks was drowned. . . . That was the foundation of the Surf and Life Saving Association — and at the cost of his life untold numbers of lives would be saved in the future.

Lyster Ormsby, foundation captain of Sydney's Bondi Club, was most instrumental in working out the earliest methods of rescue. The club's first report could proudly state that 'though started rather late in the year . . . it is now recognized by surf bathers as a body that cannot be dispensed with. Several rescues have been effected by members of the club since their advent to the beach, and there have been no accidents from drowning.'

Due to this movement, whose motto was 'vigilance and service', surfing in Australia grew to its present dimensions and the highest standards of surfing and life-saving were developed.

These are demonstrated in the annual surf carnival (inaugurated in Manly, Sydney, in 1908), with competitions and exhibitions in swimming, surfing, and, not least, life-saving skill.

To the young and strong, of top physical fitness, continually practising, and giving many hours of duty, life-saving became a highly prized and voluntary service. It has been said of the Surf Life Saving Association of Australia that 'no one man made it, but it has made thousands of men'. A story all its own is the development of its methods of rescue and resuscitation and Australia's example has set the standard for the whole world.

The first life line was a human chain, with men interlocked by their hands, the best swimmer forming the seaward end and the sturdiest the anchorage in the sands. Then a pole was set up at the centre of the beach to which was attached a rope with a life-buoy, used to bring back the swimmer in distress. Feats of endurance and dramatic rescues were performed by life-savers, battling their way through towering waters to people in difficulty.

Cork jackets were tried out — and discarded. Life lines of sisal hemp were replaced in 1914 by cotton. But something more than a line was needed, and the greatest advance was the introduction of the reel, displayed first on Bondi Beach in 1906.

The claim that Lyster Ormsby and Percy Flynn, of the Bondi Club, were its inventors, making the initial miniature scale model out of two bent hairpins and an empty cotton reel, was challenged by G. H. Olding, a coach-maker and the manufacturer of the first life-line reels who asserted that he was the real inventor of this mobile and revolving life-saving 'machine'. To add to the confusion George B. Philip made an identical claim.

An early method of resuscitation was that advised by the English physician and physiologist Dr Marshall Hall. He suggested the promotion of breathing 'by exciting the nostrils with snuff, hartshorn or volatile salts, or by tickling the throat with a feather'. This was soon rejected as ineffective and for more than forty years Australian life-savers adopted Edinburgh Professor Schafer's pressure method, in which the patient was placed face downwards in a prone position with the head lower than the body. By the application of systematic pressure the water was drained from the lungs and stomach. Eventually, mouth-to-mouth resuscitation was introduced.

This procedure actually was not as novel as most people imagine. The Bible gives an account of the identical treatment in a desperate and successful effort to restore life, when the prophet Elisha stretched himself over the body of a dead boy and 'put his mouth upon his mouth . . . and the flesh of the child waxed warm'.

In the papers of James Boswell dealing with the period of his life when he practised law (1769-1774), there is an interesting reference to the same method of restoring life. When all his advocacy had failed to have the sentence of hanging commuted for his client, John Reid (a sheep stealer), Boswell determined to rescue the unfortunate man's body from the gallows and revive him by mouth-to-mouth breathing. (Death in those days was brought about by strangulation).

Ignoring his friends' urging to let the law take its course, he hired a room near the gallows and went ahead with all necessary preparations for his clandestine plan. However, in the end he had to abandon the idea.

The Australian lifesavers' solicitude for victims of the surf is epitomized by the story of a candidate for the club who in reply to the examiner's question of how long he would continue his attempts at resuscitation of an apparently hopeless case answered: 'Until a doctor pronounced the man dead — and for two hours afterwards!'

Chapter 38

SWIMMING

Most animals are born swimmers, but man has had to learn to swim. He possibly did so in earliest times by watching animals in the water and his most primitive style was thus that of 'animal paddling' or the 'dog paddle' stroke. To begin with, he might have held on to a floating log, trying to propel himself by movements with his legs as if he were walking or running.

Ancient monuments and records uncovered by archaeologists depict him moving along or beneath the water. These prove that swimming was practised by many races in that early period of civilization.

Obviously, swimming at first was not a sport or a health-giving exercise, but a life saver and part of warfare. Man took to the water of necessity. He swam to take his foes by surprise, to make his escape (from man or beast), or to save himself from drowning. Swimming was part of early military training.

Its technique imitated the animals' movements. The swimmers thrashed the water with hands, arms, and legs, and though their speed was slow they were able to reach the shore if the distance was not too great. Man, however, swam 'with the strength of fear rather than with his own.' It was inevitable that he soon experienced the exhilaration of swimming and adopted it as a healthy pastime. Once he had mastered the art of staying afloat, his competitive instinct led him to develop the sport, step by step.

Hieroglyphic symbols, ancient Assyrian sculptures,

Greek legend, Roman documents, and the Bible, all testify to the early existence of swimming. Thousands of years ago man had learned to use inflated animal bladders as an aid to keep himself afloat.

In Egyptian writing the sign for 'swim' show a man's head and one arm forward and the other back, a position anticipating the Trudgen stroke. The British Museum treasures Assyrian stone carvings depicting men swimming, upheld by inflated bladders. Three warriors can be seen crossing a stream in flight from their foe, trying to reach their fortress. Two of them make use of blown-up skins, while the third, wounded by an arrow, is struggling against the current, apparently having lost his support. The portrayal carries the telling legend: 'They fled — like fishes crossed the river.'

Well known is the Greek myth of young Leander, who fell in love with beautiful Hero, priestess of Aphrodite. As such she could not marry and the two lovers had to meet secretly. That is how Leander was forced to pursue his courtship in most uncommon ways and difficult circumstances.

They were separated by the waters of the Hellespont (later to be known as the Dardanelles). Secretly, every night, Leander swam across to his lady love, to spend at least a few hours with her and to return home before dawn.

Leander had to cover a considerable distance (of at least two miles — 3.20 km —) each night and his feat may be considered the earliest marathon swim. He must have been a great athlete, and we may well wonder how he was able each day to conceal his fatigue from the previous night's swim.

Hero, anxiously waiting for Leander's arrival, guided him to the shore with a lamp. One night when a storm put out the light, Leander lost his bearings and was drowned. When Hero eventually saw his body floating in the surf, heart-broken she threw herself into the Hellespont.

Through the centuries, many had doubted the possibility of Leander's achievement. After all, they said, the story was a mere myth. Lord Byron, however, an expert swimmer himself, on his visit to the Dardanelles in 1810, was determined to test the feasibility of such a swim. He decided to cross the Hellespont, as he later wrote to his mother from Athens, 'in imitation of Leander, though without his lady'. Lieutenant Ekenhead joined him in the adventure.

They succeeded, and that same day (3 May), proud of his deed and in great exhilaration, Byron wrote to Henry Drury from aboard the frigate Salsette:

> This morning I swam from Sestos to Abydos. The immediate distance is not above a mile, but the current renders it hazardous; so much so that I doubt whether Leander's conjugal affection must have been a little chilled in his passage to Paradise. I attempted it a week ago, and failed, — owing to the north wind, and the wonderful rapidity of the tide, — though I have been from my childhood a strong swimmer. But this morning, I succeeded and crossed the 'broad Hellespont' in an hour and ten minutes.

Six days after the event, while the frigate was still lying at anchor at the historic site, he recalled his exploit. With poetic licence he claimed that his verses had been penned immediately after the swim:

Written After Swimming From Sestos To Abydos

If, in the month of dark December,
    Leander, who was nightly wont
(What maid will not the tale remember?)
    To cross thy stream, broad Hellespont!

If, when the wintry tempest roar'd,
    He sped to Hero, nothing loth,
And thus of old thy current pour'd,
    Fair Venus! how I pity both!

For *me*, degenerate modern wretch,
    Though in the genial month of May,
My dripping limbs I faintly stretch,
    And think I've done a feat today.

A note which he added to the poem, stated: 'The only thing that surprised me was that, as doubts have been entertained of the truth of Leander's story, no traveller had ever endeavoured to ascertain its practicability.' In a controversy, roused by this claim, he was forced to admit that, after all, he had not been the first to re-enact Leander's swim. He had been preceded by four others. In the years to follow, his example was emulated by more than a hundred swimmers who embarked not as Leander 'for love', but as Byron, 'for glory'.

Romans were renowned for their mastery of the water. Horatius, holding back the Etruscans from a wooden bridge until it could be demolished, is said to have dived into the Tiber to swim across it to safety in spite of his wounds and his armour. Even his foes had to admire his prowess.

No less, Julius Caesar was a superb swimmer. Whenever on his campaigns rivers obstructed his advance, it is said, he was the first, ahead of his legions, to have dived into the water and to have crossed them with a powerful stroke. Well known is the tradition that, when ship-wrecked off Alexandria, Caesar jumped overboard to swim ashore. Carrying his sword between his teeth, he held his *Commentaries* with this left hand above the water while beating it with his right.

Shakespeare makes Cassius in *Julius Caesar* relate:

> Caesar said to me, 'Dar'st thou, Cassius, now
> Leap in with me into this angry flood,
> And swim to yonder point?' Upon the word,
> Accoutred as I was, I plunged in,
> And bade him follow; so indeed, he did.

Romans regarded swimming as part of their education. A Latin definition could say of an uncultured person that 'he learnt neither to read nor to swim.'

Just as the Assyrians had done earlier, so the Romans too used animal bladders to support learner-swimmers. When Horace in his *Satires* in 35 BC discussed hard and easy ways of training, he referred to the use of animal bladders which he called water wings. 'It is one method,' Bacon wrote, 'to practise swimming with bladders and another to practise dancing with heavy shoes.'

Northern races, such as the Scandinavians, also knew how to swim.

Swimming, certainly, was well known in biblical days and taken for granted. The prophet Isaiah employed a graphic picture of a swimmer's powerful arm stroke. He could not have done so without assuming that his listeners were acquainted with it and, hence, immediately grasped the meaning of his metaphor. The Hebrews had mastered the art, and used it in war and peace.

Jonathan, one of the Maccabean heroes, swam the Jordan to evade his pursuers, and Josephus, first-century Jewish military leader and historian, tells in his autobiography how after he and a group of priests had been shipwrecked on their way to Rome, they swam all through the night until another ship picked them up. Rabbi Akiba, second-century luminary of the synagogue, ruled that it was a father's sacred duty to teach his sons to swim.

Other evidence comes from the New Testament. St John's Gospel (Chapter XXI) contains the story of how Peter, while fishing with friends on the lake of Tiberias, saw Christ manifesting himself on the shore. He jumped into the water and swam the hundred yards (91 m) or so that separated their boat from land.

When St Paul's ship was wrecked off the Maltese coast, the centurion commanded that, to save their lives, all men able to swim should do so. The fact that the whole company, including Paul, safely reached the shore proves they were efficient swimmers.

The first book on swimming is attributed to a German professor of languages, Nicolaus Wynmann, who published in Latin, in 1538, a volume in the then popular dialogue form. He called it (rather ponderously but convinced of its value), *The Diver, or A Dialogue Concerning the Art of Swimming, Both Pleasant and Joyful to Read.*

More humble and scientific was a treatise produced in 1696 by a Frenchman, M. Thevenot, called simply, *The Art of Swimming*. The method described clearly pictures the traditional breast stroke. Certainly, this did not give the swimmer much speed, but its popularity was due to other advantages. It did not obstruct the swimmer's vision and helped him to breathe freely. By moving his arms under the water, he did not splash his face. Altogether, the stroke gave the swimmer a feeling of security and it is not surprising that it was retained everywhere for many centuries.

It is not certain who introduced swimming into the British Isles. It might have been the Phoenicians, Vikings, or Romans. Or the Britons may have learned swimming independently. After all, they had many opportunities.

The first literary evidence of the art is contained in the seventh- or eighth-century epic poem *Beowulf*. For five days its hero is made to swim in a tempestuous sea, killing sea monsters with his sword. In 1531, Sir Thomas Elyot published *The Boke Named The Governour*. He referred to 'the Usefulness of Swymmynge', though his concern was limited to times of war.

The first actual book on swimming in England stems from Everard Digby, a Master of Arts at Cambridge University. Written in 1587, in Latin, it contained a weird assortment of woodcuts. In 1595 it was translated into English. He recorded that in his days the art had been much neglected and as 'it hath nat bene of longe tyme moche used, specially amonge noble men, perchance some reders wyll litle esteme it'. Curiously, Digby expressed the opinion which provoked much justified opposition that man swam 'naturally'. His fallacious notion was equalled, centuries later, by an absurd assertion made in a passage attributed to Benjamin Franklin, though since described as an interpolation. This held that a swimmer could not open his eyes under water.

Europe's Dark Ages took the joy out of aquatic sports. Sport, generally, was discredited and anything pertaining to the body held in contempt. Most of all, diseases, especially the epidemics that decimated Europe's population in frightening measure, were thought to be spread by the water. No wonder that ordinary people began to shun outdoor bathing and swimming for fear of catching a fatal sickness. Yet members of the nobility, it appears, did not give up swimming. They felt that it was not only a military necessity but that its skill and art were part of the true gentleman.

Nevertheless, the association of plague, death, and water lingered. It took many centuries for the prejudice to die out and for swimming to capture people's imagination once again. Only the nineteenth century saw a revival of aquatic sports.

The world owes the rebirth of swimming to Britain. The opening of the first swimming baths at Liverpool in 1828 was soon emulated elsewhere. London is said to have been the first city to introduce competitive swimming and about 1837, the city owned six pools. The contests then held were supervised by the National Swimming Society.

Not until the 1860s were swimming clubs established, and the Serpentine Club claims to be one of the oldest. Soon interclub competitions followed. In 1869 the Metropolitan Swimming Association was formed. It changed its name later to the London Swimming Association.

In 1875, Captain Matthew Webb, of Shropshire, became the first person to swim the English Channel. He swam from Dover to Calais in 21 hours and 45 minutes, a feat that caused a world-wide sensation.

Naturally, the rivalry between the various clubs created a wish to increase speed. It was realized that the traditional breast stroke could not serve this purpose. Coaches everywhere began to experiment to discover a faster style. That is how, eventually, the breast stroke was replaced by the side stroke.

Bets and cash prizes added to the excitement of swimming, but brought unruliness into the sport. When the Amateur Swimming Association was established in 1886, it laid down strict rules. Within three years, it outlawed betting of any kind. The stage was set for a faster evolution of the reborn pastime, which no doubt received its greatest impetus from the first modern Olympic Games in 1896.

Meanwhile (the exact date is uncertain) J. Arthur Trudgen, an English amateur swimmer, had visited South America. There he had learned from the natives a completely new style. On his return to Britain he copied and developed it into the famous double-overhead stroke. At first, people referred to it as the 'alternating over-arm stroke'. But he made it so famous that eventually it became known by his name, the Trudgen.

But no other stroke had equalled the revolution brought about by the Australian gift to the world of swimming — the crawl. Really, it was nothing new. It had been practised — either unknown or unheeded — among indigenous American tribes, including the Aztecs, as well as in western Africa, and on the islands of the South Pacific.

In 1844 North American Indians used the style when competing for a silver medal in London. A London newspaper report, often quoted since in various books on swimming, gave a vivid account of the race, in which Flying Gull defeated Tobacco. Their method of swimming was described as 'totally un-European'. They were said to have lashed the water violently with their arms, 'like the sails of a windmill', and, blowing forcefully, to have beaten the water downwards with their feet. Altogether, the spectacle appeared to the writer as a performance of 'grotesque antics'.

The Cavill family developed the crawl in Australia and were responsible for its worldwide adoption. London-born Frederick Cavill had excelled in swimming in his own country. Twice he attempted to emulate Captain Webb in crossing the Channel. Each time using the breast stroke, he had failed within sight of his goal.

In 1879, he emigrated to Australia with his family. He built and owned in Sydney a floating swimming pool. Styling himself Professor, he trained numerous people in the sport, including his six sons.

There are slight variations in accounts of how the Cavills first adopted the crawl. It is told that on a trip to the South Sea Islands they were so impressed by the Polynesians' manner of propelling themselves in the water that on returning to Australia they introduced the new style.

Others claim that it was Aleck Wickham, a Solomon Islander living in Sydney and employed there as house-boy to a doctor, who had given the Cavills the idea when they saw him swim at Bronte baths.

The Cavills certainly used every means to promote the style and display its effectiveness. Dick, the youngest son and the crawl's real pioneer, used ingenious methods to achieve this aim. He demonstrated the advantages of the crawl by giving starts to the fastest swimmers, while himself swimming with his legs tied above the knees.

At first, people called the crawl the 'splash stroke'. How it gained the name 'crawl' also has been variously explained. According to one tradition, it stems from the answer Dick had given when asked what it felt like to swim the stroke. 'Like *crawling* through the water,' he said. Other sources have suggested that the movement reminded people of an infant's crawl, and that this was the origin of its name. Finally, a local official at the baths has been cited as its author. Watching Wickham he had remarked: 'Look at that boy crawling over the water.'

In 1902, Richard Cavill went to England, having won eighteen Australian and twenty-two New South Wales championships. He had become the first man to swim 100 yards in less than a minute. It was a foregone conclusion that his crawl stroke would conquer. Indeed, in competitive simming, it enabled him to leave everyone else behind.

Sydney St Leonards, the fifth Cavill son, became a swimming coach in the United States where for twenty-five years he trained numerous champions. The American Daniels, using the Cavill's stroke as a model, further developed the crawl, which in its new form was renamed the 'American crawl'.

The Australian crawl in one form or another became

most popular everywhere and the results it achieved proved its value. The speeded-up stroke led to records. Miss Gertrude Ederle, a young American girl, used the crawl when she swam the Channel in 14 hours 31 minutes, improving Webb's time by more than seven hours.

Later years brought further refinements in swimming styles and ever more records. It is hard to believe that still as late as 1880 a rhyme, of unknown authorship, could have read:

> Mother, may I go out to swim?
> Yes, my darling daughter;
> Hang your clothes on a hickory limb,
> But don't go near the water.

Chapter 39

TABLE TENNIS (*Ping-Pong*)

Devised as a kind of miniature tennis only toward the end of the last century, table tennis really goes back to the twelfth-century Royal Tennis. Who first invented table tennis as it is played today is not known, nor is the country of its origin quite definite.

Britain, the United States, as well as India, and South Africa have each been named as the birthplace of this popular sport, but most people concede that it began in England. Even those who suggest that table tennis was played first in India or South Africa agree that British army officers stationed there were probably responsible for its introduction into those countries.

The simplicity of its rules and the fact that its equipment was (and is) so easily and cheaply obtained has made table tennis a most popular sport enjoyed both by the young and not so young, the man in the street and royalty.

King George VI had a table installed at Buckingham Palace and, at the outbreak of World War II, provided his daughter (then the young Princess Elizabeth) with facilities for the game at Balmoral Castle.

Likewise, the late Shah of Persia, Pundit Nehru, and the former King Farouk of Egypt were protagonists of table tennis. Sportsmen of every type found and still find it an excellent way of conditioning themselves for their own individual pursuit.

This is not surprising, as table tennis combines so many features. It gives agility to the player, demands good footwork and lightning speed, and promotes faster reflexes. Altogether, it is a most exhilarating sport.

Industrial psychologists have stressed the game's great contribution to higher efficiency in people's work, having found that after a good game of table tennis they have returned to their task refreshed and with increased energy. Table tennis, equally, has been considered a valuable means in attaining a better co-ordination of the eye and the mind.

Table tennis began, though not under that name, as a parlour game in Victorian homes. The equipment used in those early days was mostly improvised and home-made. The ball was made of string, while books, placed on a table, represented the net. The racket or bat was cut out of a piece of thick cardboard.

Early literature on the game advised that the room chosen for it should be sparsely furnished and that such furniture as there was, should be covered up to avoid wear and tear.

Commercial interests soon spied a chance of exploiting the new pastime and began to produce equipment more suitable than the hitherto home-made variety. Rivalry between the various manufacturers stimulated the game all the more.

An American firm, Parker Bros of Salem, Massachusetts, who made all types of sporting goods, are said to have been one of the first to develop what they called 'Indoor Tennis'. They exported their sets to England, where their British agent, Hamley Bros, of London, first marketed them.

Meanwhile, other English companies had registered their own patents, such as Ayres Ltd (who advertised the sport as 'The Miniature Indoor Lawn Tennis Game') and Charles Barker of Gloucestershire.

The balls supplied then were either of rubber or cork and frequently were covered with a knitted web or a piece of cloth to prevent damage to furniture and give a spin to the ball.

Bats still continued to be of various shapes, materials and weight. Their handles were exceedingly long and their blades, which were hollow, were covered with parchment or leather, giving them the appearance of small drums.

Sometimes the net was stretched across the table between the backs of two chairs. A game was completed when one of the players scored twenty-one points, or two clear points after twenty-twenty.

It was the introduction of the hollow, celluloid ball which completely revolutionized the game, giving it new impetus, extraordinary speed, and split-second precision.

Tradition relates that a player named James Gibb (or, according to others, an unidentified clergyman), on a visit to the United States, had come across such coloured balls, used by children as toys. On his return to Britain, he tried them out at table tennis and discovered their great advantage. He lost no time in telling a business acquaintance who dealt in sporting goods about them who, realizing at once their great potentialities, began to sell them. Inevitably, the innovation further boosted the game.

Business competition was vigorous, and the various firms patented their particular set of equipment. Among the names chosen were such fancy descriptions as (the now obsolete) Gossima, Whiff Whaff, and Flim Flam. Parker Bros adopted the tradename Ping-Pong.

In fact this was the second time that a sport was called onomatopoetically. The name 'ping-pong' imitated the two sounds the ball made: when the racket hit the ball, the sound was a *ping;* then, when the ball hit the table, it was a *pong.*

In no time it took people's fancy, and ping-pong became a real craze, both in America and Britain as well as other countries. Every home that wished to keep up with the Joneses, as it were, contained facilities for the sport. Not everyone, however, approved of the fad and some newspapers of the time regretted its popularity, regarding the fascination it exercised on strong men as much as on women as a sign of decadence.

After some time, as always happens to such fads, people tired of ping-pong, whiff whaff, or by whatever name it was called. It went into decline until one day a man named E. C. Goode gave the game a new lease on life.

According to the story told at the time, the sudden surge of interest in table tennis was due to a headache suffered by Goode, who had not yet lost the love of the game. Searching for a remedy for his pain, he had gone to a chemist and, when paying for whatever drug he had purchased, he noticed a studded rubber cash-mat on the shop counter. The thought came to him that it would make an ideal surface for a ping-pong bat, as it should give the player much greater control over the ball. His headache forgotten, he bought the mat from the chemist and, trimming it to the right proportions, glued it to a ping-pong bat.

He lost no time in starting to practice and soon proved the vast superiority of his improved implement with which he became so efficient that at the national final he challenged the English table tennis champion and was able, through the novel bat alone, to beat him by fifty points to three!

From that day onward, ping-pong never looked back. Aristocrats and the people took it up again with new verve. Private tournaments as well as public contests became the vogue and countries all over Europe joined enthusiastically in the sport. Well-known players took due advantage of the revolutionary bat with its fascinating ball control by introducing many new techniques which gave the game a totally different appearance.

Once again, however, table tennis lost its appeal — around 1904 — and did not revive till after World War I when, in 1921, the Ping-Pong Association was established in Britain. Realizing that a commercially patented name was being used, it was changed in the following year to the Table Tennis Association.

The Hon Ivor Montagu, a son of Lady Swaythling, then studying at Oxford University, became a table tennis enthusiast. Other undergraduates caught the fever and joined in lively contests. Soon the first inter-Varsity match, Oxford vs. Cambridge, was played.

It was through Ivor Montagu's initiative that his mother donated the Swaythling Cup which, like the Davis Cup in Lawn Tennis, has become the much coveted and treasured international table tennis trophy.

A world congress held in Berlin in 1926 resulted in the foundation of the International Table Tennis Federation which, by 1939, included more than thirty nations with England still leading, having 260 leagues with almost 3000 clubs. At long last the game's rules and equipment were standardized.

Britain did not retain the prime position she had held in the game. Other nations began to catch up and even surpassed her, notably Japan and China but also the Americans, Czechs and Hungarians.

Chapter 40

TENNIS

Tennis may refer to two totally different types of game: the original court or royal tennis (also mistakenly known as 'real' tennis) and its modern adaptation, lawn tennis. The history of the game goes back into the distant past, and there are various explanations of its origin.

In the very beginning, tennis was played not as a pastime, but — as most other ball games — as a solemn fertility rite in Egypt and elsewhere in the Middle East. Some authorities link it with a game of handball, mentioned explicitly in Homer's writings, as being played by Nausicaa, King Alcinous' daughter, and her personal maid servants in Phaecia where Odysseus was shipwrecked.

Other authorities have traced tennis to an early kind of polo, played on horseback and with rackets at the Byzantine court. However, it is clear that the Crusaders brought tennis to Europe from the Middle East, and that the game was taken up and elaborated in France.

Philologists have suggested that the name tennis was adopted from the French exclamation *tenez*, 'hold!' or 'pay heed!', which was the player's call to his opponent before serving the ball. Englishmen, it is said, watching 'the game with the palm' (*jeu de paume*), as it was known among the French, and hearing the call repeatedly, took it up to describe the game by that very expression.

Another view associates the term tennis with an Egyptian town on the Nile, known as Tinnis in Arabic, and Tanis in Greek. The city was famous for its fine linen

and the earliest balls were made of that material. Therefore, it is not so far-fetched to assume that 'tennis'
preserved, and very gratefully so, that early source of
tennis balls, the fabrics of Tanis. There are many similar
examples of words deriving from place names, such as
Tuxedo, China, Eau de Cologne, Homburgs, Frankfur-
ters, and Hamburgers.

Other derivations trace the name to Greek, Latin, and
German roots. Tennis was linked with the Latin verb
tenere — 'to catch' — a feature of the game. On the
other hand, the 'dance' of the ball, from one side of
the court to the other, led some writers to imagine that
the German *Tanz* (dance) was the origin of 'tennis'.
Again, it was said that just like the game of Fives took
its name from the number of players, so *ten*nis had been
called after an early number of ten players. The variety
of (possible and unlikely) explanations of the word certainly seems unending.

Together with court tennis the twelfth-century Crusaders brought some of its terms to Europe. Thus, racket
is derived from the Arab *rahat* for 'the palm of the hand'.
'Hazard', also belonging to the terminology of the game,
has been traced to the Arab description of dice and
chance. Deuce, however, is the Anglicized version of
the French *à deux* (two), implying that two successive
points must be gained to win the game.

The early practice to ask a servant to deliver the first
ball may account for the introduction of the term 'service'
into tennis.

Records confirm that tennis was played in France in
the twelfth century, at first with the palm of the hand
only. Rackets then were still unknown. That is why the
logical Frenchman came to call the sport not tennis but
'the game of the hand'.

Those enjoying the pastime soon felt that to strike
the ball with their bare hands could hurt very much.
Therefore, to soften the blow, players began to wear
gloves. It was found that not only did the glove guard
against injury, it gave the ball greater impetus.

The next ingenious development was the stretching

of strings crosswise on the glove. (Its meshed pattern has been suggested as yet a further explanation of the game's name. The glove was compared with a sieve, which in French is *tamis*). The result was that the ball could be struck with greatly increased power.

This marked the birth of the racket. All that was further needed was to take off the improved glove and add a handle to it. That happened in the sixteenth century. As if to remind us of the true origin of the bat, we continue to call it by the original Arab description of the hand — racket.

Court tennis, no doubt, started in France, introduced into the country by French knights. But, to begin with, it was played by monks. Many features of its walled outsize court — its openings, projections, and 'corridors' — are derived from the architecture of the monastery. The sloping roofs on three of its walls (making up the so-called penthouse), its galleries, the tambour of its columns, and the 'grille' — these are all vestiges of the monastery: its cloisters, flying buttresses, cowsheds, and buttery hatch!

Literary evidence supports the ecclesiastical claim of the source of tennis and indicates the popularity of the game among churchmen. Twelfth-century records tell of bishops joining in the game at Christmas and Easter time and evolving a ball ceremonial.

One cleric, indeed, enjoyed volleying the ball so much that he did not turn up at worship. It is not surprising therefore that the priests' indulgence in tennis (not rarely leading to the neglect of their duties) was resented, with the result that, finally, they were asked to abstain from the game. In 1245 the Archbishop of Rouen issued an edict forbidding all clergy to play tennis.

By then the love of the game had spread to the nobility and the royal court. It had become a favourite sport of kings and as such, in one case at least, had proved fatal. Louis X of France died at the age of twenty-seven from a chill he had caught while playing tennis. Because of the enthusiasm with which kings and their courts pursued the game, the sport came to be called 'royal tennis', a description which somehow, by usage or misunderstanding, was corrupted into 'real' tennis! However, there is also a suggestion that the word stems from the Italian *reale,* for 'royal'.

It was inevitable that the general population as well took up the game. Among the masses it deteriorated into a gambling pursuit, eventually becoming so unruly that Charles V of France banned tennis in Paris, at least for some time.

The Frenchness of tennis is reflected in Shakespeare's *Henry V* (Act I, scene 2), based on the famous incident in 1414 when the French Dauphin Lewis sent tennis balls to the English king. This insulting gift suggested that Henry should forego dukedoms in lieu of a 'tun of treasure' — tennis balls. Recalling the occasion, Shakespeare makes Henry V reply to the French ambassador:

> His present, and your pains, we thank you for:
> When we have match'd our rackets to these balls,
> We will, in France, by God's grace, play a set,
> Shall strike his father's crown into the hazard.
> Tell him, he hath made a match with such a wrangler,
> That all the courts of France will be disturb'd
> With chases.

The sport was established in the British Isles, about the fourteenth century, possibly reaching England via Scotland. And if the French were the fathers of court tennis, the English were their most apt pupils.

Tennis was first mentioned in English literature by Geoffrey Chaucer. An edict of 1389 prohibited play in order to promote archery, but it was impossible to suppress the game permanently. In 1530, Henry VIII built a court at his Hampton Court Palace. His keenness for the sport was equalled by that of Charles II a hundred years later. The sixteenth and seventeenth centuries in fact saw tennis rise to its greatest popularity. The first generally accepted rules were laid down by Forret, a Frenchman, in 1592.

After 1800, court tennis began to experience a decline. Its place was to be taken by lawn tennis, its modern adaptation and developed not only because its courts were so much cheaper to build but, even more so, by men's wish to pursue a game out of doors that was lively and exciting. Of course, there was croquet. This, however, appeared much too tame, sedate and leisurely.

Several claims have been made as to who invented lawn tennis. Undoubtedly, it is an evolution of racquets and court tennis. It can easily be imagined how on a balmy summer's day, players moved from the indoor court out into the open air to continue their game there. Various records exist both in France and England of some such sort of game being played and described as Long, Open, or Field Tennis. It is also known that in 1868 Major T. H. Gem and J. B. Pereira played some game of a similar kind at Edgbaston. But the man who truly popularized (if not invented) the game and patented it as a 'garden party' was Walter C. Wingfield, an English major.

A well-seasoned soldier who had commanded a cavalry troop in China, he was aware that the people longed for a good outdoor sport and felt that perhaps he could provide it, with no little advantage to himself. The easiest way, he considered, was to make use of court tennis which then was played only on the lawns of great country estates. However, to make the new game profitable to himself, it was essential to add something new.

Though Wingfield's game embodied many of the elements of traditional tennis, such as the bat, the ball, and the net, he gave each different specifications. The court had always been rectangular. Wingfield's court provided the novel touch he had sought. It was in the shape of an hourglass and thus was narrower at the net than at the ends. (This peculiar contour of the court, it has been suggested, Wingfield adopted from one of the early games of Badminton, played either in the drawing-room of the Duke of Beaufort's estate in Britain or in a hall in far-off Karachi, India.) To make the new design even more conspicuous, the major added a couple of sidewings, though they really served no practical purpose.

Finally, there was the need of an attractive name. Wingfield had heard of an ancient Greek outdoor sport called *sphairistike* (from *sphaira*, Greek for 'ball'). No one knew how it was played and Wingfield rightly reasoned that the very strangeness of the word and the general ignorance of the game's nature would prove an advantage. So he called his new sport sphairistike.

The story of how, eventually, this Greek word was changed into 'lawn tennis' has been told by the fifth Marquis of Landsdowne. He related how in 1869 the young artillery captain (as Wingfield was then) had approached him and, telling him all about his invention, had expressed the wish to demonstrate it in front of his house at Berkeley Square, London. Landsdowne, very interested in the proposition, had invited two friends — Walter Long and Arthur Balfour — for the following afternoon (with himself and the captain) to make up a foursome to play the first game on his lawn. He recalled that 'we found it good exercise and quite interesting, even with the crooked racquet and plain uncovered balls of that day'. They liked the game so much indeed that they met on many other occasions during that summer, and the more they played the more they enjoyed it.

The Marquis and his two friends also soon realized that the Greek name was far too ponderous, too difficult to remember, let alone to pronounce. So Walter Long said one day: 'Look here, if you want your game to catch on, you must find a more reasonable name for it'. All agreed but were at a loss for a suitable substitute till Arthur Balfour suggested: 'Why not call the game lawn tennis?' And that is how, at least according to this version, the game acquired its new name. It was a vivid and simple description of a sport played with a plain rubber ball and an oval-shaped racket on a grass court. Wingfield applied for a patent in February 1874 for this 'New and Improved Court for Playing the Ancient Game of Tennis', which was granted in July of that year.

Meanwhile, he had ordered the manufacture of sufficient balls and rackets to meet any demand. The boxes in which they were sold were conspicuously labelled with both the old and the new names of the game.

The major had not miscalculated. People's love of novelty combined with their longing for an outdoor sport made lawn tennis an instant success. In no time, it became the most fashionable game in England, and the fact that society adopted it made it the more popular.

Within two years, the All England Croquet Club introduced lawn tennis at Wimbledon, where the first championship won by A. W. Gore, was held in 1877. Twenty-two competitors took part and the finals were watched by 200 spectators who each paid one shilling entrance fee. Enthusiasm for the game was such that in the same year the name of the club was extended to include the new vogue, lawn tennis.

The alcove-like side courts, as was only to be expected, proved of no practical value, and were dropped, as was also an original service crease. The court's hourglass shape and the game's unpronounceable Greek name also disappeared. In the third edition of his book, Wingfield just omitted the Greek title, and it has been lawn tennis ever since.

The US Lawn Tennis Association was formed in 1881, when the first US championships were held. In fact, lawn tennis spread throughout the States almost faster than any other game had done previously. In 1900, it enthused Dwight Davis so much that he presented the Cup which ever since has been the symbol of world tennis supremacy — the Davis Cup.

SEEDING

Who plays whom in tennis could be determined by drawing a lot and be left thereby completely to chance. It was realized that this was not the way to make games in a tournament exciting. On such occasions, it was much better to arrange the matches with forethought, avoiding having ranking players or teams meet in the early rounds.

In 1911, this system of allocation of games was first

described (in the United States) as 'seeding'. Opinions differ as to why this particular term was chosen. Some believe that no other word could have described more adequately what was being done. In its original application in agriculture, 'seeding' denoted the separation of the seeds from the straw — and was not that exactly the procedure followed in the matching of players and teams?

Others, however, deny any connection between the seeding in tennis and that practised in the agrarian field. The term was the result of a fault, they said; not in the game but in speaking. Originally, this method was very simply called the 'conceding' of a position to certain players or teams. Slovenly speech made people drop or swallow the first syllable. As the remaining 'ceding' made no sense in the circumstances, it was soon confused with the well-known seeding and, sounding alike, eventually spelled that way.

SCORING

Playing tennis, some wits have suggested, goes back to the Garden of Eden, when Eve 'served' an apple to Adam: the first 'fault'.

Scoring in tennis, so different from all other sports, has mystified many. Its units of '15', and '60' for game, in fact, stem from 'paume', the forerunner of modern tennis.

In paume, as in present-day tennis, the field was divided by a net. Each half was subdivided into fifteen sections individually numbered. As still nowadays, ordinarily the ball was not permitted to bounce more than once. However, if the player could not return the ball on the first bounce, he was still allowed to do so on the second, so long as he was able to hit it into a sector of his opponent's field of a lower number. For instance, if he returned the ball from his sector 7 he had to make sure for it to land into a sector not higher than 6.

The scoring in the sequence of 15, 30, 40 and game, which tennis has also adopted from paume, fundamentally is a legacy of ancient Babylonian culture of thousands of years ago, when no one ever dreamt of a game like tennis. This introduced to the world the sexagesimal system which has left its impact in diverse ways. Babylonians believed in the cosmic significance of the figure 60 (*sexaginta* later in the Latin) which made man divide every hour into sixty minutes. Subdivided into quarters, it made 15 a popular unit generally.

It was for this reason that fourteenth-century France chose it as the basis of its monetary system. A coin was valued 60 sous. By means of an embossed cross, the coin could be divided into four quarters, each worth 15 sous. It so happened that at the very time the 'game with the palm' had become a favourite pastime of the French. They played it for money, mostly for a sixty sous piece which, prior to the game, they either handed for safe keeping to a spectator friend or placed under the net. No wonder, having the beckoning prize in mind, they did not score in simple numbers — 1, 2, 3 and game — but in the 15 (sous) units for each quarter, totalling up to 60 (sous) for the game.

Maybe psychology played its part as well in the rather inflated scores. To gain 1, 2 or 3 points sounded not very much. But to be able with one hit to obtain a score of 15 was something worthwhile and was an extra incentive to a player.

It was a practical reason that eventually reduced the 45 score to a mere 40. In calling out the figure (whether in French, English or, for that matter, in any tongue) forty was so much more euphonic and rolled more easily from the tongue than the ponderous forty-five.

That in the vocabulary of the game 'love' means 'nothing' is far removed from amorous considerations. Though, how this type of love on the court really started is still uncertain. There are two possible explanations. In Shakespeare's language 'love' expressed 'nothing', as is shown in such phrases as 'a labour of love' and 'neither for love nor money'. The French have staked a claim here as well. The shape of the figure zero resembles the egg, which in French is called *l'oeuf*. On English tongues, *l'oeuf* soon changed into 'love'. Probably, this was the origin of the term.

Chapter 41

TEN-PIN BOWLING

The sport of ten-pin bowling was the result of a move to circumvent a law on gambling. Like lawn bowling it had its roots in man's innate wish to throw or roll an object toward a target, and the story of its evolution is colourful and complex.

Nine-pin bowling or, as it is sometimes called, skittles, was the immediate forerunner of ten-pin bowling. Today an innocuous game enjoyed by young and old, centuries ago it was banned as inimical to national defence and as the cause of hooliganism and gambling. On the other hand, it was greatly developed by the Christian Church and especially Martin Luther, founder of German Protestantism.

Throughout many centuries, skittles was referred to merely as bowling, a word used equally for lawn bowling at a jack. Thus, in old documents dealing with bowling, it is often uncertain which type is meant.

Even Stone Age man must have enjoyed a very crude version of the game. Probably all he did was aim stones at other stones to pass his time. Historically, it is known that a kind of pin bowling was practised 7000 years ago in Egypt. When Sir Flinders Petrie excavated an Egyptian child's grave dating back to 5200 BC, he discovered among the objects entombed items that undoubtedly had belonged to a game very similar to modern, ten-pin bowling. Other archaeological finds in turn brought to light big skittles of pottery and stone.

The South Sea Islands have some evidence of the same

game, called by the natives *ula maika*. Polynesians have been known to join in a game with elliptical balls and round, flat, stone discs. This game was not only very much like skittles, but it demanded that stones be bowled a distance of sixty feet (18 m) — the stipulation of modern, ten-pin bowling.

Bowling of one kind or another became a popular pursuit and even a vogue in Europe, especially so in Germany. There the game was known as *Kegeln*, a term which was adopted also, at least for a time, in other parts of the world. Literally, it referred to the 'pin'.

A *Kegel* was an almost all-purpose utensil. Germans used it as a cudgel to defend themselves, as a tool (instead of a hammer), and as a gadget in physical exercise to strengthen the muscles of their hands, wrists, and arms. No wonder that they carried it with them (like knights did their swords) wherever they went, even to church.

Priests, always ready to reinforce their message, soon discovered in their congregants' *Kegels* a wonderful means to dramatize man's constant struggle against the Devil and evil. Indeed, it has been claimed that ecclesiastics had first introduced bowling at pins, an assertion supported by an ancient chronicle of the German cathedral city of Paderborn.

The clergy personified the *Kegel* as standing for the pagan adversary and wickedness, calling it by the German word *Heide* — 'heathen'. In the way modern ministers of religion might use gimmicks and 'visuals' to attract and impress their flock, German priests invited them to play 'nine-pins' within the church precincts — but not for entertainment. The game was intended to illustrate their fight against sinfulness, how they must knock down the Devil within and without. It was an extraordinary type of participatory worship, with the congregation learning their 'lesson' by play.

Eventually, it was regarded as a test of a man's innocence and pure life. If he was able to hit the target placed at the end of the 'runway' (whether an aisle or — much more likely — a cloister), he had struck down, as it were, the heathen and thereby proved that he was a

God-fearing man. If he failed to do so, it was taken as irrefutable proof of guilt and a sinful life.

Only regular attendance at services could remedy his offence and he was requested to appear again for further trials until eventually, it was hoped, he would succeed in knocking down the pin. It was a peculiar enforcement of practice at pin-bowling, certainly pursued with religious fervour in every sense of the word.

The long cloisters of the monasteries and churches provided an ideal runway, not very unlike the modern alley, a later term derived from the French *aller*, meaning 'to go'.

Once the tests were concluded, those who had scored a hit were congratulated and joined in a thanksgiving dinner.

With the passing of time, the clerics themselves must have realized that, apart from serving as a religious test, the practice was rather enjoyable for its own sake. They too began to throw the ball, to pass leisure time pleasantly. Their students were not slow in acquiring skill and love of the game. That is how the first real bowling contests took place within the church.

It was not surprising that those who had succeeded in hitting the pin in the cloister wished to try their skill outside the supervision and precincts of the church. The game became secular and popular far and wide and developed many local traditions. The pin had several shapes and sizes before it could be defined as 'a piece of wood like a sugar loaf'. It did not take players long to find out that the game would be all the more exciting if, instead of using a single pin, each *Kegler* (player) put up his own so that there were as many pins as players, each of whom tried to knock down all the pins with one throw.

There were variations in the pattern in which the pins were arranged, and in the system of scoring. The pebble first used for a ball was replaced by large, round stones, and then by the modern, wooden ball. At first, the ball could be either rolled or thrown, according to the surface of the skittle alley which consisted, to begin with, of baked clay or of slate blocks and, finally, of wood.

Bowling became part of German social life and was enjoyed on almost every festive occasion, whether in celebration of a baptism or at a country fair. Wealthy citizens built private alleys to entertain guests.

Individual cities did much to foster the game. They arranged public contests and provided good prizes. Gamblers, however, bet heavily on games and gambling reached such proportions that some cities felt the need to restrict bets.

No wonder a game that belonged so much to German life contributed its fair share to German phrases and ideas as well. Some of them, of course, are difficult to translate. A boor was compared to someone who could not hit a pin. To have neither kith nor kin was expressed by saying that he had neither children nor pins (*Kind oder Kegel*), while to move with *Kind und Kegel* (child and pin) came to mean with one's entire family and belongings. *Kegel* was also a metaphor for an illegitimate child. On the other hand, the noise of a thunderstorm was due, the young were told, to St Peter (or the angels) bowling.

With all its ecclesiastical background, it does not seem strange that Martin Luther, the great German reformer, took a liking to the game himself. At the time, the number of pins was not yet generally fixed but differed from city to city, irrespective of the number of players. Some used as many as sixteen pins and others as few as three. Methodically, Luther began to investigate possibilities of improving the game, searching for the ideal number of pins. This, eventually, he found to be nine which — one claim suggests — led to the birth of nine-pin bowling. Luther thus left his mark not only on the religious movements throughout the world but on its playing fields as well, though that kind of fame was soon forgotten.

From Germany bowling spread to adjacent countries. In England the game was known at first (in the thirteenth century) as *kayles* (or *keels*). The Scots called it *kyles*. Those in authority repeatedly tried to outlaw the game as a cause of gambling and hooliganism, and a potential danger to the practice of archery. They described it as something 'dishonourable, useless and unprofitable'.

Nevertheless, kings and nobles sponsored pin bowling. Henry IV had an alley built in the gardens of Old Northumberland House, London, and Henry VIII at Whitehall Palace. Indeed, John Aylmer, Bishop of London in 1576, enjoyed bowls so much that he played it on Sunday afternoons! No wonder that the English tongue, too, has been enriched by the game. We still speak, and paradoxically so in the age of ten-pin bowling, of someone 'going down like a nine-pin', and call the pivot of anything the 'king-pin' after the tallest central pin.

Originally, all bowling took place in the open. The obvious next step was the erection of some kind of shelter, to protect players and spectators at one end of the alley and the pin boy at the other. The first indoor bowling alley was built as early as 1455, in London not surprisingly, considering the vagaries of the English climate. Of course, at that time the halls were very crudely constructed — mere shacks. To expedite play, the ball was returned to the player by means of a sloping lane parallel with the alley.

From Europe, bowling found its way to the New World. In 1626, the Dutch first introduced it to Manhattan Island, though all agree that it was then the lawn variety.

Early Puritan settlers objected to the game and tried their utmost to have it banned. Nevertheless, even some of their own kin could not resist its lure. In 1658, a Puritan felt compelled to confess:

> To those concerned, I hereby say, I should not make confessions which are likely to be read from this page at some future time by public eyes but my conscience is troubling me, so I seek this way to ease it.
>
> The weather is tantalizing warm, but I was tempted to do what I have refrained from doing before. This game of bowls has bewitched me, I fear. For I played

it today and for funds. Yet, I was fortunate, for the bet was £10. Woe unto me! My fellow Puritans will be shocked if they hear of this, but the more reason for my confession.

I like the game, my own ability to win, and the fine folks I meet on the greens. May this confession do my soul good.

The exact time and place of the first 'bowling at pins' in the United States is uncertain. Its earliest literary reference is contained in Washington Irving's *Rip Van Winkle*, published in 1819. This speaks of the thunder of the balls colliding with pins, showing that by then the game must have been generally known.

In the late 1830s its popularity had extended far beyond New York into many other parts of the country. However, gamblers and crooks soon took advantage of the vogue for their own enrichment.

Huge bets were wagered. Bowling alleys became the haunting place of shady types whose behaviour gave the game an evil name.

Matches were rigged and those who refused to play a fixed game were victimized. Refusing to be beaten in the match, they were subsequently beaten up by the thugs who tried to run the game for their own financial gain and that of their cronies.

Things became so bad that the authorities, especially in New York, Massachusetts, and Connecticut, felt obliged to intervene and to classify the game as gambling and, as such, illegal. The Legislature of Connecticut introduced an Act outlawing bowling at nine-pins.

The wording of this and similar edicts was responsible for the birth of ten-pin bowling. The very preciseness of the ban gave those anxious to carry on the game, a loophole. To sidestep the law, they added a tenth pin to the original nine and described the old-new game as 'ten-pin bowling'. No law-enforcing officer could now object. That is how ten-pin bowling came into existence.

In 1895, in New York, the American Bowling Congress was established. Ever since, it has been known by its initials as the A.B.C.

The sport was revolutionized when modern, technological knowledge was applied and ten-pin bowling became completely mechanized.

For centuries, the pinboy had fulfilled various tasks, such as setting up the pins, calling out the number knocked down, and returning the ball to the player. Now he became redundant, being replaced by intricate machinery. Even the score was registered mechanically on a screen known as the pindicator.

Intriguing is the variety and picturesque the expressiveness of the glossary of terms that developed in modern ten-pin bowling. Pins are 'wooden bottles' and the ball the 'apple'. A good ball becomes 'a honey'. A 'barmaid' serves for a hidden pin, while 'No. 7 pin' has become synonymous with a 'mother-in-law'.

Lanes that prove easy for making a hit are 'cheesecakes', while their opposite number, taxing the player's skill, are 'graveyards'. Those so overanxious to succeed that they miss the mark altogether, 'choke'. Pins that survive the first ball are a 'Christmas tree'.

In its new garb bowling at pins (now termed 'indoor bowling') returned from the US to Europe. Britain's first ten-pin bowling centre was established at Stamford Hill, London, by the American Machine and Foundary Company in 1960. A meeting convened at the Conway Hall, London, in 1961, and attended by more than a hundred enthusiasts, resulted in the formation of the British Bowling Organization. Its constitution adopted the rules and regulations of its American parent body and it was spared the teething troubles of a new venture.

No doubt, ten-pin bowling has become commercial, a feature in which it does not differ from such other sports as greyhound racing or professional football. Neither can anyone deny that its world-wide boom was due, to a large degree, to efficient business promotion. And yet, its tremendous popularity, it has been suggested, was the result of whole families being able to join in the game. Ten-pin bowling appealed to every age and to men and women alike. It could be played in all weather and at all times.

Chapter 42

TROTTING

Trotting, or, as it is known in the United States, harness-racing, goes back to the ancient chariot races and may have preceded racing 'in saddle' by many centuries. Even when horse races were first included in the Panhellenic Games, these were still run 'in harness'. It needed many more years for horseback races to be featured in the Olympics.

Even, after that, for a considerable time, chariot races remained the more popular type of equestrian contest then to disappear and only after more than 2000 years to make a comeback. Harness-racing owes its modern development and form almost exclusively to America. Trotting races of a primitive kind were held in the country's early colonial days, particularly in New England, and grew almost accidentally out of people's love of their horses and need of diversion. Young settlers who owned a fast horse that could trot, liked to show it off and prove its superiority in speed against others. To do so they staged the first races along the early rough roads as completely private and improvised contests, watched, perhaps, by interested, friendly neighbours who were glad of a break in their still very lonely existence.

Man's competitive spirit and his delight in rivalry (whether as actual participant or mere observer) led eventually to trotting races being arranged solely for enjoyment. And so in America harness-racing gradually evolved from a local pastime into an independent sport. It was taken up at various places, though records of the first public events are missing. There is implied evidence, however, of their popularity in edicts which were issued in several parts of the country. These either totally outlawed the sport (as in Maryland in 1747), or restricted it to certain days of the year (as in New Jersey in 1748). The very fact that bans were considered necessary indicates that trotting then must have been in existence for some time, and that it had drawn large crowds.

Strangely, it was religion which more than fifty years later unintentionally promoted trotting most of all. Fervent Puritans in New England and along the Atlantic coast had become deeply concerned with people's preoccupation with horse racing and, no doubt, the gambling that accompanied it. They condemned the sport as injurious to spiritual health and detrimental to morals. Their pleas and agitation did not go unheeded and in 1802 they resulted in the closing down of all racing tracks in that part of the country.

However, the religious zealots, in their wrath about racing and its evil effects, had completely ignored the trotting 'field'. The reason for this omission can only be surmised. Perhaps the trotting horse, with its stately gait, did not appear to them to run over-fast, and thus they did not regard trotting as racing. Another possible explanation is that at the time fewer people were attracted by (or made bets on) this different type of equestrian competition. It is likely, too, that the puritanical spoilsports had simply overlooked trotting.

When people could no longer enjoy the 'sport of kings', they found themselves looking for an alternative amusement. They immediately turned to its not-frowned-upon substitute and, by force of the circumstances of the time, trotting assumed a new standing. By its own merit it soon became a most popular pastime. The New York Trotting Club, founded in 1825, laid down the first rules ever for the new sport.

Trotting proper is a gait in which the horse strikes the ground with each diagonally opposite pair of feet alternately: moving one front and the opposite rear leg, together. With a minimum of jerking, the gait ensures a much smoother ride than the gallop.

A story is told of an eighteenth-century Englishman who discovered, quite by chance, the pleasure of riding a trotter. He had purchased a new horse — a thoroughbred — and was trying it out. Never before had he experienced such a comfortable ride. Naturally, he sought an explanation. Dismounting, he ordered one of his grooms to get up on the horse and put it through a variety of manoeuvres, all the time carefully watching its behaviour. He soon realized that the horse did not move in the usual manner, but was 'trotting'. When he told his friends about it, they tried to make their own horses trot but, as the natural gait of a horse is the gallop, they did not succeed.

Whether this apocryphal tale is true or not, a newspaper report in England shows that a trotting event definitely did take place along the Essex road in 1791.

In pacing, the gait of a horse is lateral: both legs on the same side move together. The various gaits of the horse were known in early times. Indeed, they are depicted on the famous fifth-century BC Parthenon frieze, known as the Elgin Marbles, exhibited in the British Museum. Horses carrying Greek soldiers are shown galloping, trotting, and pacing. The cavalry horses of the Roman legions paced. The majority of medieval knights rode horses which trotted.

Trotting is not a natural but an acquired gait which not every horse can be taught. The English learned to hobble a horse to stop it from galloping and encourage it to take to the pacing habit. Once it had grown accustomed to this gait, it was no longer difficult to teach it to trot. At first, Americans did as the English had done.

For trotting to become a success, however, the right type of foundation sire was needed. It was by a strange quirk of nature that America received this precious gift.

American trotting horses as a breed trace back to an English thoroughbred which itself neither paced nor trotted. *Messenger* (which was its name) was a grey stallion, taken to America in 1788 to sire gallopers and certainly not to breed trotters. No one at the time ever imagined that this horse, a descendant of *Darley Arabian*, was to make history on the American trotting field. As intended, for many years all of his offspring were gallopers.

Life must be lived forward but can be understood only backward, as the Danish philosopher Kierkegaard said. It seems that this applies — sometimes — even to the life of a horse. When *Messenger* had grown old, it was felt that he could no longer sire the best thoroughbreds. However, his owner now mated it with mares of a different breed, mostly Canadian thoroughbreds, descended from French Normans.

Meanwhile, men interested in trotting were scouring the country for horses that took easily to this gait and could be trained to perfect it. They found what they were looking for in the crossbreds of *Messenger*. These fulfilled their most ardent hopes as, by some extraordinary phenomena of genetics and inter-breeding, they were born with a natural pacing gait and were able to transmit their potent ability to their progeny. And to convert a pacer into a trotter was not difficult.

As a sire of thoroughbreds *Messenger* had become a celebrated horse and was duly honoured on his death in 1808 after twenty years at stud. A volley was fired over his grave. As so often in life, however, *Messenger's* supreme value as the progenitor of the most perfect trotters was appreciated only after he had passed away.

John H. Wallace was responsible for the coining of the term 'standardbred'. It refers to the 'standard' rules a horse had to meet in its performance to be included in the *Trotting Register,* the first volume of which Wallace published in 1871. Originally, it was stipulated that to qualify for registration as a standardbred, a horse had to be able to trot a mile (1.60 km) in 2.3 minutes. The name standardbred was finally adopted as the official description of the trotting horse by the National Association of Trotting Horse Breeders in 1879.

As the country developed, improved roads enabled farmers and their friends to run much faster trotters. With an increasing wealth, many began to own horse-drawn vehicles and gradually these supplanted saddle horses in transport. Naturally enough it did not take long for people to want to match the two-wheeled carriages in a race. They felt that this was even greater fun than outdistancing each other in the saddle.

To let a horse gallop in harness was out of the question. This gait rocked the cart too much. Pacing, on the other hand, would make the gig sway all the time. The only suitable gait for the purpose was the trot, which ensured a smooth, continuous movement even at fast speed.

Experience soon taught that the ordinary sort of road-cart, or gig, was not made for harness-racing. And thus, carriage makers, at first as a sideline, began to manufacture gigs specially suitable for racing. They had to be designed for speed, comparative lightness, and safety. To avoid unnecessary vibration they had no springs. By a process of trial and error Americans were eventually presented with the 'sulky', which was first used on the country's racing tracks in 1845. It was a high-wheeled carriage for one, with iron tyres, but still rather heavy (weighing about 75 lbs — 33.75 kg.)

Of course, any innovation at first is inevitably opposed by 'experts'. No wonder, therefore, that horsemen began to decry the new contraption and heaped ridicule on the men who dared to ride in it instead of on the horse itself. Their jeers soon died down and harness-racing so caught the imagination of people that trotting in saddle no longer proved an attraction and soon after 1850 was almost completely replaced by the 'horse-powered' racing cart.

Meanwhile another development had occurred. With the ever-increasing traffic, public roads no longer offered the ideal racing course. Such was racing's popularity that it now needed its own track and proper trotting courses were established, giving the sport its final setting. In 1870 the National Trotting Association was formed as the governing body.

There was still much room for improvement. For example, the original, heavy sulky was superseded in 1892 by a much more streamlined model, the 'bicycle sulky'. By the many advantages this presented, it revolutionized trotting. Constructed entirely of tubular steel and equipped with pneumatic tyres on ball-bearing wheels, it weighed between 25 lbs and 30 lbs (11.25 kg and 13.50 kg) — only about one-third the weight of the original gig. Much easier to handle, this 'skeleton carriage' enabled the trotter to race at speeds which had previously been regarded as unattainable.

Harness-racing had been perfected and now fulfilled the most fervent hopes of all devoted to the sport. Dearly loved and widely pursued all over the country, it became America's great contribution to the outdoor sports of the world. Indeed, the trotter has even been called the national horse of America.

Chapter 43

WATER POLO

The name water polo is almost a complete misnomer. In the first place, the game has nothing to do with horses. Nor is the ball used in the water made of wood, the original meaning of the Tibetan word *pulu*. The only correct reference in water polo is to its being an aquatic sport. However, although it was played in clear water, in its early years it was the dirtiest of all team games, in point of rough play.

The story is told that it all began in 1876 by accident; more specifically, through a misfired shot. Members of the Bournemouth Rowing Club were idly tossing a medicine ball about for no other reason than to fill in time. When one of the rowers miscalculated a throw the ball 'landed' in the water. Others jumped after it and soon were engaged in throwing it to each other in the sea.

They enjoyed the diversion so much that they decided, there and then, that this would be a new game.

It is a good story, but alas quite untrue. The only facts it contains are that water polo was devised in England and developed by the Bournemouth Rowing Club.

Actually, water polo was first played with the intention of creating a new water sport. It is one of the few sports which did not grow out of small, haphazard beginnings.

Water polo had its origin in a slump in swimming. Promoters were very concerned because swimming competitions had become so monotonous that they no longer attracted crowds, and business was at an all-time low.

What was needed was a new, spectacular game that would give swimming fresh appeal and excitement. Clearly, swimming was in desperate need of a shot in the arm.

In 1869, patrons who had busied themselves with finding a new stimulus, conceived the idea of 'football in water'. The rules of water polo in fact are based on those of soccer. England had been the first country in the world to make swimming a competitive sport and the first nation to build indoor pools. Now it became the first to combine football and swimming in the new game of water polo.

Its description as such came later. In its infancy, water polo was known by other, perhaps more appropriate names, such as aquatic football, aquatic handball, and water soccer.

The game's very nature gave much room for foul play. After all, a referee could not well observe what was going on under water, and players often took advantage of his restricted view. Water polo became one of the roughest and crudest of sports, marred by wholly unsporting tactics. In the beginning, of course, there were no rules at all. All that mattered was the scoring of a goal, by fair means or foul.

To wrest the ball from a swimmer who was making for the goal, players sometimes did not hesitate to apply what was described without much exaggeration as drowning tactics. They held the man in possession in a tight grip under the water until he let go the ball. Again, players were often dunked at the outset for a considerable time in order to weaken them. Water polo frequently deteriorated into a wrestling match, with the more ruthless team, not the more capable, winning.

It was these factors that led to the laying down of the first rules. These aimed especially at making water polo a clean, but nevertheless virile, sport. There were other considerations as well. The fusion of good handball with skilful, fast swimming made great demands on the players. They had to excel at getting about in the water while catching and throwing an elusive ball, all the time in an element that gave them no firm footing. The goalkeeper had to 'jump from nothing' to reach high shots. Throughout the game the players had to keep the head high above the water to follow the progress of the ball.

In short, the players had to reach a high point of efficiency in two sports simultaneously. They had to be alert, speedy swimmers and top handball players as well. They had to be superbly fit so that their swimming was almost automatic and unflagging in all kinds of situations.

The development of water polo owes most to William Wilson, of Glasgow, a fervent sportsman who has even been called its founder.

In 1870 a committee of members from the London Swimming Club agreed on the first rules of water soccer. These had little resemblance to the present-day code. Each team then consisted of only three players.

In the years that followed, several attempts were made to popularize the game. The first really official match took place at the Crystal Palace, London, in 1874. We are fortunate that an account of a contest arranged in 1876 by the Bournemouth Rowing Club has been preserved. It was of an unexpectedly short duration and terminated when vigorous handling of the flimsy rubber ball made it burst. A newspaper reported:

> The Bournemouth Premier Rowing Club carried out the first of a series of aquatic hand-ball matches off the pier. Goals were marked by four flags moored at the west of the pier, fifty yards apart. After a severe struggle, the ball burst, but the players, nothing daunted and properly habited, displayed their aquatic accomplishments for some time.

The number of players was now fixed at seven a side and the size of teams has remained the same ever since. The area of play, hitherto undefined, was also determined, and a referee and two goal judges were appointed.

There were no proper goals yet, and to make a score,

players had to place the ball on a floating platform or a shelf at the end of the playing area. The game was still so rough that men were kept in reserve to take the place of injured team mates. Nevertheless, water polo by now had proved its potential and those anxious to see it gain firm place in popularity ratings set to work to organize it more efficiently.

The laws eventually agreed upon were still unwritten. With the exception of the goalkeeper, players were to use only one hand to throw the ball and, in doing so, could not stand on the bottom. Everyone, however, could duck an opponent and swim under water, with or without the ball. This new code was adopted by swimming clubs all over Britain.

The rules were still much too loose so that the many teams which had come into existence interpreted them in their own way, causing bitter controversy and much confusion. As a result, the game lacked status. In fact, for several years the English Amateur Swimming Association refused to recognize water polo as a separate and proper sport. It sanctioned it in 1885. Taking control of the game, the association introduced new rules and demanded their strict observance. These provided among other things that:

- the game's duration was to be twenty minutes.
- the ball should be passed from player to player and could be carried either on or below the surface of the water.
- no player was permitted to interfere with the goalkeeper, whether in or out of the water, or to hold his opponent unless he was in possession of the ball.
- penalties for infringements were to be a free throw from the spot where the foul occurred.
- a goal was scored when the ball had been fairly placed on a floating stage or a boat, used for that purpose.
- on the scoring of a goal, the umpire had to blow a whistle, which terminated play for the time being.

But even these rules were far from final. Throughout the years, and on many occasions, they were amended.

A proper goal was prescribed: eight feet (2.40 m) wide and extending six feet (1.80 m) above the water. Most of all, those anxious to see the game prosper aimed at removing its many rough features and making it a contest distinguished by great skill and stamina.

The first International Match was played between England and Scotland in 1890, the Scots winning by four goals to none. Five years later, the biennial match between England and Ireland came into being. Meanwhile, the sport had spread to the United States where two types of water polo developed. One was 'soft ball polo', appropriately and better known also as 'American water polo'. But because of the extreme roughness of play in this version, it soon declined and gave way to the second type, known as 'hard ball polo'. This was the original European game with a fully inflated, leather-covered ball. Its final adoption in the Olympic Games (for the first time in Paris in 1900) gave it world prestige.

From 1893 onward water polo was gradually adopted all over Europe: first in Germany and Austria and next in Hungary. It was in Eastern European countries especially that the game enjoyed its greatest boom. There the sport was fostered at tremendous expense and most ambitious training programs were drawn up. Players from Hungary, Yugoslavia, Rumania, and the Soviet Union became among the finest in the world. Their intense practice was pursued almost continuously for many hours each day.

The first European water polo championship tournament took place in Budapest in 1926. The year 1950 saw the establishment of the International Water Polo Board, responsible for a unified draft of rules on a worldwide scale, thereby stopping, once and for all, the haphazard growth, with rules and play differing from country to country.

It was in the same year that a new regulation drastically changed the sport and basically divided its history into two definite periods. Until then, all play stopped when a foul occurred and the referee blew his whistle. All players had to remain stationary until the ball had been thrown back into play. This, naturally, caused periods of inaction and tended to render the game uninteresting, especially from the spectators' viewpoint. The new code, however, allowed all, except the man taking the free throw, to keep moving. This speeded up the game considerably and changed its style completely.

Water polo is really still a young sport. Its rules continue to be amended periodically with the aim of emphasizing the importance of tactical play and of adding to the game's popular appeal.

Chapter 44

WATER SKIING

Claims clash as to who invented water skiing, and France vies with the United States for the honour. And there is some confusion in another respect. The sport's very name indicates that its beginnings can be traced either to the water or to the snow — to the enthusiasm of aquaplanists or of snow skiers.

Quite possibly water skiing was conceived independently and almost simultaneously in both France and the US, arising from different circumstances in each country. Without doubt, technical improvements to speedboats (and the consequent reduced costs) gave some the idea of exploring new possibilities for sport on water. The water ski itself is an evolution of the snow ski (known for more than 5000 years) and the aquaplane (very much in evidence around 1914). While, however, in snow skiing the propelling power was in the skier's own exertion, in water skiing it was in the engine of the boat.

Man, always in search of new adventure, will make use of any opportunity offered him to add to the thrills of life by adopting some new method to propel him faster through the air, along the ground, across or beneath the water. It is not surprising therefore that when launches became motorboats with speeds up to 16 mph (25.60 km), some adventurous young man (or woman) conceived the idea of being pulled along the surface of the water at an ever accelerated speed. All that was needed was a flat board on which to stand, and a rope to link the plane with the boat.

Undoubtedly, that is how aquaplaning came into existence. To ride on a plank, usually five to six feet (1.50
m to 1.80 m) in length, ranging in shape from circular
to rectangular (or just a door or a garbage-can cover)
and be towed by a speedboat, was thus described by
a combination of the Latin word for water — *aqua* —
and 'planing', a term that denoted the act of riding on
the surface of the water, rather than displacing it.

It was in pursuit of this sport, so it is told, that
'accidentally' water skiing was invented. It, too, belongs
to that category of progress in civilization where a mishap
is responsible for something entirely new. Count Maximilian Pulaski, the story goes, was aquaplaning with
a lady friend at Juan les Pins, on the French Riviera.
His companion lost her balance and fell into the water.
It is not told how far the Count went out of his way
to help the Mademoiselle, who somehow must have
reached dry land safely. However, her empty board got
into the way of the Count, bumping his plane. Trying
to push it aside with one foot, he stepped on it and
at that moment learned the delight of water skiing.

Realizing the potentialities of what he had discovered
through the mishap, with a few friends the Count developed two smaller shaped aquaplanes which were bound
to the feet. The best shape and the convenience of holding
the ropes in one's hands were discovered after some
experimentation.

Among those who had watched the Count was Jay
Gould, an American millionaire, then living at Juan les
Pins. He had actually developed the resort by building
its casino and Grand Hotel. An astute businessman, he
at once grasped the new sport's great future and, with
his wife, lost no time in putting it on a proper basis.
From the French Riviera it made its way into Spain
and down the Italian coast to the Isle of Capri.

Even in France the Count is not the sole claimant.
The invention of water skiing is also linked with officers
of the famous *Chasseurs Alpins*, French ski shock troops.
On leave in Cannes (some records date it to 1929), they
were enjoying *skijoring*, the thrilling sport of being pulled

on skis over ice and snow by a horse, on the shores of Lake Annecy. In a spirit of fun, some friends suggested that the officers take their snow skis on to the water to be pulled along by a motor boat.

The men took up the challenge, although it had never been meant seriously. At first, they fell into the water as a result of the speed the tow boat travelled and learned, as a consequence, their skis were too narrow. One of the officers shortened and widened the skis and altered the position of the binding to his feet, at the same time modifying the curving toe of the ski — and this led to success, the birth of water skiing.

Another French claim, also associated with the Riviera, asserts that one day in 1920, playboys and their friends discussed how they could transfer the principles of snow skiing to the water. With this purpose in mind they joined a pair of snow skis by means of a small board and on this H-shaped contraption made trial runs, pulled by a motor launch. It was in the wake of these pioneers that water skiing developed, eventually taking the place of aquaplaning.

Completely different from these various European traditions, some of which are certainly amusing if not apocryphal, the American story of water skiing is simple and well substantiated. It goes back to one man, Fred Waller of Long Island, whose inventive genius has also given the world the cinerama. His is the credit for water skiing as we know it today.

In 1924, Waller became definitely the first man in the New World to make his own water skis, and ride behind a boat (on Long Island Sound). Soon afterwards he took out the original patent for his Dolphin Akwa Skees. They were twice the length of the snow ski, and the earliest models made were very similar to the French ones.

His new sport greatly resembled aquaplaning, as the tips of each ski were linked with a bridle (to keep the two ropes apart) which in turn was attached by a single line to the launch. The rider balanced himself by means of two ropes joined to the bow-end of each ski.

Waller eventually discarded this and evolved a type more or less identical with the modern Free Tow Boards. Its advantage was that the skis were no longer pulled directly by the boat. The rider himself held the tow-rope while his feet were secured to the skis by shoe-like bindings.

Another pioneer was Don Ibsen, of Bellevue, Washington, who made his first pair of skis in the early 1930s. He steamed a couple of cedar boards over a five-gallon (22.70 l) can of boiling water, and then moulded his skis to the desired shape around the end of a telegraph pole. Instead of the foot binding which was used later, he merely mounted a block of wood on each ski, against which to press his feet. He then replaced the blocks with tennis shoes tied to the skis with rubber bands.

The development of much cheaper outboard craft, its fast acceleration, and the fact that it produced a much smaller wake than inboards, contributed to the sudden popularity of water skiing. All age groups (from seven to seventy, it was said) could enjoy skimming across water on skis, either singly or in groups, just for the sake of rushing along at high speed, or in competition with others.

Very rapidly the sport developed many new features. These included riding in pairs, being towed backward, and riding on one ski. The last named, referred to as mono-skiing, may have been introduced through another accident: a rider losing one ski and realizing that he could still maintain balance on the other.

The sport took its terminology from snow skiing and many of water skiing's thrilling features were adaptations from it. In the slalom, the water skier had to run a multiple S course between buoys (replacing the original flags of the snow field known as 'gates'). These were spaced at varying intervals and the water skier zigzagged through the wake of the tow-boat.

Dick Pope, Sr, creator of Florida Cypress Gardens, and one of the great American pioneers of water skiing, introduced jumping into the sport when he made the first leap from a low slanted ramp off Miami Beach in 1928. Referring to it in his book on *Water Skiing* he wrote: 'Sometimes the first person to do something sets off a reaction that reverberates through the world. My "first" did just that . . . The record I set was twenty-five feet as I soared through the air thinking I would never come down.' Charles R. (Chuck) Sleigh, an American furniture manufacturer, was the first person to do turn-arounds. He used ordinary skis with the fins removed.

The earliest record of trick skiing belongs to the United States as well — to John H. (Jack) Andresen, an engineer, who took up the sport in 1933 after seeing a picture of a French water skier. His demonstrations, and those of the Pope brothers, won over many former aquaplanists.

The more efficient the skier became, the smaller his skis grew. Eventually, skis were replaced by 'shoes' and then — the ultimate in water skiing — nothing was used underfoot. When approaching a speed of 25 mph (40 km/h) the rider slid off his skis and continued to travel over the water on the soles of his bare feet. Dick Pope, Jr, is said to have been the first to display the new art of barefoot skiing in 1947. It was a feat so unbelievable that when a correspondent to the 'Live Letters' of the London *Daily Mirror* inquired whether it was possible to water ski without skis, the editor replied that he would not think so but that 'of course, it depends on the size of your feet'. Contrary to what most people would surmise, barefoot skiing cannot possibly damage the soles of the feet. Neither is it restricted (another false notion) to skiers with large, flat feet.

Barefoot skiing clubs became among the most exclusive in the world. Only those who had skied barefoot for a minimum of sixty seconds (a figure halved in the case of juniors and women) were eligible for membership.

The immense popularity of the sport was due not least to its promotion by Dick Pope, Sr, who also was an expert at aquaplaning. It was his philosophy that anyone who could walk could learn to water ski in minutes. Displays and stunts he performed with his brother Malcolm led people all over the world to adopt the sport, and not without reason he was called the true father of American water skiing.

The outbreak of World War II temporarily halted the remarkable rise of the new aquatic pastime. In 1946 organizations throughout the world combined in the International Water Ski Union which sponsored the first world championship in Juan les Pins, France, in 1949. The sport thus returned, fully grown, to its (alleged) birthplace.

Riders developed their own sign language to communicate with the skipper of their boat. The universal signal of an 'O' made with the forefinger and thumb, indicated that everything was 'OK'. A request to cut the motor was conveyed by drawing a finger across the throat in a cutting motion. An upward movement of the open palms told the captain to 'speed up', if both hands were in use, a nod of the head was all that was needed.

Chapter 45

WRESTLING

Surrounded by jungle inhabited by wild beasts, experience taught prehistoric man that proficiency in wrestling could save his life, and so he practised the art with members of his own family and tribe.

Wrestling is one of the most ancient recorded sports. It is an innate wish of man to prove himself superior to his fellows and in primitive times he could best do so by displaying his physical prowess and forcing his opponent, literally, on to the ground. Men wrestled long before the invention of arms or armour.

In warfare, especially, it took its early significant place when victory in battle was determined not by the mass clash of armies, but by individual combat.

At first, wrestling was more a test of brute strength than of skill, and victory often went to the heavier and more ruthless adversary. A tribe's champion wrestler was greatly honoured and matches were often arranged with the experts of other tribes.

About 5000 years ago, in ancient Assyria and Egypt, the technique of wrestling was highly developed and practically all present-day holds were known.

Numerous monuments testify to the sport's early existence. A bronze statue excavated in the former Mesopotamia, from a temple near Baghdad, shows two wrestlers in action. (The same archaeological site has yielded one of the earliest representations of boxing.)

Vivid paintings discovered on the walls of the temple tombs of Beni Hasan on the Nile depict a great variety of wrestling positions and almost every type of hold. A wrestler, painted red, can be seen struggling with another painted black. Another such pair is shown with one man grasping the other around the waist, and so on through all the well-known holds of today.

From Assyria and Egypt, wrestling found its way to Greece, although later legend ascribed its introduction there to the Athenian hero, Theseus. He was the first, it was said, to understand and lay down the principles of the sport, and it was this knowledge that enabled him to overcome, not by strength but by skill, the murderous Cercyon.

Greek mythology tells how this ancient king, who had put to death his own daughter, used to challenge strangers passing through Eleusis, a city-state fourteen miles (22.40 km) west of Athens. When Theseus entered the city and came face to face with Cercyon, he accepted the challenge. Boldly, he dashed his opponent to the ground and killed him.

Classic contests are described by Homer. The match between Ajax and Odysseus is the most famous of all.

Wrestling belonged to the life of the Greeks. They made it both a science and an art and it was regulated by strict rules. Manuals of wrestling were published, carefully explaining every detail. Fragments of such an early textbook have been discovered in the form of an ancient Egyptian papyrus. Wrestling eventually became so popular that, just as nowadays we may invite a friend for a round of golf or a game of bowls, Greeks asked each other to go wrestling together.

The rules varied for men and boys. The different holds, throws, and movements were taught systematically, advancing from the simplest to the most complex style. Some states included women as wrestlers and even permitted them to compete with men.

With the growth of the sport, individual schools developed their own methods. One favoured upright wrestling. The aim was to throw the opponent to the ground who after three 'throws' had to concede defeat. Another type permitted the struggle to continue on the ground to end only when one of the wrestlers was pinned down by both shoulders.

Wrestlers used to oil their bodies before starting a match. Why they did so has been variously explained. The suggestion that its purpose was to render the body so slippery that the opponent should be unable properly to get a hold is incorrect. It was done for hygienic reasons: to cover the pores of the skin lest the sand and dust of the arena clog them. This view is confirmed by the additional practice after oiling the body to rub it in with fine powdered clay, which certainly helped the wrestlers to gain a better grip. Aristophanes alludes to some cunning and unsportsmanlike wrestler who, apparently unobserved, rubbed off the dust from his shoulders so that his adversary should not be able to get a grip on this vulnerable part of the body.

The arena was covered with a thick layer of sand to soften the impact of falls. As matches were held in the open air and therefore were subject to weather conditions, at times (fights then took place exclusively in summer) heavy downpours changed the ring into a mud bath. To be prepared for such eventualities, training was pursued in two types of ring, one the customary sandy arena, the other 'wet', colloquially described as 'bees' wax'. In the training, wrestlers changed over from one ring to the other, giving rise to a vivid phrase, speaking of going 'out of the sand into the mud', anticipating by millennia our own saying, 'out of the frying pan into the fire'.

Wrestlers were very conscious of the hold their hair could provide and therefore (also possibly to avoid injuries to the head) donned a protective headcover. We know that in at least one case such a leather cap was sent as a gift to a wrestler — by the Latin poet Martial. Using his art of poetry, he penned his accompanying note in the form of a verse, explaining that the cap would be able to cover his friend's oiled locks, lest the mud of the ring soil his sleek hair.

Wrestling became a popular feature of almost all Greek feasts and sporting events, particularly of the

Olympic Games. Greek poets, such as Pindar, claimed that actually the Olympic Festival came into existence in 776 BC as the the direct result of a wrestling match between the gods Zeus and Cronos.

Historically, however, wrestling was introduced into the Olympic Games only in the eighteenth Olympiad in 704 BC as part of the *Pentathlon.* A competition in five events, it was devised to suit the all-round athlete. Probably only those who proved themselves superior in running, jumping, throwing of the javelin, and the discus were permitted to wrestle.

A special feature was known as the *Pancratium,* from the Greek, meaning 'all strength'. This contest combined wrestling and boxing. The fighters were naked and their struggle was brutal. The bout ended only when one of the contestants yielded or, as was frequently the case, with his death.

Milon of Croton who lived in the sixth century BC, was the most renowned of all Greek wrestlers. An athlete of extraordinary strength, he was six times victor in wrestling at the Olympic, and six times at the Pythian Games.

The widespread practice of wrestling is confirmed by the Bible. Perhaps it was mastery of the art that enabled Samson, the biblical Hercules, to subdue with his bare hands the lion in the vineyards of Timnah.

The best-known reference of all is the passage that relates to 'wrestling Jacob'. Indeed, his combat with the mysterious being has been cited as the explanation of the very name Israel, thought to mean 'a wrestler with God'.

Jacob was returning home after many years of self-imposed exile, having fled from Esau's wrath. He was still not certain whether, even after that long absence, his brother had forgiven him for stealing their father's blessing. Then, one night, before crossing the river Jabbok 'there wrestled a man with him until the breaking of the day'.

The match seemed to go on indefinitely, with neither contestant gaining the upper hand. When at the breaking of dawn, Jacob finally managed to hold his adversary in a grip so firm that escape seemed impossible, the unidentified foe suddenly grasped his thigh, and dislocated it. The fight was ended. Apparently, Jacob was still the winner. But he could be seen, with his thighbone out of joint, walking with a distinct limp.

In memory of this wrestling injury, as related in the Bible, observant Jews to this day abstain from eating the part of an animal's body containing the thigh vein, traditionally explained as the sciatic nerve. Only when this has been completely removed is that portion of the animal ritually permitted for human consumption. It is a millennia-old perpetuation of the memory of a biblical wrestling match!

Probably all wrestling referred to in the Bible took the form of belt-wrestling. Its principle was to make a hold on a special belt worn by the contestants. All men of rank owned it as treasured, personal property showing individual marks of distinction. That is why, for instance, it served Judah, with his staff and signet, as a means of unmistakable identification.

A knowledge of belt-wrestling is even an aid to the proper understanding of the imagery used in some biblical phrases. A typical example is Isaiah's picture of the Davidic king in the Messianic Age. His belt (or girdle, as other translations render the Hebrew word) would be that of righteousness.

'To gird one's loins' is yet another Hebrew phrase which, through the Bible, has become part of English idiom, in the sense of preparing oneself for vigorous action. According to some, it, too, might be a linguistic survival of ancient belt-wrestling.

The New Testament, in the Epistle to the Ephesians (VI:10) speaks of the spiritual warrior who, in face of the Devil's wiles, strong in the Lord is equipped with God's armour. This fight, too, is dramatically pictured as a wrestling match: 'our wrestling is not against flesh and blood but . . . against the world-rulers of this darkness . . . Stand therefore, having girded your loins with truth.'

When the Romans had conquered Greece, they continued her wrestling matches but adapted them to their own traditions. They refined the sport and barred some of its most cruel features. Their new style became known as Graeco-Roman.

With the fall of the Roman Empire, wrestling lost much of its popularity and for some time at least, was looked upon with disdain. It was the spiritual and mental part of man that mattered and not his body.

Meanwhile, wrestling had spread all over Europe where eventually once again it became a noble sport and a royal pastime. Rulers prided themselves on their champion wrestlers. Matches were popular and international tournaments noteworthy events. For a medieval king to count among his subjects a victorious wrestler was deemed irrefutable proof of his people's superiority. From the Middle Ages on the sport was practised ever more systematically.

Nations adopted their own systems and rules. These even differed in essential details in the countries themselves, just as they had done in ancient Greece.

Wrestling caught on in Britain from the earliest days. The Saxons and Celts were partial to it.

The historic bout between King Henry VIII and Francis I of France, said to have taken place in 1520, has been variously described. One tradition tells, how, from their royal box, both kings watched their men engaged in a fight. When the English easily gained the upper hand, Henry gloated over their victory and lightheartedly made fun of their French opponents. This enraged the French king so much that he jumped from his seat and, in full view of the crowd, grappled with Henry. Fortunately, onlookers stopped the bout, which could have had disastrous results.

Another version relates that during the month-long festival of the Field of the Cloth of Gold, Henry challenged his royal colleague, saying: 'Brother, we wolle wrestle.' Francis could not refuse without loss of face. Soon the English king's superior strength became apparent. The Frenchman was well aware that his opponent had a bad leg. Suddenly he grasped it, and pinned Henry. The French rejoiced at their king's unfair victory, while Henry's followers sat in glum silence.

Accounts of the time mysteriously add that 'the blackened face of His Grace was turned to the Queen'. We are left to wonder why. Was it in search of a word of comfort or perhaps to use her as a scapegoat . . . maybe as an excuse for her later execution? Whatever the answer, many feared that the wrestling match might precipitate a war.

The English developed many local styles. Most distinct among them were those of the west country (Cornwall and Devon), Lancashire, and, best-known of all, Cumberland and Westmoreland. Almost every public holiday was marked by matches attended by the noble and great.

In the Cumberland and Westmoreland style a firm hold is taken at the very beginning of the contest. Whoever loses the grip first, or touches the ground with any part of his body, is declared defeated. Should both contestants fall and it is not possible to judge who touched the ground first, such a 'dog fall', as it is termed, necessitates a repetition of the bout.

Lancashiremen, on the other hand, employed a technique which is the forerunner of the modern catch-as-catch-can, already known among Indians, Chinese, and Greeks. There is almost no limit to what fighters can do. They may grasp any part of each other's body. Tripping is permitted, but deliberate kicking, scratching, or biting, and all dangerous holds and strangleholds are fouls. A bout ends when one wrestler succeeds in forcing his opponent's two shoulder-blades on the mat simultaneously.

In Cornish and Devon wrestling, fighters had to throw their opponent in such manner that he would touch the ground with three 'points', for instance with his two shoulders and a hip.

Sir Thomas Parkyns (d. 1741) was a famous protagonist of Cornish wrestling. An author and an able athlete himself, he established an annual wrestling match in the park of his ancestral estate at Bunny Park, Nottinghamshire, England. The prizes he offered were a gold-laced hat, valued at twenty-two shillings, for the winner, and three shillings for the second best. Though the amounts were small, it was said, the glory was great.

Sir Thomas admonished wrestlers to be sober men. 'Whoever would be a complete wrestler,' he wrote, 'must avoid being overtaken in drink, which very much enervates, or, being in a passion at the sight of his adversary, or having received a fall, in such cases he is bereaved of his senses, not being master of himself is less of his art, but sheweth too much play, or none at all, or rather pulleth, kicketh, and ventureth beyond all reason and his judgement when himself.

> That man's a fool, that hopes for good,
> From flowing bowls and feverish blood.'

One of the queer habits of the noble lord, certainly unique of its kind, was collecting stone coffins. These were to be a reminder of mortality, teaching his champion wrestlers that, no matter what happened, the great wrestler, Death, would be the final victor.

Prizes awarded in the early 1820s were of three types. Most common was a leather belt, inscribed with the winner's name and where and when the match had taken place. Another, rather odd, trophy was a length of cloth or buckskin out of which the winner could make himself a pair of breeches. On occasions, a silver cup was presented.

American Indians were acquainted with wrestling long before the advent of the white man. It became popular among America's early pioneers and accounts abound of their matches with Indians. Many years before Abraham Lincoln became President of the United States, he was famed for his wrestling ability.

Wrestling was always most popular in Asia. The Mongolians and Chinese made it part of religious celebrations. Continuous practice gave their hands extraordinary power and included a simple daily exercise, repeated innumerable times: closing the fingers as tightly as possible around a handful of wet sand.

The Japanese excelled in the sport and developed their own indigenous style known as Sumo. An ancient myth tells that the Japanese people were given their homeland as the result of a Sumo match in which a Shinto god defeated an aborigine.

The earliest fights were to the death. The first recorded match dates back to 23 BC and Sukune, its winner, has been revered ever since as the patron of wrestlers. In AD 858 succession to the Japanese throne is said to have been determined by a Sumo contest between two princes.

Wrestlers engaged in the fight almost completely in the nude; all they wore was a silken girdle. They learned to observe a strict and solemn ritual before actually joining in combat. To drive away evil spirits, they stamped with their feet the ground which they sanctified with handfuls of salt. To purify themselves they washed their mouths, and to assure all that they were hiding no weapon, they stretched out their hands and their arms. Only after the completion of these various acts was the sign given for the contest to begin. As was only to be expected, Sumo became part of the training of the Samurai.

Japanese wrestlers always prided themselves on their weight, often tipping the scales at 450 lbs. (202.50 kg). For centuries they chose their wives from their own circle, as they were convinced that only by inbreeding would they maintain their strong physique.

As practised today, wrestling can be divided into several main categories. There are the Cumberland and Westmoreland style and catch-as-catch-can, the immediate successor of the Lancashire technique. The modern Graeco-Roman style is not, as the name suggests, the original classical wrestling. In fact, it little resembles it. Extensively used in European countries, its holds are limited to the body above the waist, and neither legs nor feet may be used to bring about a fall, in which both shoulders must touch the ground.

All-in wrestling combines the greatest variety of features, including the painful and dangerous holds barred in all other types. Added to them are some prominent forms of ju-jitsu as well. In short almost anything is legitimate to bring about defeat. The bout ends when an adversary is held in such a position that he cannot disengage himself. Apparently savage, this is the most spectacular type of wrestling, which has come to rely frequently more on showmanship than sportsmanship.

Wrestling is a combative sport and a manly art, a game of wits and rapid thinking. Misapplied, it can lead to brutality or commercialized entertainment, where money comes first and the sport second. Performed with skill and a determined spirit, it can rate not only as one of the oldest but also as one of the most dramatic sports.

Chapter 46

OLYMPICS

Early in the history of Greece, the practice of athletics and gymnastics became a national pursuit. Second to none was the importance the Greeks attached to seeking a healthy mind in a healthy body and they glorified sporting champions in their epics and poems, as the writings of Homer testify.

They believed that contests of strength not only invigorated the body but moulded the mind; that they were not simply peaceful preparations for winning wars (of which there were plenty), but that they helped to renew the spirit of the departed and to win the aid of the gods.

No wonder, therefore, that the Olympic Games, once they had been regularly established, began to dominate Greek life, so much so indeed that the Greeks counted their years according to the Olympiads. In a nation that made even its calendar subject to sport, it was not surprising that traditions arose that regarded the Games not only as a national institution, but being of divine origin, or linked at least with the earliest national heroes. Greek mythology contains many legends which trace the beginnings of the Games into the distant past. This in itself could explain the sacred character with which they were invested.

Linked with the very mist of legend is the tradition that Zeus himself was the creator of the Games. He and Cronos were then the most powerful gods and in a titanic struggle wrestled with each other on the lofty peaks for possession of the Earth. Zeus won the combat and to celebrate his victory, and commenorate it for all time, the Games were held in the valley below.

Best known is the myth that associates the birth of the Olympics with the cleaning of a cowshed — the saga of Augeas, King of Elis and owner of a herd of 3000 oxen. His rule extended over the very district in which Olympia is situated. Rich pasture land had enabled a multitude of cattle and horses to flourish, resulting in such an enormous amount of filth that the countryside, as well as the stables, were overflowing with it. In fact, Augeas' stables had not been cleaned for thirty years.

It seemed that only someone endowed with super-human power could carry out the task. The hero Heracles, who had just completed yet another (the fourth) of his famous feats, undertook to clean the stables in a single day. Augeas agreed to pay him one tenth of his herds, if he did so in that period.

Heracles gladly accepted the challenge and carried out his contract — in a most unexpected manner. He diverted the rivers Alpheus and Peneus so that they ran straight through the 'Augean stables', flushing out all the filth and dung.

Augeas certainly did not like the way Heracles had won his prize, and outwitted him. In anger, he gathered a force to attack and kill Heracles. However, he himself was slain. To perpetuate his victory, Heracles consecrated the grove of Olympia and inaugurated the Games which ever since have been called by its name.

Two generations further back in the Greek mystical past is another legend which links the Olympic Games with Pelops, the grandfather of Heracles, whose name is recalled by the Peloponese peninsula in the south of Greece. Pelops had fallen in love with Hippodameia and asked Oenomaus, her father, for her hand. This was refused. Some suggest that an oracle had warned Oenomaus that he would be killed by his son-in-law or his offspring. Others claim that he himself was in love with his daughter. Who then could blame him if, on either count, he raised strong objections to any suitor?

Yet to do so without giving a feasible reason, was

out of the question. So, cunningly, he contrived a scheme which he was sure would work to his advantage. A champion charioteer and owning the swiftest horses, he challenged each suitor to a chariot race extending from Olympia to the Isthmus of Corinth. The prize was Hippodameia, the penalty of defeat for the suitor, death. To appear more than fair, he gave the prospective son-in-law a head start, while he offered a sacrifice at the mountain. In thirteen contests the race was his and on each occasion he slew the luckless suitor when overtaking him.

In Pelops, however, he found his match, if not in racing the chariot, in cunning. Before the race, Pelops succeeded in bribing Oenomaus' groom, who substituted wax pins in the axles of his regal master's chariot with the result that it crashed during the race, and Oenomaus was killed.

Pelops wedded Hippodameia and on the hallowed ground of Olympia established the Games in celebration and as a thanksgiving for his treble triumph: his victory, his marriage, and his father-in-law's death. It was rather a homicidal beginning of a contest pursued now for peace.

Another myth, recorded by the Greek writer Pausanias, credits a different Heracles with the inauguration of the Games. He was the eldest of the five Dactyl brothers who had protected the infant Zeus on Mount Ida, in Crete. The five had gone to Elis to pay homage to Cronos, who had been the lord of the universe before the time of the Olympic gods. Heracles had then organized a footrace at Olympia with his brothers, and crowned the winner with a wreath of wild olive branches he had brought from a far-off land. Thus the Games and the beautiful custom of awarding the victor a crown of wild olives originated. Because the brothers were five ('the five fingers of Ida'), the Games were held every fifth year.

(This apparently differs from our tradition that the Games take place every fourth year. It must be realized, however, that the ancient Greeks determined the date of the festival by the passage of four full years from the previous celebration, so that actually the next Games were scheduled in the fifth year. A carving of five inter-locked rings on an altar in the stadium of Delphi sym-bolized this five-year cycle. In fact, this very design has become the modern symbol of the Olympic Games. Reinterpreted, it is now understood to represent the five continents and a contest in which men and women of the most diverse races and nations meet and compete.)

Surely, as Strabo, the Greek historian, noted two thousand years ago, all of these myths must be dis-counted as unreal. Yet they indicate the veneration that was paid to the Olympic Games in those distant days. Also, there is no doubt that out of the mystery and obscurity of the mythology that surrounds their incep-tion, many a grain of truth can be gathered as to how it all began.

The choice of Olympia for the site of the Games had its manifold reasons: theological, political, and practical. So closely linked with the gods, it was a most sacred region, ensuring the gods' presence and protection. It also was, at it were, politically neutral territory and therefore would not arouse feelings of jealousy as would have happened had the Games been held in any of the participants' own cities. Finally, the vastness of the plain bounded by the rivers Alpheus and Cladeus made it possible for large crowds to assemble.

When the 'first' Olympic Games were held in 776 BC, they were not truly the first of their kind but are only described as such because the oldest records of winners stem from that time. The Games were patterned on much more ancient, sacred rites, tracing back thousands of years, to the Asian steppes, to funeral games to honour and propitiate the departed. It is quite probable that Indo-European races when eventually they invaded Greece from the north, brought with them the strange tradition.

The ancient Greeks already believed that man's death did not mean his complete extinction. His spirit survived in some 'shady' form and he continued to dwell near his former abode. Thus, honouring the dead still so near, and thereby keeping their goodwill, was not just piety but an anxious concern for self-preservation.

For this purpose, early Greek chieftains appointed certain days or seasons during which, they were convinced, the spirits of the dead would join them and, though invisible themselves, watch them closely.

The living therefore considered it their solemn duty to entertain the dead as living persons by taking part in what had been the favourite pursuit of the departed on earth. The setting aside of a special day for this would give the dead greatest pleasure, and reinforce their waning strength. Chieftains, or their delegates, went around anxiously collecting data on essential items for the program, whose range grew very wide indeed.

Early Greek civilization had taught men to sharpen their wits in rhetorical bouts, to create outstanding beauty in the form of sculptures, and to compose music that would lend grace and health to body and soul. Hence, to please the disembodied spirit, it was only proper and wise to hold rhetorical contests, exhibit new sculptures, write and recite poetry, and vie with each other in the performance of musical compositions.

Surpassing everything else, of course, was the Greeks' love of athletics and it was small wonder that the various branches known then — running, jumping, wrestling, and throwing — became a major part of the program. There was no doubt in the Greek mind that the better the performance, the more graciously it would be received by the spirits. To serve them was the sole object of the forerunner of the Olympics.

According to this explanation, the Games were therefore held first of all to honour an ancestor hero, or god, and to please and appease his spirit. Neglect to do so might have most unpleasant consequences for the survivors. That is why, too, as those sharing this view have pointed out, the earliest Games took place beside the actual tomb of a national figure of renown, or a monument to him.

Studying ancient traditions and myths, scholars have suggested other sources which, they argued, were the more likely origin of the Games.

Some still linked those earliest sporting events with death. However, the researchers reasoned that it was not the purpose of the athletes to gain the good will of otherwise dangerous spirits, but to cheer the hearts of the mourners. Just as in an Irish wake in modern times the bereaved drink whisky to lighten the burden of their sorrow, so, in olden times, they indulged in sporting competitions, and from the excitement of the contests learned to sublimate (if not to forget) their grief. The Games could thus be regarded as akin to an ancient method of mental hygiene and grief therapy — a psychological cure for one's distraught mind, particularly when honouring the passing of a national hero.

Another suggestion is that the Games evolved out of a fertility rite in which the winner of a footrace represented the spirit of fruitfulness and, subsequently, the sun. A further theory, advanced with fervour, if not convincing proof, is that the Olympics originally and essentially were a religious New Year's ritual in the ancient chronology of the Greeks, performed to promote the prospects of the vintage and olive harvest.

It has been claimed by Sir James Frazer, in *The Golden Bough*, that the purpose of the first footrace that started off the Olympic Games was the selection of 'the king of the year'. This was a sacred contest for the throne. The regal head periodically had to defend his position against 'suitors' who claimed his daughter's hand, and his crown. Out of this primitive racing rite — 'run for no less a prize than a kingdom' — developed the elaborate system of the Olympic Games, according to Frazer.

Much more realistic to the modern mind is another conjecture. Hellas, as Greece was first known, was not then a united country but a conglomeration of many city-states and tribes, with their own rulers and ambitions. Each guarded its independence jealously and many a time clashed in battle with its neighbour. There were constant wars.

The country's sages realized that their land would be doomed, and that civilization would vanish, unless they could join the various groups together. The problem was how to achieve such a bond.

There was one interest all of them passionately shared: sport and their wish to excel in it. Why not approach the separate rulers and infuse them with the idea of a mammoth contest, in which all could take part, sending their finest champions to prove their worth?

That is how, this hypothesis claims, the Panhellenic Games were born, to become the Olympics. As had been hoped, they created one people out of the many splinter groups and changed men's warring instinct into a contest of exhilarating sporting events.

In fact, early Greek tradition and historical documents express an identical notion, linking it, however, with supernatural agency and only a later revival of the original Games. These authorites say that the final site, Olympia, was once the shrine of an ancient oracle, and that the Games there were held as far back as the second millennium BC. But in the early days, they took place also at many other centres throughout Greece, in honour of local heroes and deities. However, gradually they grew into the one festival at Olympia, in worship of Zeus, the father of all gods and men. Then they lapsed altogether until, in the ninth century BC, Iphitus became king of Elis.

Greatly perturbed by constant wars, it is said, he anxiously sought counsel from the oracle at Delphi. This oracle told him that the only way to stop the fights and to bring unity to the people was to re-establish the former Games. And so, this claim asserts, they were revived. From that period certainly dates the 'sacred truce' introduced for the purpose of promoting goodwill and peace. At first, the truce merely guaranteed safe conduct to all contestants going to the Games. Eventually, it was extended to last an entire 'holy month', during which warfare and even the presence of armed men were forbidden.

Many interesting features belong to the early story of the Olympics. To begin with, the Games were confined to one day — the day of the first full moon after the summer solstice. During the first thirteen Games recorded, the footrace was the sole event. It was won in 776 BC by Coroebus, a cook by calling.

Even the origin of the footraces leads back to religion in the far-distant past. Then they were not run for the sake of running. They had another purpose. They were part of a solemn religious rite, performed once again in honour of the god Zeus. To worship him, and thereby to gain his aid, animals were sacrificed and then burned, together with fruit. The ascending smoke, as in biblical lore, was considered sweet odour to the lord of heaven.

The rite was prepared meticulously. Priests heaped the slain beasts and the fruit on Zeus' altar, adding wood ready to be lit. Meanwhile, chosen youths aligned themselves at a specified distance (approximately 200 yards — 182 m — away) and, at a given signal, raced towards the altar. The first to reach it was handed a flaming torch by the priest, with which he set fire to the pyre. The torch itself, tradition relates, was lit not by human hand but by priests focusing the sun's rays into a polished metal bowl. It was believed that thus the sun-god himself had been the source of the flame. It is a long way indeed that the race and the torch have travelled to become a modern sporting event and a symbolic torch linking the present world Olympics with ancient Greece . . .

For many centuries, the festival was for free Greek men only. Slaves, though not eligible for competition, nevertheless could come as spectators. Women (except on certain days) were forbidden even to watch the games! An early law ruled that any woman apprehended in the arena should be thrown to her death from a nearby mountain.

Competing athletes at first wore loin cloths. But one day, so the story goes, a youth lost his. However, unashamed and unperturbed, he carried on and, being unimpeded, excelled all his rivals. As a result of his superlative performance, from then on all participants in the games competed in the nude. (This is still recalled by our word gymnast, in which *gumnos* means 'naked'.) This practice also ensured that women could not take part disguised as men. This original discrimination against the female sex led later to the formation of the Greek Women's Games, known as Heraea. They were held in honour of Hera, the great woman divinity of Olympus and queen of heaven.

Athletes chosen for the contests had to restrict their diet and in a certain period could partake only of cheese and wine, though later meat was added. For at least ten months before the Olympics they had to undergo strenuous training. They well realized that they were to participate in a sacred rite and that is why, in their individual prayer for victory, they specified their petition that this should be theirs 'only if I am best'.

Victors were looked upon with awe as men whom the gods had favoured with invincibility. They were crowned with a garland of twigs from the wild olive tree. This wreath — the forerunner of all our modern medals — was not merely decorative and symbolic of victory. Greeks firmly believed in the myth that it had been plucked from a sacred tree Heracles himself had brought from the land of the Hyperboreans, a country of perpetual sunshine, free from disease, violence, and war. He had planted it in the sacred grove near the temple of Zeus at Olympia. It possessed magical qualities, imparting some of its sanctity to the wearer. As in the case of a king, the crown bestowed on the recipient divine honour and 'likened him to the great god Zeus himself, whose glorious image at Olympia wore a similar wreath'.

As the years passed, winners of the contests were awarded additional privileges, including tax-exemption for life and a permanent seat of honour in the local theatre. At the expense of his native city, a life-sized statue of each victor could be erected in the sacred grove of the plain of Elis. Nothing equalled the triumphant homecoming of a victor. The most famous poets praised him in odes and all joined in hymns exalting him. He was driven in a chariot drawn by white horses to the temple of the chief deity of his city. There he placed on the altar, as a thanksgiving, the wreath he had won.

For many centuries the Olympics prospered and grew ever more in importance and extent. In 708 BC the Pentathlon (from the Greek meaning 'five-contest') was introduced. It consisted of five (*pente*) separate events: the footrace, leaping, spear-throwing, discus-hurling, and wrestling. Then (in 688 BC) boxing and (in 680 BC) chariot races became part of the Games as well and eventually they included twenty-four different competitions. This indeed was a majestic growth out of small, obscure beginnings.

After an existence of almost 1200 years, the decline of Greek culture and the conquest of Greece by Rome led to the deterioration of the Games. The new Christian teaching of the sinfulness of the body, and its abhorrence of heathen practice, dealt the deathblow to the Games, which were finally banned in AD 393 by the Christian Emperor, Theodosius I, as 'pagan idolatry'. When, to his horror, his grandson, Theodosius II, learned that in spite of the prohibition the contests were still being held at Olympia, he had its buildings burned to he ground and the last physical traces of the Olympics thus disappeared. For the Games to have existed almost uninterruptedly for twelve centuries is in itself a proud record, unequalled in the annals of history. Certainly paradoxical is the fact that while one religion had given birth to the Olympic Games, in the name of another they were destroyed.

It took 1502 years to revive the Games. Baron Pierre de Coubertin, founder of the modern Games, was inspired by their ancient aim to create good will and peace among men.

He was not an athlete himself, but a scholar and educationist. His 'revivalist' enthusiasm had been roused by several experiences and factors. On a visit to England he had been impressed by the practice of sport at schools, particularly so at 'Rugby'. A Scottish friend had fired his imagination with the Olympic ideal. Even more so, he had been deeply affected by the excavation of the actual ancient Olympic site by German archaeologists (1875-81). At the time the subject of Free Trade was hotly argued about by politicians who strongly advocated the abolition of tariffs in the movement of goods from one country to another. The French Baron, with the archaeologists' triumph vivid in his mind, then declared: 'Let us export our oarsmen, our runners, our fencers, into other countries. This is the true Free Trade of the future, and the day it is introduced into Europe the cause of peace will have gained a strong ally.'

At first, however, there was opposition to his proposal. Undaunted, Coubertin, deeply concerned with the future of man, pursued his aim. Instead of merely talking about it, in 1894 he sent out invitations to all sporting organizations in the world to an international athletic congress to be held at the Sorbonne University, in Paris. He wrote: 'Re-establishment of the Olympic Games under conditions conformable to the needs of modern life would bring together every four years representatives of all nations, and it is permissible to suppose that these peaceful and courteous contests would thus supply the best of internationalism.'

Though acceptances were slow in coming, the meeting took place as arranged and was attended by an enthusiastic group of sportsmen. However, the Baron had learned his lesson. He was not only cautious, but shrewd. At least so some people suggested. In the agenda drawn up for the meeting in the famous French university, the main object in Coubertin's mind — the Olympics' revival — was listed only eighth.

Things went even better than the Baron had expected in his most sanguine mood. When, after much wearying discussion of the preceding seven topics, the meeting eventually reached item 'number eight', all were so tired and anxious to conclude that no one tried to argue, and the motion was carried easily. It was also agreed to offer Greece the honour of being host nation for the first of the resurrected Games. This, of course, was out of deference to their Greek beginnings.

Two years later, on 6 April 1896, in the presence of a crowd of 50,000, the King of Greece declared the first of the new series of Olympic Games open, for men to unite from the four corners of the earth in the pursuit of excellence or, in the words of the ancient Olympic motto, to be *faster, higher, stronger.* The Bishop of Pennsylvania, in a sermon preached in London on the occasion of the 1908 Olympics there, epitomized the true spirit of the Games (and, indeed, of all sports) in an often quoted observation that 'the important thing in the Olympic Games is not winning, but taking part, for the essential thing in life is not so much conquering as fighting well'.

The story of the Olympics thus leads from small, parochial gatherings to propitiate gods and the spirits of departed heroes to a universal contest in the service of peace and brotherhood. And as such, sport can make its greatest contribution yet to our world.

Chapter 47

AUSTRALIAN BEGINNINGS

Australia is one of the most sports-minded countries in the world. Her contributions to sport are manifold and almost unparalleled. They include the life-savers' movement and the 'Australian crawl'. Australians gave the totalizator to the world of horse racing and made Australian Rules Football a sport all of its own. Australians created motorcycle speedway racing and introduced the Fairbairn style into rowing.

Australia, indeed, became the home of almost every sport, taking it up, sooner or later, with fervour and enthusiasm, and not rarely excelling in it. Australians became world champions in running, tennis, cricket and racquets, to mention just a few examples. That Australia, too, of all nations was the first to wrest the America's Cup from the Americans, merely was another symptomatic event.

Alone among all primitive people of the world, the Australian Aborigines, because of their superior boomerang, never knew the bow and arrow as a means of hunting or fighting. Europeans introduced them towards the middle of last century and Wilbraham Liardet, a London-born publican who had opened an hotel at the future site of Port Melbourne, inaugurated **archery** contests for the entertainment of his guests. From 1840 onward, he even provided those interested with the necessary equipment.

Badminton was a late-comer. The first club was formed in Perth, Western Australia, around the turn of the century. However, only in the late 1920s did the game gain popularity.

Baseball was first played by American gold miners in 1856 who, in search of wealth, had come to the fields of Ballarat. Australians themselves took up playing the game three decades later.

Victoria was the first State — in 1930 — to establish a **basketball** association, though thirty years earlier a rudimentary sort of the game was first played in the YMCA in Melbourne.

Lack of the necessary implements gave **billiards** a late start in Australia. Thomas Spencer was the first to open — in 1851 — a saloon in Sydney, with one imported table and one which he had made locally. It was the Lindrum family, dominating the game for four generations and well over 120 years — an all-time record in any sport — that put Australia on the map of billiards. Walter Lindrum became the world's greatest billiards exponent: 'a wizard at the billiard cue'. His skill won him altogether fifty-seven world records. On one occasion he scored 4819 points in four hours. He gave exhibitions at Buckingham Palace before King George V and Queen Mary.

During the 1880s members of the Indian army brought **snooker** to Australia, with the manager of the billiard room of the Sydney Hotel Australia becoming the game's ardent pioneer.

Boxing was popular from the early days of the colonization. The first recorded boxing match dates back to 1814, to a two-hour fight over fifty-six rounds at the Sydney Race Course. A peculiar feature of the match was that, before it, both men had to run half a mile (0.80 km).

Though **bullfights** never took place in Australia, there were at least two Australian bullfighters. The first was Alan Brown, though his career was exceedingly brief. After learning the art in England (!) in 1959, he went to Spain for his first — and last — corrida, on a village green near Madrid. On the first pass he was badly gored and never again attempted to master a bull. Christopher

D. Meagher, a Sydney solicitor, fared much better. He had visited Spain as a tourist towards the end of 1959. While in the country, bullfighting caught his imagination. He stayed on and became a member of the Syndicate of Toreros. Earning his living as a teacher in English and as an interpreter, he acquired the art of bullfighting in his spare time. He appeared in various bullfighting centres throughout Spain and, altogether, he confronted thirty bulls and on each occasion 'dispatched' them. Appropriately he was billed as *El Australiano*, the only matador in the world ever to have been called thus.

Cock-fighting found its place early in the life of the Australian settlement, where it gained wide popularity. According to a report of 1810, published in the *Sydney Gazette*, 'a number of good battles' were fought then in Parramatta. Australia bred its own game cock which, it was claimed, was the result of judicious crossing of the blood of the Malay, the Aseel and British fighting fowl.

There is no doubt that even members of the First Fleet played **cricket.** If they did not bring their bats with them from England, they improvised them as soon became the custom, from local timber that was strong enough to withstand hitting the ball. Soldiers were the first players. Cricket was then a crude game with gloves and pads unknown. But no one minded. All that mattered was the game itself. The earliest organized match in Australia took place in 1803. It was arranged by the officers of HMS Calcutta at the present-day Hyde Park, Sydney, which soon was to become the venue for many sports.

Australia was the first country to conceive the idea of international **croquet** contests, early described as Test Matches. The first club had been formed in South Australia, at Kapunda, in 1868. Australians became so proficient in the game that a visit of one of its teams to England was at the season's conclusion praised by the commentary that 'we all have something to learn from the Australians, if it is only how to win quickly if one is fated to win, and to lose good-honouredly if it is one's lot to lose'.

Because betting on cycle races had been illegal throughout the Commonwealth except in Victoria, its pioneering State and chief promoter, it has been explained, Australians were late in becoming enthusiastic on **cycling**. Melbourne's Boneshaker Club organized Australia's first cycling race in 1869, which was only within one year of the first race of its kind to be held anywhere (at Hendon, England). A crowd of 12,000 spectators watched the historic occasion. Australia has had many 'firsts' in world cycling. What is believed to have been the first women's cycling race ever held was the two-mile title event conducted in 1888 at Ashfield, NSW.

A wallaby, so the story goes, was responsible for the introduction of **dog racing**. It did so quite inadvertently, when it crossed the path of a party which was on its way home after a full day's 'enjoyment' hunting kangaroos around Mayhall, South Australia. When the wallaby suddenly appeared out of the bush, the pack of eleven hounds at once gave chase. But the wallaby proved itself superior by far and, one by one, the dogs dropped out. One of the hunters witnessing the spectacle, within a year (in 1868) organized Australia's first Waterloo Cup. During the early period not hares but wallabies and kangaroo rats were used for coursing.

Though, no doubt, British army personnel were the first to practise **fencing** in Australia, the first proper fencing instructions were given only at the beginning of this century by the German-trained Albert Schuch. A former member of the German army, he worked as a masseur in Sydney, on the site of the future Salvation Army headquarters.

Football of a kind dates back to a very early period in Australia's history. A Sydney newspaper report of 1829 recorded how 'the privates in the barracks are in the habit of amusing themselves with the game and ... the ball can be daily descried repeatedly mounting higher or lower, according to the skill and energy of the bold military kickers thereof'.

Soccer was brought to Australia by J. W. Fletcher, an English schoolmaster, who had made his home in Sydney and who, with a friend, convened a meeting in 1880 'to consider and promote the introduction of the English Association Game into New South Wales', founding the Wanderers' Club.

Rugby Union began in NSW in 1864 and in less than ten years was played by at least 100 clubs. It started at the University of Sydney, with matches arranged among the students themselves, or against visiting war ships. **Rugby League** began only in 1907, the year in which Rugby Union had reached its height.

Tradition has it that **golf** was introduced by Scottish migrants from Fifeshire. A club must have been in existence in 1847, as James Graham, himself a Fifeshireman, made an entry in one of his ledgers showing that he had paid £2 as his annual subscription 'to the [Melbourne] Golf Club'. The democratization of golf popularized the game so much that it was to become no longer the hobby of a few rich but the pastime of many. Proportionately, Australia has more public golf courses than any other nation.

The forerunner of hockey in Australia was **hurley**. Irish goldminers brought it to Victoria where by 1880 they had established several clubs. Only gradually was hurley replaced by **hockey** which was first played on Australian soil by members of the Royal Navy, while their ships were in port.

Love of **horses** and horsemanship have belonged to the Australian people from the very inception of the colony. In January 1788, the First Fleet, with its convicts and soldiers, brought also the first horses: one stallion, three mares, and three colts. Most races were run along the Windsor and Parramatta roads, at times over a distance of sixteen miles (25.60 km). The first specific race meeting was held in 1810 at what was to become Hyde Park, Sydney. It has been suggested that the immediate reason was not only the wish to soften the harsh life of the penal settlement, but the hope that the event would cause people to forget all their antagonism and tensions engendered by the Rum Rebellion. The first Melbourne Cup was run on 7 November 1861. A fearful accident almost marred the occasion. As the horses rounded the turn, coming into the straight, three fell. Two of them were killed on the spot and their riders were badly injured. Nevertheless, the day ended on a happy note with the spectators attending spectacular shows, specially put on for the occasion in Melbourne's theatres. Among the performances was a Chinese drama, performed by 'dinkum' Chinese actors.

Aborigines had perfected the art of **hunting** which was so essential for their survival. In its pursuit, they dexterously employed boomerangs, throwing clubs and most of all, special hunting spears. If for no other reason, it was to supplement their sparse food supply that the early European colonists took up hunting, in which many a convict excelled. In fact, in the early days of the colony hunting became one of the principal sporting amusements, greatly fostered by the arrival of the 73rd Regiment in 1810 whose officers brought their own packs of hounds to assist them in the hunting of both the kangaroo and the dingo. The earliest account of a hunt with hounds goes back to January 1811. A kangaroo hunted on forest ground at the Nepean was killed 'after an exciting run of two hours'.

Ice hockey was first played in 1908, in the Melbourne and Sydney Glaciariums.

Dunbar Poole, a Scotsman from Glasgow and at the time one of the world's finest **ice skating** promoters, was instrumental in establishing the sport in Australia when visiting Adelaide in 1904.

Judo was first practised in Queensland, where the visit of Rugora Shima greatly fostered it. Dr A. J. Ross claimed to have founded the first judo club in 1928, doing so also in Queensland. New South Wales was the first State to establish — in 1956 — an Australian Society of Ju-jitsuans.

Karate came to Australia as late as 1962. It found its place very slowly and without any definite, preconceived plan, taking advantage of the advice and tuition by occasional Japanese visitors.

Lacrosse was introduced in 1872 when L. L. Mount brought some sticks from Canada to Victoria.

Lawn bowling was enjoyed from the colony's early days onward, first played by enthusiastic Englishmen arriving in New South Wales who brought their bowls with them. Following the English pattern, bowling greens were laid out adjacent to, and as part of, hotels. Innkeepers put them down not only as a new type of amenity for their patrons but as a clever means of increasing their trade. Australians not only learned to play the game second to none, they also knew how to produce equipment for it of unsurpassed quality. Australian-made bowls are now acknowledged to be among the best in the world and are exported to countries far and wide.

Bushwalkers were the first to take up **mountaineering**. This was a natural result of their exploration of the countryside which began in the 90s of last century. Sometimes their path was obstructed by steep mountains and precipitous rocks. However, determined to get to their destination, they learned to scale the heights and to master the slippery boulders. It was chiefly in Tasmania that real mountaineering could be practised. Curiously, the first book written on Australian mountaineering is in German and its author, Franz Malcher, was an Austrian who in 1913 related his experiences *As Mountaineer and Skier in the Fifth Continent*.

British army officers have been credited to have brought **polo** to Australia where it was played first in the 1870s. British cavalry regiments in India imported many of their mounts from Australia. Coming from New South Wales, they were called 'Walers'. Hardy bush horses, they proved very suitable as polo ponies. This fact led the officers when on buying visits 'down under', to suggest that Walers be used to try out the game in this country. Records speak of 'the first polo in Australia' being played in Albert Park, Melbourne, in 1875. In some small way Australia even contributed to the efficiency of the game by inventing an 'instrument' to be used by umpires for picking up balls. This saved them from having to dismount, and hence speeded up the game.

Among the chief promoters of **roller skating** were the boxer 'Larry' Foley (possibly best remembered by the Australianism 'happy as Larry') and George Wirth of circus fame. Australia's most fashionable and spectacular rink, the Palladium, was opened in Sydney in 1912.

The Australians' excellence as oarsmen might well derive in part from the early colonial days when ships returning to harbour after a long voyage were anxious to restock their food supplies, especially meat. This was the time of the 'butcher boats'. Butchers, keen to make sales, rowed out to the vessels, vying with each other to get there first. These spontaneous races had a commercial incentive and certainly trained the men for future regattas. The first known **rowing** race with local men took place in 1818 on a course that extended from Bradley's Head to Sydney Cove. It was won by John Piper, to whose enthusiasm and zeal Australian rowing and yachting owe a great debt. The first rowing regatta took place in Tasmania on the river Derwent at Hobart in 1827.

The winning of the America's Cup was only the culmination of Australians' love of **sailing.** In the early days of the colony it could rightly be said that 'next to the outside of a horse, your true Australian was most at home in a boat'. Among the many achievements was the design of several new classes of sailing boats, notably the famous Eighteen Footers.

Skis, crudely made from local timber, were first used in the 1830s by Tasmanian fur trappers.

Australia pioneered public courts for **squash**, the first of which was opened in Melbourne in 1835. Anyone, whether a member or not, could play there at any time by simply paying a small fee. This gave squash the widest popularity and, no other nation, it is claimed, counts as many women squash players and clubs as this country. Though among the youngest sports in Australia (the first court having been built at a Sydney gymnasium as late as 1919), it is nevertheless a fact that Australians soon excelled in squash racquets and became its world leaders, with Heather Blundell a champion.

Swimming belongs to the Australian way of life. No other country can claim a finer record or achievements and produced proportionately more champions. Even the early Aborigines excelled in swimming. A record tells of an incident concerning a native who was one of Governor Phillip's servants. One day he was taken by ship from Sydney. When a fair way out at sea, he suddenly panicked, jumped into the water, and struck out for shore... Dawn Fraser was the first swimmer to win an Olympic title three consecutive times.

Table tennis caught on towards the end of the last century and 'ping-pong' championships were played in 1898 in Adelaide. By the early 1900s table tennis was played in most of the capital cities and it almost seemed as if the game was becoming a craze.

Australians began to play the earlier form of **tennis** around 1850, and the game was enjoyed by all sections of the community, with 'every residence of consequence' having its tennis court. A popular construction material in the early days, particularly in country districts, was the ant-heap. A student returning from Britain is said to have brought the new tennis to Australia soon after 1874. At first, this was played on private lawns. Club tennis was started in 1878 by the Melbourne Cricket Club. Australia took up the challenge of the Davis Cup in 1905. Within two years, Norman E. Brookes carried home the trophy, thus starting an unequalled Australian record.

An illustration of 1855 shows that Ballarat, Victoria, had a bowling alley. No doubt **nine-pin bowling** was a pastime followed early in various parts of Australia, especially among German settlers in the Barossa Valley, South Australia. The history of **ten-pin bowling** began only in May 1960. Jack Carthy of Glenelg, SA, who had never seen a game played but had read about it in American books, took such a fancy to the novel sport that he was determined to introduce it in his home town. He converted a local old cinema into the first ten-pin bowling alley. The first fully automatic bowling centre was opened at Hurstville, Sydney, in 1960 as well. Australia added its own particular features.

When an American leading bowler inspected the Australian alleys, he was struck by the custom for everyone to pay before the game, a precaution then not adhered to elsewhere. Yet another Australian-created difference was the practice to book lanes by time.

Trotting began haphazardly, in private and improvised contests. Owners of horses that could pace or trot liked to display their ability and ran races against each other. Trotting races became part of Australian sporting events soon after 1800. The Parramatta meeting on 30 April 1810 featured Captain Piper's 'famous *Miss Kitty*', which won a race in a style praised as 'scarcely to be surpassed by some of the first trotters in England'. Nothing did more to make trotting popular than the introduction of night meetings on flood-lit tracks, the first held in Perth in 1914.

Water polo was already played during the latter half of the last century. Eventually, it became highly popular, specially in Sydney which leads the world in the number of teams, including school teams, playing regularly.

A short film and an enthusiastic viewer who owned a speed boat and a weekender on the banks of the Hawkesbury River, NSW, combined to give birth to Australian **water skiing**. Reg Johnston, a resident photographer at Prince Alfred Hospital, Sydney, quite by chance one day saw an American film of the sport. He took an immediate fancy to it and on the spur of the moment decided to try it out himself on homemade skis. He and his wife were to become the pioneers of water skiing in Australia. At the end of World War II, Johnston's work took him to the United States. When he returned home, it was merely a matter of spreading his first hand knowledge. In 1947 the Aqua Club was formed and the sport soon caught on throughout the country.

Wrestling became a favourite competitive pastime in Australia soon after the landing of the First Fleet. Matches — often mere impromptu bouts — took place between soldiers and convicts. Professional wrestling began in the 1880s.

Ever since the inauguration of the modern **Olympic Games** in 1896, Australians have participated on each occasion, a distinction shared by only three other nations — Britain, the United States, and Greece. The total of medals won reflected Australians' love of sportsmanship and striving to set ever new records in this specific area of human creativity.

INDEX

Abel, 131

Aborigines, Australian, and barracking, 158

Accident, and shuttlecock, 21; at cricket, 85; in cycling, 117-18, at dog races, 126; and origin of Rugby, 148-49; and ice skating, 224; at polo, 275; and water polo, 377; and water skiing, 384

Actium, battle at, 302

Adam, 120

Aeneas, 287

Africa, pygmies and archery, 8; Zulus and bull, 63: surfing in, 330; and crawl, 346

Aggressiveness, and sport, 1

Agincourt, battle at, 14

Aiguille, Mount, 264

Ailsa Craig, and curling, 104

Ajax, 390

Akbar, the Great, and polo, 275

Akiba, Rabbi, on swimming, 343

Albatross, in golf, 170-71

Albert, Prince, and curling, 100-01

Alexander the Great, and unarmed combat, 246; and polo, 275; and skiing, 318

Algonquin Indians, and lacrosse, 248

All Blacks, 147

Allen, Sir Montagu, 219

Alley, bowling, 366

Alpenstock, 267

Alps, Australian, 321; French, 264; New Zealand, 271; Swiss, 265, 266, 267, 268, 270-71

Altcar Club, 127

Amenophis II, Pharoah, 5

America, and cock-fighting, 79; and curling, 102; and horse's birthday, 201; and ice hockey, 216; and skating, 227; *see also* United States

American Bowling Congress, 369

American football, 151-53; and soccer, 143

American Indians, and archery, 8; and football, 139; and hockey, 173-74; and the horse, 182; and hunting, 207; and lacrosse, 248; and boats, 286, and crawl, 346; and wrestling, 396

America's Cup, 308-10

Amsterdam, 225, 304, 305

Amulets, on horse, 196-97

Anacharsis, and billiards, 46

Anchises, 287

Andes, 271

Andresen, John H., 387

Anecdotes, on Ascham's treatise on archery, 15; Abraham Lincoln and baseball, 37; origin of billiards, 45, 49; origin of curling 95-6; pneumatic tyre, 115; cycling, 117-18; dog and man, 120; origin of golf, 159; modern golf ball, 164; three racing prizes, 186; steeplechase, 199; dark horse, 200: totalizator, 204; Mount Pilatus, 265-66; polo, 275; roller skating, 283; origin of schooner, 313; modern table tennis bat, 352; naming of lawn tennis, 359; first trotter, 373; origin of water polo, 377; wrestling match, 394-95

Angling, 4

Anglo Saxon, and cricket, 86; and wicket, 86; and starboard, 313

Anne, Queen, of England, and racing, 187

Antony and Cleopatra, and billiards, 47

Apollo, and sport, 4, 123, 210

Appalachian Mountain Club, 269

Aquaplane, 384, 385

Arabs, and archery, 12; and cock's crow, 74; and greyhound, 124; and racket, 279; and sail, 302; and tennis, 354; and hazard, 355

Archaeology, and archery, 8, 10; bullfighting, 62; and bicycle, 109; and greyhound, 123; and fencing, 136; and bridle, 194; and skates, 222; and unarmed combat, 245; and boats, 301; and skis, 316, and bowling, 364; and wrestling, 389; and modern Olympic Games, 409

Archery, 2, 8-19; and golf, 160; and hockey, 176; and bowling, 256; and skittles, 367 68

Aristophanes, on wrestlers, 391

Aristotle, on horseshoe, 195

Armada, and bowls, 255

Army, and game of poona, 22; and origin of snooker, 52; and bowls, 63; and cock-fighting, 75–6; and curling, 103–4, 109; and football cheer, 152; and barracking, 158; and ice hockey, 216–17; and polo, 273, 276; and skiing, 318–19; and water skiing, 384–85; and wrestling, 389; *see also* Warfare

Arrian, 124–25

Arrowroot, 18

Ascham, Roger, on archery, 14–5

Ashdown Park Meeting, 127

Ashes, the, 87–8

Asia, cock fighting in, 76; and the sabre, 135; and hockey, 173; and the horse, 179–80, 182; and the chariot, 183; and saddle, 193; and ice skating, 222

Asklepios, and cock, 74

Assam, and tug-of-war, 3; and polo, 276

Association Football, 145

Assurbanipal, and archery, 10

Assyrians, and archery, 10; and dog, 121; and horse, 180; and swimming, 342; and wrestling, 389

Athelstan, 303

Athenaeum Club, London, and billiards, 52

Athletics, 6–7

Atonement, Jewish Day of, and sacrifice of cock, 74

Attila, and horse, 182; and polo, 274

Auckland, New Zealand, 204

Augeas, king of Elis, 400

Australia, and the Ashes, 87–8; and cricket, 88; and the rabbit, 128; and Rugby, 147; and football, 153–57; and monkey crouch, 193; and horse's birthday, 201; and totalizator, 202–5; and motorcycle speedway races, 259; and rowing, 298; and America's Cup, 310; and skiing, 321–22; and Davis Cup, 326; and surfing, 335–37; and life saving, 335–38; and crawl, 346–49

Australian Rules Football, 153–57; and soccer, 143

Austria, and mountaineering, 269; and skiing, 319, 321; and water polo, 381

Aylmer, John, Bishop of London, 368

Aztecs, and dog, 121–22; and hockey, 173; and horse, 182; and jai alai, 231; and crawl, 346

Babcock, J. C., 297

Babylonians, and bull, 61; and bicycle, 109; and horse, 180

Baden, Duke of, 110–11

Badminton, 20–6; library, 20, 25–6; drink, 26; magazine and football, 150; and lawn tennis court, 358

Baggataway, 248

Baghdad, 54, 389

Bail, in cricket, 84, 86

Ball, its history, 137; in football, 138, 147, 156; in lacrosse, 217, 251–52; in polo, 273, 274; in squash, 325; in table

tennis, 351, 352; in water polo, 377

Ball games, and Makah Indians, 3; cosmic significance, 3–4; divining future, 20; and bat, 32; of Mayas and Toltecs, 43–4; and religion, 172–73

Banderilla, 66

Bandy ball, 174

Baptism, with bull's blood, 62

Barefoot water skiing, 387

Barker, Charles, 350

Barracking, 157–58

Baseball, 2, 27–39

Basketball, 40–4

Basques, and jai alai, 231

Bastille, and billiards, 49

Bat, story of cricket, 85–6

Bath, England, and badminton, 24; and billiards, 50

Battledore and shuttlecock, 20–1

Beaufort, Duke of, and badminton, 20, 23; and sports library, 26; and lawn tennis court, 358–59

Becket, Thomas à, 181

Beers, Dr George W., 251

Belfast, Ireland, 114

Belgium, and roller skating, 283

Bells, on horses, 197

Belle Vue, Manchester, England, 129

Belmonte, Juan, 69

Beni Hassan, 389–90

Beowulf, on swimming, 344

Berlin, Germany, 284, 353

Bernardino, 59

Berners, Juliana, on hunting with dogs, 125

Betting, and cock-fights, 78–9, 82; in curling, 99; and dog races, 127; on horses, 184, 185, 187; and bookmaker, 200; and totalizator, 202–5; in jai alai, 233; and bowling, 256, 364, 367, 369; and America's Cup, 309; and surfing, 333; and trotting, 372

Bias, in bowls, 257

Bible, and sport, 5–6; on archery, 12; and the Veronica, 71; and cock's crow, 73; and cricket bat, 85; name of curling stone, 103; dog in, 122, 123–24; and duel, 131; and football, 137; and horseshoe, 195; and eating of meat, 206; and hunting, 210; mountains in, 263; and modern resuscitation, 337; and swimming, 343; and wrestling, 392–93

Bicycle, its names, 108

Billiards, 45–52

Birthday, of horses, 201

Bizet, G., 68

Blackheath, 146, 167, 177

Black pool, and snooker, 53

Blaine, encyclopedia of sports, 25

Bligh, Ivo, and the Ashes, 88

Blood, of bull, 62–3

Boadicea, Queen, 184

Boat, its history, 86–7, 295–97; sailing, 301–2, 303–4

Boat racing, 287-88, 293-97
Bondi, Sydney, Australia, and surf clubs, 336
Boneshaker, 108, 113
Bonspiel, 96
Bookmaker, 200
Borneo, and dog, 121
Boston, and baseball, 32; and yachting, 333
Boswell, James, and resuscitation, 337
Bournemouth, England, rowing and water polo, 377, 379-80
Bowler hat, 197-98
Bowling, *see* Lawn bowling; Skittles; Ten-pin bowling
Bowls, history of, 257
Boxing, 5, 54-60; Shaolin, 245, 246; and Olympic Games, 408
Bradman, Sir Donald, 326
Brahma, and swordsmanship, 131
Brasses, horse, 196-97
Bridle, 194
Brighton, England, and billiards, 51
Britain, and archery, 12-17; and shuttlecock, 21-2; and billiards, 50-52; and boxing, 56-60; and cock-fighting, 76-7; and love of cricket, 83; and croquet, 91; and bicycle, 112-15; and greyhound racing, 125-29; and football, 138, 140-51; and barracking, 158; and golf ball, 162-63; and hockey, 175-78; and horse-racing, 184-91; and ice hockey, 217, 220; and skating, 227-28; and lacrosse, 250-53; and bowling, 255-58; and mountaineering, 268-69; and polo, 273, 276-77; and racquets, 278-81; and roller skating, 284-85; and rowing, 289, 290-96; and the sliding seat, 297; and yachting, 307-8; and America's Cup, 308-9; and skiing, 321; and sport, 323-24; and squash, 325-28; and swimming, 344-46; and table tennis, 349, 351-53; and Royal tennis, 257-60; and skittles, 367; and ten-pin bowling, 370; and trotting, 373; and water polo, 377-81; and wrestling, 394-96
Broom, for curling, 104-6
Broughton, Jack, and his rules, 57-8
Browning, Robert, 165
Buccaneer, 312-13
Buckingham Grade School, and basketball, 42
Buckingham Palace, table tennis at, 349
Budapest, and water polo, 381
Buddhism, and archery, 12; and bicycle, 118; and unarmed combat, 246
Bull, baiting, 18; eye, 18; sacred, 61; fighting, 61-71
Bunbury, Sir Charles, and the Derby, 190
Bunker, in golf, 168
Bushido, 239
Bushnell, E. W., 226-27
Byerly Turk, 187
Byron, Lord, at Harrow, 324; as swimmer, 341, 342
Byzantium, and saddle, 193; and tennis, 354

Caddie, in golf, 169
Cadets, army, and snooker, 52
Caesar, Julius, and bullfighting, 66; and cha-rioteers, 184; and boats, 289; as swimmer, 342
Caillois, Roger, 262
Cain, 131
Cairnie, John, 100, 101, 107
Cairo, Egypt, 231, 274
Calcutta, India, 276
Calendar, English racing, 188; and horse's birth-day, 201; and Olympic Games, 401-2
California, southern, and surfing, 334-35
Caligula, and horse, 179
Calvary, Mount, 263
Cambridge, University, England, and soccer, 143-44; and Rugby, 146; and racquets, 280; and boat races, 294-95; and squash, 326
Camp, Walter, and American football, 153
Canada, and basketball, 40; and curling, 98-9, 102-4; and Rugby, 147; and American football, 152-53; and ice hockey, 216-20; and lacrosse, 218; and racquets, 281; and squash, 327
Cannes, 384
Canter, 181
Canterbury Tales, 181
Car racing, 5; *see also* Speedway racing
Carmel, Mount, 263
Carmen, opera, 68
Carol, and football, 140
Carr, John, 50-1
Cartwright, Alexander Joy, 35-6
Carver, Robin, 32
Cassius, 342
Catamaran, 301
Catherine, of Braganza, 89
Caucasus, 271
Cave paintings, and archery, 8-9; and hunting, 208
Cavill, Frederick, 346; Richard, 347; Sydney St Leonard, 347
Cayus, Dr, 123
Cemeteries, and yew trees, 13
Centaur, the, 182
Cerberus, 121
Cercyon, 390
Cestero, 233
Cestus, 55
Chadwick, Henry, and baseball, 27, 38
Chalk, 'twisting', in billiards, 50
Chamberlain, Nevil Bowles, and snooker, 52
Chamillart, M. de, and billiards, 49
Channel, English, swimming of, 345
Character, training of, and sports, 323-24
Charles I, and dog trials, 126; and golf, 161; and horse-racing, 186; expert bowler, 257
Charles II, and cock-fighting, 77; and Pall Mall, 89; and Newmarket, 186; and skating, 225; and sailing, 306; as tennis player, 357
Charles V, of France, banned tennis, 357

Charles VIII, and mountaineering, 264
Charmian, 47
Charms, at hunt, 209
Chaucer, Geoffrey, and canter, 181; on priests hunting, 214; first mention of tennis in English literature, 357
Cheer, at football, 152
Chester, England, 186
Chicago, and sliding seat, 297
Chichen Itza, Mexico, and ball game, 43–4
Chimborazo, 271
Chin Gen Pin, 235
China, and bullfights, 61; and football, 138; saddle and stirrup, 193–94; and falconry; 212; and jai alai, 231; and ju-jitsu, 234; and unarmed combat, 242; and polo, 274, 275; and ski, 318; and table tennis, 353; and wrestling, 396
Christ, *see* Jesus
Christchurch, New Zealand, 203
Christian, King of Denmark, and cock-fighting, 76
Christiania, 319, 321
Christianity, and ancient Olympic Games, 408; *see also* Church, Gospels, Religion
Church, and the cock, 75; and cock-fights, 77; and curling, 98; and steeplechase, 199; and skittles, 365, 366; *see also* Christianity
Churchill, Sir Winston, 324
Cid, the, 66
Clairvoyance, and horse, 196
Clasper, Henry, 296
Cleopatra, Queen, 302
Clergy, and basketball, 40–2; and boxing, 59; and curling, 98; and golf ball markings, 163; and totalizator, 202–3; and hunting, 214; and mountaineering, 266–67, 269–71; and surfing, 333; and tennis, 356; and skittles, 365–66
Climate, and sport, 2
Club, in golf, 161–62
Cock, its crow, 73; its symbolism in religion, 73–4; of gun, 80–1
Cock-fighting, 72–82
Cockpit, 72, 77
Coleta 70
Colours, at horse races, 184; at boat races, 295
Commandments, ten, of sport, 7
Commodus, Emperor, and ostrich hunt, 11
Compleat Gamester, and billiards, 46, 49
Connecticut, state of, and ten-pin bowling 369
Conquistadores, Spanish, and use of horse, 180, 182
Constantinople, 193, 274
Cook, Captain James, on surfing, 331
Cook, Mount, New Zealand, 271
Cooperstown, U.S.A., and baseball, 28–9, 31
Corinthians, Epistle to, and sport, 5
Cork, Ireland, and yachting, 306, 307
Cornell University, 42
Cornish wrestling, 395–96
Corridas, 61, 64, 67, 71

Cortes, Hernando, and horse, 182, 231
Cosmonautics, 4
Cotton, Charles, on billiards, 46, 49
Coubertin, Baron de, Pierre, 408–9
Coursing, 124–29
Court tennis, 356–58
Coventry Sewing Machine Company, and bicycle, 113
Cowes, 303
Crampit, 107
Crawl, the, 346–49
Creag, and cricket, 85
Crécy, the battle of, 14
Creighton, J. G. A., 217
Crete, and bullfight, 63; and greyhound 125
Cricket, 83–88; and Australian Rules Football, 154; poem on, 324
Critchley, General A. C., 129
Cromwell, Oliver, and cock-fights, 77–8; lover of greyhounds, 126; and football, 142
Croquet, 89–94; and cricket, 86; and lawn tennis, 360
Crusaders, and billiards, 46; and tennis, 355
Cuba, jai alai in, 231
Cuchulain, 175
Cue, evolution of billiards, 49
Cumberland, wrestling style, 395, 397
Cumberland, Duke of, 57, 307
Cup, in golf, 166
Curling, 95–107
Curry, Duncan F., 35
Customs, of yew tree in cemetery, 13; cock on church steeple, 73; of football cheer, 152; of bowler hat, 197–98; calling ship a 'she', 315; saluting quarter deck, 315; funeral games, 402–3
Cycling, 108–119
Cypress Gardens, Florida, 386
Czechs, and table tennis, 353

Dactyl, brothers, the, 401
Dance, and hunt, 208
Danes, and archery, 12; and head of as football, 137; and skiing, 319
Daphne, 123
Dardanelles, 340–41
Darley, Thomas, 187
David, King, 12, 131
Davis Cup, 360
Davis, Dwight, 360
Davis, J. W., 36
Death, and cock, 74; by cricket ball, 85; at cricket match, 87; and dog howling, 120; at dog races, 126; at polo, 275; through tennis, 356–57; and Olympic Games, 402–4
Deborah, and horseshoe, 195
Defence, and sport, 2; and boxing, 54; and fencing, 130; and judo, 235; and karate, 247
Delmonico's, New York City, 27

Delphi, 4, 210, 405

Demons, expulsion of, 3; and tug of war, 3; and archery, 10; and cock, 73-4; and horse, 196

Denmark, and badminton, 24

Derby, of coursing, 137; football at, 138; 12th Earl of, 189; the, 189-90; hat, 197-99; roller, 285; skiing, 321

Deuce, 355

Devon, England, 139

Devon, type of wrestling, 395

Diamond, of baseball, 36

Dickens, Charles, on hunting, 215; on racquets, 279

Digby, Everard, on swimming, 344

Disraeli, Benjamin, and badminton drink, 26; and 'dark horse', 200

Dogs, boxer, 59-60; and man, 121-22; racing of, 123-39; and hunt, 213

Doggett, Thomas, 293-94

Dolphin Akwa Skees, 385

Doncaster, the, 189, 191

Doubleday, Abner, 28, 30-1

Dove, Dame Frances, 253

Doyle, Conan, on Australian Rules Football, 157

Drais, Baron Karl von, 108, 110-11

Draisine, 108, 111

Drake, Sir Francis, 255

Duck's egg, 86

Duddingston, the, 99

Duel, 131-32

Dumfries, Scotland, 112

Dunlop, John Boyd, 114-15

Dunn, Tom, 168

Dutch, and sloop, 133; and golf, 159, 160; and tee, 165; and putt, 165; and skates, 225; and roller skating, 282; and sailing, 302, 303-4; and yacht, 302; and filibuster, 312; and bowling in America, 368

Dutch East India Company, 304, 306

Eagle, in golf, 170-71

Easter, games on, 83

Edda, on skating, 222-23

Ederle, Gertrude, 348

Edinburgh, curling in, 100; Dunlop and cycle, 115; golfers, 167; skating, 225

Edward I, and cricket, 84-5

Edward II, bans football, 142

Edward III, bans hockey, 176; and bowling, 256

Egypt, and sporting picture in temple, 5; and archery, 10; and billiards, 47; and bullfight, 62; and bicycle, 109; and dog, 121; and greyhound, 123; and fencing, 130; and football, 138; and horse, 182; and saddle, 192; and hunt, 210; and karate, 245; and bowling, 254; and polo, 274; and boating, 286; and rowing, 289; and sailing, 300-2; and swimming, 340; and tennis, 354; and skittles, 364; and wrestling, 389

Eighteen holes, in golf, 166-68

Eleusis, 390

Elgin marbles, 373

Elijah, and mountains, 263

Elis, 400, 401, 407

Elisha, and resuscitation, 337

Elizabeth I, Queen, and Ascham, 14-5; and coursing, 125; and sailing, 303; and Harrow, 324

Elizabeth II, Queen, and mountaineering, 271

Ellis, William Webb, 145-46

Elyot, Sir Thomas, 344

Elysian Field, Hoboken, N. J., and baseball, 36

Empedocles, and mountain, 263-64

Encyclopedia of Sports, 25

'English', in billiards, 50

Épée, 135

Ephesians, Epistle to, 393

Epsom Downs, 189, 191

Errors, of, toreador, 68; red rag to bull, 69-70; meaning of 'football', 138; and riders, 182; thoroughbred, 187; horseshoe, 195; hockey, 220; skiing as sport, 312; swimming, 344; 'real' tennis, 354, 357; water polo, 377; first Olympic Games, 402

Esau, 210, 392

Eskimos, and games, 3; and skates, 222

Etna, Mount, 263

Eton, playing fields of, 324

Etruscans, 342

Etymology, of, sport, 1; game, 6; score, 6; umpire, 6; amateur, 6; athlete, 6; toxophily, 14; toxic, 18; bull's eye, 18; baseball, 33; billiards, 45, 48; cue, 49; cannon in billiards, 52; snooker, 52; pugilism, 58-9; boxing ring, 59; boxing, 59; Bantam weight, 60; corrida, 61; torero, 66-7; picador, 68; matador, 68; Pall Mall, 89; croquet, 91; curling, 96; loofie, 102; curling tee, 106; curling rink, 107; velocipede, 108; bicycle, 108; Draisine, 111; pneumatic, 114; greyhound, 122-23; fencing, 130; foil, 135; football, 138; soccer, 145; scrummage, 147-48; Rafferty's rules, 157; barracking, 157-58; golf, 159; putting, 165; golf tee, 165; caddie, 169; hockey, 172; shinty, 175; Philip, 179; racing, 181; furlong, 182; jockey, 191-92; stirrup, 194; bridle, 194; bowler, 197-98; debonair, 212; riot, 213; sleuth, 213-14; skates, 222; fives, 231; judo, 234, 241; ju-jitsu, 239; lacrosse, 248; bowls, 255; polo, 273, 377; jodhpurs, 276; racquets, 279; regatta, 295; catamaran, 301; yacht, 303-4; posh, 312; grog, 312; filibuster, 312; buccaneer, 312-13; sloop, 313; schooner, 313; starboard, 313; tonnage, 314; ballast, 314; fo'c'sle, 314; ski, 317; stretcher, 319; moko, 321-22; squash, 325; crawl, 347; ping-pong, 351; tennis, 354; racket, 355; deuce, 355; 'royal' tennis, 357;

love in tennis, 362–63; alley in bowling, 366, Pancratium, 392; gymnast, 407; Pentathlon, 408

Euphrates, and boating, 301

Eve, 120

Evelyn, John, on skating, 225; on sailing, 306

Everest, Mount, 271

Excavations, *see* Archaeology

Fairbairn, Steve, 298

Falconry, 212

Farouk, King of Egypt, and table tennis, 349

Featherie, 163

Fencing, 130–36

Fertility, and bull, 61–2; of cock, 73, 74; and horseshoe, 196

Fertility rites and sport, 2; and games, 3; and football, 138–40; and ball games, 172–73; and horse races, 181; and hunting, 208; and polo, 274; and tennis, 354; and Olympic Games, 404

Field hockey, 90

Figg, Jim, 56–7

Filibuster, 312

Finland, 228, 318

Firdusi, and polo, 275

First, book in English on archery, 14; fine for swearing in baseball, 37; glove in baseball, 37; description of billiards, 46; public billiard room, 52; boxing ring, 55; modern boxing glove, 58; bull ring, 66; cricket score, 85; horse-racing trophy, 186; sweepstake, 187; mechanically refrigerated ice rink, 229; keelless boat, 296; sliding seat, 297; yachting club, 206; ski jump, 320; surf life saving assocation, 335; reel, 336, 337; swimming of Channel, 345; Olympic Games, 402

Fitzgerald, G. R., 135

Fitzstephen, William, on cockfight, 77; football, 140; hockey, 176; skating, 223

Fives, at Harrow, 231

Flagstick, in golf, 169–70

Fletcher, 17

Floyd, Gilbert, 117

Fly Creek, and baseball, 30

Flying, 5

Flynn, Percy, 336

Foil, in fencing, 135

Football, 2, 159–71; 'in water', 378

Footraces, 5–6, 404, 406

Ford, Alexander H., 334

Ford, Horace A., 16–7

Forret, and tennis, 357

Frampton, Tregonwell, 187

France, caves in, and archery, 8; and archery, 14; and Pall Mall, 90; and cycling, 109–10, 113, 118–19; and fencing, 134; and Rugby, 147; and caddie, 169; and totalizator, 204; and rock paintings of hunting, 208; and roller skating, 283; and court tennis, 356; and scoring in tennis, 362; and

water skiing, 383–85

Francis I, of France, his wrestling bout, 394–95

Franklin, Benjamin, 344

Frazer, Sir James, on archery, 10; bull worship, 62–3; cock-fights, 74–5; horse racing, 181; Olympic Games, 404

Frederick, Prince of Wales, and cricket, 85

Frederik, Don, 225

Freeth, George, 335

French, and cricket, 86; Pall Mall, 89; croquet, 91; *bonspiel*, 96; épée, 135; hockey, 172; debonair, 212; lacrosse, 248; racquets, 279; grog, 312; buccaneer, 313; tonnage, 313; tennis, 354; deuce, 355; 'love', 362–63

Freshfield, D. W., 271

Freud, Sigmund, and bullfight, 65

Fronton, 232

Fuji, Mount, 262

Funakoshi, Gichin, 246–47

Furlong, 182

Gaelic, and tee, 165; and shinty, 174; and hurling, 175

Gaelic football, 153, 155

Galen, on football, 137

Galway, Ireland, statutes of, 172

Gambling, and bowling, 367, 369; and trotting, 372; *see also* Betting

Games, for rain, 3; cosmic significance, 4; etymology, 6; on Shrove Tuesday, 21, 77, 139, 140, 141; 'one old cat', 33–34; at Easter, 83; 'cat and dog', 83–4; stool ball, 83; and character, 323–24; funeral, 402–4

Gauls, and bull worship, 63; and saddle, 193

Gem, Major T. H., 358

George III, and lacrosse, 250

George IV, and horses, 190

George VI, and table tennis, 349

German, and curling, 96; *bonspiel*, 96; greyhound, 122; golf, 159; schooner, 313; larboard, 314; tennis, 355; *Kegel*, 365, 367

Germany, and, bicycle, 110–11; arms control, 236; skis, 317; skittles, 365–66; water polo, 381; Olympic Games, 409

Gesner, Professor Conrad, 266

Ghenghis Khan, 180

Gibb, James, 351

Gilboa, battle of, 12

Gingerbread, 311

Glasgow, Scotland, and, curling, 98; bicycle, 112; lacrosse, 253

Gloucester, England, and hockey window, 176

Godfrey, Captain, on Figg, 56

Godolphin, Earl of, 187

Goethe, Johann W. von, on skates, 230

Golden Bough, the, on, archery, 10; bull sacrifice, 62; Olympic Games, 404

Goldsmith, Oliver, at Harrow, 324

Goldwin, William, and cricket, 85

Golf, 159–71

Goliath, 131

Gonzalo de Cordoba, 133
Good Friday, football on, 139
Goode, E. C., 352
Gore, A. W., 360
Gospels, and, the Veronica, 71; cock's crow, 73; mountains, 263; swimming, 343; wrestling, 393; *see also* Bible
Gould, Jay, 384
Graeco-Roman style, in wrestling, 394, 397
Graham, W. W., 271
Grant, George F, and golf peg, 165–66
Graves, Abner, and baseball, 28, 29
Gray, Thomas, 109
Greek, and athletics, 6; for archery, 14; and toxic, 18; and pugilism, 58–9; and cock, 73; and bicycle, 108; and pneumatic, 114–15; and greyhound, 122; and Pankration, 245
Greeks, and, archery, 11; billiards, 46; boxing, 55; bullfights, 61, 63; cock, 73; cock-fights, 76; spurs for cocks, 78; Pall Mall, 90; dog, 121, 123; football, 137; hockey, 174; horse-racing, 183–84; saddle, 192; horseshoe, 195; hunting, 212; jai alai, 231; Pankration, 245, 392; karate, 245; bowling, 254–55; boats, 287; rowing contests, 288; skiing, 318; sport and character, 323; swimming, 340; lawn tennis, 359; trotting and pacing, 373; wrestling, 390–92; sport, 399; *see also* Olympic Games
Green, Rev W.S., 271
Greenland, 320
Gregory XIII, Pope, and bullfights, 67
Greyhound, 122–23, 124; stud book of, 127
Grog, 312
Gulick, Dr Luther, 40–1
Gun, cock of, 80–1
Gundobald, King, and duel, 132
Guthrie, Rev William, 98
Guttie, 164

Hades, and dog, 121
Haines, Jackson, 227, 228, 284
Haiti, 313
Halifax, Canada, 217
Hall, Dr Marshall, 337
Hambledon Club, 85
Hamley Bros, London, 350
Hand, in defence, 54; as measure, 181–82
Handel, G. F., his Water Music, 292
Hare, live, racing 128; mechanical, 128–29
Harness racing, *see* Trotting
Harrison, H. C., 154, 155
Harrow College, and football, 154, 155; and racquets, 280, 324–25; as English institution, 324
Harvard, and football, 152, 153
Hat, trick in golf, 87; bowler, 197–98; derby, 197–99
Hawaii, and boxing, 54; and surfing, 331–34
Heat, the, 196
Hazard, in tennis, 355

Hebrews, Epistle to, and foot-race, 6
Hecate, goddess, 123
Hellespont, 340–41
Henderson, Robert W., and baseball claim, 31, 32
Hendon, England, and cycling, 118; and dog-racing, 128
Henie, Sonja, 228
Henley, England, regatta, 295, 296
Henry I, and horses, 185
Henry II, and horse racing, 185
Henry IV, and skittles, 368
Henry V, and archery, 14; and tennis, 357
Henry VIII, and archery, 14; and Ascham, 14–5; and cock-fights, 77; and coursing, 125; and fencing, 134; and bowling, 257; and watermen, 291–92; and tennis, 357; and skittles, 368; his wrestling bout, 394–95
Heracles, 212, 400, 401, 407
Heraea, 407
Hero, priestess, 340–41
Herodotus, on horsemanship, 180
Hieroglyphics, for, athlete, 5; dog, 121; fencing, 130–31; swimming, 340
Hiisi, 318
Hillary, Sir Edmund P., 271
Himalayas, the, 271
Hippodameia, 400–1
Hitler, Adolf, 324
Hittites, and archery, 10; and horse, 180
Hobby horse, 110–11
Hoboken, N. J., and baseball, 36
Hockey, 172–78; primitive type of, 3; and Wichita tribe, 3; and Makah Indians, 3; 'on horseback', 273, 277
Holmenkollen, 321
Homer, on archery, 11; chariot races, 183; horseshoes, 195; tennis, 354; wrestling, 390; sport, 399
Homosexuality, and archery, 10
Hood, Robin, as archer, 13
Hopman, Harry, 326
Horace, on swimming, 342–43
Horatius, 342
Horse, and bullfight, 71; dandy, 112; its history, 179–81; racing, 179–205; shoe, 195–96; bells and brasses, 196–97; its birthday, 201; and polo, 274–76; and trotting, 371, 373–74
Hoskins, J.S., 259–60
Hounslow Heath, England, and polo, 276
Huddersfield, England, 149
Hugh of Lincoln, and football, 141
Humour, of cycling, 117
Hundred years war, and archery, 14
Hungary, and fencing, 135; and skates, 222; and table tennis, 353; and water polo, 381
Huns, and horse, 180, 182; and stirrup, 194; and polo, 274
Hunting, 4, 9, 10, 206–15; and archery, 9, 10; of ostriches, 11; and dog, 122
Hunting, A. J., 260

Huntington, and steeplechase, 199
Hurley, 153, 159, 174
Hurling, 153, 174, 175
Hurlingham, England, and croquet, 92
Hurlingham Club, and polo, 277
Huseby Hill, Norway, 320
Hyperboreans, 407

Ibsen, Don, 386
Ice hockey, 216-20; hockey in U.S.A., 172
Ice skating, 221-30
Iceland, and curling, 96, 97; and skating, 222-23; and lacrosse, 148
Iceni, tribe of, 184
Ida, Mount, Crete, 401
Iliad, 183
Ilici, Spain, 63
Ilsen, battle of, 318
Impotence, healed by archery, 10
Incas, and dog, 121, 122; and horse, 182
India, and archery, 9; and game of poona, 22; and badminton, 23; snooker from, 53; and cock-fighting, 76; and swordsmanship, 131; and stirrup, 194; and unarmed combat, 246; and polo, 273, 275; and racquets, 281; and squash, 327; and surfing, 330
Iphitus, 405
Iran, see Persia
Ireland, and, billiards, 46; croquet, 91; football, 139; Australian Rules Football, 153; barracking, 158; hurling, 174-75; steeplechase, 199; yachting, 306
Irving, Washington, on nine-pin bowling, 369
Isaac, 210
Isaiah, prophet, and, football, 137; horseshoe, 195; Messianic age, 210; swimming, 343; wrestling term 393
Isfahan, Iran, 275
Ishmael, and archery, 12
Israelites, and bull worship, 61
Isthmian Games, and hockey, 174; and rowing contests, 288
Italy, and, billiards, 276; Pall Mall, 89; fencing, 133-34; bowls, 254; regatta, 295; 'royal' tennis, 357
Ithaca, 288

Jacob, wrestling, 392-93
Jai alai, 231-33
James I, of England, and battledore, 21; and cock-fights, 77; and curling, 97; and football, 142; and bowling, 257
James II, of England, and golf, 161
James II, of Scotland, and golf, 160
James IV, of Scotland, and curling, 97
James VI, of Scotland, and curling, 97
Japan, and, archery, 10, 12; sword, 131; cycle as prayerwheel, 118; judo, 234-41; ju-jitsu, 240; karate, 246-47; polo, 274; table tennis, 353; wrestling, 397
Jaques, John, and croquet, 91
Jefferson, Thomas, and cock-fighting, 79

Jesus, and, the Veronica, 71; cock's crow, 73; football, 140; mountains, 262, 263
Jews, and cock, 73-4; and dietary legislation, 210; and swimming, 343; see also Bible
Job, and archery, 12
Jockey, 191-92
Jodhpur, 276
John, King of England, and coursing, 125; and horse-racing, 185-86
Johnson, Ben, on riders, 202
Johnson, Dennis, 112
Johnson, Dr Samuel, on Ascham, 14
Jonathan, and archery, 12; the Maccabee, and swimming, 343
Jones, Robert, 226
Josephus, Flavius, on swimming, 343
Juan les Pins, 384, 388
Jubbulpore, and snooker, 52-3
Judah, 393
Judo, 2, 234-43
Ju-jitsu, 234
Julius, Sir George A., 202-5
Jungfrau, the, 268

Kahanamoku, Duke, 334, 335
Kalevala, on skiing, 318
Kano, J., 234, 240-41
Karachi, India, and badminton, 23-4; and lawn tennis court, 358
Karate, 2, 244-47
Kegeln, 365, 367
Kempo, 235, 245
Kentfield, Edwin, 51
Kentucky Derby, 199
Kerr, Rev John, 98
Kiandra, Australia, 321
Kierkegaard, S. A., on life, 374
Kingston, Canada, 216
Kirkwell, Scotland, 98
Knapp, James H., 199
Knickerbockers, and baseball, 35
Knighthood, English, and sword, 131
Kodokan Institute, Tokyo, 234
Korea, bullfights in, 61
Kumiuchi, 239

La Boëssière, 135
Lacrosse, 248-53; and ice hockey, 217
Lahore, Pakistan, 275
Lallement, Pierre, 113
Lamb, Charles, on roast pork, 221
Lancashire, wrestling style of, 395
Landsdowne, 5th Marquis of, 359
Languedoc, France, and Pall Mall, 90
Laotse, 238
Latin, and, umpire, 6; amateur, 6; pugilism, 58; bicycle, 108; tennis, 355
Latin America, bullfighting in, 61; and cock-fighting, 79; and jai alai, 231; and Trudgen, 346
Lausanne, Switzerland, 265
Lawn bowling, 254-58; and billiards, 47; on

ice', 96
Lawn tennis, 358-60; and croquet, 92
Lawson, Harry J., 114
Leaf, H., 326
Leander, his swimming exploit, 340-41
Legends, on, archery, 9, 11; origin of boxing, 55; Ailsa Craig, 104; dog, 120; divine sword, 131; first hockey, 173; Mount Pilatus, 265-66; polo, 274; *see also* Mythology
Leo XII, Pope, 225; and patron of skaters, 225
Lever, Sir Ashton, 16
Library of Sports and Pastimes, 26
Library, badminton,, 20, 25-6
Lincoln, Abraham, and baseball, 37; as wrestler, 396
Liverpool, England, and dog-racing, 127; and swimming, 345
London, and, archery, 15; Lord's, 85; Pall Mall, 89; bicycle club, 117; football, 143; Rugby Union, 146; Rugby League, 149, 150; Glaciarium, 229; Alpine Club, 268-69; Fleet Gaol and racquets, 278; first competitive swimming, 345; 'water soccer', 379; modern Olympic Games, 410
London, Jack, on surfing, 329-30, 335
Long, Walter, 359
Long Island Sound, U.S.A., 385
Longman, C. J., and publication on sports, 25-6
Longmans, Green & Co., London, and Sports Library, 25-6
Loofie, 102
Lord, Thomas, 85
Lord's, London, 85, 88
Lot, and mountains, 262
Louis X, of France, victim of tennis, 356
Louis XIV, of France, and billiards, 49; and fencing, 134
Love, in tennis, 362
Lowell, Dr William, and golf peg, 166
Lucerne, Switzerland, 266
Lunn, Arnold, 321
Luther, Martin, and skittles, 364, 367
Luxor, Egypt, and fencing, 130-31
MacKay, Robert, 280
Macmillan, Kirkpatrick, 112
Macpherson, Mrs, and croquet, 91
Madison Square Garden, New York City, and baseball, 375; and cycle races, 119; as ice rink, 229; and roller skating, 284, 285
Magic, and, sport, 2; wrestling, 3; archery, 9-10; the sun, 9-10; divining future, 22; battledore, 22; powder in billiards, 50; bull's blood, 63; cock, 73, 74-5; hockey, 172-73; horse, 196-97; hunting, 208-9; polo, 274; surfing, 332
Maiden, the, in cricket, 87
Maitland, Australia, and speedway racing, 259
Makah Indians, and hockey, 3, 173
Malden, N. C., 143
Mallory, George L, 271-72
Manchester, England, and greyhound racing,

129
Manhattan Island, N.Y., and baseball, 35; and bowling, 368
Manipur, India, 273
Manly, Australia, and surfing, 335
Mapuche Indians, and hockey, 173
Mars, sacrifice of horse, to, 181
Martial, the Latin poet, 391
Mary, Queen of Scots, and golf, 161; and caddie, 169
Marylebone Cricket Club, England 85
Mask, in baseball, 37; in fencing, 130, 135
Massachusetts, and nine-pin bowling, 369
Matador, the, 64-8
Matterhorn, Mount, 270
Mayas, and, ball games, 43-4; dog, 121; football, 138; jai alai, 231
McGeoghegan, Abbe, on billiards, 46
McGill University, Montreal, and Rugby, 153; and ice hockey, 217-19
McKinley, Mount, Alaska, 271
Medicine, and, archery as cure for homosexuality and impotence, 10; billiards, 49; cock, 74; cycling, 116; football games, 137-38; hockey, 173; polo for leprosy, 274; skis for stretcher, 319; sport as grief therapy, 404
Melbourne, Australia, and Australian Rules Football, 154-55, 158
Merlin, Joseph, 283
Mesopotamia, and, archery, 10; bullfights, 62; hunt, 123, 210; falconry, 217; karate, 245; wrestling, 389
Messenger, and trotting horse, 374
Messianic Age, and man's carnivorous habit, 210
Mexico, Zuñis of, 2; and basketball, 43-4; and horse, 182; and jai alai, 233
Meyerbeer, Giacomo, 283-84
Michaux, E., 113
Michillimackinac, Fort, 250
Miles, Henry D.,, 58
Mills, Abraham G., and claims of baseball, 27, 28-9
Milon, of Croton, 392
Mingaud, Captain, and billiards, 49-50
Minotaur, 63, 210
Mitchell, W. W., 258
Mithra, and bull sacrifice, 62
Molesey, England, 177
Molyneux, Lord, 127
Monasteries, and court tennis, 356; bowling alleys in, 366, 367
Mongolians, as horsemen, 180; as wrestlers, 396
Monkey crouch, 193
Montagu, Ivor, 353-54
Mont Blanc, 267-68
Montreal, Canada, and, curling, 103; Rugby, 147; ice hockey, 217-19; Lacrosse Club, 251
Monuments, of baseball, 29, 31, 36; a street as, 89; of Rugby, 148; of fatal polo acci-

dent, 275
Moore, James, 119
More, Catkire, and billiards, 46
Moreton on Marsh, England, and croquet, 92
Morocco, and horse, 185
Mortlock Islands, and boxing, 54
Moscow, Russia, 319
Moses, 263
Motorcycle speedway races, 259–61
Mountaineering, 262–72
Muleta, the, 68–9
Munn, Charles, 129
Museums, baseball, Cooperstown, U.S.A., 30–1; South Kensington, London, and cycle, 112; Royal Science, Edingburgh, and Dunlop tyre, 115; British, London, and greyhound, 123; and dog, 123; and football specimens, 138; and hunting horse, 180; and polo, 274; and swimming, 340; and trotting, 373; of Madrid, and sword, 133; National of Copenhagen, and hockey, 176; Djurgarden, Stockholm, and oldest skis, 316; Holmenkollen, Norway, and skiing, 321
Muthill, Perth, Scotland, and curling, 99
Muu-muu, 333
Mythology, on, Minotaur, 63; cock, 73; dog, 120–21; Cerberus, 121; hockey, 173; Centaur, 182; ice skating, 222–23; unarmed combat, 235–36; boat racing, 288; skiing, 317–18; Hero and Leander, 340; wrestling, 390; Sumo and foundation of Japan, 397; Olympic Games, 399–401

Nagasaki, and ju-jitsu, 237
Naismith, Dr James A., 40–42
Nansen, Fridtjof, and skiing, 320–21
Nassau, and boat club, 297
Nausicaa, 354
Nebel, Gerhard, on bullfight, 64–5
Nebo, Mount, 263
Nebraska Indians, and hockey, 173–74
Nehru, Pundit, and table tennis, 349
Netherby, Yorkshire, 185
Netherlands, and, curling, 185; skates, 223–24; roller skating, 282; sailing, 305; see also Dutch
Newbolt, Sir Henry, 324
New Brunswick, N. J., U.S.A., and football, 152
Newmarket, England, races at, 184, 186, 187–88
New York, and, baseball, 31–2, 35, 375; cycle races, 119; Derby hat, 199; yacht club, 308; trotting club, 372
New Zealand, and curling, 102; and Rugby, 147; totalizator in, 204; and mountaineering, 271
Niepce, M., 110
Nigeria, 3
Nile, sailing on, 302
Nimrod, and Nineveh, 180, 210

Nine-pin bowling, see Skittles
Nineveh, 180
Noah, 206
Norman, Sir John, 290
Normans, and archery, 13; and football, 140
Norse, Old, and, score, 6; sleuth, 214
Norsemen, and sailing, 302
Northumberland, Earl of, and battledore, 21
Norway, and, curling, 102; sailing, 303; skiing, 319, 321
Norwich, England, 202

Oaks, the, 189
Odysseus, and archery, 11; and boat race, 288; wrestling, 390
Oenomaus, 400–1
Okinawa, karate and Shaolin boxing in, 244–45, 246–47
Oklahoma, and hockey, 3; and football, 139
Old Blackheathens, and rugger, 146
Old cat, one, game of, 33–4
Old Freemasons Tavern, London, 144
Old Rowley, 186
Olding, G. H., 337
Olympia, 4, 400, 401, 405
Olympic Games, 4, 399–410; ancient, and, religion, 4, 402–5; hockey, 174; horse races, 183; chariot races, 185; wrestling, 391–2; their cycle, 401–2; women, 406–7; prize, 407; revival, 408–9; modern, 408–10, and, fencing, 136; hockey, 177; Kano, 242; karate, 245; yachting, 311; swimming, 345–46; water polo, 381; symbol, 402
Olympus, Mount, 262
Ordeal, trial by, 131–32
Orford, Lord, and dog racing, 126
Origin, of, sport, 1–7; yew trees in churchyard, 13; bull's eye, 18; arrowroot, 18; badminton, 20; Badminton Library, 20, 25–6; first shape of lawn tennis court, 23, 358–59; badminton 'drink', 26; diamond in baseball, 36; basketball, 42–3; billiard table, 47–8; banderilla, 66; muleta, 68–9; Veronica, 71; cock on steeple, 73; domestication of fowl, 75; cockpit, 77, 79; pit in theatre, 80; cricket stumps, 83–4; Lord's, 85; wicket, 86; the Ashes, 87–8; curling, 95–9; six day cycle races, 119; mechanical hare, 128, 129; dog-racing track, 128–9; Rugby Union, 148–49; football 'cheer', 152; golf, 159; golf cup, 166; wooden golf peg, 166; bunker, 168; hockey, 173; trousers, 179; canter, 181; horse-racing, 181; three prizes, 186; thoroughbred, 187; bowler hat, 197–98; Derby, 189–90; Derby hat, 199; steeplechase, 199; ice hockey, 216–17; puck, 219; ju-jitsu, 234; motorcycle speedway racing, 259; jodhpurs, 276; galley slave, 289; life saving reel, 336–37; table tennis ball, 351; bat, 352; water polo, 377; wreath, 407
Ormsby, Lyster, 336

Oslo, Norway, 319
Ottawa Indians, and lacrosse, 250
Outrigger, 296
Ovid, 123
Oxford, and Cambridge University boat race, 294–95

Paccard, M. G., 268
Pacific Ocean, and surfing, 330
Pacing, 373
Pall Mall, 89–90
Pankration, 245, 392
Paris, France, and, Pall Mall, 90; bicycle, 110; cycle race, 118–19; Treaty of, 250; modern Olympic Games, 409
Park Hill, England, 189
Parker Bros., Salem, Mass., U.S.A., 350
Parkyns, Sir Thomas, 395–96
Parthenon, and horses, 192, 373
Parthians, and archery, 10, 11; and horse, 180
Paul, St, and wrestling, 5–6, 393; and footrace, 6; as swimmer, 343
Pausanias, on Olympic Games, 401
Peel, Sir Robert, at Harrow, 324
Pell, Arthur, 146
Pelops, 400–1
Pelota, 231–33
Penelope, 11
Pennsylvania, and baseball, 34–5; Bishop of, and Olympic Games, 410
Penny-farthing, the, 108, 113–14
Pentathlon, 392, 408
Pepys, Samuel, on, cock-fighting, 78–9; Pall Mall, 90; skating, 225, 228; yachting, 305
Percy, Thomas, 141
Pereira, J. B., 358
Persians, and, archery, 10; bull, 62; cock, 73, 74; cock-fighting, 76; dog, 122; hockey, 174; bowler hat, 198; as hunters, 210; polo, 274–75
Peru, and dog, 121; and boating, 301
Peter, St, and cock's crow, 73; as swimmer, 343; and *Kegel*, 367
Peterkin, W. A., 105
Petrarch, and mountaineering, 264
Petrie, Sir Flinders, 364
Pett, Peter, 305
Pett, Phineas, 303
Pharaohs, of Egypt, and sport, 5: and football, 138; and sailing 302
Philip V, of Macedonia, as mountaineer, 264
Philip V, of Spain, and bullfight, 67–8
Philip, George B., 337
Phoenicians, and boats, 287
Phrases, from, *archery*: bull's eye, 18; draw long bow, 18; unstrung, 18–9; *baseball*: rain check, 38; *billiards*: behind the 8 ball, 53; *boxing*: throw in sponge, 59; come up to scratch, 59; *bullfighting*: red rag to bull, 70; *cock-fighting*: cockpit, 72, 77; battle royal, 79; pit against, 79; crestfallen, 80; show white feather, 80; cocksure, 80; cock

a weapon, 81; *croquet*: ring bell, 94; peg out, 94; *football*: Rafferty's rules, 157; *horse-racing*: straight from horse's mouth, horse-play, hold your horses, flog a dead horse, horse-sense, horse chestnut, 201–2; *hunting*: beat about the bush, 213; barking up wrong tree, 213; *sailing*: take gilt off gingerbread, 311–12; posh, 312; grog, 312; filibuster, 312; *pin-bowling*: go down like a nine-pin, 368; king pin, 368; *wrestling*: gird one's loins, 393.
Picador, 68
Pilate, Pontius, 265–66
Pilatus, Mount, 265, 269
Pindar, and wrestling, 392
Ping-pong, *see* Table tennis
Pius V, Pope, and bullfights, 67
Pizarro, F., and horse, 182
Plato, on hunting, 211; and sport, 323
Pliny, and skis, 318
Poetry, on, love of baseball, 38; croquet, 91; death of Cairnie, 101–2; curling broom, 105–6; cycling, 116; dog, 123,125; football, 141; boat race, 287–88; watermen, 290; ABC of rowing, 298–99; cricket, 324; swimming, 341,348
Poitiers, battle of, 14
Polo, 273–77; and tennis, 354; water, 377–82
Polynesians, and boating, 301; and surfing, 330; and crawl, 346; and bowling, 365
Pompeii, and bicycle, 109
Pontiac, chief of Ottawas, 250
Poona, and badminton, 22
Pope, Dick, 386–87
Porter, Luther H., on cycling, 109,116
Portugal, bullfights in, 61
Portunus, 288
Posh, 312
Poundage, 17
Princeton, and football cheer, 152
Prison, and, shuttlecock, 21; billiards, 49; racquets, 278
Psalms, and archery, 12; and dog, 123
Psychoanalysis, and bullfighting, 64
Psychology, on, bullfighting, 64–5; horse, 196; table tennis, 350
Public schools, of England, and football, 143; and racquets, 280; and sport, 323
Puck, in ice hockey, 219
Pugilism, etymology, 58; *see* Boxing
Pulaski, Count Maximilian, 384
Puritans, and bowling, 368–69; and harness racing, 372
Putt, in golf, 165
Pythian Games, 4, 392

Quebec, Canada, and curling, 103–4; and lacrosse. 248
Queensberry, Marquis of, on boxing, 58

Rabbit, and dog-racing, 128

Religion, in sport, and, demon expulsion, 3; gift of gods, 4; ball games, 4; basketball, 40; boxing and pyx, 58-9; bull, 61-2,64; cock, 72-4,75,77; curling, 103; bicycle, 109,118; dog, 123; football, 139, 140; golf ball, 163; canter, 181; steeplechase, 199; automatic totalizator, 202-3,204; hunt, 208; skating, 223, 224-25; unarmed combat, 235,236,246; lacrosse, 248-49; mountains, 262-63, 265-67; saluting quarterdeck, 315; skiing, 317-18; surfing, 331,333; court tennis, 356; skittles, 364-66,367; bowling, 368-69; trotting, 372; wrestling, 396; Olympic Games, 401,402,405,409,410; footrace, 406
Resuscitation, methods of, 337
Rhodes, Philip L., and ideal yacht, 310
Rhône, river, 265
Rhymes, divinatory, and shuttlecock, 22; see also Poetry
Richard I, and horse-racing, 185
Richard II, and bowling, 256
Richardson, L. M., 284
Riviera, French, and water skiing, 384-85
Roberts, John, and snooker, 53
Robertson, G. F., 217
Robinson, Andrew, 313
Rochester, N. Y., U.S.A., and baseball, 34
Roller skating, 282-85; derby, 285
Romans, as archers, 11; and boxing, 55-6; cult of bull, 63; bullfight, 66; cock-fight, 76; dog, 121; duel, 132; football, 137-38, 140; golf, 159; hockey, 174; horse, 180; horse sacrifice, 181; horse-racing, 184; jockey's cap, 192; stirrup, 194; jai alai, 231; bowling, 254-55; boats, 287; rowing, 289; body culture, 323; swimming, 342; wrestling, 394
Romero, Francisco, 68
Romero, Pedro, 71
Roosevelt, Franklin D., and baseball, 31
Roosevelt, Theodore, and judo, 242
Rouen, France, and cycle races, 118
Rounders, 27,28,31-2,34
Rowing, 286-99; and water polo, 377,379
Royal tennis, 356-58
Rugby, and, basketball, 40; soccer, 143; Union, 145-48; League, 148-51; American Football, 151; Australian Rules, 154; modern Olympic Games, 408
Rugger, 145-48
Russia, and cock, 74
Rutgers, and football, 152

Sabre, the, 135
Sacrifice, of, bull, 62,63; cock, 74; dog, 121; animal head at football, 140; horse, 181; hunt, 209; surfboard, 332; and footrace, 406
Saddle, the, 192-93
Sailing, 300-15
St Andrews Royal and Ancient Golf Club,

Scotland, 159,161,167-68
St George, and dragon, 211
St Leger, 188-89
St Leger, Colonel Anthony, 188-89
St Lidwina, and skating, 224-25
St Louis, Missouri, and jai alai, 231
Saluki, the, 123
Samson, as hunter, 210; as wrestler, 392
Samurai, 238-39,240,397
Sandow, Eugene, and rowing, 298
Saturnalia, and football, 140
Saul, King, 12
Saussure, H. B. de, and mountaineering, 267
Saxons, and archery, 13; and wrestling, 394
Scandinavians, and, hunting, 207; ice skating, 222; ski, 316; swimming, 343
Schafer, Professor, 337
Schooner, 313
Scoring, etymology, 6; in tennis, 361-62
Scotch College, Melbourne, Australia, and football, 154-55
Scots, and, archery, 16; cock, 74; cricket, 83; curling, 95-107; bicycle, 112-13; pneumatic tyre, 114; golf, 159-61; shinty, 174; ice skating, 225-26; bowling, 257-58; skittles, 367-68; water polo, 381
Scrummage, 147
Scythians, and archery, 10; and billiards, 46
Sefton, Earl of, and dog-racing, 127
Seltzer, Leo, and roller derby, 285
Severus Septimus, Emperor, 185
Seville, bullfights in, 71
Sex, and, sport, 2; games, 3; archery, 10; bull, 61; cock, 73,74; horseshoe, 196
Shakespeare, W., on, archery, 14; billiards, 46-7; swimming, 342; tennis, 357
Shaolin boxing, 245,246
Sheffield Club, England, and football, 144
Sherer, Major, 273
Shinty, 174-75,217
Ship, a 'she', 314-15
Shooting, 4; free-flight (archery), 17
Shoreditch, London, and archery, 15
Shrove Tuesday, shuttlecock on, 21-2; cock-fighting on, 77; football on, 139,140,141
Shuttlecock, 21,24-5
Silver, George, 134
Simler, Professor Josias, 267
Simpson, Sir W. G., 159
Sinai, Mount, 61,263
Sioux Indians, and hockey, 173
Sivrac, Chevalier M. de, 109-10
Six-day races, bicycle, 119; roller skating, 284-85
Skadi, 317
Skates, 226-27; their development, 230-31; roller, 282-85
Skiing, 316-22; water, 383-88; barefoot water, 387
Skittles, 364-69
Slalom, 321
Sleigh, Charles R., 387

Sloop, 313
Smith, Owen P., 129
Smithfield, England, and horse races, 185
Snooker, 52-3
Soccer, 143-45; water, 379
Socrates, sacrifices cock, 74
Solomon, King, 210
Somerville, Crichton, on ski jump, 320
Sorbonne University, Paris, and Olympic Games, 409
South Africa, and Rugby, 147
Southampton, England, and bowling, 255
Southsea, England, and badminton, 24
Spain, cave paintings, and, archery and hunting, 8-9,208; billiards, 46; bullfights, 61,66,71; fencing, 133; her Conquistadores and horse, 180,182; war against Dutch, 225; jai alai, 232; Armada and bowls, 255
Spalding, Albert G., and baseball, 28
Speedway races, motorcycle, 259-61
Spencer, Herbert,and billiards, 51-2
Sport, its etymology, 1; its beginnings, 1-7; as gift of gods, 4; and divination, 21; books library, 25; classification of, 262; as character builder, 323-24
Springboks, 147
Springfield, Mass., U.S.A., and basketball, 40
Spurs, for cocks, 78; for horses, 193-94
Squash, 323-28
Standardbred, the, 374
Stanley, Lord, of Preston, 219
Starboard, 313
Steeplechase, 199
Stevens, John C., 308-9,310
Stirrup, 194
Stoke Poges, Bucks., England, and bicycle, 109
Stool ball, 83
Strabo, on Olympic Games, 402
Studbook, greyhounds, 127; horses, 191
Stump, at cricket, 83-4
Sulky, evolution of, 375-76
Sumatra, cock-fights in, 75
Sumerians, and bullfights, 62
Sumo, 235,397
Surfing, 329-38
Sverra, King of Sweden, 318
Swaffham, England, coursing club at, 126
Swaythling Cup, in table tennis, 352-53
Sweden, and curling, 102; and skiing, 319
Swimming, 339-48; and water polo, 377-78,379
Switzerland, and, curling, 102; mountaineering, 266-67; skiing, 321
Sword, 130-33
Sydney, Australia, and, Australian Rules Football, 154; barracking, 158; totalizator, 204; speedway racing, 260; surfing, 335-37
Symbolism, of,bullfights, 65; cock, 74,75; sword, 131; football, 139; horseshoe, 196; horse, 196; polo ball, 274; five rings and Olympic Games, 402

Table tennis, 349-53

Taglioni, Paul, 284
Tamil, 301
Taoism, philosophy of, and unarmed combat, 238
Tara, Ireland, 175
Tattersall, Richard, 190
Tauromachy, 71
Taurus, constellation of, 61
Taylor, Matt, 296
Tee, in curling, 106; in golf, 165-66
Telemark, Norway, 320,321
Tennis, 354-63; and racquets, 278; and squash, 326
Ten-pin bowling, 5,364-70
Tensing, Sherpa, 271
Terminology, of, *baseball:* 'running to the base', 33; rain check, 38; *billiards:* cue, 49-50; cannon, 52; *boxing:* ring, 58-9; bantam weight, 60; *bullfighting:* corrida, 61; *traje de luces,* 65; 'cut the pigtail', 70; Veronica, 71; *cock-fighting:* main, 77; battle royal, 'pitted', cockpit, 79; *cricket:* stump, 83; 'laying an egg', 86; duck, 86; 'maiden over', 87; hat trick, 87; the Ashes, 87-8; *curling:* loofie, 102; sooping, 105; rink, 107; crampit, 107; *fencing:* épée, foil, sabre, 135; *golf:* putt, 165; tee, 165-66; fore!, birdie, 170-71; *horse-racing:* canter, 181; furlong, 182; jockey, 191-92; heat, 196; steeplechase, 199; bookmaker, 200; *ice hockey:* puck, 219; *jai alai:* pelota, 232; fronton, 232; cestero, 233; *mountaineering:* Alpenstock, 267; *skiing:* Christiania, Telemark, slalom, 321; moko, 321-22; *swimming:* Trudgen stroke, 340,346; breast stroke, 345; crawl, 346-49; *tennis:* racket, hazard, deuce, service, 355; seeding, 360-61; 'love', 362-63; *ten-pin bowling:* kegeln, 367; wooden bottles, apple, a honey, barmaid, mother-in-law, cheesecakes, graveyards, 370; *trotting:* standardbred, 374; *wrestling:* 'gird one's loins', 393
Tête du Pont, Ontario, Canada, and ice hockey, 216-17
Thames, river, and boating, 289,306
Themistocles, 76,174
Theodoseus I, of Rome, 193,408
Theodoseus II, of Rome, 408
Theseus, and boxing, 55; bullfight, 63; Minotaur, 210; wrestling, 390
Thessaly, 123
Thevenot, 344
Thomas, 4th Duke of Norfolk, 125
Thoroughbred, the, 187
Thring, J. C., 144
Thutmosis, Pharaoh, and charioteers, 183
Tiber, river, 265,342
Tiberias, Lake, 343
Tiberius Caesar, 265
Tibet, 236,377
Timnah, vineyards of, 210,392
Titicaca, Lake, Peru, and boating, 301

Tokyo, Japan, 234
Toltecs, and ball games, 43–4
Tonga Islands, and boxing, 54
Torero, 66–7
Totalizator, mechanical, 202–3
Town ball, 34–5
Toxophily, 14
Trajan, Emperor, 264
Traje de luces, 65
Trinity College, Cambridge, England, 143
Trojans, and boats, 288
Trophy, of, Waterloo Cup, 127; first horse-racing, 186; Stanley Cup, 219; Doggett's Coat and Badge, 294; America's Cup, 309; Swaythling Cup, 353; Davis Cup, 360; wrestling, 396; Olympics, 407
Trotting, 371–76
Trousers, origin of, 179
Troy, N. Y., U.S.A., 252
Trudgen, J. A., 346
Turks, and skis, 318
Twain, Mark, and baseball, 27

Ull, Scandinavian god of skiing, 317–18
Umpire, etymology, 6
United States, and, badminton, 24,25; baseball, 27–39; basketball, 40; goose egg in cricket, 86; curling, 102; bicycle, 117; cycling, 117,118; greyhound racing, 129; American Football, 151–53; golf, ball, 163; tee, 165–66; field hockey, 172; horse-racing, short stirrup, 193; monkey crouch, 193; Derby hat, 198–99; hunting, 214; ice hockey, 220; skating rink, 229; jai alai, 231; judo, 242; lacrosse, 252; bowling, 255; mountaineering, 269,271; polo, 277; racquets, 281; roller skate, 284–85; roller derby, 285; sliding seat, 297; rowing, 297; skis, 317; squash, 327–28; surfing, 334–35; crawl, 347; table tennis, 350–51; tennis, 360; skittles, 368–69; harness racing, 371,375; water polo, 381; water skiing, 383,384–88

Valley Forge, Pennsylvania, and baseball, 34
Van Praag, Lionel, and speedway racing 260
Vatican Hill, Rome, and bull sacrifice, 63
Vaucluse, France, 264
Vegetius, Flavius, on hunting, 211
Venice, Italy, regatta in, 295
Vernon, Admiral Edward, 312
Veronica, the, 71
Victoria, Queen, and billiards, 52; and curling, 100–1; on lacrosse, 252; against mountaineering, 270; and America's Cup, 309
Vienna, Austria, and skating, 228
Vikings, and skates, 222; and sails, 302
Virgil, on boat race, 287
Vishnu, god, and golf ball, 163

Waikiki Beach, Honolulu, and first surfing club, 334
Wallabies, the, 147

Wallace, Rev J., 98
Wallace, John H., 374
Waller, Fred, 385
Walton, Izaak, 14
Ward, John M., 37
Warfare, and, sport, 2,130,324; archery, 10,14,160; billiards, 47; man's earliest weapon, 54; bulls, 63; cock-fights, 75–7; white feather, 80; cock of gun, 80–1; evolution of bicycle, 113; practice of fencing, 130; duel, 131–32; swordsmanship, 132–34; scimitar, 135; football, 137,138; hockey, 176; horse, 180,182,274; hunting, 211; skating, 225; unarmed combat, 234,235–36, 244–47; lacrosse, 248–51; yachting, 302; fo'c'sle, 314; skis, 318–19; swimming, 340,342,343; wrestling, 389, Olympic Games, 405,410
Washington, George, and cock-fights, 79; and fox hunting, 214
Waterloo, battle of, 324
Waterloo Cup, for coursing, 127
Waterloo Hotel, Edinburgh, Scotland, and curling, 100; Liverpool, England, and dog-racing, 127
Watermen, 289–90, 292
Water polo, 377–82
Water skiing, 383–88
Weatherby, Messrs., 191
Webb, Captain Matthew, 345,346
Wechsberg, Joseph, on yachtsmanship, 308
Weight lifting, 5
Welsh, and archery, 13; and bandy, 174; Harp, Hendon, England, and mechanical hare, 128
Wembley, London, and speedway racing, 260
Westmoreland, wrestling, style of, 395,397
Westminster Palace, and cockpit, 77; and watermen, 290
Westward Ho, England, 162
Wetterhorn, Mount, 268,270
Whaling season, and sport, 3
Whitby, England, and football, 139
Whitehall, London, bowling alley at, 257,368
Whitmore, Walter James, 92
Whymper, Edward, 270
Wichita tribe, and hockey, 3,173
Wicket, in cricket, 86
Wickham, Alec, 347
Wight, Isle of, England, and America's Cup, 308
Wilde, Oscar, on fox hunting, 315
William the Conqueror, and the Stanleys, 189; and horseshoes, 195
William III, and racing, 187
Wills, Sir Alfred, 268
Wills, Thomas W., 154
Wilson, William, 379
Wimbledon, and croquet, 92; hockey club, 177; and lawn tennis, 360
Winchester College, England, and sport, 324
Windsor Castle, England, billiards at, 52; and

lacrosse, 252; and bowling, 255
Wingfield, Major Walter C., 23,92,358–59
Winnepeg, Canada, and *bonspiel*, 98–9
Women, and, golf, 161; hockey, 177–78; ice
. skating, 224–25,228–29; swimming Eng-
lish Channel, 348; Olympic Games,
406,407
Wordsworth, Charles, 294
Wordsworth, William, and skating, 229
Wrestling, 3,5,389–98; *see also* Sumo
Wright, Harry, 37
Wycliffe, John, 85
Wynman, Nicolaus, on swimming, 343

Xenophon, on, horsemanship, 183; horseshoe,
195; hunting, 211

Yachting, 4,303–8
Yale University, U.S.A., and football, 152
Yorkshire, England, and Rugby League, 149
Young Men's Christian Association, and bas-
ketball, 40–2

Zen Buddhism, and archery, 12; and unarmed
commbat, 239–40
Zeus, 4,392,399,405,406,407
Zion, Mount, 263
Zulus, and bull, 63
Zuñis, and games, 2

LLYFRGELL COLEG MENAI LIBRARY
SAFLE FFRIDDOEDD SITE
BANGOR GWYNEDD LL57 2TP